MYTHS OF
CHINA AND JAPAN

MYTHS OF CHINA AND JAPAN

BY

DONALD A. MACKENZIE

GRAMERCY BOOKS
NEW YORK • AVENEL

Publisher's Note: The text has been slightly altered for this edition,
but has not been abridged.

Foreword copyright © 1994 Random House Value Publishing, Inc.
All rights reserved.

This edition is published by Gramercy Books,
distributed by Random House Value Publishing, Inc.
40 Engelhard Avenue, Avenel, New Jersey 07001

Printed and bound in the United States of America

Library of Congress Cataloging-in-Publication Data
Mackenzie, Donald Alexander, 1873–1936.
Myths of China and Japan / Donald A. Mackenzie.
p.   cm.
Includes index.
ISBN 0–517–10163–7
1. Mythology, Chinese. 2. Mythology, Japanese.
3. Folklore—China. 4. Folklore—Japan.
5. China— Civilization. 6. Japan—Civilization. I. Title.
BL1802M33 1994
299'.51–dc20
93-46195
CIP

8 7 6 5 4 3 2 1

CONTENTS

FOREWORD

Dragons and jade, herbs and precious stones — in this book, Donald A. Mackenzie explores the fascinating mythology behind these and other symbols of the Orient. Did the Far East, so geographically isolated in ancient times, give spontaneous birth to its own unique civilizations and mythologies? Not at all, says Mackenzie, writing in the early years of this century. Contradicting the established beliefs of his day, he traces evidence of cultural influences that spread across great distances of land and sea as traders and explorers brought not only "progress" — the tools of their civilizations — but their explanations of the mysteries of the universe as well.

Mackenzie demonstrates how archaeological remains documented the movement of the potter's wheel along the routes of trade from Egypt to China, then on to Korea and from there to Japan, and he links the use of the potter's wheel to the adoption of certain myths and legends. Similarly, when an agricultural way of life was introduced into China by the Egyptians, their religious beliefs and mythological symbolism connected with agriculture were also passed along. The Chinese dragon god and the Japanese dragon, for example, are closely linked with water, which is intimately connected with agriculture. And these dragons are akin to other rain and thunder gods — Zeus of Greece, Tarku of Asia Minor, Thor of northern Europe, the Babylonian Marduk. In this book, the reader will cross cultures to find similarities in the stories of human encounters with these dragon gods, in tales of people searching for immortality and Paradise, and in myths of the mother-goddess and the tree of life, as well as in the explanations of creation, life, death, and the afterworld.

For the ancients, material wealth had religious significance. Mackenzie explores the mystical powers attributed to precious metals and stones, sea shells, pearls, and herbs, all of which were believed to provide links between the physical and spiritual worlds. The color of a plant, berry, stone, or metal imbued it with specific qualities. Gold, for instance, was revered as the essence of fire, which brings warmth, and as the essence of the sun, which promotes the growth of vegetation. One chapter in the book is devoted to folklore and tales associated with such plants as mugwort, mandrake, and ginseng, which are still used by herbalists.

Because this book was written in the early years of this century, it reflects certain accepted prejudices of the day. The modern reader will notice the author's occasional judgments about "backward" and "civilized" peoples and about what constitutes "primitive" cultures and "progress." These comments do not, however, detract from the value of Mackenzie's comprehensive scholarship. In following the threads of history and mythology from around the world, Mackenzie shows how the mythologies of China and Japan are actually a blending of influences, and how myths took on new hues and new meanings as they traveled from land to ancient land.

1994

PREFACE TO THE FIRST EDITION

This volume deals with the myths of China and Japan, and it is shown that these throw light on the origin and growth of civilization and the widespread dissemination of complex ideas associated with certain modes of life. The Far East does not appear to have remained immune to outside cultural influences in ancient times. Modern research has established that the old school of opinions which insisted on the complete isolation of China can no longer obtain. As Laufer says: "It cannot be strongly enough emphasized on every occasion that Chinese civilization, as it appears now, is not a unit and not the exclusive production of the Chinese, but the final result of the cultural efforts of a vast conglomeration of the most varied tribes, an amalgamation of ideas accumulated from manifold quarters and widely differentiated in space and time. . . . No graver error can hence be committed than to attribute any culture idea at the outset to the Chinese, for no other reason than because it appears within the precincts of their empire."

Even the Chinese records have to be regarded with caution. It is impossible nowadays to accept as serious contributions to history the inflated chronology and the obvious fables compiled and invented by Chinese scholars for political and other purposes during the Han and later dynasties. These scholars had really little knowledge of the early history of their country and people. They were puzzled even by certain existing customs and religious practices, and provided ingenious "secondary explanations" which, like their accounts of the early dynasties, do not accord with the data accumulated by archæologists and other workers in the scientific field. The complex religious ideas of the Chinese were obviously not of spontaneous generation. Many of these resemble too closely the complexes found elsewhere, and their history cannot be traced within the limits of the Chinese empire. Indeed, as is shown, some of them are undoubtedly products of human experiences obtained elsewhere, and they reveal traces of the influences to which they were subjected during the process of gradual transmission from areas of origin. Nor, would it appear, was Chinese civilization nearly as ancient as the native scholars would have us believe.

When the early Chinese entered China, they found non-Chinese peoples in different parts of that vast area which they ultimately welded into an empire. They were an inland people and did not invent boats; they did not originate the agricultural mode of life but adopted it, using the seeds and implements they had acquired; nor did they invent the potter's wheel with which they were familiar from the earliest times in China, having evidently become possessed of it, along with the complex culture associated with it, before they migrated into the province of Shensi. Nor could an agrarian people like the Chinese have been the originators of the belief in the existence of

"Isles of the Blest" in the Eastern Ocean; they were not alone in Asia in believing in a Western Paradise situated among the mountains.

The Chinese, as Laufer demonstrates in his *Jade*, did not pass through in China that culture stage called the "Neolithic". When they first settled in Shensi, they searched for and found jade, as did the carriers of bronze who first entered Europe. There was obviously an acquired psychological motive for the search for jade, and the evidence of Chinese jade symbolism demonstrates to the full that it had been acquired from those who had transferred to jade the earlier symbolism of shells, pearls, and precious metals. In the chapter devoted to jade it is shown that this view is confirmed by the evidence afforded by Chinese customs connected with jade, shells, pearls, &c.

In no country in the world are the processes of culture drifting and culture mixing made more manifest than in China. The Chinese dragon is, as Professor Elliot Smith puts it, a "composite wonder beast". Throughout this volume it is shown to yield, when dissected, remarkable evidence regarding the varied influences under which it acquired its highly complex character. The fact that a Chinese dragon charm closely resembles a Scottish serpent charm is of special interest in this connection. When, however, it is found that China obtained certain myths and practices from the area called by its writers "Fu-lin" (the Byzantine Empire), and that not only Byzantine but Ægean influences are traceable in the Celtic field, the charm-link between Gaelic Scotland and China may not, after all, be regarded as "far-fetched". The same may be said regarding the curious similarity between the myths and practices connected with shells, and especially cockle-shells, in Japan and the Scottish Hebrides. Although the West Highlanders and the inhabitants of the Land of the Rising Sun were never brought into contact, it may be that similar cultural influences drifted east and west from their area of origin, and that the carriers were the ancient mariners who introduced the same type of vessel into far-separated oceans.

As in China, we do not in Japan find a culture of purely native origin, but rather one which has grown up from a mass of imported elements as varied as the racial types that compose the present-day population. Both in China and Japan these imported elements have been subjected to the influences of time and locality and infused with national ideas and ideals. The processes of growth and change have not, however, concealed the sources from which certain of the early ideas emanated in varying degrees of development.

The early native history of Japan is, like that of China, no more worthy of acceptance than are the long-discarded English and Scottish fables regarding Brute and Scota.

The data accumulated in this volume tend to show, although we have no direct evidence of systematic missionary enterprise earlier than that of the Bhuddists, that the influential religious cults of ancient times that flourished in Mesopotamia and in the Egyptian Empire (which included part of Western Asia) appear to have left their impress on the intellectual life of even far-distant peoples. Apparently modes of thought were transmitted along direct and indirect avenues of intercourse by groups of traders. Even before trade routes were opened, religious beliefs and practices appear to have been introduced into distant lands by prospectors and by settlers who founded colonies from which later colonies " budded". When the same set of complexes are found in widely separated areas, it is difficult to accept the view that they originated from the same particular experiences and the same set of circumstances, especially when it is made manifest that the complexes in the older centre of culture reflect strictly local physical conditions, and even the local political conditions that resulted in a fusion of peoples and of their myths, symbols, and religious beliefs and practices.

DONALD A. MACKENZIE

CHAPTER I

The Dawn of Civilization

Chinese Culture—Had it Independent Origin?—Evolution in Human Affairs—Stratification Theory—The Mystery of Mind—Man's First Philosophy of Life—Influences exercised by Ancient Civilizations—Culture Mixing—The Idea of Progress—Art in the Pleistocene Age—Introduction of Agriculture—Birth of Osirian Civilization—The " Water of Greenness " as " Water of Life "—How Commerce Began—Introduction of Copper-working—The Oldest Calendar in the World—The " Kings of Mankind "—Ancient Man and Modern Man.

THE destinies of a people are shaped by their modes of thought, and their real history is therefore the history of their culture. The Chinese frame of mind has made the Chinese the people they are and China the country it is. Every section of society has been swayed by this far-reaching and enduring influence, the sources of which lie in remote antiquity. It is the force that has even been shaping public opinion and directing political movements. Emperors and leaders of thought have been uplifted by it or cast down by it.

To understand China, it is necessary that we should inquire into its inner history—the history of its culture—

1

so as to get at the Chinese point of view and look at things through Chinese eyes. That inner history is in part a record of its early experiences among the nations of the earth. There was a time when China was "in the making", when the little leaven that leavened the whole lump began to move, when that culture which spread over a vast area was confined to a small centre and to a comparatively small group of people. Who were this people, where were they situated, what influences were at work to stir them and shape their ambitions, and what secret did they learn which gave them power over the minds and bodies of about a third of the inhabitants of the globe? In short, how and where did Chinese culture originate, and how did it spread and become firmly established? Was it a thing of purely local growth? Did it begin to be quite independently of all other cultures? Does it owe its virility and distinctiveness among the cultures of ancient and modern times to the influence of the locality in which it had "independent origin"? Had it an independent origin?

These queries open up the larger problem as to the origin of civilization in the world. At this point, therefore, we must decide whether or not we are to accept the idea of evolution in human affairs. Can the principles of biological evolution be applied to the problems of ethnology (using the term in its widest sense to include the physical and cultural history of mankind)? Can we accept the theory that in isolated quarters of the globe separated communities were stirred by natural laws to make progress in adapting themselves to their environments, and that, once a beginning was made, separated communities developed on similar lines? Did each ancient civilization have its natural periods of growth and decay? Were separated communities uninfluenced during these periods by human minds and wills? Were their destinies shaped by natural laws, or by the cumulative force of public opinion? Was it a natural law that made men abandon the hunting and adopt the agricultural mode of life? Did certain communities of men, influenced by natural laws in ancient times, begin to shape their religious systems by first worshipping groups of spirits and ultimately, having passed through a sequence of well-defined stages, find themselves elevated by these natural laws to the stage of monotheism? Is it because certain races have, for some mysterious reason, been prompted to pass through these stages more quickly than others, that they have been termed "progressive" while others have been characterized as "backward"?

If these questions are answered in the affirmative, we must assume that we have solved the riddle of Mind. Those who apply the principles of biological evolution to human affairs are in the habit of referring to laws that control the workings of the human mind. But what do we really know about the workings of the human mind? This question has only to be asked so that the hazardous character of the fashion of thinking adopted by extreme exponents of the Evolution School may be emphasized. It cannot but be admitted that we know little or nothing regarding the human mind. What happens when we think? How are memories stored in the brain? How are emotions caused? What is Consciousness? How does the Will operate? Grave psychological problems have to be solved before we can undertake the responsibility of discussing with any degree of confidence the laws that are supposed to govern human thought and action.

The researches into the early history of man, of about a generation ago, were believed by some to "have revealed the essential similarity with which, under many superficial differences, the human mind has elaborated its first crude philosophy of life". It was found that similar beliefs and practices obtained among widely separated communities, and it was not suspected that the influence exercised by direct and indirect cultural contact between "progressive" and "backward" communities extended to such great distances as has since been found to be the case. Prospecting routes by land and sea were the avenues along which cultural influences "drifted". Early man was much more enterprising as a trader and explorer than was believed in Tylor's day. The evidence accumulated of late years tends to show that almost no part of the globe remained immune to the influences exercised by the great ancient civilizations, and that these civilizations were never in a state of "splendid isolation" at any period in their histories. In the light of this knowledge it is becoming more and more clear that Victorian ethnologists were inclined to make too much of resemblances, and failed to take into account the differences that a more intensive study of local cultures have revealed. There were, of course, resemblances, which suggest the influence of cultural contact and the settlement among backward peoples of colonists from progressive communities, but there were also differences of beliefs and customs which were of local origin and can hardly be characterized as "superficial". One of the results of contact was the process of "culture mixing". Customs and fashions of thinking were introduced into a country and blended with local customs and local modes of thought. In early China, as will be shown, there was "culture mixing". The Chinese people incorporated cultural elements from other sources into their belief system in remote times.

How, then, did the idea of progress originate? Is there in the human mind an instinct which stirs mankind to achieve progress? If so, how does it come about that some peoples have failed to move until brought into contact with progressive races? Why did the Melanesians, for instance, remain in the Stone Age until reached by the missionary and the sandal-wood trader? The missionaries and the traders caused them to advance in a brief period from the Stone Age to the Age of Steel and Machinery. Can it be maintained that in ancient days no sudden changes took place? Did the people, for instance, who introduced bronze-working into a country introduce nothing else? Did they leave behind their beliefs, their myths, their customs, and their stories?

When it is asked how progress originated, we can only turn to such evidence as is available regarding the early history of " Modern Man ". At a remote period, dating back in Europe to the Pleistocene Age, men lived in organized communities and pursued the hunting mode of life. Their culture is revealed by their pictorial art in the prehistoric cave-dwellings of France and Spain, and their decorative art by their finely engraved implements and weapons.[1] This art reached a high state of perfection. In some aspects it compares favourably with modern art.[2] Evidently it had a long history, and was practised by those who were endowed with the artistic faculty and had received a training. These early men, who belonged to the Cro-Magnon races, were traders as well as hunters. In some of their " inland stations " have been found shells that had been imported from the Mediterranean coast.

The hunting mode of life prevailed also among the proto-Egyptians in the Nile valley, an area which was less capable in remote times of maintaining a large popu-

[1] *Myths of Crete and Pre-Hellenic Europe*, pp. 26 *et seq.*
[2] *Ibid.* See illustrations opposite p. 20.

lation than were the wide and fertile plains of Europe. Egypt was thinly peopled until the agricultural mode of life was introduced. Someone discovered how to make use of the barley that grew wild in the Nile valley and western Asia. In time the seeds were cultivated, and some little community thus provided itself with an abundant food-supply. Men's minds were afterwards engaged in solving the problem how to extend the area available for cultivation in the narrow Nile valley. Nature was at hand to make suggestions to them. Each year the River Nile came down in flood and fertilized the parched and sun-burnt wastes. The waters caused the desert to "blossom like the rose". Intelligent observers perceived that if the process of water-fertilization were maintained, as in the Delta region, they could extend their little farms and form new ones. The art of irrigation was discovered and gradually adopted, with the result that the narrow river valley, which had been thinly peopled during the Hunting Period, became capable of maintaining a large population.

In what particular area the agricultural mode of life was first introduced, it is impossible to say. Some favour southern Palestine and some southern Mesopotamia. Those who favour Egypt[1] can refer to interesting and important evidence in support of their view. It is the only ancient country, for instance, in which there are traditions regarding the man[2] who introduced the agricultural mode of life. This was Osiris, a priest-king[3] who was deified, or a god to whom was credited the discovery, made by a

[1] Professor Cherry *The Origin of Agriculture* (Mem. and Proc. Manchester Lit. and Phil. Soc., 1920).

[2] In Babylonian legends civilization is introduced by the "goat-fish" god Ea, who came from the Persian Gulf.

[3] Those who give Osiris a Libyan origin believe his name signifies "The Old One", or "The Old Man".

man or group of men, of how to grow corn. Plutarch's version of the Egyptian legend states: "Osiris, being now become King of Egypt, applied himself towards civilizing his countrymen, by turning them from their former indigent and barbarous course of life; he moreover taught them how to cultivate and improve the fruits of the earth". Evidence has been forthcoming that the pre-Dynastic Egyptians were agriculturists. The bodies of many of them have been found preserved in their graves in the hot dry sands of Upper Egypt. "From the stomachs and intestines of these prehistoric people", writes Professor G. Elliot Smith, "I was able to recover large quantities of food materials, in fact, the last meals eaten before death." Careful examination was made of the contents of the stomachs. "Almost every sample contained husks of barley, and in about 10 per cent of the specimens husks of millet could be identified with certainty." The millet found in these bodies is nearly related to the variety "which is now cultivated in the East Indies".[1]

Here we have proof that the agricultural mode of life obtained in the Nile valley over sixty centuries ago, and that the seeds of the cultivated variety of millet, which grows wild in North Africa and southern Asia, were carried to far-distant areas by ancient traders and colonists. These facts have, as will be found, an important bearing on the early history of Chinese civilization.

Our immediate concern, however, is with the history of early civilization. In the Nile valley man made progress when he was able to provide something which he required, by the intelligent utilization of means at his disposal. No natural law prompted him to cultivate corn and irrigate the sun-parched soil. He did not

[1] *The Ancient Egyptians*, pp. 41–42.

become an agriculturist by instinct. He conducted observations, exercised his reasoning faculty, made experiments, and a great discovery was forthcoming. The man whose memory is enshrined in that of Osiris was one of the great benefactors of the human race. When he solved the problem of how to provide an abundant supply of food, he made it possible for a large population to live in a small area. It is told of Osiris that " he gave them (the Egyptians) a body of laws to regulate their conduct by ". No doubt the early hunters observed laws which regulated conduct in the cave-home as well as on the hunting-field. The fact that a great pictorial art was cultivated by Aurignacian man in western Europe, about 20,000 years ago, indicates that the social organization had been sufficiently well developed to permit of certain individuals of a class—possibly the priestly class—devoting themselves to the study of art, while others attended to the food-supply. Aurignacian art could never have reached the degree of excellence it did had there not been a school of art—apparently religious art—and a system of laws that promoted its welfare.

When, in Egypt, the agricultural mode of life was introduced, and an abundant supply of food was assured, new laws became a necessity, so that the growing communities might be kept under control. These laws were given a religious significance. Osiris " instructed them (the Egyptians) in that reverence and worship which they were to pay to the gods ". Society was united by the bonds of a religious organization, and, as is found, Nilotic religion had a close association with the agricultural mode of life. It reflected the experiences of the early farmers; it reflected, too, the natural phenomena of the Nile valley. Water—the Nile water—was the fertilizing agency. It was the " water of life ". The god Osiris was closely associated with the Nile; he was the "fresh" or the "new" water that flowed in due season after the trying period of "the low Nile", during which the land was parched by the burning sun and every green thing was coated by the sand-storms. "Ho, Osiris! the inundation comes," cried the priest when the Nile began to rise. "Horus comes; he recognizes his father in thee, youthful in thy name of Fresh Water."[1] The literal rendering is: "Horus comes; he beholds his father in thee, *greenness* in thy name of *Water of Greenness*". The reference is to the "new water" which flows quite green for the first few days of the annual inundation. The "new water" entered the soil and vegetation sprang up. Osiris was the principle of life; he was also the ghost-god who controlled the river. As the Nile, Osiris was regarded as the source of all life—the creator and sustainer and ruler in one.

When the discovery of how to grow corn was passed from people to people and from land to land, not only the seeds and agricultural implements were passed along, but the ceremonies and religious beliefs connected with the agricultural mode of life in the area of origin. The ceremonies were regarded as of as much importance as the implements.

It need not surprise us, therefore, to find, as we do find, not only North African millet in the East Indies, but North African religious beliefs connected with agriculture in widely separated countries. Osirian religious ideas and myths were, it would appear, distributed over wide areas and among various races. There is therefore a germ of historical truth in the account given by Plutarch of the missionary efforts of Osiris. "With the same disposition", we read, "he (Osiris) afterwards

---

[1] Breasted's *Religion and Thought in Egypt*, p. 18.

travelled over the rest of the world, inducing the people everywhere to submit to his discipline. . . . The Greeks conclude him to have been the same person with their Dionysos or Bacchus."[1]

In the process of time the Egyptians found that they were able to produce a larger food-supply than they required for their own needs. They were consequently able to devote their surplus to stimulating trade, so as to obtain from other countries things which were not to be had in Egypt. They were thus brought into touch with other communities, and these communities, such as the wood-cutters of Lebanon, were influenced by Egyptian civilization and stimulated to adopt new modes of life. Their food-supply was assured by the Egyptian demand for timber. They received corn from the Nile valley in payment for their labour. There are references in the Egyptian texts to the exports of wheat to North Syria and Asia Minor.

When the great discovery was made of how to work copper, the early agriculturists achieved rapid progress. Boats were built more easily and in larger numbers, new weapons were produced, and the Upper Egyptians con-quered the Lower Egyptians, with the result that Egypt was united under a single king. With this union, which was followed by a period of remarkable activity, begins the history of Ancient Egypt.

The man, remembered as Osiris, who first sowed his little corn patch, sowed also the seeds from which grew a mighty empire and a great civilization. His discovery spread from people to people, and from land to land, and a new era was inaugurated in the history of the world. Progress was made possible when mankind were led from the wide hunting-fields to the little fields of the Stone

[1] S. Squire, *Plutarch's Treatise of Isis and Osiris* (Cambridge, 1744).

Age[1] farmer, and shown how they could live pleasant and well-ordered lives in large communities.

The early Egyptian farmers found it necessary to measure time and take account of the seasons. A Calendar was introduced and adopted during the prehistoric (Palæolithic) period,[2] and was used by the Egyptians for thousands of years. Julius Cæsar adapted this Calendar for use in Rome. It was subsequently adjusted by Pope Gregory and others, and is now in use throughout much of the world. Each time we hang up a new calendar, therefore, we are reminded of the man who stimulated progress over vast areas by sowing corn, so as to provide food for his family in a distant land at a far-distant period of time.

When we consider the problem of the origin of progress, let us not forget him and others like him—those early thinkers and discoverers to whom all humanity owe a debt of gratitude. The few invent, the many adopt; the few think and lead, and the many follow.

"No abstract doctrine", writes Sir James F. Frazer in this connection, "is more false and mischievous than that of the natural equality of men. . . . The experience of common life sufficiently contradicts such a vain imagination. . . . The men of keenest intelligence and strongest characters lead the rest and shape the moulds into which, outwardly at least, society is cast. . . . The true rulers of men are the thinkers who advance knowledge. . . . It is knowledge which, in the long run, directs and controls the forces of society. Thus the discoverers of new truths are the real though uncrowned and unsceptred kings of mankind."[3]

---

[1] In Egypt this was the Solutrean stage of the so-called "Palæolithic Age".

[2] There was no "Neolithic Age" in Egypt.

[3] *The Scope of Social Anthropology* (London, 1908), pp. 12–13.

Progress has its origin in Mind. It has been manifested in the past in those districts in which the mind of man was applied to overcome natural obstacles and to develop natural resources. The histories of the great ancient civilizations do not support the idea of an evolutionary process which had its origin in human instinct. "There has", Professor G. Elliot Smith writes, "been no general or widespread tendency on the part of human societies to strive after what by Europeans is regarded as intellectual or material progress. Progressive societies are rare because it requires a very complex series of factors to compel men to embark upon the hazardous process of striving after such artificial advancement."

Professor Elliot Smith will have none of what Dr. W. H. R. Rivers refers to as "crude evolutionary ideas". "The history of man", he writes, "will be truly interpreted, not by means of hazardous and mistaken analogies with biological evolution, but by the application of the true historical method. The causes of the modern actions of mankind are deeply rooted in the past. But the spirit of man has ever been the same: and the course of ancient history can only be properly appreciated when it is realized that the same human motives whose nature can be studied in our fellow-men to-day actuated the men of old also."[1]

In the chapters that immediately follow it will be shown that separated communities were brought into close touch by traders. The term "trading", however, refers, especially in early times, chiefly to prospecting and the exploiting of locally unappreciated forms of wealth. It was not until after early traders had travelled far and wide that permanent trade routes were established. Some overland routes became less important when sea routes were ultimately opened.

[1] *Primitive Man* (Proceedings of the British Academy, Vol. VII), p. 50.

CHAPTER II

A Far-travelled Invention

The Potter's Wheel—An Egyptian Invention—The Wheel in Theology
—Clay Pots and Stone Vessels—Skilled Artisans produce Poor Pottery—The
Yakut Evidence—Female Potters—Pot Symbol of Mother-goddess—Potter's
Wheel worked by Men—Egyptian "Wheel" adopted in Crete, Babylonia,
Iran, India, and China—No "Wheel" in America—Secular and Religious
Pottery in China, Japan, India, and Rome—Coarse Grave-Pottery—Potter's
Wheel as Symbol of Creator—Chinese Emperors as Potters—Culture Heroes—
Association of Agriculture with Pottery—Egyptian Ideas in Far East.

WHAT bearing, it may be asked, have the discoveries made
in Egypt on the early history of China? Is there evidence
to show that these widely-separated countries were brought
into contact in remote times? Did the primitive Chinese
receive and adopt Egyptian inventions, and if so, how
were such inventions conveyed across the wide and difficult country lying between the Mediterranean coast and
the Yellow Sea? Is there any proof that trade routes
extended in ancient times right across Asia? Did prospecting and trading ancient mariners cross the Indian
Ocean and coast round to Chinese waters?

Interesting evidence regarding cultural contact is
afforded by the potter's wheel. This wonderful machine
was invented in Egypt some time before the Fourth
Dynasty (about 3000 B.C.), and in its area of origin it
exercised an influence not only on ceramic craftsmanship
but on religious ideas. It was regarded as a gift of the
gods, as in ancient Scotland bronze weapons, implements,

musical instruments, &c., were regarded as gifts from the fairies. Apparently the invention was first introduced in Memphis, the ancient capital, the chief god of which was Ptah, the supreme deity "of all handicraftsmen and of all workers in metal and stone". Ptah was already regarded as the creator of the primeval egg from which the universe was hatched, and of the "sun egg" and the "moon egg". He was evidently a deity whose life-history goes back to primitive times when the mother-goddess was symbolized as the goose that laid the primeval egg. The problem of whether the egg or the bird came first was solved by the priests of the Ptah cult of Memphis, who regarded their deity as the creator of the "egg". After the potter's wheel came into use, they depicted Ptah turning the "egg" upon it. The manufacture of wheel-made pottery thus came to have religious associations. It was closely connected with the culture of Egypt which had its basis in the agricultural mode of life. The arts and crafts were all stimulated by religious ideas; they were cultivated by the priestly class in temple workshops, and were essentially an expression of Egyptian beliefs and conceptions.

Before the potter's wheel came into use, the potter's art had degenerated. Vases, bowls, jars, platters, and other vessels were made of such costly stones as diorite, alabaster, and porphyry; these were drilled out with copper implements. Copper vessels were also made. The discovery of how to work copper had caused the craftsmen to neglect the potter's art, and to work with enthusiasm in the hardest stone until they achieved a high degree of skill. The coarse pottery of the pre-wheel period is therefore no indication that the civilization had reached a stage of decadence. This fact should be a warning to those archæologists who are prone to conclude that if the pottery taken from a stratum in some particular

area is "coarse", the people who produced it at the period
it represents were necessarily in a backward condition.
The evidence afforded by Yakut products is of special
interest in this connection. The Yakuts are usually
referred to as " the most intelligent and progressive
people in Siberia". They are, however, poor potters.
They never glaze their vessels or use the potter's wheel.
At the great Russian market of Yakutsk they refuse to
purchase wheel-made crockery, and purchase instead the
raw clay with which to make their own hand-made vessels,
which are almost as coarse as those of the Stone Age.
But although the technique displayed in their pottery is
crude, they are famous for their excellent wood-carving
and iron forged-work.[1] A people cannot, therefore, be
judged by their pottery alone. It may be that those
ancient peoples who are found to have been poor potters
were skilled and progressive in other spheres of activity.
Whether in their artwork, their literature, their music, or
their technical solutions to the demands of daily living,
different cultures offer different contributions to history.

After the potter's wheel was introduced in Memphis,
a new era in the history of pottery was inaugurated. The
enclosed baking-furnace came into use at the same time,
and the potter's art and technique speedily attained a
wonderfully high degree of excellence. But the old
crude, hand-made pottery was still being produced. It
was consistently produced until Egypt ceased to be a great
and independent kingdom. Indeed, it is being manufactured even in our own day.

The reason why good and bad pottery are produced
in a single country—and Egypt is no exception to this
rule—is that the manufacture of hand-made vessels was
in ancient times essentially a woman's avocation. The

[1] *The Yakut* (in Russian), Vol. I, p. 378.

potter's wheel was invented by man, and credited to a
god, and has from the beginning been worked by men
only.   There was apparently a religious significance in
the connection of the sexes with the different processes.
The clay pot was, in ancient Egypt, a symbol of the
mother-goddess.[1]   Pots used in connection with the worship of the Great Mother were apparently produced by
her priestesses.   As women played their part in agricultural ceremonies, so did they play their part—evidently a
prominent one—in producing the goddess's pot symbols.
The coarse jars in which were stored wines and oils and
food-stuffs were gifts of the Great Mother, the giver of
all; she was the inexhaustible sacred Pot—the womb of
Nature.   Domestic pottery used by women was, very
properly, the ancient folks appear to have argued, produced by women.

"It will be noted", writes O. T. Mason in this connection, "that the feminine gender is used throughout in
speaking of aboriginal potters.   This is because every
piece of such ware is the work of woman's hands.   She
quarried the clay, and, like the patient beast of burden,
bore it home on her back.   She washed it and kneaded it
and rolled it into fillets.   These she wound carefully and
symmetrically until the vessel was built up.   She further
decorated and burned it, and wore it out in household
drudgery.   The art at first was woman's."[2]

In many countries the connection of women with
hand-made and of men with wheel-made pottery obtains
even in our day.   The following statement by two American scholars, who have produced a short but authoritative
paper on the potter's art, is the result of a close investiga-

---

[1] *The Evolution of the Dragon*, G. Elliot Smith (London, 1919), pp. 178 *et seq.*
[2] O. T. Mason, *Origins of Invention*, p. 166; and *Woman's Share in Primitive Culture*, p. 91.

tion of evidence collected over a wide area, and carefully digested and summarized :[1]

" The potter's wheel is the creation of man, and therefore is an independent act of invention which was not evolved from any contrivance utilized during the period of hand-made ceramic ware.   The two processes have grown out of two radically distinct spheres of human activity.   The wheel, so speak, came from another world. It had no point of contact with any tool that existed in the old industry, but was brought in from an outside quarter as a novel affair when man appropriated to himself the work hitherto cultivated by woman.   The development was one from outside, not from within.   All efforts, accordingly, which view the subject solely from the technological angle, and try to derive the wheel from previous devices of the female potter, are futile and misleading.   It is as erroneous as tracing the plough back to the hoe or digging-stick, whereas, in fact, the two are in no historical interrelation and belong to fundamentally different culture strata and periods — the hoe to the gardening activity of woman, the plough to the agricultural activity of man.   Both in India and China the division of ceramic labour sets apart the thrower or wheel-potter, and distinctly separates him from the moulder. The potters in India, who work on the wheel, do not intermarry with those who use a mould or make images. They form a caste by themselves."[2]

The oldest wheel-made pottery is found in Egypt. There can be no doubt that the potter's wheel was invented in that country.   It was imported into Crete,

---

[1] *The Beginnings of Porcelain in China*, by Berthold Laufer and H. W. Nichols (Field Museum of Natural History Publication, 192, Anthropological Series, Vol. XII, No. 2.   Chicago, 1917).

[2] *Ibid*, pp. 153–154.

which had trading relations with the merchants of the ancient Pharaohs, as far back as about 3000 B.C. Before the wheel was adopted the Cretans made stone vessels, following Egyptian patterns, but using soft stone instead of hard. Their hand-made pottery degenerated, as did the Egyptian. "Pottery came again to its own in both countries", writes Mr. H. R. Hall, "with the invention of the potter's wheel and the baking-furnace."[1]

The potter's wheel must have found a ready market in the old days. It was adopted, in time, in western Europe; it was quickly "taken up" in Babylonia and in Iran, and was ultimately introduced into India and China. But not all Asiatic civilizations adopted it, and consequently wheel-made pottery is not found everywhere. Among the "aboriginal Americans" the wheel was never employed. It is an interesting fact that the mind of man, which is alleged to "work" on the same lines everywhere, never "evolved" a potter's wheel in Mexico or Peru.[2] Major Gordon tells that in Assam[3] "the women fashion the pots by hand; they do not use the potter's wheel". Similar evidence is obtainable in various other countries. In China there are wheel-potters and moulders, and a distinction is drawn between them by ancient writers. "This clear distinction is accentuated by Chu Yen in his treatise on pottery.[4] He justly observes also that the articles made by the wheel-potters were all intended for cooking, with the exception of the vessel *yu*, which was designed for measuring; while the output of the moulders, who made the ceremonial vessels *kuei* and *tou* by availing themselves of the plumb-line, was

[1] *The Journal of Egyptian Archæology*, April, 1914, p. 14.
[2] *Aboriginal Pottery of the Eastern United States*, p. 50 (Twentieth Annual Report, Bureau of American Ethnology, Washington, 1903).
[3] *The Khasis*, p. 61.   [4] *Tao Shuo*, chap. ii, p. 2 (new edition, 1912).

intended for sacrificial use. Also here, in like manner as in ancient Rome, India, and Japan, the idea may have prevailed that a wheel-made jar is of a less sacred character than one made by hand."[1] Here then we touch on another point which must be borne in mind by those who draw conclusions regarding ancient cultures by means of pottery. In Britain, for instance, a rather coarse pottery is found in graves. It is possible that a better pottery was made for everyday use. The conservatism of burial customs may have caused coarser pottery to be put into graves than the early folks were capable of producing during the period at which the burial took place.

The wheel-pottery was as sacred to some cults as the hand-made was to others. Even the potter's wheel was sacred. In Egypt the Ptah cult adopted it, as has been stated; in India it was a symbol of the Creator; in China (as in ancient Egypt) the idea originally prevailed that the Creator was a potter who turned on his wheel the sun and the moon, man and woman, although in time this myth became a philosophical abstraction. The symbolism of Jeremiah has similarly a history:

"O house of Israel, cannot I do with you as this potter? saith the Lord. Behold, as the clay is in the potter's hand, so are ye in mine hand, O house of Israel."—Chapter XVIII, 6.

St. Paul, too, refers to the potter:

"Nay but, O man, who art thou that repliest against God? Shall the thing formed say to him that formed it, Why hast thou made me thus? Hath not the potter power over the clay, of the same lump to make one vessel unto honour, and another unto dishonour?" (Romans, ix, 20–21.)

Chinese emperors were compared to potters. They

---

[1] *The Beginnings of Porcelain in China*, pp. 154–5. In "culture mixing" old local religious beliefs were not obliterated.

were credited with the power to control a nation as the potter controlled his wheel. The ancient peoples who adopted the Egyptian potter's wheel evidently learned that it was of divine origin. They adopted the Egyptian beliefs and myths associated with it. Withal, the wheel was associated with the agricultural mode of life, having originated in a country of agriculturists. Ptah, the divine potter, was, like all the other prominent gods of Egypt, fused with Osiris—the god who was, among other things, the "culture hero". The Chinese "culture hero", Shun, who became emperor, is said to have "practised husbandry, fishing, and making pottery jars". He manufactured clay vessels without flaw on the river bank.[1]

The Chinese culture hero, Shen-ming ("Divine Husbandman") "was regarded as the father of agriculture and the discoverer of the healing property of plants". In ancient Chinese lore "we meet a close association of agriculture with pottery, and an illustration of the fact that husbandman and potter were one and the same person during the primeval period".[2]

Memories of Ptah-Osiris clung to the potter's wheel. The trade routes must have hummed with stories about the god who had gifted this wonderful contrivance to mankind. These stories were localized in various countries, and they took on the colour of the period during which the wheel was imported. In Japan, the Ptah legend has been given a Buddhistic significance. The potter's wheel is reputed there to be the invention of the famous Korean monk, Gyōgi (A.D. 670–749). No doubt the first potter's wheel reached Japan from Korea, whence came the conquerors of the Ainus. But there is evidence

---

[1] Chavannes, *Mémoires historiques de Se-ma Ts'ien*, Vol. I, pp. 72–4.
[2] *The Beginnings of Porcelain in China*, p. 160.

that it was in use long before Buddhism "drifted" along
the sea route from the mainland in the sixth century, to
become curiously mixed up with Shintoism two centuries
later.   The priests of Buddhism, who transformed the
Shinto gods into "avatars" of Buddha, no doubt also
identified the far-carried Ptah-Osiris with their monk—
the Japanese "culture hero".

The earliest pottery in Japan was manufactured by
the Ainus and was "hand-shaped" by the women.   A
similar pottery was produced in Korea.   The wheel-made
variety made its appearance when Chinese culture spread
through Korea during the Silla kingdom period, which
began about the time (A.D. 59) when the earliest Japanese,
according to their own traditions, migrated to the islands
that bear their name.   No doubt the traders were active
on sea and land long before the Japanese conquered the
islands of the Ainus and the Chinese overran Korea.
Great migrations and conquests in ancient times were
indirectly stimulated by trade.   A new culture was
introduced into backward communities by the early
prospectors and trading colonists, and these communities
in time acquired weapons, reared the domesticated horse,
and took to the sea after having learned how to build and
navigate ships similar to those introduced by the traders.

When the potter's wheel was introduced into Korea,
the clay vessels were shaped in imitation of Chinese
pottery.   There can remain no doubt, therefore, as to
whence the wheel came.   China was the chief centre
of early civilization in the Far East, and its influence
spread far and wide.   There are some who think that
Burma was during its early period in closer touch with
China than with India ; but more evidence than is yet
available is required to establish this theory.   The earliest
civilization in southern China of which we have know-

ledge was of Indian origin.   The sea traders who had crossed the Indian Ocean reached the Burmese coast several centuries before the Christian era, as the archaic character of Burmese river boats suggests.   It may be, however, that the potter's wheel was carried along the mid-Asian trade routes long before the shippers coasted round to Chinese waters.   There can be no doubt that the potter's wheel was introduced into China at a very remote period.   Investigators are unable to discover any native legends regarding its origin.   Nor are there any traditions regarding female potters.   The culture heroes of China who made the first pots appear to have used the wheel, and the Chinese potter's wheel is identical with the Egyptian.

When the wheel was introduced into Japan, hand-made pottery was in use for religious purposes, and for long afterwards the vessels used at Shinto shrines were not turned on the wheel.   In India, hand-made pottery was similarly reserved for religious worship after the wheel-made variety came into use.[1]   The wheel did not reach southern India until its Iron Age.[2]   When the southern India Iron Age began is uncertain.   It was not, of course, an " Age " in the real sense, but a cultural " stage ".   Iron was known and apparently in use during the Aryo-Indian Vedic period in the north.[3]

The potter's wheel was introduced into Babylonia at a very remote period.   From Babylonia it was carried into Persia.   The Avestan word for kiln is *tanura*, which is believed, according to Laufer, to be a loan word from Semitic *tanur*.

There are, of course, no records regarding the intro-

---

[1] *Antiquities of India*, L. D. Barnett, p. 176.
[2] *Madras Government Museum Catalogue of Prehistoric Antiquities*, p. 111.
[3] *Vedic Index of Names and Subjects*, Macdonell and Keith, Vol. I, pp. 31, 32.

duction of the potter's wheel into Babylonia, India, or
China. All that we know definitely is that it first came
into use in Egypt, and that it was afterwards adopted in
the various ancient centres of civilization from which
cultural influences "flowed" to various areas. With the
wheel went certain religious ideas and customs. These
are not found in the areas unreached by the potter's
wheel.

China appears to have been influenced at the dawn of
its history by the culture represented by the Egyptian
wheel.

CHAPTER III

Ancient Mariners and Explorers

The Chinese Junk—Kutas—The Ancient "Reed Float" and Skin-buoyed Raft—"Two floats of the Sky"—Dug-out Canoes—Where Shipping was developed—Burmese and Chinese Junks resemble Ancient Egyptian Ships—Cretan and Phoenician Mariners—Africa circumnavigated—Was Sumeria colonized by Sea-farers?—Egyptian Boats on Sea of Okhotsk—Japanese and Polynesian Boats—Egyptian Types in Mediterranean and Northern Europe—Stories of Long Voyages in Small Craft—Visit of Chinese Junk to the Thames—Solomon's Ships.

FURTHER important evidence regarding cultural contact in early times is afforded by shipping. How came it about that an inland people like the primitive Chinese took to seafaring?

The question that first arises in this connection is: Were ships invented and developed by a single ancient people, or were they invented independently by various ancient peoples at different periods? Were the Chinese junks of independent origin? Or were these junks developed from early models of vessels—such foreign vessels as first cruised in Chinese waters?

Chinese junks are flat-bottomed ships, and the largest of them reach about 1000 tons. The poops and forecastles are high, and the masts carry lug-sails, generally of bamboo splits. They are fitted with rudders. Often on the bows appear painted or inlaid eyes. These eyes are found on models of ancient Egyptian ships.

During the first Han dynasty (about 206 B.C.) junks

24

of "one thousand *kin*" (about 15 tons) were regarded as very large vessels. In these boats the early Chinese navigators appear to have reached Korea and Japan. But long before they took to the sea there were other mariners in the China sea.

The Chinese were, as stated, originally an inland people. They were acquainted with river *kufas* (coracles) before they reached the seashore. These resembled the kufas of the Babylonians referred to by Herodotus, who wrote:

"The boats which come down the river to Babylon are circular, and made of skins. The frames, which are of willow, are cut in the country of the Armenians above Assyria, and on these, which serve for hulls, a covering of skins is stretched outside, and thus the boats are made, without either stem or stern, quite round like a shield."[1]

These kufas are still in use in Mesopotamia. They do not seem to have altered much since the days of Hammurabi, or even of Sargon of Akkad. The Assyrians crossed rivers on skin floats, and some of the primitive peoples of mid-Asia are still using the inflated skins of cows as river "ferry-boats". But such contrivances hardly enter into the history of shipping. The modern liner did not "evolve" from either kufa or skin float. Logs of wood were, no doubt, used to cross rivers at an early period. The idea of utilizing these may have been suggested to ancient hunters who saw animals being carried down on trees during a river flood. But attempts to utilize a tree for crossing a river would have been disastrous when first made, if the hunters were unable to swim. Trees are so apt to roll round in water. Besides, they would be useless if not guided with a punting-pole, expertly manipulated. Early man must have learned

[1] Book I, chap. 194.

how to navigate a river by using, to begin with, at least two trees lashed together. In Egypt and Babylonia we find traces of his first attempts in this connection. The reed float, consisting of two bundles of reeds, and the raft to which the inflated skins of animals were attached to give it buoyancy, were in use at an early period on the Rivers Nile and Euphrates. A raft of this kind had evidently its origin among a people accustomed, as were the later Assyrians, to use skin floats when swimming across rivers. There are sculptured representations of the Assyrian soldiers swimming with inflated skins under their chests.

The reed float was in use at a very early period on the Nile. Professor Breasted says that the two prehistoric floats were " bound firmly together, side by side, like two huge cigars ", and adds the following interesting note: " The writer was once without a boat in Nubia, and a native from a neighbouring village at once hurried away and returned with a pair of such floats made of dried reeds from the Nile shores. On this somewhat precarious craft he ferried the writer over a wide channel to an island in the river. It was the first time that the author had ever seen this contrivance, and it was not a little interesting to find a craft which he knew only in the Pyramid texts of 5000 years ago still surviving and in daily use on the ancient river in far-off Nubia."

In the Pyramid texts there are references to the reed floats used by the souls of kings when being ferried across the river to death. The gods " bind together the two floats for this King Pepi", runs a Pyramid text. " The knots are tied, the ferry-boats are brought together", says another, and there are allusions to the ferryman (the prehistoric Charon) standing in the stern and poling the float. Before the Egyptian sun-god was placed in a boat, he had "two floats of the sky" to carry him along the celestial Nile to the horizon.[1]

The "dug-out" canoe was probably developed from the raft. Men who drifted timber down a river may have had the idea of a "dug-out" suggested to them by first shaping a seat on a log, or a "hold" to secure the food-supply for the river voyage. Pitt Rivers suggests that after the discovery was made that a hollowed log could be utilized in water, "the next stage in the development of the canoe would consist in pointing the ends".[2]

In what locality the dug-out canoe was invented it is impossible to say with absolute certainty. All reliable writers on naval architecture agree, however, that Egypt was the "cradle" of naval architecture.[3]

"For the development of the art of shipbuilding," says Chatterton, "few countries could be found as suitable as Egypt. . . . The peacefulness of the waters of the Nile, the absence of storms, and the rarity of calms, combined with the fact that, at any rate, during the winter and early spring months, the gentle north wind blew up the river with the regularity of a Trade Wind, so enabling the ships to sail against the stream without the aid of oars —these were just the conditions that many another nation might have longed for. Very different, indeed, were the circumstances which had to be wrestled with in the case of the first shipbuilders and sailormen of Northern Europe."[4]

The early Egyptians were continually crossing the

---

[1] Breasted, *Religion and Thought in Egypt*, pp. 108, 158.

[2] *Early Modes of Navigation*, Journal of the Anthropological Institute, Vol. IV, p. 402.

[3] Holmes's *Ancient and Modern Ships*, E. K. Chatterton's *Sailing Ships and their Story*, Cecil Torr's *Ancient Ships*, Warrington Smith's *Mast and Sail in Europe and Asia*, Elliot Smith's *Ships as Evidence of the Migrations of Early Culture*, and the works of Pâris and Assmann, and Pitt Rivers (*op. cit.*).

[4] *Sailing Ships and their Story*, pp. 25-6.

river. When they began to convey stones from their quarries, they required substantial rafts. Egyptian needs promoted the development of the art of navigation on a river specially suited for experiments that led to great discoveries. The demand for wood was always great, and it was intensified after metal-working had been introduced, because of the increased quantities of fuel required to feed the furnaces. It became absolutely necessary for the Egyptians to go far afield in search of timber. The fact that they received supplies of timber at an early period from Lebanon is therefore of special interest. Their experiences in drifting rafts of timber across the Mediterranean from the Syrian coast apparently not only stimulated naval architecture and increased the experiences of early navigators, but inaugurated the habit of organizing seafaring expeditions on a growing scale. "Men", says Professor Elliot Smith, "did not take to maritime trafficking either for aimless pleasure or for idle adventure. They went to sea only under the pressure of the strongest incentives."[1]

The Mediterranean must have been crossed at a very early period. Settlements of seafarers took place in Crete before 3000 B.C.[2] On the island have been found flakes of obsidian that were imported at the dawn of its history from the Island of Melos. No doubt obsidian artifacts were used in connection with the construction of vessels before copper implements became common.

The earliest evidence of shipbuilding as an organized and important national industry is found in the Egyptian tomb pictures of the Old Kingdom period (c. 2400 B.C.). Gangs of men, under overseers, are seen constructing many kinds of boats, large and small. There are records

[1] *Ships as Evidence*, &c., pp. 5, 6.
[2] *Myths of Crete and Pre-Hellenic Europe*, pp. 146 and 191, *et seq.*

of organized expeditions dating back 500 years earlier.
Pharaoh Snefru built vessels "nearly one hundred and
seventy feet long". He sent "a fleet of forty vessels to
the Phœnician coast to procure cedar logs from the slopes
of Lebanon".[1] Expeditions were also sent across the Red
Sea. Vessels with numerous oars, and even vessels with
sails, are depicted on Egyptian prehistoric pottery dating
back to anything like 6000 B.C. In no other country
in the world was seafaring and shipbuilding practised
at such a remote period.

The earliest representations of deep-sea boats are
found in Egypt. One is seen in the tomb of Sahure,
of the Fifth Dynasty (c. 2600 B.C.). A great expedition
sailed to Punt (Somaliland) during the reign of Queen
Halshepsut (c. 1500 B.C.). Five of the highly-developed
vessels are depicted in her temple at Deir-el-Bahari.
It is of interest to compare one of these vessels with
a Chinese junk. "Between the Chinese and Burmese
junks of to-day and the Egyptian ships of about six
thousand years ago there are", writes E. Kebel Chatterton,
"many points of similarity. . . . Until quite recently,
China remained in the same state of development for
four thousand years. If that was so with her arts and
life generally, it has been especially so in the case of
her sailing craft." Both the Chinese junk and the ancient
Egyptian ship "show a common influence and a remarkable persistence in type".[2]

"Are we to believe", a reader asks, "that the ancient
Egyptian navigators went as far as China? Is there any
proof that they made long voyages? Were the ancient
Egyptians not a people who lived in isolation for a
prolonged period?"[3]

[1] Breasted's *A History of Egypt*, pp. 114–5.   [2] *Sailing Ships and their Story*, pp. 31, 32.
[3] Maspero in his *The Dawn of Civilization* protests against this view.

It is not known definitely how far the ancient Egyptian mariners went after they had begun to venture to sea. But one thing is certain. They made much longer voyages than were credited to them a generation ago. The Phœnicians, who became the sea-traders of the Egyptians, learned the art of navigation from those Nilotic adventurers who began to visit their coast at a very early period in quest of timber; they adopted the Egyptian style of craft, as did the Cretans, their predecessors in Mediterranean sea trafficking. By the time of King Solomon the Phœnicians had established colonies in Spain, and were trading not only from Carthage in the Mediterranean, but apparently with the British Isles, while they were also active in the Indian Ocean. They were evidently accustomed to make long voyages of exploration. At the time of the Jewish captivity, Pharaoh Necho (609–593 B.C.) sent an expedition of Phœnicians from the Red Sea to circumnavigate Africa. They returned three years later by way of Gibraltar. But their voyage excited no surprise in Egypt.[1] It had long been believed by the priests that the world was surrounded by water. Besides, these priests preserved many traditions of long voyages that had been made to distant lands.

There are those who believe that the early Egyptian mariners, who were accustomed to visit British East Africa and sail round the Arabian coast, founded the earliest colony in Sumeria (ancient Babylonia) at the head of the Persian Gulf. The cradle of Sumerian culture was Eridu, "the sea port". The god of Eridu was Ea, who had a ship with pilot and crew. According to Babylonian traditions, he instructed the people, as did Osiris in Egypt, how to irrigate the land, grow corn, build houses and temples, make laws, engage in trade, and so

[1] *Egyptian Myth and Legend*, p. 372.

on. He was remembered as a monster—a goat-fish god, or half fish, half man. Apparently he was identical with the Oannes of Berosus. It may be that Ea-Oannes symbolized the seafarers who visited the coast and founded a colony at Eridu, introducing the agricultural mode of life and the working of copper. Early inland peoples must have regarded the mariners with whom they first came into contact as semi-divine beings, just as the Cubans regarded Columbus and his followers as visitors from the sky. The Mongols of Tartary entertained quaint ideas about the British " foreign devils " after they had fought in one of the early wars against China. M. Huc, the French missionary priest of the congregation of St. Lazarus, who travelled through Tartary, Tibet, and China during 1844–6, had once an interesting conversation with a Mongol, who " had been told by the Chinese what kind of people, or monsters rather, these English were ". The story ran that the Englishmen " lived in the water like fish, and when you least expected it, they would rise to the surface and cast at you fiery gourds. Then as soon as you bend your bow to send an arrow at them, they plunge again into the water like frogs."[1]

Those who suppose that the Sumerians coasted round from the Persian Gulf to the Red Sea, landed on the barren African coast, and, setting out to cross a terrible desert, penetrated to the Nile valley along a hitherto unexplored route of about 200 miles, have to explain what was the particular attraction offered to them by prehistoric Egypt if, according to their theory, it was still uncultivated and in the " Hunting Age ". How came it about that they knew of a river which ran through desert country?

[1] English translation of M. Huc's *Recollections* (London, 1852), p. 21.

It is more probable that the Nilotic people penetrated to the Red Sea coast, and afterwards ventured to sea in their river boats, and that, in time, having obtained skill in navigation, they coasted round to the Persian Gulf. In pre-Dynastic times the Egyptians obtained shells from the Red Sea coast.

At what period India was first reached is uncertain. When Solomon imported peacocks from that country (the land of the peacock), the sea route was already well known. It is significant to find that all round the coast, from the Red Sea to India, Ceylon, and Burma, the Egyptian types of vessels have been in use from the earliest seafaring periods. The Burmese junks on the Irawadi resemble closely, as has been indicated, the Nile boats of the ancient Egyptians.[1]   The Chinese junks were developed from Egyptian models. More antique Egyptian boats than are found on the Chinese coast are still being used by the Koryak tribe who dwell around the sea of Okhotsk.   Mr. Chatterton says that the Koryak craft have "important similarities to the Egyptian ships of the Fourth and Fifth Dynasties (c. 3000–2500 B.C.).   Thus, besides copying the ancients in steering with an oar, the fore-end of the prow of their sailing boats terminates in a fork through which the harpoon-line is passed, the fork being sometimes carved with a human face which they believe will serve as a protector of the boat.   Instead of rowlocks they have, like the early Egyptians, thong-loops through which the oar or paddle is inserted. Their sail, too, is a rectangular shape of dressed reindeer skins sewed together.   But it is their mast that is especially like the Egyptians and Burmese." This mast is made of three poles "set up in the manner

[1] E. Kebel Chatterton's *Sailing Ships and their Story*, pp. 7 and 31, and illustra-
opposite page 8.

of a tripod ". The double mast was common in ancient
Egypt, but Mr. Chatterton notes that Mr. Villiers Stuart
"found on the walls of a tomb belonging to the Sixth
Dynasty (*c.* 2400 B.C.) at Gebel Abu Faida, the painting
of a boat with a treble mast made of three spars arranged
like the edges of a triangular pyramid".[1] Thus we find
that vessels of Egyptian type (adopted by various peoples)
not only reached China but went a considerable distance
beyond it. Japanese vessels still display Egyptian characteristics. In the Moluccas and Malays the ancient three-
limbed mast has not yet gone out of fashion. Polynesian
craft were likewise developed from Egyptian models.
William Ellis, the missionary,[2] noted "the peculiar and
almost classical shape of the large Tahitian canoes", with
"elevated prow and stern", and tells that a fleet of them
reminded him of representations of "the ships in which
the Argonauts sailed, or the vessels that conveyed the
heroes of Homer to the siege of Troy".

Various writers have called attention to the persistence of Egyptian types in the Mediterranean and in
northern Europe. "In every age and every district of
the ancient world", wrote Mr. Cecil Torr, the great
authority on classic shipping, "the method of rigging
ships was substantially the same; and this method is first
depicted by the Egyptians."[3]

The Far Eastern craft went long distances in ancient
days. Ellis tells of regular voyages made by Polynesian
chiefs which extended to 300 and even 600 miles. A
chief from Rurutu once visited the Society Islands in
a native boat built "somewhat in the shape of a cres-
cent, the stem and stern high and pointed and the sides

[1] *Sailing Ships and their Story*, pp. 32–3.
[2] *Polynesian Researches*, First Edition, 1829, Vol. I, p. 169.
[3] *Ancient Ships*, p. 78.

deep ".[1]   Sometimes exceptionally long voyages were
forced by the weather conditions of Oceania.   " In
1696 ", Ellis writes, " two canoes were driven from
Ancarso to one of the Philippine Islands, a distance of
800 miles." He gives other instances of voyages of
like character. A Christian missionary, travelling in
a native boat, was carried " nearly 800 miles in a south-
westerly direction ".[2]   Reference has already been made
to the long and daring voyage made by the Phœnicians
who circumnavigated Africa. Another extraordinary
enterprise is referred to by Pliny the elder,[3] who quotes
from the lost work of Cornelius Nepos. This was a voyage
performed by Indians who had, before 60 B.C., embarked
on a commercial voyage and reached the coast of Germany. It is uncertain whether they sailed round the
Cape of Good Hope and up the Atlantic Ocean, or went
northward past Japan and discovered the north-east
passage, skirting the coast of Siberia, and sailing round
Lapland and Norway to the Baltic. They were made
prisoners by the Suevians and handed over to Quintus
Metellus Celer, pro-consular governor of Gaul.

In 1770 Japanese navigators reached the northern
coast of Siberia and landed at Kamchatka. They were
taken to St. Petersburg, where they were received by the
Empress of Russia, who treated them with marked kind-
ness. In 1847–8 the Chinese junk *Keying* sailed from
Canton to the Thames and caused no small sensation on
its arrival. This vessel rounded the Horn and took 477
days to complete the voyage.

Solomon's ships made long voyages : " Once every

---

[1] *Polynesian Researches*, First Edition, 1829, Vol. I, pp. 181, 2.   The crescent-shaped
vessel is quite Egyptian in character.

[2] *Ibid*, Vol. II, pp. 50, 51.   [3] Book II, 67.

three years came the navy of Tarshish, bringing gold, and silver, ivory, and apes, and peacocks ".[1]

As in the case of the potter's wheel, cultural elements were distributed far and wide by the vessels of the most ancient of mariners. Before tracing these elements in China, it would be well to deal with the motives that impelled early seafarers to undertake long and adventurous voyages of exploration and to found colonies in distant lands.

[1] 1 Kings, x, 22.

CHAPTER IV

The World-wide Search for Wealth

Religious Incentive of Quest of Wealth—Sacredness of Precious Metals and Stones—Gold and the Sky Deities—Iron as the Devil's Metal—Chinese Dragons and Metals—Gold good and Silver bad in India—Dragons and Copper—Sulphuret of Mercury as "Dragon's Blood" and Elixir of Life—Dragons and Pearls—The "Jewel that grants all Desires"—Story of Buddhist Abbot and the Sea-God—"Jewels of Flood and Ebb"—Japan and Korea—Sea-god as "Abundant Pearl Prince"—Pearl Fishers—Early History of Sea-trafficking—Traders and Colonists—Cow, Moon, Shells, and Pearls connected with Mother-goddess—The Sow Goddess—Shell Beliefs—Culture Drifts and Culture Complexes.

THERE can be no doubt as to the reasons why Solomon sought to emulate the maritime activities of the Phœnicians who had been bringing peacocks from India, silver from Spain, and gold from West Africa and elsewhere long before his day.

"And King Solomon made a navy of ships in Ezion-geber, which is beside Eloth, on the shore of the Red Sea, in the land of Edom.   And Hiram sent in the navy his servants, shipmen that had knowledge of the sea, with the servants of Solomon.   And they came to Ophir, and fetched from thence gold, four hundred and twenty talents, and brought it to King Solomon."[1]

When the Queen of Sheba visited Jerusalem she was accompanied by "camels that bare spices, and very much gold, and precious stones".[2]   About seven centuries before Solomon's day, Queen Hatshepsut of Egypt, to

[1] 1 Kings, ix, 26-8.   [2] 1 Kings, x, 2.

36

whom reference was made in the last chapter, had emu-
lated the feats of her ancestors by sending a fleet to Punt
(Somaliland or British East Africa) to bring back, among
other things, myrrh trees for her new temple.   The
myrrh was required " for the incense in the temple
service ".[1]   Ancient mariners set out on long voyages,
not only on the quest of wealth, but also of various
articles required for religious purposes.   Indeed, the
quest of wealth had originally religious associations.
Gold, silver, copper, pearls, and precious stones were
all sacred, and it was because of their connection with the
ancient deities that they were first sought for.   The so-
called " ornaments " worn by our remote ancestors were
charms against evil and ill luck.   Metals were similarly
supposed to have protective qualities.   Iron is still regarded
in the Scottish Highlands as a charm against fairy attack.
In China it is a protection against dragons.   The souls of
the Egyptian dead were " charmed " in the other world by
the amulets placed in their tombs.   When the Pharaoh's
soul entered the boat of the sun-god he was protected by
metals.   " Brought to thee ", a Pyramid text states, " are
blocks of silver and masses of malachite."[2]   Gold was the
metal of the sun-god and silver of the deity of the moon.
Horus had associations with copper, and Ptah, the god of
craftsmen, with various metals.   Iron was " the bones of
Set ", the Egyptian devil.   In Greece and India the mythical ages were associated with metals, and iron was the
metal of the dark age of evil (the Indian " Kali Yuga ").

In China the metals have similarly religious associations.   The dragon-gods of water, rain, and thunder are
connected with gold of various hues—the "golds" coloured
by the alchemists by fusion with other metals.   Thus we

[1] Breasted's *A History of Egypt*, p. 274.
[2] Breasted's *Religion and Thought in Ancient Egypt*, p. 279.

have Chinese references to red, yellow, white, blue, and black gold, as in the following extract :

"When the yellow dragon, born from yellow gold a thousand years old, enters a deep place, a yellow spring dashes forth; and if from this spring some particles (fine dust) arise, these become a yellow cloud.

"In the same way blue springs and blue clouds originate from blue dragons, born from blue gold eight hundred years old; red, white, and black springs and clouds from red, white, and black dragons born from gold of same colours a thousand years old."[1]

In Indian Vedic lore gold is a good metal and silver a bad metal. One of the Creation Myths states in this connection :

"He (Prajapati) created Asuras (demons). That was displeasing to him. That became the precious metal with the bad colour (silver). This was the origin of silver. He created gods. That was pleasing to him. That became the precious metal with the good colour (gold). That was the origin of gold."[2]

The dragon of the Far East is associated with copper as well as gold. In the Japanese *Historical Records* the story is told how the Emperor Hwang brought down a dragon so that he might ride on its back through the air. He first gathered copper on a mountain. Then he cast a tripod. Immediately a dragon, dropping its whiskers, came down to him. After the monarch had used the god as an "airship", no fewer than seventy of his subjects followed his example. Hwang was the monarch who prepared the "liquor of immortality" (the Japanese "soma") by melting cinnabar (sulphuret of mercury, known as "dragon's blood"). Chinese dragons, according to Wang Fu in '*Rh ya yih*, dread iron and like precious

---

[1] Quoted from a Chinese work by Dr. W. M. W. de Visser in *The Dragon in China and Japan* (Amsterdam, 1913).

[2] Muir's *Sanskrit Texts*, Vol. I, p. 516 (1890).

stones. In Japan the belief prevailed that if iron and filth were flung into ponds the dragons raised hurricanes that devastated the land. The Chinese roused dragons, when they wanted rain, by making a great noise and by throwing iron into dragon pools. Iron has "a pungent nature" and injures the eyes of dragons, and they rise to protect their eyes. Copper has, in China, associations with darkness and death. The "Stone of Darkness" is hollow and contains water or "the vital spirit of copper".[1] Dragons are fond of these stones and of beautiful gems.[2]

The dragon-shaped sea-gods of India and the dragon-gods of China and Japan have close associations with pearls. In a sixth-century Chinese work,[3] it is stated that pearls are spit out by dragons. Dragons have pearls "worth a hundred pieces of gold" in their mouths, under their throats, or in their pools. When dragons fight in the sky, pearls fall to the ground. De Groot[4] makes reference to "thunder pearls" that dragons have dropped from their mouths. These illuminate a house by night. In Wang Fu's description of the dragon it is stated that a dragon has "a bright pearl under its chin".

A mountain in Japan is called Ryushuho, which means "Dragon-Pearl Peak". It is situated in Fuwa district of Mino province, and is associated in a legend with the Buddhist temple called "Cloud-Dragon Shrine". When this temple was being erected, a dragon, carrying a pearl in its mouth, appeared before one of the priests. Mountain and sanctuary were consequently given dragon names.

The "jewel that grants all desires" is known in India, China, and Japan. A Japanese story relates that once upon a time an Indian Buddhist abbot, named Bussei

---

[1] Dr. W. M. W. de Visser, *The Dragon in China and Japan*, p. 69.
[2] *Ibid.*, p. 223. [3] *Shi i ki*, chap. ii.
[4] *Religious System of China*, Vol. V, p. 867.

(Buddha's vow), set out on a voyage with purpose to obtain this jewel (a pearl) which was possessed by "the dragon king of the ocean". In the midst of the sea the boat hove to while Bussei performed a ceremony and repeated a charm, causing the dragon-king to appear. The abbot, making a mystic sign, then demanded the pearl; but the dragon deceived him and nullified the mystic sign. Rising in the air, "the King of the Ocean" caused a great storm to rage. The boat was destroyed and all on board it, except Bussei, were drowned. Bussei afterwards migrated from southern India to Japan, accompanied by Baramon ("Wall-gazing Brahman").

The "Jewels of Flood and Ebb" were jewels that granted desires. In Japanese legend these were possessed by the dragon king (*Sagara*), whose kingdom, like that of the Indian Naga monarch and that of the Gaelic ruler of "Land Under-Waves", is situated at the bottom of the sea. The white jewel is called "Pearl of Ebb", and the blue jewel "Pearl of Flood".

A Japanese story relates that the Empress Jingo obtained from a sea-god a "jewel that grants all desires". During her reign a great fleet went to Korea to obtain tribute. The Korean fleet went out to meet it, but when it was drawn up for battle, a Japanese god cast into the sea the "Pearl of Ebb", and immediately the waters withdrew, leaving both fleets stranded. The resolute King of Korea, not to be daunted, leapt on to the dried sea-bed, and, marshalling his troops there, advanced at the head of them to attack and destroy the Japanese fleet. Then the Japanese god flung the "Pearl of Flood" into the sea. No sooner was this done than the waters returned and drowned large numbers of Koreans. Then a tidal wave swept over the Korean shore, while the troops prayed for their lives in vain. Not until the "Pearl of Ebb" was thrown once again into the sea did the waters retreat from the land.

After these miraculous and disastrous manifestations, the King of Korea was glad to make peace, and sent out three vessels laden with tribute to the empress, who had conquered the enemy without the loss of a single Japanese soldier or sailor, or even a single drop of Japanese blood.

Other names of the Japanese sea-god *Sagara*[1] are *Oho-watatsumi* ("sea lord, or sea snake"), and *Toyo-tama hiko no Mikoto* ("Abundant Pearl Prince"), and he has a daughter named *Toyo-tama-bime* ("Abundant Pearl Princess").[2] During storms, sailors threw jewels into the sea to pacify the dragon king.

Chinese emperors, like the Egyptian Pharaohs, had dragon boats which were used in connection with religious rain-getting ceremonies. They had also the bird boats called "yih". Mr. Wells Williams refers to the yih as "a kind of sea-bird that flies high, whose figure is gaily painted on the sterns of junks, to denote their swift sailing". He adds that "the descriptions are contradictory, but its picture rudely resembles a heron".[3]

It will be gathered from the evidence summarized above that the seafaring activities of the Chinese and Japanese had close associations with the search for precious metals and stones and pearls on the part of those who introduced the Egyptian type of vessels into their waters. With these ships went many customs and beliefs that became mixed with local customs and beliefs. New modes of life were introduced, and, with these, new modes of thought. Nothing persists like immemorial customs,

---

[1] This is the name of the Indian Naga king.
[2] *The Dragon in China and Japan*, p. 139.
[3] *Chinese-English Dictionary*, p. 1092.

myths, and religious beliefs associated with a particular mode of life.

Before the culture-complexes of China and Japan are investigated, so that local elements may be sifted out from the overlying mass of imported elements, it would be well to deal with the history of the search for wealth across the oceans of the world.

It is necessary, therefore, to turn back again to the cradle of shipbuilding and maritime enterprise—to ancient Egypt with its wonderful civilization of over 3000 years that sent its influences far and wide. Whether or not the Egyptians ever reached China or Japan, we have no means of knowing. Pauthier's view in this connection has come in for a good deal of destructive criticism. He referred to a Chinese tradition that about 1113 B.C. the Court was visited by seafarers from the kingdom of " Nili", and suggested that they came from the Nile valley.[1] The "Nili", " Nĕlĕ", or " Nĕrĕ " folk, according to others, came from the direction of Japan or from beyond Korea. References to them are somewhat obscure. It does not follow that because Egyptian ships reached China, they were manned by Egyptians. Ships were, like potter's wheels, adopted by folks who may never have heard of Egypt. A culture flows far beyond the areas reached by those who have given it a definite character, just as the Bantu dialects have penetrated to areas in Africa far beyond Bantu control.

What motives, then, stimulated maritime enterprise at the dawn of the history of sea-trafficking? What attracted the ancient mariners? If it was wealth, what was " wealth " to them?

The answer to the last query is that wealth was something with a religious significance. Gold was searched

[1] *Chine Ancienne*, pp. 94 *et seq.*

for, but not, to begin with, for the purpose of making coins. There was no coinage. Gold was a precious metal in the sense that it brought luck, and to the ancient people " luck " meant everything they yearned for in this world and the next.

As far back as the so-called " Palæolithic period " in western Europe, there was, as has been noted, a systematic search for wealth in the form of sea-shells. The hunters in central Europe imported shells from the Mediterranean coast and used them as amulets. These imported shells are found in their graves. In Ancient Egypt, shells were carried from the Red Sea coast, as well as from the Mediterranean coast, long before the historical period begins. The evidence of the grave-finds shows that Red Sea pearl-shell and Red Sea cowries were in use for religious purposes. " Millions of them ", as Maspero has noted, have been found in Ancient Egyptian graves. In time, pearls came into use, not only pearls from Nile mussels, but from oysters found in the southern part of the Gulf of Aden. As shipping developed, the pearl-fishers went farther and farther in search of pearls. The famous ancient pearl area in the Persian Gulf was discovered and drawn upon at some remote period. No doubt the pearls worn by Assyrian and Persian monarchs came, in part, from the Persian Gulf. At what period Ceylon pearls were first fished for it is impossible to say. Of one thing we can be certain, however. They were fished for by men who used the Egyptian type of vessel.

The migrating and trading pearl-fishers carried their beliefs with them from land to land. Almost everywhere are found the same beliefs and practices connected with shells and pearls. These beliefs and practices are of a highly complex character—so complex, indeed, that they must have had an area of origin in which they reflected the beliefs and customs of a people with a history of their own. The pearl, for instance, was connected with the moon, with the goddess who was the Great Mother, and with the sun and the sun-god. Venus (Aphrodite) was sea-born. She was lifted from the sea, by Tritons, seated on a shell. She was the pearl—the vital essence of the magic shell, and she was the moon, the "Pearl of Heaven". The pearl, like the moon, was supposed to exercise an influence over human beings. In Egypt, the Mother Goddess was symbolized by a cow, and cow, moon, pearl, and shell were connected in an arbitrary way.

In those areas in which the Mother Goddess was symbolized by the sow, the shell was likewise connected with her. The Greeks applied to the cowry a word that means "little pig"; this word had a special reference to the female sex. The Romans called the shell "porci", and porcelain has a like derivation.[1] As has been shown, women were connected with hand-made pottery, and the pot was a symbol of the Great Mother. In Scotland, certain shells are still referred to as "cows" and "pigs". They were anciently believed to promote fertility and bring luck. The custom of placing shells on window-sills, at doors, in fire-places, and round garden plots still obtains in parts of England, Scotland, and Ireland. Some low-reliefs of mother goddesses with baskets of fruit, corn, &c., surviving from the Romano-British period, which have been found in various parts of Britain, have shell-canopies. The Romans "took over" the goddesses of the peoples of western Europe on whom they imposed their rule, as they took over the Greek pantheon.

Following the clues afforded by the evidence of ships, it is found that the early pearl-fishers coasted round from

[1] Elliot Smith, *The Evolution of the Dragon*, pp. 216 *et seq.*

the Red Sea to the Persian Gulf, round India to the Bay of Bengal, round the Malay Peninsula to the China Sea, northwards to the Sea of Okhotsk, and on to the western coast of North America. Oceania was peopled by the ancient mariners, who appear to have reached by this route the coast of South America. As we have seen, Africa was circumnavigated. Western and north-western Europe and the British Isles were reached at a very early period.

The ancient seafarers searched not only for pearls and pearl-shell, but also for gold, silver, copper, tin, and other metals and for precious stones. They appear to have founded trading colonies that became centres from which cultural influences radiated far and wide. From these colonies expeditions set out to discover new pearling grounds and new mineral fields. The search for wealth, having a religious incentive, caused, as has been said, the spread of religious ideas. In different countries, imported beliefs and customs became mingled with local beliefs and customs, with the result that in many countries are found "culture complexes" which have a historical significance —reflecting as they do the varied experiences of the peoples and the influences introduced into their homelands at various periods.

In the next chapter it will be shown how the dragon of China has a history that throws much light on the early movements of explorers and traders who carried the elements of complex cultures into far distant lands.

CHAPTER V

Chinese Dragon Lore

Dragon Rain-god and Tiger-god of Mountains and Woods—Thunder-gods of East and West—Shark-gods as Guardians of Treasure—Dragon and Whale — Fish Vertebræ as Charms — Dragon and Dugong, Crocodile, Eel, &c. — Polynesian Dragon as "Pearl-mother"—Chinese Dragon and "Stag of the Sky"—Babylonian Sea-god and the Antelope, Gazelle, Stag, and Goat —Babylonian Dragon-slayers—Egyptian Gazelle- and Antelope-gods—Osiris as a Sea-god—African Antelope and Asiatic Dragon—The Serpent as "Water Confiner" in Egypt and India—Chinese Dragon has "Nature of Serpent"—Ancient Attributes of Far-Eastern Dragon—Dragon Battles—Dragons in East and West—Stones as "Dragon Eggs"—Dragon Mother and World Dragon —Dragons and Emperors.

THE Chinese dragon is a strange mixture of several animals. Ancient native writers like Wang Fu inform us that it has the head of a camel, the horns of a stag, the eyes of a demon, the ears of a cow, the neck of a snake, the belly of a clam, the scales of a carp, the claws of an eagle, and the soles of a tiger. On its head is the *chi'ih muh* lump that (like a "gas-bag") enables it to soar through the air. The body has three jointed parts, the first being "head to shoulders", the second, "shoulders to breast", and the third, "breast to tail". The scales number 117, of which 81 are imbued with good influence (*yang*) and 36 with bad influence (*yin*), for the dragon is partly a Preserver and partly a Destroyer. Under the neck the scales are reversed. There are five "fingers" or claws on each foot. The male dragon has whiskers, and under the chin, or in the throat, is a luminous pearl.

There is no denying the importance and significance of that pearl.

A male dragon can be distinguished from a female one by its undulating horn, which is thickest in the upper part. A female dragon's nose is straight. A horned dragon is called *k'iu-lung* and a hornless one *ch'i-lung*. Some dragons have wings. In addition there are horse-dragons, snake-dragons, cow-dragons, toad-dragons, dog-dragons, fish-dragons, &c., in China and Japan. Indeed, all hairy, feathered, and scaled animals are more or less associated with what may be called the "Orthodox Dragon". The tiger is an enemy of the dragon, but there are references to tiger-headed dragons. The dragon is a divinity of water and rain, and the tiger a divinity of mountains and woods.[1] The white tiger is a god of the west.

Like the deities of other countries, the Chinese dragon-god (and the Japanese dragon) may appear in different shapes—as a youth or aged man, as a lovely girl or an old hag, as a rat, a snake, a fish, a tree, a weapon, or an implement. But no matter what its shape may be, the dragon is intimately connected with water. It is a "rain lord" and therefore the thunder-god who causes rain to fall. The Chinese dragon thus links with the Aryo-Indian god Indra and other rain- and thunder-gods connected with agriculture, including Zeus of Greece, Tarku of Asia Minor, Thor of northern Europe, the Babylonian Marduk (Merodach), &c. There are sea-dragons that send storms like the wind-gods, and may be appeased with offerings. These are guardians of treasure and especially of pearling-grounds. Apparently the early pearl-fishers regarded the shark as the guardian of pearls. It seized and carried away the "robbers" who dived for

[1] De Visser, *The Dragon in China and Japan*, p. 109.

oysters.   The chief sea-god of China sometimes appeared
in shark form—an enormous lion-headed shark.

Procopius, a sixth-century writer, says in this connection: "Sea-dogs are wonderful admirers of the pearl-
fish, and follow them out to sea. . . . A certain fisherman, having watched for the moment when the shell-fish
was deprived of the attention of its attendant sea-dog . . .
seized the shell-fish and made for the shore.   The sea-
dog, however, was soon aware of the theft, and, making
straight for the fisherman, seized him.   Finding himself
thus caught, he made a last effort, and threw the pearl-
fish on shore, immediately on which he was torn to
pieces by its protector."[1]

In Polynesia the natives have superstitious ideas
about the shark.   "Although", says Ellis, "they would
not only kill but eat certain kinds of shark, the large
blue sharks, *Squalus glaucus*, were deified by them, and,
rather than attempt to destroy them, they would endea-
vour to propitiate their favour by prayers and offerings.
Temples were erected, in which priests officiated, and
offerings were presented to the deified sharks, while
fishermen, and others who were much at sea, sought
their favour."[2]   Polynesian gods, like Chinese dragons,
appeared in various shapes.   "One, for instance," writes
Turner, "saw his god in the eel, another in the shark,
another in the turtle, another in the dog, another in the
owl, another in the lizard; and so on throughout all the
fish of the sea, and birds, and four-footed beasts and
creeping things.   In some of the shell-fish, even, gods
were supposed to be present."[3]   Here we meet again

---

[1] Quoted by Prof. G. Elliot Smith, *The Evolution of the Dragon*, p. 160.

[2] Ellis, *Polynesian Researches*, First Edition, Vol. I, p. 178.

[3] Rev. George Turner's *Nineteen Years in Polynesia* (1861), pp. 238–9.   The god
emerging from the shell-fish is found in Mexico.   Jackson's *Shells as Evidence of the
Migrations of Early Culture*, p. 52.

with the shell beliefs. The avatars of dragons had pearls.
In an old Chinese work the story is told of a dragon that
appeared in the shape of a little girl sitting at the entrance
of a cave and playing with three pearls. When a man
appeared, the child fled into the cave, and, reassuming
dragon form, put the pearls in its left ear.[1] As the
guardian of pearls, the Chinese dragon links with the
shark-god of the early pearl-fishers. There were varieties
of these sea-gods. In Polynesia "they had", Ellis has
recorded, "gods who were supposed to preside over the
fisheries, and to direct to their coasts the various shoals
by which they were periodically visited. The Polynesians
invoked their aid "either before launching their canoes,
or while engaged at sea". It is of interest to find in
this connection that the dragon had associations with the
whale. Ancient mariners reverenced the whale. The
Ligurians and Cretans carried home portions of the back-
bones of whales.[2] The habit of placing spines of fish in
graves is of great antiquity in Europe. The early seafarers who reached California during its prehistoric age
perpetuated this very ancient custom. Beuchat gives an
illustration of a kitchen-midden grave in California in
which a whale's vertebra is shown near the human
skeleton.[3] The swashtika appears among the pottery
designs of early American pottery.[4] The ancient Peru-
vians worshipped the whale, and the Maori dragon was
compared to one.[5] In Scottish folk-lore witches sometimes assume the forms of whales.

[1] De Visser, *The Dragon in China and Japan*, p. 88.

[2] *Myths of Crete and Pre-Hellenic Europe*, pp. 306–7. Pierced fish vertebræ have
been found in Malta, Italy, the south-east of Spain, and Troy. See *Malta and the
Mediterranean Race*, R. N. Bradley (London, 1912), p. 136.

[3] *Manuel d'Archéologie Américaine*, Fig. 21, p. 114.

[4] *Ibid.*, p. 169.   [5] *Ibid.*, p. 169.

The dolphin, the bluish dugong[1] (probably the "semi-human whale" referred to by Ælian), and other denizens of the sea were regarded as deities by ancient seafarers. De Groot, in his *The Religious System of China*, quoting from the *Shan hai King*, relates that in the Eastern Sea is a "Land of Rolling Waves". In this region dwell sea-monsters that are shaped like cows and have blue bodies. They are hornless and one-legged. Each time they leave or enter the waters, winds arise and rain comes down. Their voice is that of thunder and their glare that of sun and moon.

The reference to the single leg may have been suggested by the fact that when the dugong dives the tail comes into view. This interesting sea-animal has been "recklessly and indiscriminately slaughtered" in historic times.

Classical writers referred to some of the strange monsters seen by their mariners as "sea-cows". In like manner the Chinese have connected denizens of the deep with different land animals.

The religious beliefs associated with various sea and land animals cling to that composite god the dragon. In dealing with it, therefore, we cannot ignore its history, not only in China but in those countries that influenced Chinese civilization, while attention must also be paid to countries that, like China, were influenced by the early sea and land traders and colonists.

In Polynesia the dragon is called *mo-o* and *mo-ko*. "Their (the Polynesian) use of this word in traditions", says W. D. Westervelt,[2] "showed that they often had in mind animals like crocodiles and alligators, and some-

---

[1] This mammal belongs to the order *Sirenia*, which includes manatees. It is native to Indian seas. A variety has been found in the Red Sea.
[2] *Legends of Gods and Ghosts (Hawaiian Mythology)*, 1915, pp. 255–6.

times they referred the name to any monster of great
mythical powers belonging to the man-destroying class.
Mighty eels, immense sea-turtles, large fish of the ocean,
fierce sharks, were all called *mo-o*. The most ancient
dragons of the Hawaiians are spoken of as living in pools
or lakes." Mr. Westervelt notes that "one dragon
lived in the Ewa lagoon, now known as 'Pearl Harbour'. This was *Kane-kua-ana*, who was said to have
brought the pipi (oysters) to Ewa. She[1] was worshipped
by those who gather the shell-fish. When the oysters
began to disappear about 1850, the natives said the
dragon had become angry and was sending the oysters to
Kahiki, or some far-away foreign land." It is evident
that such a belief is of great antiquity. The pearl under
the chin of the Chinese dragon has, as will be seen, an
interesting history.

But, it may be asked here, what connection has a
mountain stag with the ancient pearl-fishers? As Wang
Fu reminds us, the pearl-guarding Chinese dragon has
"the horns of a stag". It was sometimes called, De
Groot states,[2] "the celestial stag"—the "stag of the sky".
This was not merely a poetic image. The sea-god Ea of
ancient Babylonia was in one of his forms "the goat
fish", as some put it. Professor Sayce says, in this
conection, "Ea was called 'the antelope of the deep',
'the antelope the creator', 'the lusty antelope'. He was
sometimes referred to as 'a gazelle'. *Lubin*, 'a stag',
was a reduplicated form of *elim*, 'a gazelle'. Both words
were equivalent to *sarru*, 'king'."[3] Whatever the Ea
land animal was—whether goat, gazelle, antelope, or stag
—it was associated with a sea-god who, according to
Babylonian belief, brought the elements of culture to the

[1] A form of the mother-goddess. [2] *The Religious System of China*, Vol. III, p. 1143.
[3] *Hibbert Lectures*, pp. 280-84.

ancient Sumerians, who were developing their civilization at the seaport of Eridu, then situated at the head of the Persian Gulf, in which pearls were found. Ea was depicted as half a land animal and half a fish, or as a man wrapped in the skin of a gigantic fish as Egyptian deities were wrapped in the skins of wild beasts. One of Ea's names was Dagan, which was possibly the Dagon worshipped also by the Philistines and by the inhabitants of Canaan before the Philistines arrived from Kaphtor (the land of Keftiu, i.e. Crete).

Ea was associated with the dragon Tiamat, which his son Marduk (Merodach) slew. It is stated in Babylonian script that Ea "conferred his name" on Marduk. In other words, Marduk supplanted Ea and took over certain of his attributes, and part of his history. He was the god of Babylon, which supplanted other cities, formerly capitals; he therefore supplanted the chief gods of these cities.

Ea was originally the slayer of the dragon Tiamat and the conqueror of the watery abyss over which he reigned, supplanting the dragon.[1] He became the dragon himself —the "goat fish" or "antelope of the deep"—the composite deity connected with animals deified by ancient hunters and fishers whose beliefs were ultimately fused with those of others with whom they were brought into close association in centres of culture. Ea, who had a dragon form, was connected with the serpent, or "worm", as well as with the fish.

In Egypt Horus, Osiris, and Set were associated with the gazelle. Osiris was, in one of his forms, the River Nile. He was not only the Nile itself, but the controller of it; he was the serpent and soul of the Nile, and he was the ocean into which the Nile flowed, and the

[1] *Legends of Babylonia and Egypt*, Leonard W. King, pp. 116–7 (1918).

leviathan of the deep. In the Pyramid texts Osiris is addressed: "Thou art great, thou art green, in thy name of Great-green (sea); lo, thou art round as the Great Circle (Okeanos); lo, thou art turned about, thou art round as the circle that encircles the Hauneba (Ægeans)".[1] Osiris was thus the serpent (dragon) that, lying in the ocean, encircled the world. His son Horus is at one point in the Pyramid texts (Nos. 1505–8) narrative "represented as crossing the sea".[2] Horus was sometimes depicted riding on the back of a gazelle or antelope. The Egyptian antelope-god was in time fused with the serpent or dragon of the sea. Referring to the evidence of Frobenius[3] in this connection, Professor Elliot Smith says that "in some parts of Africa, especially in the west, the antelope plays the part of the dragon in Asiatic stories".[4] When we reach India, it is found that the wind-god, Vayu, rides on the back of the antelope. Vayu was fused with Indra, the slayer of the dragon that controlled the water-supply, and, indeed, retained it by enclosing it as the Osiris serpent of Egypt, or the serpent-mother of Osiris, enclosed the water in its cavern during the period of "the low Nile", before the inundation took place.[5] After Osiris, as the water-confining serpent (dragon) was slain, the river ran red with his blood and rose in flood. Osiris, originally "a dangerous god",[6] was the "new" or "fresh" water of the inundation. "The tradition of his unfavourable character", Breasted comments, "survived in vague reminiscences long centuries after he had gained wide popularity." Osiris ultimately became "the kindly

---

[1] Breasted, *Religion and Thought in Ancient Egypt*, p. 20.   [2] *Ibid.*, p. 26.
[3] *The Voice of Africa*, Vol. II, p. 467.   [4] *The Evolution of the Dragon*, p. 130.
[5] See illustration of the serpent enclosing the waters in the *shrine of the Nile*, from a bas-relief in the small temple of Philæ. Maspero's *The Dawn of Civilization*, p. 39.
[6] Breasted, *op. cit.*, p. 38.

dispenser of plenty", and his slayer, Set, originally a beneficent deity, was made the villain of the story and fused with the dragon Apep, the symbol of darkness and evil. This change appears to have been effected after the introduction of the agricultural mode of life. The Nile, formerly the destroyer, then became the preserver, sustainer, and generous giver of "soul substance" and daily bread.

When the agricultural mode of life was introduced into China the horned-dragon, or horned-serpent (for the dragon, Chinese writers remind us, has "the nature of a serpent"), became the Osiris water-serpent.

How a snake becomes a dragon is explained in the *Shu i ki*, which says: "A water-snake after 500 years changes into a *kiao*, a *kiao* after 1000 years changes into a *lung*;[1] a *lung* after 500 years changes into a *kiohlung*,[2] and after 1000 years into a *ying-lung*.[3]" In Japan is found, in addition, the *p'an-lung* ("coiled dragon"), which has not yet ascended to heaven.[4] The "coiled dragon" is evidently the water-retaining monster.

The Chinese dragon is as closely connected with water as was the serpent form of Osiris with the Nile in ancient Egypt, and as was Indra with the "drought dragon" in India. The dragon dwells in pools, it rises to the clouds, it thunders and brings rain, it floods rivers, it is in the ocean, and controls the tides and causes the waters to ebb and flow as do its magic pearls (the "Jewels of Flood and Ebb"), and it is a symbol of the emperor. The Egyptian Pharaoh was an "avatar" of Osiris, or Horus,[5] and the Chinese emperor was an "avatar" or incarnation

---

[1] A kiao-lung is a dragon with fish scales.
[2] A horned dragon.   [3] A dragon with wings.
[4] De Visser, *The Dragon in China and Japan*, pp. 72 *et seq.*
[5] Horus while alive, and Osiris after he died, as Dr. Gardiner insists.

of the dragon. As water destroys, the dragon is a destroyer; as water preserves and sustains, the dragon is a preserver and sustainer.

The dragon, as has been indicated, is essentially the Chinese water-god. "The ancient texts . . . are short," says de Visser, "but sufficient to give us the main conceptions of old China with regard to the dragon. He was in those early days, just like now, the god of water, thunder, clouds, and rain, the harbinger of blessings, and the symbol of holy men. As the emperors are the holy beings of earth, the idea of the dragon being the symbol of imperial power is based upon this ancient conception."[1]

The Chinese "dragon well" is usually situated inside a deep mountain cave. It was believed that the well owed its origin to the dragon. De Visser quotes, in this connection, from an ancient sage, who wrote: "When the yellow dragon, born from yellow gold a thousand years old, enters a deep place, a yellow spring dashes forth, and if from this spring some particles (fine dust) arise, these become a yellow cloud". A famous dragon well is situated at the top of Mount Pien, in Hu-cheu. It flows from a cave, and is called "Golden Well Spring". The cave is known as the "Golden Well Cave", and is supposed to be so deep that no one can reach the end of it. There was a dragon well near Jerusalem.[2] Other dragon wells are found as far west as Ireland and Scotland. A cave with wells, called the "Dropping Cave", at Cromarty, has a demon in its inner recesses. The Corycian cave of the Anatolian Typhoon is one of similar character. According to Greek legend, this hundred - headed monster, from whose eyes lightning flashes, will one day send hail, floods, and rivers of fire

---

[1] *The Dragon in China and Japan*, p. 42.   [2] Nehemiah, ii, 13.

to lay waste Sicilian farms.[1]   The floods of the River Rhone were supposed to be caused by the "drac".   In Egypt Set became the "roaring serpent", who crept into a hole in the ground, "wherein he hid himself and lived".   He had previously taken the shapes of the crocodile and the hippopotamus to escape Horus, the Egyptian "dragon slayer".

In China the season of drought is winter.   The dragons are supposed to sleep in their pools during the dry spell, and that is why, in the old Chinese work, *Yih Ling*, it is stated that "a dragon hidden in water is useless".   The dragons are supposed to sleep so that they may "preserve their bodies".   They begin to stir and rise in spring.   Soon they fight with one another, so that there is no need for a Horus, a Merodach, or an Indra to compel them, by waging battle, to bring benefits to mankind.   The Chinese welcome what they called a "dragon battle" after the dry season.   Thunderstorms break out, and rain pours down in torrents.   If a number of dragons engage in battle, and the war in the air continues longer than is desired, the rivers rise in flood and cause much destruction and loss of life. As the emperor was closely connected with the chief dragon-god, social upheavals and war might result, it was anciently believed, in consequence of the failure of the priests and the emperor (the holiest of priests) to control the dragons.   The dynasty might be overthrown by the indignant and ruined peasantry.

Among the curious superstitions entertained in China regarding dragon battles, is one that no mortal should watch them.   It was not only unlucky but perilous for human beings to peer into the mysteries.   De Visser quotes a Chinese metrical verse in this connection:

---

[1] Æschylus, *Prometheus Vinctus*, 351–72.

When they fight, the dragons do not look at us;
Why should we look at them when they are fighting?
If we do not seek the dragons,
They also will not seek us.[1]

In Gaelic Scotland the serpent, which is associated with the goddess Bride, sleeps all winter and comes forth on 1st February (old style), known as "Bride's day". A Gaelic verse tells in this connection:

The serpent will come from the home
On the brown day of Bride,
Though there should be three feet of snow
On the flat surface of the ground.[2]

As in China, a compact was made with the Bride serpent or dragon:

To-day is the Day of Bride,
The serpent shall come from his hole,
I will not molest the serpent,
And the serpent will not molest me.

It is evident that some very ancient belief, connected with the agricultural mode of life, lies behind these curious verses in such far-separated countries as Scotland and China. Bride and her serpent come forth to inaugurate the season of fruitfulness as do the battling dragons in the Far East.

When Chinese dragons fight, fire-balls and pearls fall to the ground. Pearls give promise of abundant supplies of water in the future. It is necessary, if all is to go well with the agriculturist, that the blue and yellow dragons should prevail over the others. The blue dragon is the chief spirit of water and rain, and this is the deity that presides during the spring season.

[1] *The Dragon in China and Japan*, p. 46.
[2] Dr. A. Carmichael, *Carmina Gadlica*, Vol. I, p. 169.

A glimpse is afforded of the mental habits of the early searchers for precious or sacred metals and jewels by the beliefs entertained in China regarding the origin of the dragon-gods. These were supposed to have been hatched from stones, especially beautiful stones. The colours of stones were supposed to reveal the characters of the spirits that inhabited them. In Egypt, for instance, the blue turquoise was connected with the mother-goddess Hathor, who was, among other things, a deity of the sky and therefore the controller of the waters above the firmament as well as of the Nile. She was the mother of sun and moon. She was appealed to for water by the agriculturists and for favourable winds by the seafarers. The symbol used on such occasions was a blue stone. It was a "luck stone" that exercised an influence on the elements controlled by the goddess. In the Hebrides a blue stone used to be reverenced by the descendants of ancient sea-rovers. Martin in his *Western Isles* tells of such a stone, said to be always wet, which was preserved in a chapel dedicated to St. Columba on the Island of Fladda. "It is an ordinary custom," he has written, "when any of the fishermen are detained in the isle by contrary winds, to wash the blue stone with water all round, expecting thereby to procure a favourable wind, which, the credulous tenant living in the isle says, never fails, especially if a stranger wash the stone." Why a "stranger"? Was this curious custom introduced of old by strangers who had crossed the deep? Had the washing ceremony its origin in the custom of pouring out libations practised by those who came from an area in which a complex religious culture had grown up, and where men had connected a deity, originally associated with the water-supply and therefore with the food-supply, with tempests and ocean-tides and the sky?

The Chinese, who called certain beautiful stones. "dragon's eggs", believed that when they split, lightning flashed and thunder bellowed and darkness came on. The new-born dragons ascended to the sky. Before the dragons came forth, much water poured from the stone. As in the Hebrides, the dragon stone had, it would appear, originally an association with the fertilizing water-deity.

The new-born Chinese dragon is no bigger than a worm, or a baby serpent or lizard, but it grows rapidly. Evidently beliefs associated with the water-snake deities were fused with those regarding coloured stones. The snake was the soul of the river. Osiris as the Nile was a snake. His mother had, therefore, a snake form.

The haunting memory of the goddess-mother of water-spirits clings to the "dragon mother" of a Chinese legend related by ancient writers, a version of which is summarized by de Visser.[1] Once, it runs, an old woman found five "dragon eggs" lying in the grass. When they split (as in Egypt "the mountain of dawn" splits to give birth to the sun), this woman carried the little serpents to a river and let them go. For this service she was given the power to foretell future events. She became a sibyl—a priestess. The people called her "The Dragon Mother." When she washed clothes at the river-side, the fishes, who were subjects of dragons, "used to dance before her".

In various countries certain fish were regarded as forms of the shape-changing dragon. The Gaelic dragon sometimes appeared as the salmon, and a migratory fish was in Egypt associated with Osiris and his "mother". When the Chinese "Dragon Mother" died, she was buried on the eastern side of the river. Why, it may

[1] *The Dragon in China and Japan*, p. 89.

be asked, on the eastern side? Was it because, being originally a goddess, she was regarded as the "mother" of the sun-god of the east—the mother who was "the mountain of dawn" and whose influence was concentrated in the blue stone? The Chinese dragon of the east is blue, and the blue dragon is associated with spring—the first-born season of the year. But apparently the dragons objected to the burial of the "Dragon Mother" on the eastern bank. The legend tells that they raised a violent storm, and transferred her grave to the western bank. Until the present age the belief obtains that there is always wind and rain near the "Dragon Mother's Grave". The people explain that the dragons love to "wash the grave".

Here we find the dragons pouring out libations, as did the worshippers of the Great Mother who came from a distant land.

The god of the western quarter is white, and presides over the autumn season of fruitfulness. Just before the "birth" of autumn the Chinese address their prayers to the mountains and hills.

In ancient Egypt the conflict between the Solar and Osirian cults was a conflict between the "cult of the east" and the "cult of the west". Professor Breasted notes that although Osiris is "First of the Westerners" (the west being his quarter) "he goes to the east (after death) in the Pyramid texts (of the solar cult) and the pair, Isis and Nepthys (the goddess), carry the dead into the east". The east was the place where the ascent to the sky was made. In Egyptian solar theology it combined with the south. The rivalry between the two cults is reflected in one particular Pyramid text in which "the dead is adjured to go to the west in preference to the east, in order to join the sun-god!" But to the solar cult the east was "the most sacred of all regions". In the Pyramid texts it is found that "the old doctrine of the 'west' as the permanent realm of the dead, a doctrine which is later so prominent, has been quite submerged by the pre-eminence of the east".[1]

This east-and-west theological war, then, had its origin in Egypt. How did it reach China, there to be enshrined in the legend of the Dragon Mother? Can it be held that it was "natural" the Chinese should have invented a legend which had so significant and ancient a history in the homeland of the earliest seafarers?

The dragon-gods that presided over the seasons and the divisions of the world were five in number. At the east was the blue (or green) god associated with spring, at the west the white god associated with autumn, at the north the black god associated with winter (the Chinese season of drought), and at the south were two gods, the red and the yellow; the red god presided during the greater part of summer, the rule of the yellow god being confined to the last month.

The dragons were life-givers not only as the gods who presided over the seasons and ensured the food supply, but as those who gave cures for diseases. The "Red Cloud herb" and other curative herbs were found after a thunderstorm beside the dragon-haunted pools. De Groot[2] tells that fossil bones were called "dragon bones", and were used for medicinal purposes. The dragons were supposed to cast off their bones as well as their skins. Bones of five colours (the colours of the five dragons) were regarded as the most effective. White and yellow bones came next in favour. Black bones were "of inferior quality". The *Shu King*, a famous Chinese

[1] Breasted, *Religion and Thought in Ancient Egypt*, pp. 99 *et seq.*
[2] *The Religious System of China*, Vol. VI, p. 1087.

historical classic,[1] tells that the dragons' bones come from Tsin land. It is noted that the five-coloured ones are the best. The blue, yellow, red, white, and black ones, according to their colours, correspond with the viscera, as do the five *chih* (felicitous plants), the five crystals (*shih ying*), and the five kinds of mineral bole (*shih chi*). De Groot[2] gives the colours connected with the internal organs as follows:

1. Blue—liver and gall.
2. White—lungs and small intestines.
3. Red—heart and large intestines.
4. Black—kidneys and bladder.
5. Yellow—spleen and stomach.

Apparently the special curative quality of a dragon's bone was revealed by its colour. The gods of the various "mansions" influenced different organs of the human body.

In ancient Egypt the internal organs were placed in jars and protected by the Horuses of the cardinal points. The god of the north had charge of the small viscera, the god of the south of the stomach and large intestines, the god of the west of liver and gall, and the god of the east of heart and lungs. The Egyptian north was red and symbolized by the Red Crown, and the south was white and symbolized by the White Crown.

In Mexico the colours white, red, and yellow were connected with different internal organs, and black with a disembowelled condition.

It is evident that the sea and land traders carried their strange stocks of medical knowledge over vast areas. It is not without significance to find in this connection that,

---

[1] See English translation by Walter Gorn Old (London, 1904).
[2] *The Religious System of China*, Vol. IV, p. 26.

according to Chinese belief, there was an island on which dragons' bones were found.

The dragons are not only rain-gods and gods of the four quarters and the seasons, but also "light-gods", connected with sun and moon, day and night. In the *Yih lin* there is a reference to a black dragon which vomits light and causes darkness to turn into light. The mountain dragon of Mount Chung is called the "Enlightener of Darkness". "When it opens its eyes it is day, when it shuts its eyes it is night. Blowing he makes winter, exhaling he makes summer. The wind is its breath."[1]

In like manner the Egyptian Ra and Ptah are universal gods, the sun and moon being their "eyes". Even Osiris, as far back as the Pyramid period, was the source of all life and a world-god. He was addressed: "The soil is on thy arm, its corners are upon thee as far as the four pillars of the sky. When thou movest the earth trembles. . . . As for thee, the Nile comes forth from the sweat of thy hands. Thou spewest out the wind. . . ."[2] Osiris sent water to bring fertility as do the dragons, air for the life-breath of man and beast, and also light, which was, of course, fire (the heat which is life).

The idea of the life-principle being in fire and water lies behind Wang Fu's statement: "Dragon fire and human fire are opposite. If dragon fire comes into contact with wetness, it flames; and if it meets water, it burns. If one drives it (the dragon) away by means of fire, it stops burning and its flames are extinguished."[3] Celestial fire is something different from ordinary fire.

[1] De Visser, *The Dragon in Japan and China*, p. 62.
[2] Breasted's *Religion and Thought in Ancient Egypt*, p. 21.
[3] *The Dragon in China and Japan*, p. 67.

The "vital spark" is of celestial origin—purer and holier than ordinary fire. Dragon skins, even when cast off, shine by night. So do pearls, coral, and precious stones "shine in darkness" in the Chinese myths.

One traces the influence of the solar cult in the idea that the dragon's vital spirit is in its eyes. It is because iron blinds a dragon that it fears that metal. In Egypt the eye of Horus is blinded by Set, whose metal is iron.

There is a quaint mixture of religious ideas in the Chinese custom of carrying in procession through the streets, on the 15th of the first month, a dragon made of bamboo, linen, and paper. In front of it is borne a red ball. De Groot says that this is the azure dragon, the head of which rose as a star to usher in spring at the beginning.[1] In like manner the Egyptian "spring" is ushered in by the star Sirius, the mother of the sun, from which falls a tear that causes the inundation. But although the red ball may have been a solar symbol, it is also connected with the moon. The Chinese themselves call the ball "The Pearl of Heaven"—that is, "the moon". An inscription on porcelain brings this out clearly. Mr. Blacker has translated the text below two dragons rushing towards a ball as "A couple of dragons facing the moon".[2] The dragons were not only moon- and sun-"devourers" who caused eclipses, but guardians of these orbs in their capacities as gods of the four quarters.

The all-absorbing dragon appears even as a vampire. A tiger-headed dragon with the body of a snake seizes human beings, covers them with saliva, and sucks blood from under their armpits. "No blood is left when they stop sucking."[3] In Japanese legends dragons as white

---

[1] De Groot's *The Religious System of China*, Vol. I, p. 369.
[2] *Chats on Oriental China* (London, 1908).
[3] De Visser, *The Dragon in China and Japan*, p. 79.

eels draw blood from the legs of horses that enter a river.[1]
Evil or sick dragons send bad rain.

The gods ride on dragons, and therefore emperors
and holy men can also use them as vehicles. Yu, the
founder of the Hea Dynasty, had a carriage drawn by two
dragons. Ghosts sometimes appear riding on dragons
and wearing blue hats. The souls of the dead are
conveyed to the Celestial regions by the winged gods.
Dragons appear when great men are born.[2] Emperors
had dragon ancestors. The Emperor Yaou was the son
of a red dragon ; one Japanese emperor had a dragon's
tail, being a descendant of the sea-god.[3]

In the next chapter it will be shown that in Chinese
dragon-lore it is possible to detect with certainty the
sources of certain "layers" that were superimposed on
primitive conceptions regarding these deities.

[1] *The Dragom in China and Japan*, p. 112.
[2] A dragon appeared at the birth of Confucius.
[3] De Visser, *The Dragon in China and Japan*, p. 145.

CHAPTER VI

Bird and Serpent Myths

Culture Complexes in Dragon-lore—Polynesian Dragon Beliefs—Oceanic and African Fish-gods—Reptile Deities where no Reptiles are found—Chinese Dragons and Indian Nagas—Dragon-links between India, Tibet, China, and Japan—Birds and Snakes—Distribution of Egyptian "Winged Disk"—Horus and the "Secretary Bird"—Indian Mungoose supplants "Secretary Bird"—Mungoose form of God of Riches and Death—Bird and Serpent combined in Dragon—Babylonian Dragon was a combination of Eagle, Serpent, and Lion—Tree Forms of the Chinese Dragon, the Polynesian Mo-o, and the Indian Nagas—The Dragon, the Salmon, the Tree, and the "Thunder-bird".

THE intensive study of a country's beliefs and ideas, as revealed in its myths and legends, is greatly facilitated by the adoption of the comparative method. It may not always be found possible to identify areas in which certain beliefs had origin, but when we detect, as we do in China, myths similar to those found in other lands, and especially highly complex myths, that had origin in one particular country and received additions in another, the imported elements may be sifted out from a local religious system without much difficulty.

The Chinese dragon has distinct and outstanding Chinese characteristics, but it is obviously not entirely a Chinese creation. Attached to the "composite wonder beast" are complex ideas that have a history outside China, as well as those ideas that reflect Chinese natural phenomena and Chinese experiences and habits of life and thought. The fused beliefs, as symbolized by the dragon,

66

have passed through a prolonged process of local development, but those that were imported have not, it is found, been entirely divested of their distinctive characteristics, and remain preserved as flies are in amber.

Interesting and important evidence that throws light on the history of the Chinese dragon is found in Polynesia, India, and Babylonia, and even in Egypt and Europe. The cultural influence of Babylonia, which radiated over a wide area for a score of centuries or longer, is traceable in India, and, as is well known, Buddhist India exercised a strong cultural influence on China. But, as will be shown, Babylonian influence reached the Shensi province of China long before the Aryans entered India. Buddhist ideas regarding the pearl-protecting dragon-god of water and fire were evidently superimposed in China upon earlier Babylonian ideas regarding the water-dragon, which had no particular connection with pearls. At any rate, there is no mention of pearls in the Babylonian myth.

When it is found that many of the ideas connected with the Chinese dragon were prevalent in Polynesia, what conclusion is to be drawn? There is no evidence that Chinese culture was an active force in New Zealand or Hawaii, for instance. It cannot have been from China that the Polynesians derived their dragon, or their beliefs connected with the serpent, a reptile unknown to the islanders at first hand. The only reasonable conclusion that can be drawn is that the Chinese and the Polynesians were influenced at an early period by intruders from other lands. The Polynesian intruders must necessarily have been sea-traders. Of course, the Polynesians may themselves have imported their dragon beliefs from their homeland. That homeland, however, was certainly not China.

The Polynesian Mo-o or Mo-ko (dragon) had, as was shown in the last chapter, a connection with pearls. "On Maui", writes W. D. Westervelt,[1] "the greatest dragon of the island was Kiha-wahine. The natives had the saying, 'Kiha has *mana*, or miraculous power, like Mo-o-inanea'. She lived *in a large, deep pool* on the edge of the village Lahaina, and was worshipped by the royal family of Maui as their special guardian." Royal families were invariably the descendants of intruding conquerors. It is of special interest, therefore, to find the Polynesian dragon-god connected with a military aristocracy.

The Rev. George Brown, missionary and explorer, refers to similar dragon beliefs among the people of New Britain. He tells of a spring connected with the woman (goddess) who caused the deluge. The natives "say that an immense fish lives in it, which will come out when they call it". The belief obtains among the Melanesians "that the creator of all things was a woman". She "made all lands" and "the natives prayed" to her "when an eclipse of the sun or the moon took place".[2] The king of Samoan gods was a dragon. "This god", Brown tells, "had the body of a man to the breast only, and the body of an eel (*muræna*) below. This eel's body lies down in the ocean, and from the chest to the head lies down in the house. This is the god to whom all things are reported. The inferior gods are his attendants."[3]

Gods half human and half reptile, or half human and half fish, are found in various countries. In the British Museum are bronze reliefs of the King of Benin (as the representative of his chief deity) half shark and half man The kings of Dahomey were depicted as sharks with bodies

[1] *Legends of Gods and Ghosts* (Hawaiian Mythology, 1915), p. 258.
[2] *Melanesians and Polynesians* (London, 1910), pp. 334-5.
[3] *Ibid.*, p. 364.

covered with scales; their statues are in the Trocadero, Paris.[1]

That the Polynesian reptile deities were imported there can be no doubt. As early as 1825 Mr. Bloxam, the English naval chaplain, drew this necessary conclusion. In his *The Voyage of the Blonde* he says: "At the bottom of the Parre (pali) there are two large stones, on which even now offerings of fruit and flowers are laid to propitiate the Aku-wahines, or goddesses, who are supposed to have the power of granting a safe passage". Referring to the female mo-o, or reptile deities, Mr. Bloxam says it was difficult for him to get an explanation of their name, the Hawaiians having "nothing of the shape of serpents or large reptiles in their islands".[2]

But the closest analogy to the Chinese dragon is found in India. The Nagas (serpent-gods), which were taken over by the Buddhists, and the Chinese dragons have much in common. "Cobras in their ordinary shape," writes Dr. Rhys Davids of the Nagas, "they lived beneath the waters like mermen and mermaids, in great luxury and wealth, more especially of gems." Sometimes the tree-spirits (dryads) are called Nagas. "They could at will, and often did, adopt the human form; and though terrible if angered, were kindly and mild by nature."[3] Kerns says "that the Nagas are water-spirits represented, as a rule, in human shapes, with a crown of serpents on their heads", and also as "snake-like beings resembling clouds".[4] They are "demi-gods". Like the Chinese dragons, the Nagas are guardians of the four quarters of the universe. There are withal Nagas in the sea who control winds and tides, and one of the Naga kings is Sagara, who is a Neptune in

[1] *Indo-China and its Primitive People*, London (trans.), p. 192.
[2] *Hawaiian Mythology*, p. 257.   [3] *Buddhist India*, pp. 222-3.
[4] *Manual of Indian Buddhism*, pp. 593 *et seq.*

Japan.   The Nagas are also "Lords of the Earth", and send drought and disease when offended or neglected.   Ea, the sea-god of the early Babylonians, was known also as Enki, "The Lord of the Earth".

In Buddhist art the Naga is shown in three forms: (1) as a human being with a snake on or poised over the head, reminding one of the Egyptian kings or queens who wear the uræus symbol on their foreheads; (2) as half human and half snake (the "mermaid form"); and (3) as ordinary snakes.   The first form is found not only in India, but in Tibet, China, and Japan.   Human-shaped Nagas are depicted worshipping Buddha, as they stand in water.

In Tibet, the Naga is shown with the upper part of the body in human shape and the lower in snake shape; there are horns on the head and wings spreading out from the shoulders.   The same form is found in Japan.

This Tibetan link between the Indian Naga and the Chinese Dragon is important.   The bird-god has been blended with the snake-god.   In India the bird-gods (Garudas) are enemies of the Nagas (snakes), and Garudas in "eagle shape" are found depicted in low relief, carrying off Nagas in snake shape.   This eternal conflict between eagle-like birds and serpents is one of the features of Babylonian mythology.

The story of Zu, the Babylonian Eagle-god, is found on tablets that were stored in the library of the great Assyrian King, Ashur-bani-pal.   Zu, it is related, stole from the gods the "tablets of destiny", and was pursued and caught by Shamash, the sun-god.   In one version of the myth Zu, the eagle, is punished by the serpent, which conceals itself in the body of an ox.   When the eagle comes to feast on the flesh it is seized by the serpent and slain.

In Polynesia the eternal conflict between bird-god and serpent-god is illustrated in wood-carvings. The Egyptian winged disk, as adopted by the islanders, shows the bird in the centre with a struggling snake in its beak. The Central American peoples had likewise this bird-and-serpent myth. Indeed, it figures prominently in their mythologies. In Mexico the winged disk was placed, as in Egypt, above the entrances to the temples.

The bird-and-sepent myth is to be found even in the *Iliad*. When Hector set forth with his heroes to break through the wall of the Achæan camp, an eagle appeared in the air, bearing in its talons "a blood-red monstrous snake, alive and struggling still". The writhing snake manages to sting the eagle, which immediately drops it.[1]

In ancient Egyptian myths the bird was the Horus hawk and the serpent was Set. Horus assumed, in his great battle against the snake, crocodile, and other enemies of Ra, the winged disk form—the winged sun, protected by the two snake-goddesses of Upper and Lower Egypt.

This strange combination of deities in the "winged disk" symbol was as distinctively an Egyptian cultural and political complex as the Union Jack is distinctively a British complex. As the Union Jack has been carried to many a distant land, so was the Egyptian winged disk, "the flag" of Egyptian culture. In those areas in which the winged disk is found, are found also traces of Egyptian ideas which, of course, were not necessarily introduced by the Egyptians themselves.

How did this myth of the struggle between bird and serpent have origin? The only country in the world in which a great bird hunts serpents is Africa. The bird in question is the famous secretary bird (*Serpentarius secretarius*), which is nowadays domesticated by South African

---

[1] *Iliad*, Book XII (Lang's, Leaf's, and Dyer's Trans.), p. 236.

farmers so as to keep down snakes. It is found in East and West Africa. "In general appearance it looks like a modified eagle mounted on stilts."[1] The bird attacks a snake with wings outspread, and flaps them in front of its body to prevent itself from being bitten during the conflict. Early Egyptian seafarers were no doubt greatly impressed when, "in the land of Punt", they saw these strange birds, with heads like eagles or hawks, standing over snakes they had clutched in their talons, and then flying away with them dangling from their beaks. The mariners' stories about the snake-devouring bird appear to have crept into the mythology of Egypt, with the result that the Horus hawk became the hunter of Set in his "hissing serpent" form. Above the hole in the ground into which the Set serpent fled for concealment and safety was set a pole surmounted by the head of the Horus hawk. As Dr. Budge puts it : "Horus, the son of Isis, stood upon him (Set) in the form of a pole or staff, on the top of which was the head of a hawk".[2] But, one may urge, it could not have been until after Egyptian vessels visited the coasts haunted by the secretary bird that the bird and serpent variation of the Horus-Set myth was formulated in the land of Egypt, whence, apparently, it was distributed far and wide. Horus was not necessarily an enemy of serpents, seeing that there are two in his disk.

In Tibet, as has been stated, the bird and serpent were combined, and the "composite beast" was given a human head with horns. The horned and winged dragon of China is thus, in part, a combination of the original secretary bird and the snake.

[1] *The Natural History of Animals* (Gresham, London), Vol. III, p. 176 and pp. 46 *et seq.*
[2] Budge, *The Gods of the Egyptians*, Vol. I, p. 481.

The later blending process was, no doubt, due to Buddhistic influence. Both Nagas (snakes) and Garudas (eagles or secretary birds) were included in northern India among the gods and demons who worshipped Buddha. The Nagas understood the language of birds. They gave charms to human beings so that they might share this knowledge. In European and Arabian stories folk-heroes acquire the language of birds, or of all animals, after eating the hearts of dragons. A Naga king causes an Indian king to understand what animals say.[1]

"The jewel that grants all desires" is possessed by the Indian Nagas, as it is by Chinese and Japanese dragons. In the *Mahábhárata*, the Pandava hero Arjuna is, after being slain in combat, restored to life by his Naga wife, who had obtained this magic jewel from the Naga king.[2]

The Nagas are guardians of pearls, and the females have many pearl necklaces.

Note may here be taken of interesting Indian evidence that throws light on the process of transferring to a local animal complex ideas associated with another animal figuring in an imported myth. The great enemy of African snakes is, as has been said, the secretary bird; the Indian enemy is the mungoose. In early Buddhist art the mungoose, spitting jewels, is placed in the right hand of Kubera, god of wealth, who stands on the back of a Yaksha (a bird demon). By devouring snakes (Nagas) the mungoose (according to the myth) "appropriates their jewels, and has hence developed into the attribute of Kubera".[3] Here the pearl-guarding shark, having become a jewel-guarding dragon-snake, is sub-

---

[1] Chavanne's *Contes et Apologues*.   [2] *Indian Myth and Legend*, pp. 314–5.
[3] Laufers, *The Diamond: a study in Chinese and Hellenistic Folk-lore*, p. 7 (Chicago, 1915).

stituted by the jewel-spitting mungoose which has "devoured" its attributes.

The god Kubera has a heaven of its own, and is a form of Yama, god of death. In his form as Dharma, god of justice, Yama figures in the *Mahâbhârata*[1] as a "blue-eyed mungoose with one side of his body changed into gold", his voice being "loud and deep as thunder". Here Yama links with Indra, god of thunder, who, having a heaven of his own, is also a god of death. Egypt had its "blue-eyed Horus".[2] The god Horus was the living form of Osiris. The living Pharaoh was a Horus, and the dead Pharaoh an Osiris, as Dr. Gardiner reminds us.

The combination of bird and serpent is found in Persia as well as in Tibet. On an archaic cylinder seal from the ancient Elamite capital of Susa, the dragon is a lion with an eagle's head and wings; the forelegs are those of the eagle, and the hind legs those of a lion.

A form of the god Tammuz, namely the god Nin-Girsu ("Lord of Girsu") of the Sumerian city of Lagash (Girsu appears to have been a suburb), was a lion-headed eagle.[3] The god Ea had a dragon form.[4] The dragon of the Ishtar gate of Babylon is a combination of eagle, serpent, and lion, and is horned.

There can remain little doubt that the Chinese dragon has an interesting history, not only in China but outside that country. It cannot be held to have independent origin. At a remote period dragon beliefs reached China, India, and Polynesia, and even America.[5]

In each separated area the dragon took on a local

---

[1] *Açwamedha Parva*, Section XC, Sloka 5.
[2] Budge, *Gods of the Egyptians*, Vol. II, p. 107.
[3] *Myths of Babylonia and Assyria*, p. 120.   [4] *Ibid.*, p. 62.
[5] *The Evolution of the Dragon*, G. Elliot Smith, pp. 83 *et seq.*

colouring, but the fundamental beliefs connected with it remained the same. It was closely connected with water (the "water of life"), and also with trees (the "trees of life"). Thus we find that in China a dragon might assume "the shape of a tree growing under water";[1] a boat once collided with drift-wood which was found to be a dragon. Crocodiles are sometimes mistaken for logs of wood.

In Hawaii two noted dragons (mo-o) lived in a river. "They were called 'the moving boards' which made a bridge across the river."[2]

The Indian Nagas were not only water deities but tree spirits, as Dr. Rhys Davids has emphasized.[3]

Behind dragon worship is a complex of beliefs connected with what is usually called "tree and well worship". In Gaelic stories, the sacred tree is guarded by the "beast" in the sacred well, and a form of the "beast" (dragon) is the salmon; in the tree is the "thunder bird". Dragon, tree, and bird are connected with the god of thunder who sends rain.

When Buddhism reached China, imported Naga beliefs were superimposed on earlier Chinese beliefs connected with the dragon-god who controlled the rain-supply, as Osiris in Egypt controlled the Nile, and the Babylonian Ea the Euphrates.

In the next chapter various beliefs connected with the dragon are brought out in representative legends.

---

[1] De Visser, *The Dragon in China and Japan*, p. 130.
[2] Westervelt's *Legends of Gods and Ghosts*, p. 258.
[3] *Buddhist India*, pp. 224–5.

CHAPTER VII
Dragon Folk-stories

How Fish became Chinese Dragons—-Fish forms of Teutonic and Celtic Gods—Dragon-slayers eat Dragons' Hearts—-The "Language of Birds"—Heart as Seat of Intelligence—Babylonian Dragon-Kupu—Polynesian Dragon-Kupua—Dragons and Medicinal Herbs—Story of Chinese Herbalist and "Red Cloud Herb"—"Boy Blue" and Red Carp as Forms of Black Dragon—Ignis Fatuus as "Dragon Lanterns"—"Heart Fire"—Story of Priest and Dragon-woman—The "Fire Nail" in Japan and Polynesia—The "Faith Cure" in Japan—The Magic Rush-mat—Grave Reed-mats, Skins, and Linen Wrappings—The Ephod—Melusina in Far East—Story of Wu and the Thunder Dragon.

In Chinese and Japanese folk-stories the dragons have fish forms or avatars. They may be eels, carps, or migratory fish like the salmon. It is believed that those fish that ascend a river's "dragon gate" become dragons, while those that remain behind continue to be fish. Dragons are closely associated with waterfalls. They haunt in one or other of their forms the deep pools below them.

In western European stories, dragons and gods of fire and water assume the forms of fish, and hide themselves in pools. Loki of Icelandic legend has a salmon form. When the gods pursue him, he hides in Franang's stream, or "under the waters of a cascade called Franangurfors".[1] After he is caught and bound, Loki is tortured by a serpent. When he twists his body violently, earthquakes are caused. He is closely associated with

---

[1] *Teutonic Myth and Legend*, p. 174 *et seq.*

the " dragon-woman ", and is the father of monsters, including the moon-swallowing wolf-dragon.

Andvari, the guardian of Nibelung treasure, has a pike form.[1]

In Gaelic legend the salmon is the source of wisdom and of the power to foretell events. Finn (Fionn) tastes of the " Salmon of Knowledge " when it is being cooked, and immediately becomes a seer. Michael Scott, in like manner, derives wisdom from the " juices " of the white snake. The salmon is, in Gaelic, a form of the dragon. The dragon of Lough Bel Séad[2] (Lake of the Jewel Mouth), in Ireland, was caught " in the shape of a salmon ".

Sigurd, the dragon-slayer of Norse Icelandic stories, eats the dragon's heart, and at once understands the language of birds. So does Siegfried of Germanic romance. The birds know the secrets of the gods. They are themselves forms of the gods. Apollonius of Tyana acquired wisdom by eating the hearts of dragons in Arabia.

In ancient Egypt the heart was not only the seat of life, but the mind, and therefore the source of " words of power ". The Hebrews and many other peoples used " heart " when they wrote of " mind ".[3] Ptah, god of Memphis, was the " heart " (mind) of the gods. The " heart " fashioned the gods. Everything that is came into existence by the thought of the " heart " (mind).

The Egyptian belief about the power of the " heart " (the source of magic knowledge, and healing, and creative power) lies behind the stories regarding heroes eating dragons' hearts. In an Egyptian folk-tale the dragon-

---

[1] *Teutonic Myth and Legend*, p. 286.

[2] The Irish term *sed* (pronounced "shade "), the old form of which is *set*, signified a cow, a measure of value, property, and " a pearl, a precious stone, or a gem of any kind ". Joyce, *Irish Names of Places*, p. 355 (Dublin, 1875).

[3] Breasted, *A History of Egypt*, p. 357.

slayer does not eat the heart of the reptile god, but gets possession of a book of spells, and, on reading these, acquires knowledge of the languages of all animals, including fish and birds.[1]

When, however, we investigate the dragon beliefs of ancient Babylonia, we meet with a reference to the Ku-pu as the source of divine power and wisdom. After Merodach (Marduk) the dragon - slayer kills Tiamat, the "mother dragon", a form of the mother-goddess, he "divides the flesh of the Ku-pu, and devises a cunning plan". As the late Mr. Leonard W. King pointed out,[2] Ku-pu is a word of uncertain meaning. It did not signify the heart, because it had been previously stated in the text that Merodach *severed her inward parts, he pierced her heart*.

Jensen has suggested that Ku-pu signifies "trunk, body". It is more probable that the Ku-pu was the seat of the soul, mind, and magical power; the power that enabled the slain reptile to come to life again in another form.[3]

It may be that a clue is afforded in this connection by the Polynesian idea of Kupua. Mr. Westervelt, who has carefully recorded what he has found, writes regarding the Mo-o (dragons) of the Hawaiians:

"Mighty eels, immense sea turtles, large fish of the ocean, fierce sharks, were all called mo-o. The most ancient dragons of the Hawaiians are spoken of as living in pools or lakes. These

---

[1] *Egyptian Myth and Legend*, pp. 341, 342.   [2] *Seven Tablets of Creation.*
[3] The belief that the cat has nine lives may be cited, and also the belief that if an eel or a serpent is cut in two it will come to life again. A Chinese dragon may revive after being cut up and buried. The story is told in Japan of a man who killed a snake-dragon, cut it into three pieces, and buried them, but thirteen years later, on the same day of the year on which he slew the dragon, he cried out "I drink water," choked, and died. His death was caused by the dragon he had endeavoured to kill (de Visser, *The Dragon in China and Japan*, p. 195). The "Deathless Snake" in an ancient Egyptian story comes to life until the severed parts are buried separately.

dragons were known also as Kupuas, or mysterious characters, who could appear as animals, or human beings, according to their wish.   The saying was, 'Kupuas have a strange double body!'"

The Polynesian beliefs connected with the Kupuas are highly suggestive.   Mr. Westervelt continues:

"It was sometimes thought that at birth another natural form was added, such as an egg of a fowl or a bird, or the seed of a plant, or the embryo of some animal which, when fully developed, made a form which could be used as readily as the human body. These Kupuas were always given some great magic power. They were wonderfully strong, and wise, and skilful.

"Usually the birth of a Kupua, like the birth of a high chief, was attended with strange disturbances in the heavens, such as reverberating thunder, flashing lightning, and severe storms which sent the abundant red soil of the islands down the mountain-sides in blood-red torrents, known as ka-ua-koko (the blood rain). The name was also given to misty, fine rain when shot through by the red waves of the sun."

All the dragons of Hawaii were descended from Mo-o-inanea (the self-reliant dragon), a mother-goddess. She had a dual nature, "sometimes appearing as a dragon, sometimes as a woman ".   Hawaiian dragons also assumed the forms of large stones, some of which were associated with groves of hau trees; on these stones ferns and flowers were laid and referred to as "kupuas".[1]

In China the dragon's kupua (to use the Polynesian term) figures in various stories.   We meet with the "Red Cloud herb", or the "Dragon Cloud herb", which cures diseases.   It is the gift of the dragon, and apparently a dragon kupua.   Other curative herbs are the "dragon-whisker's herb" and the "dragon's liver", a species of gentian, which is in Japan a badge of the Minamoto family.   The "dragon's spittle" had curative qualities,

[1] *Legends of Gods and Ghosts (Hawaiian Mythology)*, pp. 256–7.

the essence of life being in the body moisture of a deity. The pearl, which the dragon spits out, has, or is, "soul substance". The plum tree was in China connected with the dragon. A story tells that once a dragon was punished by having its ears cut off. Its blood fell on the ground, and a plum tree sprang up; it bore fleshy fruit without kernels.[1] When in an ancient Egyptian story the blood of the Bata bull falls to the ground two trees containing his soul-forms grow in a night.[2]

A Chinese "Boy Blue" story deals with the search made by Wang Shuh, a herbalist, for the Red Cloud herb. He followed the course of a mountain stream on a hot summer day, and at noon sat down to rest and eat rice below shady trees beside the deep pool of a waterfall. As he lay on the bank, gazing into the water, he was astonished to see in its depths a blue boy, about a foot in height, with a blue rush in his hand, riding on the back of a red carp, without disturbing the fish, which darted hither and thither. In time the pair came to the surface, and, rising into the air, turned towards the east. Then they went swiftly in the direction of a bank of cloud that was creeping across the blue sky, and vanished from sight.

The herbalist continued to ascend the mountain, searching for the herb, and when he reached the summit was surprised to find that the sky had become completely overcast. Great masses of black and yellow clouds had risen over the Eastern Sea, and a thunder-storm was threatening. Wang Shuh then realized that the blue boy he had seen riding on the back of the red carp was no other than the thunder-dragon. He peered at

---

[1] *The Dragon in China and Japan*, p. 127. See also the Egyptian Bata story *Egyptian Myth and Legend*, pp. 49–56.
[2] *Egyptian Myth and Legend*, p. 55.

the clouds, and perceived that the boy and the carp[1] had been transformed into a black *kiao* (scaled dragon). He was greatly alarmed, and concealed himself in a hollow tree.

Soon the storm burst forth in all its fury. The herbalist trembled to hear the voice of the black thunder-dragon and to catch glimpses of his fiery tongue as he spat out flashes of lightning. Rain fell in torrents, and the mountain stream was heavily swollen, and roared down the steep valley. Wang Shuh feared that each moment would be his last.

In time, however, the storm ceased and the sky cleared. Wang Shuh then crept forth from his hiding-place, thankful to be still alive, although he had seen the dragon. He at once set out to return by the way he had come. When he drew near to the waterfall he was greatly astonished to hear the sound of sweet humming music. Peering through the branches of the trees, he beheld the little blue boy riding on the back of the red carp, returning from the east and settling down on the surface of the pool. Soon the boy was carried into the depths and past the playful fish again.

Struck with fear, the herbalist was for a time unable to move. When at length he had summoned sufficient strength and courage to go forward, he found that the boy and the carp had vanished completely. Then he perceived that the Red Cloud herb, for which he had been searching, had sprung up on the very edge of the swirling water. Stooping, he plucked it greedily. As soon as he had done so, he went scampering down the side of the mountain. On reaching the village, Wang told his friends the wonderful story of his adventure and discovery.

[1] The Dragon's Kupuas.

Now it happened that the Emperor's daughter—
a very beautiful girl—was lying ill in the royal palace.
The Court physicians had endeavoured in vain to restore
her to health. Hearing of Wang Shuh's discovery of
the Red Cloud herb, the Emperor sent out for him.
On reaching the palace, the herbalist was addressed by
the Emperor himself, who said: " Is it true, as men
tell, that you have seen the black *kiao* in the form of
a little blue boy riding on a red carp?"

" It is indeed true," Wang Shuh made answer.

" And is it true that you have found the dragon herb
that sprang up during the thunder-storm?"

" I have brought the herb with me, Your Majesty."

" Mayhap," the Emperor said, " it will give healing
to my daughter."

Wang Shuh at once made offer of the herb, and
the Emperor led him to the room in which the sick
princess lay. The herb had a sweet odour,[1] and Wang
Shuh plucked a leaf and gave it to the lady to smell.
She at once showed signs of reviving, and this was
regarded as a good omen. Wang Shuh then made a
medicine from the herb, and when the princess had
partaken of it, she grew well and strong again.

The Emperor rewarded Wang Shuh by appointing
him his chief physician. Thus the herbalist became a
great and influential man.

To few mortals comes the privilege of setting eyes on
a dragon, and to fewer is the vision followed by good
fortune.

In this quaint story the Red Cloud herb is evidently

---

[1] The odour of the herb was the body odour of the dragon. It helped to restore
vitality, as did incense, when burned before an Egyptian mummy. Gods were similarly
" fed " by offerings of incense. The Babylonian Noah burned incense, and the gods smelt
the sweet savour. The gods gathered like flies about him that offered the sacrifice.
—King, *Babylonian Religion*, p. 136.

a kupua of the thunder-dragon. It had "soul substance" (the vital essence). Another kupua or avatar was the carp.

In China and Japan there are references in dragon stories to pine trees being forms assumed by dragons. The connection between the tree and dragon is emphasized by the explanation that when a pine becomes very old it is covered with scales of bark, and ultimately changes into a dragon. By night "dragon lanterns" (ignis fatuus) are seen on pine trees in marshy places, and on the masts of ships at sea.

The pine trees at Buddhist temples and Shinto shrines are said to be regularly illuminated by these "supernatural" lights. The "lanterns" are supposed to come from the sea. Japanese stories tell that when a lantern appears on a pine, a little boy, known as the "Heavenly Boy", is to be seen sitting on the topmost branch. Some lights were supposed to be the souls of holy men. In Gaelic stories are told about little men being seen in these wandering lights.

There is an evil form of the fire which is supposed to rise from the blood of a suicide or of a murderer's victim. The "heart fire" (the "vital spark") in the blood is supposed to rise as a flame from the ground. A similar superstition prevailed in England. If lights made their appearance above a prison on the night before the arrival of the judges of assize, the omen was regarded as a fatal one for the prisoners. The belief is widespread in the British Isles that lights (usually greenish lights) appear before a sudden death takes place.

Wandering lights seen on mountains were supposed by the Chinese and Japanese to be caused by dragons. A Japanese legend associates them with a dragon woman, named Zennyo, who appears to have the attributes of a fire-goddess. It is told regarding a Buddhist priest who lived beside a dragon hole on Mount Murōbu. One day, as he was about to cross a river, a lady wearing rich and dazzling attire came up to him and made request for a magic charm he possessed. She spoke with averted face, telling who she was. The priest repeated the charm to her and then said: " Permit me to look upon your face".

Said the dragon woman: " It is very terrible to behold. No man dare gaze on my face. But I cannot refuse your request."

The priest had his curiosity satisfied, but apparently without coming to harm. Priestly prestige was maintained by stories of this kind.

As soon as the priest looked in her face the dragon woman rose in the air, and stretched out the small finger of her right hand. It was not, however, of human shape, but a claw that suddenly extended a great length and flashed lights of five colours. The " five colours " indicate that the woman was a deity. Kwan Chung, in his work *Kwantsze*, says: " A dragon in the water covers himself with five colours. *Therefore, he is a god (shin).*"[1]

The " fire nail " figures prominently in Polynesian mythology. In the legend of Maui, that hero-god goes to the old woman (the goddess), his grandmother, to obtain fire for mankind. " Then the aged woman pulled out her nail; and as she pulled it out fire flowed from it, and she gave it to him. And when Maui saw she had drawn out her nail to produce fire for him, he thought it a most wonderful thing."[2]

The reference in the Japanese story to the averted face of the dragon woman may be connected with the ancient belief that the mortal who looked in the face of

[1] De Visser, *The Dragon in China and Japan*, p. 63.   Kwan Chung died in 645 B.C.
[2] *Polynesian Mythology*, Sir George Grey, p. 33.

a deity was either shrivelled up or transformed into stone, as happened in the case of those who fixed their eyes upon the face of Medusa. Goddesses like the Egyptian Neith were "veiled". A Japanese legend tells of a dragon woman who appeared as a woman with a malicious white face. She laughed loudly, displaying black teeth. She was often seen on a bridge, binding up her hair.[1] Apparently she was a variety of the mermaid family, and this may explain the reference to her being "one legged". The people scared her away by forming a torch-light procession and advancing towards her. Dragons were sometimes expelled by means of fire. In Europe, bon-fires were lit when certain "ceremonies of riddance" were performed.

British mermaids are credited, in the folk-tales, with providing cures for various diseases, and especially herbs,[2] and in this connection they link with the dragon wives of China and Japan. Some dragon women lived for a time among human beings as do swan-maidens, nereids, mer-maids, and fairies in the stories of various lands.

A Japanese legend tells of an elderly and mysterious woman who had the power to cure any ill that flesh is heir to. When a patient called, she listened attentively to what was told her. Then she retired to a secret chamber, sat down and placed a rush mat[3] on her head.

---

[1] De Visser, *The Dragon in China and Japan*, p. 174.

[2] A Galloway herbalist who was searching for herbs to cure a consumptive girl, named May, saw a mermaid rising in the sea. According to the folk-story, the mermaid recommended mugwort (southernwood) as a cure by singing:

> Would you let bonnie May die in your hand,
> And the mugwort flowering in the land?

[3] Jade disks, decorated with the rush pattern, were in China images of Heaven and badges of rank. The rain-dragon in human form carries in his right hand a blue rush. The rush was connected with water—the water below the firmament and the water above the firmament. Reeds were likewise connected with the deities. In Babylonia, priests had visions in reed huts and the dead lay on reed mats. The reed and river-mud were used by Marduk when he created man. Apparently, the reed was an

After sitting alone for a time (apparently engaged in working a magic spell) she left the chamber and returned to the patient. She recommended the "faith cure". Making the pretence that she was handing over a medicine, she said: "Believe that I have given you medicine. Now, go away. Each day you must sit down and imagine that you are taking my medicine. Come back to me in seven days' time." Those who faithfully carried out her instructions are said to have been cured. Large numbers visited her daily.

It was suspected that this woman was possessed by the spirit of a water-demon. A watch was set upon her, and one night she was seen going from her house to a well in which, during the day, she often washed her head while being consulted by patients. Those who watched her told that she remained in human shape for a little time. Then she transformed herself into a white mist and entered the well. Protective charms were recited, and she never returned. For many years afterwards, however, her house was haunted.

De Groot relates a story about one of the wives of an Emperor of China who practised magic by means of reptiles and insects. Her object was to have her son selected as crown prince. She was detected, and she and her son were imprisoned. Both became dragons before they died.

Dragons sometimes appear in the stories in the rôle of demon lovers. A Japanese legend tells of two boys who were the children of a man and a dragon woman. In time they changed into dragons and flew away. The

---

avatar of the water deity: it contained "soul ·substance". Linen made from flax was sacred and inspiring. It was wrapped round the dead, instead of animal skins, in pre-Dynastic Egypt. The linen ephod was inspiring; like the "prophet's mantle" it gave the wearer power to foretell events.

woman herself came to her lover in the shape of a snake, and then transformed herself into a beautiful maiden.

This is a version of a very widespread story, found in the Old and New World, which was possibly distributed by ancient mariners and traders. Its most familiar form is the French legend of Melusina, the serpent woman, who became the wife of Raymond of Poitou, and the mother of his disfigured children.[1]

A Chinese legend of the Melusina order deals with the fall of the Hea Dynasty. A case of dragon foam which had been kept in the royal palace during three dynasties was one day opened, and there issued forth a dragon in the form of a black lizard. It touched a young virgin, who became the mother of a girl whom she bore in secret and abandoned in a wood. It chanced that a poor man and his wife, who were childless, hearing the cries of the babe, took her to their house, where they cared for her tenderly. But the magicians came to know of the dragon's daughter, of whom it had been prophesied that she would destroy the dynasty. Search was made for the child, and the foster-parents fled with her to the land of Pao. They presented her to the king of the land, and she grew up to be a beautiful maid who was called Pao Sze. The king loved her dearly, and when she gave birth to a son, he made her his queen, degrading Queen Chen and her son, the crown prince. Poh Fuh, the son of the dragon woman, then became crown prince instead.

Now Pao Sze, although very beautiful, was always sad of countenance. She never smiled. The king did everything in his power to make her smile and laugh. But his efforts were in vain.

"Fain would I hear you laugh," said he.

But she only sighed and said: "Ask me not to laugh."

[1] S. Baring-Gould's *Curious Myths of the Middle Ages*, pp. 471 *et seq.*

One day the king, in his endeavours to break the spell of sadness that bound his beautiful queen, arranged that his lords should enter the palace and declare that an enemy army was at hand, and that the life of the king was in peril.

This they did. The king was at the time making merry when his lords entered suddenly and said: " Your Majesty, the enemy have come, while you sit making merry, and they are resolved to slay you."

The king's sudden change of countenance made the dragon woman laugh. His Majesty was well pleased.

Then, as it chanced, the enemy came indeed. But when the alarm was raised, the lords thought it was a false one. The army took possession of the city, entered the palace, and slew the king. Pao Sze was taken prisoner, because of her fatal beauty; but she brought no joy to her captor and transformed herself into a dragon, departing suddenly and causing a thunder-storm to rage.

To those who win their favour, the dragons are pre-servers even when they come forth as destroyers. The story is told of how Wu, the son of a farmer named Yin, won the favour of a dragon and rose to be a great man in China. When he was a boy of thirteen, he was sitting one day at the garden gate, looking across the plain which is watered by a winding river that flows from the mountains. He was a silent, dreamy boy, who had been brought up by his grandmother, his mother having died when he was very young, and it was his habit thus to sit in silence, thinking and observing things. Along the highway came a handsome youth riding a white horse. He was clad in yellow garments and seemed to be of high birth. Four man-servants accompanied him, and one held an umbrella to shield him from the sun's bright rays. The youth drew up his horse at the gate and, addressing Wu, said: "Son of Yin, I am weary. May I enter your father's house and rest a little time?"

The boy bowed and said: "Enter."

Yin then came forward and opened the gate. The noble youth dismounted and sat on a seat in the court, while his servants tethered the horse. The farmer chatted with his visitor, and Wu gazed at them in silence. Food was brought, and when the meal was finished, the youth thanked him for his hospitality and walked across the courtyard. Wu noticed that before one of the servants passed through the gate, he turned the umbrella upside down. When the youth had mounted his horse, he turned to the silent, observant boy and said: "I shall come again to-morrow."

Wu bowed and answered: "Come!"

The strangers rode away, and Wu sat watching them until they had vanished from sight.

When evening came on, the farmer spoke to his son regarding the visitors, and said: "The noble youth knew my name and yet I have never set eyes on him before."

Wu was silent for a time. Then he said: "I cannot say who the youth is or who his attendants are."

"You watched them very closely, my son. Did you note anything peculiar about them?"

Said Wu: "There were no seams in their clothing; the white horse had spots of five colours and scaly armour instead of hair. The hoofs of the horse and the feet of the strangers did not touch the ground."[1]

Yin rose up with agitation and exclaimed: "Then they are not human beings, but spirits."

[1] A similar belief regarding supernatural beings prevailed in India. See story of Nala in *Indian Myth and Legend*.

Said Wu: "I watched them as they went westward. Rain-clouds were gathering on the horizon, and when they were a great distance off they all rose in the air and vanished in the clouds."[1]

Yin was greatly alarmed to hear this, and said: "I must ask your grandmother what she thinks of this strange happening."

The old woman was fast asleep, and as she had grown very deaf it was difficult to awaken her. When at length she was thoroughly roused, and sat up with head and hands trembling with palsy,[2] Yin repeated to her in a loud voice all that Wu had told him.

Said the woman: "The horse, spotted with five colours, and with scaly armour instead of hair, is a dragon-horse. When spirits appear before human beings they wear magic garments. That is why the clothing of your visitors had no seams. Spirits tread on air. As these spirits went westward, they rose higher and higher in the air, going towards the rain-clouds. The youth was the Yellow Dragon. He is to raise a storm, and as he had four followers the storm will be a great one. May no evil befall us."

Then Yin told the old woman that one of the strangers had turned the umbrella upside down before passing through the garden gate. "That is a good omen," she said. Then she lay down and closed her eyes. "I have need of sleep," she murmured; "I am very old."[3]

---

[1] The appearance of four servants (the gods of the four quarters) with the dragon-god, indicates that the coming storm is to be one of exceptional violence.

[2] The deep slumberer in a folk-tale is usually engaged "working a spell". As will be gathered from the story, the boy received his knowledge and power from his grandmother. She resembles the Norse Vala and the Witch of Endor.

[3] The Norse Vala makes similar complaint when awakened by Odin. It looks as if this Chinese story is based on one about consulting a spirit of a "wise woman" who sleeps in her tomb.

Heavy masses of clouds were by this time gathering in the sky, and Yin decided to sit up all night. Wu asked to be permitted to do the same, and his father consented. Then the boy lit a yellow lantern, put on a yellow robe that his grandmother had made for him, burned incense, and sat down reading charms from an old yellow book.[1]

The storm burst forth in fury just when dawn was breaking dimly. Wu then closed his yellow book and went to a window. The thunder bellowed, the lightning flamed, and the rain fell in torrents, and swollen streams poured down from the mountains. Soon the river rose in flood and swept across the fields. Cattle gathered in groups on shrinking mounds that had become islands surrounded by raging water.

Yin feared greatly that the house would be swept away, and wished he had fled to the mountains.

At night the cottage was entirely surrounded by the flood. Trees were cast down and swept away. " We cannot escape now," groaned Yin.

Wu sat in silence, displaying no signs of emotion. " What do you think of it all?" his father asked.

Wu reminded him that one of the strangers had turned the umbrella upside down, and added: " Before the dragon youth went away he spoke and said: ' I shall come again to-morrow '."

" He has come indeed," Yin groaned, and covered his face with his hands.

Said Wu: " I have just seen the dragon. As I looked towards the sky he spread out his great hood above our home. He is protecting us now."

" Alas! my son, you are dreaming."

[1] An interesting glimpse of the connection between colour symbolism and magic. Everything is yellow because a yellow dragon is being invoked.

"Listen, father, no rain falls on the roof."

Yin listened intently.   Then he said: "You speak truly, my son.   This is indeed a great marvel."

"It was well," said Wu, "that you welcomed the dragon yesterday."

"He spoke to you first, my son; and you answered, 'Enter'. Ah, you have much wisdom. You will become a great man."

The storm began to subside, and Wu prevailed upon his father to lie down and sleep.[1]

Much damage had been done by storm and flood, and large numbers of human beings and domesticated animals had perished.   In the village, which was situated at the mouth of the valley, only a few houses were left standing.

The rain ceased to fall at midday.   Then the sun came out and shone brightly, while the waters began to retreat.

Wu went outside and sat at the garden gate, as was his custom.   In time he saw the yellow youth returning from the west, accompanied by his four attendants. When he came nigh, Wu bowed and the youth drew up his horse and spoke, saying: "I said I should return to-day."

Wu bowed.

"But this time I shall not enter the courtyard," the youth added.

"As you will," Wu said reverently.

The dragon youth then handed the boy a single scale which he had taken from the horse's neck, and said: "Keep this and I shall remember you."

Then he rode away and vanished from sight.

The boy re-entered the house.   He awoke his father

---

[1] This sleep appears to be as necessary as that of the grandmother.

and said: "The storm is over and the dragon has returned to his pool."[1]

Yin embraced his son, and together they went to inform the old woman. She awoke, sat up, and listened to all that was said to her. When she learned that the dragon youth had again appeared and had spoken to Wu, she asked: "Did he give you ought before he departed?"

Wu opened a small wooden box and showed her the scale that had been taken from the neck of the dragon horse.

The woman was well pleased, and said: "When the Emperor sends for you, all will be well."

Yin was astonished to hear these words, and exclaimed: "Why should the Emperor send for my boy?"

"You shall see," the old woman made answer as she lay down again.

Before long the Emperor heard of the great marvel that had been worked in the flooded valley. Men who had taken refuge on the mountains had observed that no rain fell on Yin's house during the storm. So His Majesty sent couriers to the valley, and these bade Yin to accompany them to the palace, taking Wu with him.

On being brought before the Emperor, Yin related everything that had taken place. Then His Majesty asked to see the scale of the dragon horse.

It was growing dusk when Wu opened the box, and the scale shone so brightly that it illumined the throne-room so that it became as bright as at high noon.

Said the Emperor: "Wu shall remain here and become one of my magicians. The yellow dragon has imparted to him much power and wisdom."

Thus it came about that Wu attained high rank in

---

[1] The latest spell had been worked, and it was not necessary that the father should sleep any longer.

the kingdom. He found that great miracles could be worked with the scale of the dragon horse. It cured disease, and it caused the Emperor's army to win victories. Withal, Wu was able to foretell events, and he became a renowned prophet and magician.

The farmer's son grew to be very rich and powerful. A great house was erected for him close to the royal palace, and he took his grandmother and father to it, and there they lived happily until the end of their days.

Thus did Wu, son of Yin, become a great man, because of the favour shown to him by the thunder-dragon, who had wrought great destruction in the river valley and taken toll of many lives.

It will be gathered from this story that the Chinese dragon is not always a "beneficent deity", as some writers put it. Like certain other gods, he is a destroyer and preserver in one.

CHAPTER VIII

The Kingdom under the Sea

The Vanishing Island of Far-Eastern Dragon-god—Story of Priest who visited Underworld—Far-Eastern Dragon as "Pearl Princess"—Her Human Lover—An Indian Parallel—Dragon Island in Ancient Egyptian Story—The Osirian Underworld—Vanishing Island in Scotland and Fiji—Babylonian Gem-tree Garden—Far-Eastern Quest of the Magic Sword—Parallels of Teutonic and Celtic Legend—"Kusanagi Sword", the Japanese "Excalibur" —City of the Far-Eastern Sea-god—Japanese Vision of Gem-tree Garden— Weapon Demons — Star Spirits of Magic Swords — Swords that become Dragons—Dragon Jewels—Dragon Tranformations.

THE palace of the dragon king is situated in the Underworld, which can be entered through a deep mountain cave or a dragon-guarded well. In some of the Chinese stories the dragon palace is located right below a remote island in the Eastern Sea. This island is not easily approached, for on the calmest of days great billows dash against its shelving crags. When the tide is high, it is entirely covered by water and hidden from sight. Junks may then pass it or even sail over it, without their crews being aware that they are nigh to the palace of the sea-god.

Sometimes a red light burns above the island at night. It is seen many miles distant, and its vivid rays may be reflected in the heavens.

In a Japanese story the island is referred to as "a glowing red mass resembling the rising sun". No mariner dares to approach it.

There was once a Chinese priest who, on a memorable

night, reached the dragon king's palace by entering a deep cave on a mountain-side. It was his pious desire to worship the dragon, and he went onward in the darkness, reciting religious texts that gave him protection. The way was long and dark and difficult, but at length, after travelling far, he saw a light in front of him. He walked towards this light and emerged from the cavern to find that he was in the Underworld. Above him was a clear blue firmament lit by the night sun. He beheld a beautiful palace in the midst of a garden that glittered with gems and flowers, and directed his steps towards it. He reached a window the curtain of which rustled in the wind. He perceived that it was a mass of gleaming pearls. Peering behind it, as it moved, he beheld a table formed of jewels. On this table lay a book of Buddhist prayers (sutras).

As he gazed with wonder and reverence, the priest heard a voice that spake and said: "Who hath come nigh and why hath he come?"

The priest answered in a low voice, giving his name, and expressing his desire to behold the dragon king, whom he desired to worship.

Then the voice made answer: "Here no human eye can look upon me. Return by the way thou hast come, and I shall appear before thee at a distance from the cavern mouth."

The priest made obeisance, and returned to the world of men by the way he had come. He went to the spot that the voice had indicated, and there he waited, reading sacred texts. Soon the earth yawned and the dragon king arose in human shape, wearing a red hat and garment. The priest worshipped him, and then the dragon vanished from sight. On that sacred spot a temple was afterwards erected.

Once upon a time the daughter of the dragon king, who was named "Abundant Pearl Princess", fell in love with a comely youth of Japan. He was sitting, on a calm summer day, beneath a holy tree, and his image was reflected in a dragon well. The princess appeared before him and cast a love spell over his heart. The youth was enchanted by her beauty, and she led him towards the palace of the dragon king, the "Abundant Pearl Prince". There she married him, and they lived together for three years. Then the youth was possessed by a desire to return to the world of men. In vain the princess pleaded with him to remain in the palace. When, however, she found that his heart was set on leaving the kingdom of the Underworld, she resolved to accompany him. He was conveyed across the sea on the back of a *wani* (a dragon in crocodile shape). The princess accompanied him, and he built a house for her on the seashore.

The "Abundant Pearl Princess" was about to become a mother, and she made the youth promise not to look upon her until after her child was born. But he broke his vow. Overcome with curiosity, he peered into her chamber and saw that his wife had assumed the shape of a dragon. As soon as the child was born, the princess departed in anger and was never again beheld by her husband.

This story, it will be noted, is another Far-Eastern version of the Melusina legend.

An Indian version of the tale relates that the hero was a sailor, the sole survivor from a wreck, who swam to a small island in the midst of the sea. When he reached the shore, he set out to look for food, but found that the trees and shrubs, which dazzled him with their beauty, bore beautiful gems instead of fruit. At length, however, he found a fruit-bearing tree. He ate and was well content.   Then he sat down beside a well.   As he stooped to drink of its waters, he had a vision of the Underworld in all its beauty.   At the bottom of the well sat a fair sea-maid, who looked upwards with eyes of love and beckoned him towards her.   He plunged into the well and found himself in the radiant Kingdom of Ocean.   The maid was the queen, and she took him as her consort.   She promised him great wealth, but forbade him to touch the statue of an Apsara[1], which was of gold and adorned with gems.   But one day he placed his hand on the right foot of the image.   The foot darted forth and struck him with such force that he was driven through the sea and washed ashore on his native coast.[2]

The oldest version of this type of story comes from Egypt.   It has been preserved in a papyrus in the Hermitage collection at Petrograd, and is usually referred to as of Twelfth Dynasty origin (c. 2000 B.C.).   A sailor relates that he was the sole survivor from a wreck.   He had seized a piece of wood and swam to an island.   After he recovered from exhaustion, he set out to search for food.   "I found there figs and grapes, all manner of good herbs, berries and grain, melons of all kinds, fishes and birds."   In time, he heard a noise "as of thunder", while "the trees shook and the earth was moved".   The ruler of the island drew nigh.   He was a human-headed serpent "thirty cubits long, and his beard greater than two cubits; his body was as overlaid with gold, and his colour as that of true lapis-lazuli".

The story proceeds to tell that the sailor becomes the guest of the serpent, who makes speeches to him and introduces him to his family.   It is stated that the island "has risen from the waves and will sink again".   After

---

[1] Indian fairy girl.   There are apsaras in the Paradise of Indra.
[2] *Indian Fairy Stories* (London, 1915), pp. 47 *et seq.*

a time the sailor is rescued by a passing vessel.[1]   This ancient Egyptian tale links with the Indian and Chinese versions given above.   The blue serpent resembles closely the Chinese dragon; the vanishing island is common to Egypt and China.   Like much else that came from Egypt, the island has a history.   Long before the ancient mariners transferred it to the ocean, it figured in the fused mythology of the Solar and Osirian cults. Horus hid from Set on a green floating island on the Nile.   He was protected by a serpent deity.   His father, Osiris, is Judge and Ruler of the Underworld, and has a serpent shape as the Nile god and the dragon of the abyss.   The red light associated with the Chinese dragon island of ocean recalls the Red Horus, a form of the sun-god, rising from the Nile of the Underworld, on which floated the green nocturnal sun, "the green bed of Horus" and a form of his father Osiris as the solar deity of night.

The Osirian underworld idea appears to have given origin to the widespread stories found as far apart as Japan and the British Isles regarding "Land-under-Waves" and "the Kingdom of the Sea".   The green floating island of Paradise is referred to in Scottish Gaelic folk-tales.   In Fiji the natives tell of a floating island that vanishes when men approach it.[2]

In some Chinese legends Egyptian conceptions blend with those of Babylonia.   The Chinese priest who, in the dragon-king story, reached the Underworld through a deep cave, followed in the footsteps of Gilgamesh, who went in search of the "Plant of Life"—the herb that causes man "to renew his youth like the eagle".[3]   Gil-

---

[1] *Egyptian Tales* (first series), W. H. Flinders Petrie (London, 1899), pp. 81 *et seq.*
[2] *Folk Lore Journal*, Vol. V, p. 257.
[3] *Myths of Babylonia and Assyria*, pp. 177 *et seq.*

gamesh entered the cave of the Mountain of Mashi (Sunset Hill), and after passing through its night-black depths, reached the seaside garden in which, as on the island in the Indian story, the trees bore, instead of fruit and flowers, clusters of precious stones. He beheld in the midst of this garden of dazzling splendour the palace of Sabitu, the goddess, who instructed him how to reach the island on which lived his ancestor Pir-naphishtum (Utnapishtim). Gilgamesh was originally a god, the earlier Gishbilgames of Sumerian texts.[1]

The Indian Hanuman (the monkey-god) similarly enters a deep cave when he goes forth as a spy to Lanka, the dwelling-place of Ravana, the demon who carried away Sita, wife of Rama, the hero of the *Ramayana*. A similar story is told in the mythical history of Alexander the Great. There are also western European legends of like character. Hercules searches for the golden apples that grow in the Hesperian gardens.[2] In some Far Eastern stories the hero searches for a sword instead of an herb. " Every weapon," declares an old Gaelic saying, " has its demon." The same belief prevailed in China, where dragons sometimes appeared in the form of weapons, and in India, where the spirits of celestial weapons appeared before heroes like Arjuna and Rama.[3] In the Teutonic Balder story, as related by Saxo Grammaticus,[4] the hero is slain by a sword taken from the Underworld, where it was kept by Miming (Mimer), the god, in an Underworld cave. Hother, who gains possession of it, goes by a road " hard for mortal man to travel ".

In the Norse version the sword becomes an herb—the mistletoe, a " cure-all ", like the Chinese dragon herb and

[1] L. W. King, *Legends of Babylonia and Egypt* (London, 1918), p. 146.
[2] See references in *Myths of Babylonia and Assyria*, pp. 184 *et seq.*
[3] *Indian Myth and Legend*, p. 256 and p. 381.   [4] Book III.

the Babylonian "Plant of Life". *Excalibur*, the sword
of King Arthur, was obtained from the lake-goddess (a
British "Naga"), and was flung back into the lake before
he died:

> So flashed and fell the brand Excalibur:
> But ere he dipped the surface, rose an arm
> Clothed in white samite, mystic, wonderful,
> And caught him by the hilt, and brandished him
> Three times, and drew him under in the mere.[1]

The Japanese story of the famous Kusanagi sword is
a Far-Eastern link between the Celestial herb- and weapon-
legends of Asia and Europe. It tells that this magic
sword was one of the three treasures possessed by the
imperial family of Japan, and that the warrior who wielded
it could put to flight an entire army. At a naval battle
the sword was worn by the boy-Emperor, Antoku Tennō.
He was unable to make use of it, and when the enemy
were seen to be victorious, the boy's grandmother, Nu-
no-ama, clutched him in her arms and leapt into the
sea.

Many long years afterwards, when the Emperor Go
Shirakawa sat on the imperial throne, his barbarian
enemies declared war against him. The Emperor arose
in his wrath and called for the Kusanagi sword. Search
was made for it in the temple of Kamo, where it was supposed to be in safe-keeping. The Emperor was told,
however, that it had been lost, and he gave orders that
ceremonies should be performed with purpose to discover
where the sword was, and how it might be restored. One
night, soon afterwards, the Emperor dreamed a dream, in
which a royal lady, who had been dead for centuries,
appeared before him and told that the Kusanagi sword

---

[1] Tennyson's *The Passing of Arthur*.

was in the keeping of the dragon king in his palace at the bottom of the sea.

Next morning the Emperor related his dream to his chief minister, and bade him hasten to the two female divers, Oimatsu and her daughter Wakamatsu, who resided at Dan-no-ura, so that they might dive to the bottom of the sea and obtain the sword.

The divers undertook the task, and were conveyed in a boat to that part of the ocean where the boy-Emperor, Antoku Tennō, had been drowned. A religious ceremony was performed, and the mother and daughter then dived into the sea. A whole day passed before they appeared again. They told, as soon as they were taken into the boat, that they had visited a wonderful city at the bottom of the sea. Its gates were guarded by silent sentinels who drew flashing swords when they (the divers) attempted to enter. They were consequently compelled to wait for several hours, until a holy man appeared and asked them what they sought. When they had informed him that they were searching for the Kusanagi sword, he said that the city could not be entered without the aid of Buddha.

Said the Emperor's chief minister: "The city is that of the god of the sea."

"It is very beautiful," Oimatsu told him; "the walls are of gold, and the gates of pearl. Above the city walls are seen many-coloured towers that gleam like to precious stones. When one of the gates was opened, we perceived that the streets were of silver and the houses of mother-of-pearl."

Said the Emperor's chief minister: "Fain would I visit that city."

He looked over the side of the boat and sighed, "I see naught but darkness."

"When we dived and reached the sea-bottom,"

Oimatsu continued, "we beheld a cave and entered it. Thick darkness prevailed, but we walked on and on, groping as we went, until we reached a beautiful plain over which bends the sky, blue as sapphire. Trees growing on the plain bear clusters of dazzling gems that sparkle among their leaves."

"Were you not tempted to pluck them?" asked the minister.

"Each tree is guarded by a poisonous snake," Oimatsu told him, "and we dared not touch the gems."

On the following day the divers were provided with sutra-charms by the chief priest of the temple of Kamo.

They entered the sea again, and told, on their return next morning, that they had visited the city, and reached the palace of the dragon king, which was guarded by invisible sentries. Two women came out of the palace and bade them stand below an old pine tree, the bark of which glittered like the scales of a dragon. In front of them was a window. The blind was made of beautiful pearls, and was raised high enough to permit them to see right into the room.

One of the palace ladies said, "Look through the window."

The women looked. In the room they saw a mighty serpent with a sword in his mouth. He had eyes bright as the sun, and a blood-red tongue. In his coils lay a little boy fast asleep.[1] The serpent looked round and, addressing the women, spoke and said: "You have come hither to obtain the Kusanagi sword, but I shall keep it for ever. It does not belong to the Emperor of Japan. Many years ago it was taken from this palace by a dragon prince who went to dwell in the river Hi. He was slain

---

[1] Like the Indian god Vishnu, who lies asleep on the Naga. This sleep, like that of magicians, is a spell-working or power-accumulating sleep.

by a hero of Japan.[1] This hero carried off the sword and presented it to the Emperor. After many years had gone past a sea-dragon took the form of a princess. She became the bride of a prince of Japan, and was the grandmother of the boy-Emperor with whom she leapt into the sea during the battle of Dan-no-ura. This boy now lies asleep in my coils."

The Emperor of Japan sorrowed greatly when he was informed regarding the dragon king's message. "Alas!" he said, "if the Kusanagi sword cannot be obtained, the barbarians will defeat my army in battle."

Then a magician told the Emperor that he knew of a powerful spell that would compel the dragon to give up the sword. "If it is successful," the Emperor said, "I shall elevate you to the rank of a prince."

The spell was worked, and when next the female divers went to the Kingdom under the Sea, they obtained the sword, with which they returned to the Emperor. He used it in battle and won a great victory.

The sword was afterwards placed in a box and deposited in the temple of Atsuta, and there it remained for many years, until a Korean priest carried it away. When, however, the Korean was crossing the ocean to his own land, a great storm arose. The captain of the vessel knew it was no ordinary storm, but one that had been raised by a god, and he spoke and said, "Who on board this ship has offended the dragon king of Ocean?"

Then said the Korean priest, "I shall throw my sword into the sea as a peace-offering."

He did as he said he would, and immediately the storm passed away.

---

[1] Like the Egyptian hero who slays the river serpent which guards the box containing magic spells. Sigurd, Siegfried, and other dragon-slaying heroes may be compared with this Far-Eastern hero.

The dragon king caused the sword to be replaced in the temple from which the Korean had stolen it. There it lay for a century. Then it was carried back to the palace of the dragon-god in his Kingdom under the Sea.

Magic or supernatural swords were possessed by the spirits of dragon-gods.

According to a Chinese story in the Books of the Tsin Dynasty, an astrologer once discovered that among the stars there shone the spirits of two magic swords, and that they were situated right above the spot where the swords had, in time past, been concealed. Search was made for these, and deep down in the earth was found a luminous stone chest. Inside the chest lay two swords that bore inscriptions indicating that they were dragon swords. As soon as they were taken out of the box, their star-spirits faded from the sky.

These dragon swords could not be retained by human beings for any prolonged period. Stories are told of swords being taken away by spirit-beings and even of swords leaping of their own accord from their sheaths into rivers or the ocean, and assuming dragon shape as soon as they touched water.[1]

Similarly dragon jewels might be carried away by dragons who appeared in human shape—either as beautiful girls or as crafty old men.

It was fortunate for mortals when dragons appeared as human beings, as animals, or as fish that spoke with human voices. Dragons were unable to change their shapes when angry, or when they intended to avenge a wrong. A transformed dragon was therefore quite harmless.

[1] De Visser, *The Dragon in China and Japan.*

CHAPTER IX

The Islands of the Blest

Souls on Islands—Wells of Life and Trees or Plants of Life in China, Ancient Egypt, Babylonia, &c.—How Islands were Anchored—The Ocean Tortoise—A Giant's Fishing—The Mystery of Fu-sang—Island of Women—Search for Fabled Isles—Chinese and Japanese Stories—How Navigation was Stimulated — Columbus and Eden — Water of Life in Ceylon, Polynesia, America, and Scotland—Delos, a Floating Island—Atlantis and the Fortunate Isles—Celtic Island Paradise—Apples and Nuts as Food of Life—America as Paradise—The Indian Lotus of Life — Buddhist Paradise with Gem-trees — Diamond Valley Legend in China and Greece—Luck Gems and Immortality.

The Chinese and Japanese, like the Egyptians, Indians, Fijians, and others, believed, as has been shown, in the existence of a floating and vanishing island associated with the serpent-god or dragon-god of ocean. They believed, too, that somewhere in the Eastern Sea lay a group of islands that were difficult to locate or reach; which resembled closely, in essential particulars, the "Islands of the Blest", or "Fortunate Isles", of ancient Greek writers. Vague beliefs regarding fabulous countries far across the ocean were likewise prevalent.

In some native accounts these Chinese Islands of the Blest are said to be five in number, and named Tai Yü, Yüan Chiao, Fang Hu, Ying Chou, and P'ēng-lai; in others the number is nine, or ten, or only three. A single island is sometimes referred to; it may be located in the ocean, or in the Yellow River, or in the river of the Milky Way, the Celestial Ho.

106

The islands are, in Chinese legend, reputed to be inhabited by those who have won immortality, or by those who have been transported to their Paradise to dwell there in bliss for a prolonged period so that they may be reborn on earth, or pass to a higher state of existence.

It is of special interest to note in connection with these islands that they have Wells of Life and Trees or Herbs of Life. The souls drink the water and eat the herb or fruit of the tree to prolong their existence. One Chinese "plant of life" is *li chih*, "the fungus of immortality". It appears on Chinese jade ornaments as a symbol of longevity. "This fungus", writes Laufer, "is a species of *Agaric* and considered a felicitous plant, because it absorbs the vapours of the earth. In the *Li Ki* (ed. Couvreur, Vol. I, p. 643) it is mentioned as an edible plant. As a marvellous plant foreboding good luck, it first appeared under the Han Dynasty, in 109 B.C., when it sprouted in the imperial palace Kan-ts'üan. The emperor issued an edict announcing this phenomenon, and proclaimed an amnesty in the empire except for relapsing criminals. A hymn in honour of this divine plant was composed in the same year."[1]

Like the Red Cloud herb the *li chih* had evidently a close connection with the dragon-god.

The question arises whether the idea of an island of paradise was of "spontaneous origin" in China, or whether the ancient Chinese borrowed the belief from intruders, or from peoples with whom they had constant trading relations. There is evidence that as far back as the fourth century, B.C., a Chinese explorer set out on an expedition to search for the island or islands of Paradise

[1] *Jade: A Study in Chinese Archæology and Religion*, Berthold Laufer (Chicago, 1912), pp. 209–10.

in the Eastern Sea. But it is not known at what precise period belief in the island arose and became prevalent.

The evidence afforded by the ancient Egyptian Pyramid Texts is of special interest and importance in connection with the problem of origin. As far back as *c.* 2500 B.C. "the departed Pharaoh hoped to draw his sustenance in the realm of Re (Paradise)" from "the tree of life in the mysterious isle in the midst of the Field of Offerings". The soul of the Pharaoh, according to the Pyramid Texts, set out, soon after death, in search of this island "in company with the Morning Star. The Morning Star is a gorgeous green falcon, a solar divinity, identified with Horus of Dewat." The Egyptian story of the soul's quest goes on to tell that "this King Pepi . . . went to the great isle in the midst of the Field of Offerings over which the gods make the swallows fly. The swallows are the Imperishable Stars. They give to this King Pepi the tree of life, whereof they live, that ye (Pepi and the Morning Star) may at the same time live thereof." (Pyramid Texts, 1209–16). Sinister enemies " may contrive to deprive the king of the sustenance provided for him. . . ." Charms were provided to protect the fruit of immortality. " The enemy against which these are most often directed in the Pyramid Texts is serpents." In the Japanese story of the Kusanagi sword, the gem-trees of the Otherworld are protected by dragons.

The Pyramid Texts devoted to the ancient Egyptian King Unis tell that a divine voice cries to the gods Re and Thoth (sun and moon), saying, " Take ye this King Unis with you that he may eat of that which ye eat, and that he may drink of that which ye drink." The magic well is referred to as " the pool of King Unis ".[1] The soul of the Pharaoh also sails with the unwearied stars in

[1] Breasted, *Religion and Thought in Egypt*, pp. 133–7.

the barque of the sun-god, not only by day but by night, and as the Egyptian night sun was green, " the green bed of Horus ", the idea of the floating solar island on the Underworld Nile became fused with that of the island with the Well of Life and the Tree of Life. In the Pyramid Texts the Celestial Otherworld " is ", as Breasted says, " not only the east, but explicitly the east of the sky ".[1] Similarly the fabulous continents of the Chinese were situated to the east of the mythical sea.

The Sumerians and early Babylonians had, like the Egyptians, their Islands of the Blest. Gilgamesh, who reaches these islands by crossing the mythical sea, finds dwelling on one of them Ut-napishtim (the Babylonian Noah) and his wife. Ut-napishtim directs the hero to another island on which there is a fountain of healing waters and a magic plant that renews youth. Gilgamesh finds the Plant of Immortality, but as he stoops to drink water from a stream, a serpent darts forth and snatches the plant from him. This serpent was a form of " the Earth Lion " (the dragon).[2]

The Gilgamesh legend dates back beyond 2500 B.C. Like the Egyptian one enshrined in the Pyramid Texts, it has two main features, the Well of Life and the Tree or Plant of Life, which are situated on an island. The island in time crept into the folk-tales. It was no doubt the prototype of the vanishing island of the Egyptian mariner's story already referred to.

In the *Shih Chi* (Historical Record) of Ssŭ-ma Ch'ien, " the Herodotus of China ", a considerable part of which has been translated by Professor Ed. Chavannes,[3] the three Chinese Islands of the Blest (*San, Shen, Shan*) are

---

[1] Breasted, *Religion and Thought in Egypt*, p. 102.
[2] *Myths of Babylonia and Assyria*, pp. 181-3.
[3] *Mémoires Historiques de Se-ma Ts'ien* (1895-1905).

named P'ēng-lai, Fang Chang, and Ying Chou. They
are located in the Gulf of Chihli, but are difficult to
reach because contrary winds spring up and drive vessels
away in the same manner as the vessel of Odysseus was
driven away from Ithaca. It is told, however, that in
days of old certain fortunate heroes contrived to reach
and visit the fabled isles. They told that they saw there
palaces of gold and silver, that the white men and
women, the white beasts and the white birds ate the
Herb of Life and drank the waters of the Fountain of
Life. On the island of Ying Chou are great precipices
of jade. A brook, the waters of which are as stimulating as wine, flows out of a jade rock. Those who can
reach the island and drink of this water will increase the
length of their lives. When the jade water is mixed
with pounded "fungus of immortality" a food is provided
which ensures a thousand years of existence in the body.

Chinese legends tell that the lucky mariners who
come within view of the Isles of the Blest, behold them
but dimly, as they seem to be enveloped in luminous
clouds. When vessels approach too closely, the islands
vanish by sinking below the waves, as do the fabled
islands of Gaelic stories.

Lieh Tze, alleged to be an early Taoist writer,[1] but
whose writings, or those writings attributed to him, were
forged in the first or second century A.D., has located the
islands to the east of the gulf of Chihli in that fathomless
abyss into which flow all the streams of the earth and the
river of the Milky Way. Apparently this abyss is the
Mythical Sea which was located beyond the eastern horizon—a part of the sea that surrounds the world. Into
this sea or lake, according to the ancient Egyptian texts,

---

[1] He figures as a character (not a real one) in the writings of Kwang-tze, who was
born in the fourth century B.C.

pours the celestial river, along which sails the barque of
the sun-god.   The Nile was supposed by the Ancient
Egyptians to be fed by the waters above the firmament
and the waters below the earth.   The Pyramid Texts,
when referring to the birth of Osiris as "new water"
(the inundation), say:

> The waters of life that are in the sky come;
> The waters of life that are in the earth come.
> The sky burns for thee,
> The earth trembles for thee.[1]

In India the Ganges was likewise fed by the celestial
Ganges that poured down from the sky.

Lieh Tze's Islands of the Blest are five in number,
and are inhabited by the white souls of saintly sages who
have won immortality by having their bodies rendered
transparent, or after casting off their bodies as snakes
cast off their skins.   All the animals on these islands are
likewise white and therefore pure and holy.   The spirit-
dwellings are of gold and jade, and in the groves and
gardens the trees and plants bear pearls and precious
stones.   Those who eat of the fungus, or of perfumed
fruit, renew their youth and acquire the power of floating
like down through the air from island to island.

At one time the islands drifted about on the tides of
ocean, but the Lord of All who controls the Universe,
having been appealed to by the Taoist sages who dwelt
on the isles, caused three great Atlas-turtles to support
each island with their heads so that they might remain
steadfast.   These turtles are relieved by others at the
end of sixty thousand years.   In like manner, in Indian
mythology, the tortoise Kurma, an avatar of the god
Vishnu, supports Mount Meru when it is placed in the

[1] Breasted, *Religion and Thought in Ancient Egypt*, p. 145.

Sea of Milk. The Japanese Creator has a tortoise form that supports the world-tree, on the summit of which sits a four-armed god. In China the tortoise had divine attributes. Tortoise shell is a symbol of unchangeability, and a symbol of rank when used for court girdles. The tortoise was also used for purposes of divination.[1]

A gigantic mythical tortoise is supposed, in the Far East, to live in the depths of ocean. It has one eye situated in the middle of its body. Once every three thousand years it rises to the surface and turns over on its back so that it may see the sun.

Once upon a time, a legend tells, the Atlas-turtles that support the Islands of the Blest suffered from a raid by a wandering giant. As the Indian god Vishnu and the Greek Poseidon could cross the Universe at three strides, so could this giant pass quickly from country to country and ocean to ocean. One or two strides were sufficient for him to reach the mythical ocean from the Lung-po mountains. He sat on the mountain summit of one of the Islands of the Blest, and cast his fishing-line into the deep waters.[2] The Atlas-turtles were unable to resist the lure of his bait and, having hooked and captured six of them, he threw them over his back and returned home in triumph. These turtles had been supporting the two islands, Tai Yü and Yüan Chiao, which, having been set free, were carried by powerful tides towards the north, where they stranded among the ice-fields. The white beings that inhabited these islands were thus separated from their fellow saints on the other three islands, Fang Hu, Ying Chou, and P'ēng-lai. We are left to imagine how lonely they felt in isolation. No

---

[1] Dr. J. Legge, *Chinese Classics*, Vol. III, Part I, p. 240, and Part II, p. 554.

[2] In Scottish giant-lore giants sit on mountains in like manner and fish for whales, using trees as fishing-rods.

doubt, they suffered from the evils associated with the north—the "airt" of drought and darkness. The giant and his tribesmen were punished by the Lord of the Universe for this act by having their stature and their kingdom greatly reduced.

On the fabled islands, the white saints cultivate and gather the "fungus of immortality", as the souls in the Paradise of Osiris cultivate and harvest crops of barley and wheat and dates. Like the Osirian corn, the island fungus sprouts in great profusion. This fungus has not only the power to renew youth but even to restore the dead to life. The "Herodotus of China" has recorded that once upon a time leaves of the fungus were carried by ravens to the mainland from one of the islands, and dropped on the faces of warriors slain in battle. The warriors immediately came to life, although they had lain dead for three days. The "water of life" had similarly reanimating properties.

The famous magician, Tung-fang Shuo, who lived in second century B.C., tells that the sacred islands are ten in number, there being two distinct groups of five. One of the distant islands is named Fu-sang, and it has been identified by different western writers with California, Mexico, Japan, and Formosa. Its name signifies "the Land of the Leaning Mulberry". The mulberries are said to grow in pairs and to be of great height. Once every nine thousand years they bear fruit which the saints partake of. This fruit adds to their saintly qualities, and gives them power to soar skyward like celestial birds.

Beyond Fu-sang is a country of white women who have hairy bodies. In the spring season they enter the river to bathe and become pregnant, and their children are born in the autumn. The hair of their heads is so

long that it trails on the ground behind them.   Instead
of breasts, they have white locks or hairy organs at the
back of their necks from which comes a liquor that
nourishes their children.   These women, according to
some accounts, have no husbands, and take flight when
they see a man.   A historian who, by the way, gives
them husbands, has recorded that a Chinese vessel was
once driven by a tempest to this wonderful island.   The
crew landed and found that the women resembled those
of China, but that the men had heads like dogs and voices
that sounded like the barking of dogs.   Evidently the
legends about the fabled islands became mixed up with
accounts of the distant islands of a bearded race reached
by seafarers.

There are records of several attempts that were made
by pious Chinese Emperors to discover the Islands of
the Blest, with purpose to obtain the " fungus of immortality".   One mariner named Hsu Fü, who was sent to
explore the Eastern Sea so that the fungus might be
brought to the royal palace, returned with a wonderful
story.   He said that a god had risen out of the sea and
inquired if he was the Emperor's representative.   " I
am," the mariner made answer.

" What seek ye ? " asked the sea-god.

" I am searching for the plant that has the power to
prolong human life," Hsu Fü answered.

The god then informed the Emperor's messenger
that the offerings he brought were not sufficient to be
regarded as payment for this magic plant.   He was
willing, however, that Hsu Fü should see the fungus
for himself so that, apparently, the Emperor might be
convinced it really existed.

The vessel was then piloted in a south-easterly direction until the Islands of the Blest were reached.   Hsu

Fü was permitted to land on P'ĕng-lai, the chief island, on which was situated the golden palace of the dragon king of ocean. There he saw newly-harvested crops of the "fungus of immortality" guarded by a great brazen dragon of ferocious aspect. Not a leaf could he obtain, however, to bring back to China.

The pious mariner knelt before the sea-god and asked him what offering he required from the Emperor in return for the fungus. He was informed that many youths and girls would have to be sent to P'ĕng-lai.

On ascertaining the price demanded by the god for the magic fungus, the Emperor dispatched a fleet of vessels with three thousand young men and virgins. Hsu Fü was placed in command of the expedition. But he never returned again to China. According to some, he and his followers still reside on P'ĕng-lai; others assert that he reached a distant land, supposed to be Japan, where he founded a state over which he reigned as king.

Other Chinese Emperors were similarly anxious to discover the fabled islands, and many expeditions were sent to sea. One exasperated monarch is said to have had nearly five hundred magicians and scholars put to death because their efforts to assist him in discovering the islands had proved to be futile.

Another Emperor fitted out a naval expedition which he himself commanded. Each vessel was packed with soldiers who in mid-ocean raised a great clamour, blowing horns, beating drums, and shouting in chorus, with purpose to terrify the gods of ocean and compel them to reveal the location of the Isle of Immortality. In time the dragon-god appeared in his fiercest shape, with the head of a lion and a shark-like body 500 feet in length. The Emperor ordered his fleet to surround the god, who had apparently come with the intention of preventing the ships going any farther. A fierce battle ensued. Thousands of poisoned arrows were discharged against the god, who was so grievously wounded that his blood tinged the sea over an area of 10,000 miles. But despite this victory achieved by mortals, the famous island on which grew the herb of immortality was never reached. On the same night the Emperor had to engage in single combat with the dragon-god, who came against him in a dream. This was a combat of souls, for in sleep, as was believed, the soul leaves the body. The soul of the Emperor fared badly. On the day that followed his majesty was unable to rise from his couch, and he died within the space of seven days.

In Japanese stories the island of P'ēng-lai is referred to as Horaizan. It has three high mountains, on the chief of which, called Horai, grows the Tree of Life. This tree has a trunk and branches of gold, roots of silver, and gem-leaves and fruit. In some stories there are three trees, the peach, the plum, and the pine. The "fungus of immortality" is also referred to. It grows in the shade of one or another of the holy trees, usually the pine. There is evidence, too, of the belief that a "grass of immortality" grew on the sacred island as well as the famous fungus. The life-giving fountain was as well known to the Japanese as it was to the Chinese and others.

A story is told of a Japanese Gilgamesh, named Sentaro, who, being afraid of death, summoned to his aid an immortal saint so that he might be enabled to obtain the "grass of immortality". The saint handed him a crane made of paper which, when mounted, came to life and carried Sentaro across the ocean to Mount Horai. There he found and ate the life-giving grass. When, however, he had lived for a time on the island he became discontented. The other inhabitants had already grown weary of immortality and wished they could die. Sentaro himself began to pine for Japan and, in the end, resolved to mount his paper crane and fly over the sea. But after he left the island he doubted the wisdom of his impulsive resolution. The result was that the crane, which moved according to his will, began to crumple up and drop through the air. Sentaro was greatly scared, and once again yearned so deeply for his native land that the crane, straightened and strengthened by his yearning, rose into the air and continued its flight until Japan was reached.

Another Japanese hero, named Wasobioye, the story of whose wanderings is retold by Professor Chamberlain,[1] once set out in a boat to escape troublesome visitors. The day was the eighth of the eighth month and the moon was full. Suddenly a storm came on, which tore the sail to shreds and brought down the mast. Wasobioye was unable to return home, and his boat was driven about on the wide ocean for the space of three months. Then he reached the Sea of Mud, on which he could not catch any fish. He was soon reduced to sore straits and feared he would die of hunger, but, in time, he caught sight of land and was greatly cheered. His boat drifted slowly towards a beautiful island on which there were three great mountains. As he drew near to the shore, he found, to his great joy, that the air was laden with most exquisite perfumes that came from the flowers and tree-blossoms of that wonderful isle. He landed and found a sparkling well. When he had drunk of the water his strength was revived, and a feeling of intense pleasure tingled in his veins. He rose up refreshed and happy and, walking inland, soon met with Jofuku the

---

[1] *Transactions of the Asiatic Society of Japan.*

sage, known in China as Hsu Fŭ, who had been sent to the Island of the Blest (P'ēng-lai) by the Emperor She Wang Ti to obtain the "fungus of immortality", with the youths and virgins, but had never returned.

Wasobioye was taken by the friendly sage to the city of the immortals, who spent their lives in the pursuit of pleasure. He found, however, that these people had grown to dislike their monotonous existence, and were constantly striving to discover some means whereby their days would be shortened. They refused to partake of mermaid flesh because this was a food that prolonged life; they favoured instead goldfish and soot, a mixture which was supposed to be poisonous. The manners of the people were curious. Instead of wishing one another good health and long life, they wished for sickness and a speedy death. Congratulations were showered on any individual who seemed to be indisposed, and he was sympathized with when he showed signs of recovering.

Wasobioye lived on the island for nearly a quarter of a century. Then, having grown weary of the monotonous life, he endeavoured to commit suicide by partaking of poisonous fruit, fish, and flesh. But all his attempts were in vain. It was impossible for anyone to die on that island. In time he came to know that he could die if he left it, but he had heard of other wonderful lands and wished to visit them before his days came to an end. Then, instead of eating poisonous food, he began to feast on mermaid flesh so that his life might be prolonged for many years beyond the allotted span. Thereafter he visited the Land of Shams, the Land of Plenty, &c. His last visit was paid to the Land of Giants. Wasobioye is usually referred to as the "Japanese Gulliver".

The search for the mythical islands with their "wells of life" and "trees" or "plants of life" is referred to in the stories of many lands and even in history, especially the history of exploration, for the world-wide search for the Earthly Paradise appears to have exercised decided influence in stimulating maritime enterprise in mediæval as well as prehistoric times. Columbus searched for the island paradise in which the " well" and " tree" were to be found. He sailed westward so as to approach the paradise " eastward in Eden ",[1] through " the back door " as it were, and wrote: " The saintly theologians and philosophers were right when they fixed the site of the terrestrial paradise in the extreme Orient, because it is a most temperate clime; and the lands which I have just discovered are the limits of the Orient." In another letter he says: " I am convinced that there lies the terrestrial paradise ".[2]

As Ellis reminds us, " the expedition which led to the discovery of Florida was undertaken not so much from a desire to explore unknown countries ", as to find a " celebrated fountain, described in a tradition prevailing among the inhabitants of Puerto Rico, as existing in Binini, one of the Lucayo Islands. It was said to possess such restorative powers as to renew youth and the vigour of every person who bathed in its waters. It was in search of this fountain, which was the chief object of their expedition, that Ponce de Leon ranged through the Lucayo Islands and ultimately reached the shores of Florida."

Ellis refers to this voyage because he found that the mythical island and well were believed in by the Polynesians. He refers, in this connection, to the " Hawaiian account of the voyage of Kamapiikai to the land where

[1] Genesis, ii, 8.
[2] Navarrette, *Coll. de Documents*, I, p. 244, quoted in *Curious Myths of the Middle Ages*, p. 525.

the inhabitants enjoyed perpetual health and youthful beauty, where the *wai ora* (life-giving fountain) removed every internal malady, and every external deformity or paralysed decrepitude, from all those who were plunged beneath its salutary waters ".   Ellis anticipates the views of modern ethnologists when dealing with the existence of the same beliefs among widely-separated peoples.   He says: " A tabular view of a number of words in the Malayan, Asiatic, or the Madagasse, the American, and the Polynesian languages, would probably show that, at some remote period, either the inhabitants of these distant parts of the world maintained frequent intercourse with each other, or that colonies from some one of them originally peopled, in part or altogether, the others ". He adds, " Either part of the present inhabitants of the South Sea Islands came originally from America, or tribes of the Polynesians have, at some remote period, found their way to the (American) continent ".[1]

W. D. Westervelt, in his *Legends of Old Honolulu*, heads his old Hawaiian story " The Water of Life of Ka-ne ", which he himself has collected, with the following extract from the Maori legend of New Zealand:

When the moon dies, she goes to the living water of Ka-ne, to the water which can restore all life, even the moon to the path in the sky.

In the Hawaiian form of the legend the hero, who found the water so that his sick father, the king, might be cured, met with a dwarf who instructed him where to go and what to do.

A russet dwarf similarly figures in the Gaelic story of Diarmaid's search for the cup and the water of life so that the daughter of the King of Land-under-Waves

[1] William Ellis, *Polynesian Researches* (1st edition, London, 1829), Vol. II, pp. 47 *et seq.*

might be cured of her sickness.   This dwarf takes the
Gaelic hero across a ferry and instructs him how to find
the cup and the water.[1]

The Polynesians' ghosts went westward.   In their
Paradise was a bread-fruit tree.   "This tree had two
branches, one towards the east and one towards the west,
both of which were used by the ghosts.   One was for
leaping into eternal darkness into Po-pau-ole, the other
was a meeting-place with the helpful gods."[2]   Turner
tells that "some of the South Sea Islanders have a tradition of a river in their imaginary world of spirits, called
the 'water of life'.   It was supposed that if the aged,
when they died, went and bathed there, they became
young and returned to earth to live another life over
again."[3] Yudhishthira, one of the heroes of the Aryo-Indian
epic the *Mahábhárata*, becomes immortal after bathing in
the celestial Ganges.[4]   In the *Æneid*, the hero sees souls
in Paradise drinking of the water of Lethe so that they
may forget the past and be reborn among men.

Sir John de Mandeville, the fourteenth-century
traveller and compiler of traveller's stories, located the
fountain of life at the base of a great mountain in Ceylon.
This "fayr well . . . hathe odour and savour of all
spices; and at every hour of the day, he chaungethe his
odour and his savour dyversely.   And whoso drinkethe
3 times fasting of that watre of that welle, he is hool
(whole) of alle maner (of) sykenesse that he hathe.   And
they that duellen (dwell) there and drynken often of that
welle, thei nevere hau (have) sykenesse, and thei semen

[1] Campbell, *Popular Tales of the West Highlands*, Vol. III, Tale LXXXVI.

[2] *Legends of Gods and Ghosts*, p. 246.   [3] *Nineteen Years in Polynesia*, p. 353.

[4] *Swargaro-hanika Parva*, Section III (Roy's translation), p. 9.   The chief of the
gods says to Yudhishthira: "Here is the celestial river. . . . Plunging into it, thou
wilt go to thine own regions (Paradise)."   Having bathed, the hero "cast off his human
body" and "assumed a celestial form".

(seem) alle weys yonge." Sir John says that he drank of
the water on three or four occasions and fared the better
for it. Some men called it the "Welle of Youthe".
They had often drunk from it and seemed "alle weys yongly
(youthful)" and lived without sickness. "And men
seyn that that welle comethe out of Paradys, and therefore it is so vertuous." The "tree of life" is always situated
near the "well of life" in mediæval literature. At Heliopolis in Egypt a well and tree are connected by Coptic
Christians and Mohammedans with Christ. When Joseph
and Mary fled to Egypt they rested under this tree,
according to Egyptian belief, and the clothes of the holy
child were washed in the well. Heliopolis, the Biblical
On, is "the city of the sun", and the Arabs still call the
well the "spring of the sun". According to ancient
Egyptian belief the sun-god Ra washed his face in it
every morning. The tree, a sycamore, was the mother-
goddess.

That European ideas regarding a floating island or
islands were of Egyptian origin and closely connected
with the solar cult, is suggested by the classical legend
regarding Delos, one of the Cyclades. It was fabled to
have been raised to the surface of the sea at the command
of Poseidon, so that the persecuted goddess Latona, who
was pursued from land to land by a python, as the
Egyptian Isis was pursued by Set, might give birth there
to Apollo. On Delos the image of Apollo was in the
shape of a dragon, and delivered oracles. It was unlawful
for any person to die on Delos, and those of its inhabitants who fell sick were transported to another island.

Delos was a floating island like the floating island of
the Nile, "the green bed of Horus" on which that son
of Osiris and Isis hid from Set. The most ancient
Apollo was the son of cripple Hephaistos. Cripple

Horus was, in one of his forms, a Hephaistos and a metal-worker.   Homer knew of the fabled island of Apollo.   The swineherd, addressing Odysseus, says,[1] " There is a certain isle called Syria . . . over above Ortygia, and there are the turning places of the sun.   It is not very great in compass, though a goodly isle, rich in herds, rich in flocks, with plenty of corn and wine. Dearth never enters the land, and no hateful sickness falls on wretched mortals."

The later Greeks located the island Paradise in the Atlantic, and it is referred to as " Atlantis ", the Islands of the Blest and the Fortunate Isles (fortunatae insulae). Hercules set out to search for the golden apples, the fruit of immortality that grow in

> those Hesperian gardens famed of old,
> Fortunate fields and groves and flowery vales.

The garden of Paradise, cared for by those celebrated nymphs, the daughters of Hesperus, brother of Atlas— Hesperus is the planet Venus as an evening star—was also located among the Atlas mountains in Africa.   There the tree of life, which bore the golden apples, was guarded by the nymphs and by a sleepless dragon, like the gem-trees in the Paradises of China and Japan.

According to Diodorus, the Phœnicians discovered the island Paradise.   Plutarch placed it at a distance of five days' voyage to the west of Brittia (England and Scotland), apparently confusing it with Ireland (the " sacred isle " of the ancients), or with an island in the Hebrides.

The island of immortals in the western ocean is found in Gaelic folk- and manuscript-literature.

Among the Gaelic names of Paradise is that of

[1] *Odyssey*, XV (Butcher and Lang's trans.), p. 253.

"Emain Ablach" (Emain rich in apples).   In one description a youth named Conla and his bride Veniusa are referred to.   "Now the youth was so that in his hand he held a fragrant apple having the hue of gold; a third part of it he would eat, and still, for all he consumed, never a whit would it be diminished.   The fruit it was that supported the pair of them and when once they had partaken of it, nor age nor dimness could affect them."   A part of this Paradise was reserved for "monarchs, kings, and tribal chiefs".   Teigue, a Celtic Gilgamesh who visited the island, saw there "a thickly furnished wide-spreading apple tree that bore blossom and ripe fruit" at the same time.   He asked regarding the great tree and was informed that its fruit was "meat" intended to "serve the congregation" which was to inhabit the mansion.[1]   The rowan berry and hazel nut were also to the Gaels fruits of immortality.   There once came to St. Patrick "from the south" a youth wearing a crimson mantle fixed by a fibula of gold over a yellow shirt.   He brought "a double armful of round yellow-headed nuts and of beautiful golden-yellow apples".[2]   The Gaelic Islands of the Blest are pictured in glowing colours:

> Splendours of every colour glisten
> Throughout the gentle-voiced plains.
> Joy is known, ranked around music
> In the southern Silver-cloud Plain.
> Unknown is wailing or treachery . . .
> There is nothing rough or hoarse . . .
> Without grief, without sorrow, without death,
> Without sickness, without debility . . .
> A lovely land
> On which the many blossoms drop.[3]

[1] S. H. O'Grady, *Silva Gadelica*, Vol. II, pp. 393–4.
[2] *Ibid.*, Vol. II, p. 113.   [3] The Voyage of Bran.

The hero Bran sets out to search for the islands, and, like one of the Chinese mariners, meets with the sea-god, who addresses him and tells of the wonders of the island Paradise with its trees of life.

> A wood laden with beautiful fruit . . .
> A wood without decay, without defect,
> On which is a foliage of a golden hue.[1]

The green floating and vanishing island and the well of life are common in Scottish Gaelic folk-lore. It was believed that the life-giving water had greatest potency if drunk at dawn of the day which was of equal length with the night preceding it, and that it should be drunk before a bird sipped at the well and before a dog barked. The Scandinavians heard of the Gaelic Island of the West during their prolonged sojourn in the British Isles and Ireland, and referred to it as "Ireland hit Mikla" ("The Mickle Ireland"), and the mythical island was afterwards identified with Vinland, believed to be America, which was apparently reached by the hardy sea-rovers.

The Earthly Paradise was also located in Asia. In the mythical histories of Alexander a hero sets forth like Gilgamesh on the quest of the Water of Life. He similarly enters a cavern of a great mountain in the west which is guarded by a monster serpent. In one version of the tale this hero carries a jewel that shines in darkness —a jewel that figures prominently in Chinese lore (Chap. XIII)—and passes through the dark tunnel. He reaches the Well of Life and plunges into it. When he came out he found that his body had turned a bluish-green colour, and ever afterwards he was called "El Khidr", which means "Green".[2]

---

[1] *Ancient Irish Poetry*, p. 8.

[2] *The Life and Exploits of Alexander the Great*, trans. by E. Walter Budge, pp. 11 *et seq.*, and 167 *et seq.*

The Well of Life is referred to in the Koran. Commentators explain a reference to a vanishing fish by telling that Moses or Joshua carried a fried fish when they reached the Well of Life. Some drops of the water fell on the fish, which at once leapt out of the basket into the sea and swam away.

In the Aryo-Indian epic, the *Mahábhárata*, the hero Bhima sets out in search of the Lake of Life and the Lotus of Life. He overcomes the Yaksha-guardians of the lake, and when he bathes in the lake his wounds are healed.[1]

There are glowing descriptions in Buddhist literature of the Paradise reached by those who are to qualify for Buddhahood. A proportion of the Chinese Taoist inhabitants of the Islands of the Blest similarly wait for the time when they will pass into another state of existence. A similar belief prevailed in the West. Certain Celtic heroes, like Arthur, Ossian, Fionn (Finn), Brian Boroimhe, and Thomas the Rhymer, live in Paradise for long periods awaiting the time when they are to return to the world of men, as do Charlemagne, Frederick of Barbarossa, William Tell, and others on the Continent.

In the Buddhist Paradise the pure beings have faces " bright and yellowish ", yellow being the sacred colour of the Buddhist as it is the colour of the chief dragon of China. In this Paradise is the Celestial Ganges and the great Bodhi-tree, " a hundred yoganas in height ", which prolongs life and increases " their stock of merit ". Their " merit " may " grow in the following shapes, viz. either in gold, in silver, in jewels, in beryls, in shells, in stones, in corals, in amber, in red pearls, in diamonds, &c., or in any one of the other jewels; or in all kinds of perfumes, in flowers, in garlands, in ointment, in incense-

---

[1] "Vana Parva" of *Mahábhárata*, and *Indian Myth and Legend*, pp. 105-9.

powder, in cloaks, in umbrellas, in flags, in banners, or in lamps; or in all kinds of dancing, singing, and music ".[1]

The gem-trees abound in this Paradise. "Of some trees", one account runs, "the trunks are of coral, the branches of red pearls, the small branches of diamonds, the leaves of gold, the flowers of silver, and the fruits of beryl."[2] In the "eastern quarter" there are "Buddha countries equal to the sand of the River Ganga (Ganges) ". The purified beings in the lands "surpass the light of the sun and moon, by the light of wisdom, and by the whiteness, brilliancy, purity, and beauty of their knowledge ".[3] There are references to "the king of jewels that fulfils every wish ". It has "golden-coloured rays excessively beautiful, the radiance of which transforms itself into birds possessing the colours of a hundred jewels, which sing out harmonious notes ".[4] The purified may become like Buddha "with bodies bright as gold and blue eyes ", for "the eyes of Buddha are like the water of the four great oceans; the blue and the white are quite distinct ".[5] The imaginations of the Buddhists run riot in their descriptions of the Land of Bliss, and the stream of glowing narrative carries with it many pre-Buddhist beliefs about metals and precious stones, "red pearls, blue pearls ", and so on, and "nets of gold adorned with the emblems of the dolphin, the svastika (swashtika), the nandyāvarta, and the moon ".[6] In their Paradise even the river mud is of gold. The religious ideas of the early searchers for "soul substance " in the form of metals and gems are thus found to be quaintly blended with Buddhist conceptions of the Earthly Paradise.

---

[1] Description of Sukhāvāti, the Land of Bliss, in *Buddhist Mahayama Texts* (*Sacred Books of the East*, Vol. XLIX), pp. 16, 17.
　[2] *Ibid.*, p. 35.　　[3] *Ibid.*, p. 56.　　[4] *Ibid.*, p. 174.　　[5] *Ibid.*, p. 180.　　[6] *Ibid.*, p. 50.

In some Chinese and Japanese stories the souls of the
dead are carried to Paradise by birds, and especially by the
crane or stork, which takes the place of the Indian man-
eagle Garuda (Japanese Gario, the woman-bird with
crane's legs), and of the Babylonian eagle that carried
the hero Etana to heaven. The saints who reach the
Indian Paradise of Uttara Kuru, situated at the sources
of the River Indus, among the Himalayan mountains, and
originally the homeland of the Kuru tribe of Aryans, are
supposed to have their lives prolonged for centuries.
When they die their bodies are carried away by gigantic
birds and dropped into mountain recesses. The belief
enshrined in stories of this kind may be traced to the
wide-spread legend of the Diamond Valley. Laufer notes
that a version of it occurs in the *Liang se kung ki*, "one of
the most curious books of Chinese literature". A prince
is informed by scholars regarding the wonders of distant
lands. "In the west, arriving at the Mediterranean,"
one Chinese story runs, "there is in the sea an island of
two hundred square miles. On this island is a large
forest, abundant in trees with precious stones, and inhabited by over ten thousand families. These men show
great ability in cleverly working gems, which are named
for the country Fu-lin (Syria). In a north-westerly
direction from the island is a ravine, hollowed out like
a bowl, more than a thousand feet deep. They throw
flesh into this valley. Birds take it up in their beaks,
whereupon they drop the precious stones." Here Fu-lin,
in the Mediterranean area, is referred to as early as the
beginning of the sixth century.

The Chinese Diamond Valley story is "an abridged
form of a well-known Western legend". In a version
of it in the writings of Epiphanius, Bishop of Constantia
in Cyprus (*c.* 315–403), the valley is situated in "a

desert of great Scythia", and the precious stones are gathered on the mountains, whence the eagles carry them. The eagle-stone is "useful to women in aiding parturition". Laufer notes that Pliny knew about the parturition stone, and that the beliefs associated with it are found in Egypt and India. In the latter country it occurs in legends about the combats between the eagle and serpent.[1]

A Scottish Gaelic folk-story tells of a man who had a combat with an eagle which carried him away to the floating island of the blest. He was killed, but came to life again after drops of the water from the well of life were thrown on his body. Stones found in eagles' or ravens' nests, according to Scottish belief, imparted to their possessors the power of prophecy or healing.

The gems from the trees of Paradise in Babylonian, Indian, Chinese, and Japanese literature were supposed to confer special powers on those who became possessed of them. To this class belongs the "Jewel that grants all Desires", the "gem that shines in darkness", the prophet's or priest's jewel or jewels, &c. Gems were searched for in ancient times because they were supposed to possess what has been called "soul substance". They protected those who wore them from all evil, they assisted birth, they prolonged life. Precious metals were similarly believed to be "luck-bringers", and to early man luck meant everything he wished for, including good health, longevity, plentiful supplies of food, a knowledge of the future, offspring, and so on.

In the stories of the Islands of the Blest the happy souls are, in the ancient sense of the term, "lucky souls".

[1] B. Laufer, *The Diamond* (*A Study in Chinese and Hellenistic Folk-lore*) (Chicago, 1915).

Paradise was a land in which life-giving water and fruit, and innumerable gems were to be found, and those who reached it became wise as magicians and prophets, and lived for thousands of years free from sickness and pain. It was the land of eternal youth and unlimited happiness.

CHAPTER X

The Mother-goddess of China and Japan

Food for the Dead—Milk, Bread, and Beer in Paradise—The Western Tree of Life in Egypt—Tree of Life in Greece, Britain, and Polynesia—The Underworld Paradise—The "Wonderful Rose Garden"—Chinese Cult of the West—Biblical Tree Parable—Chinese Peach Tree of Longevity—The "Royal Mother of the West"—Visit of the Chinese Emperor—A Far-Eastern El-Khidr—The Sacred Chrysanthemum—The Cassia Tree Cult—Celestial Yellow River—Moon Myths—Lunar Elixir in China, India, and Scandinavia—Chinese Star Maiden—The Sun Barque—"Island of Blest" in Celestial River—Moon-girl Story—The "Makara" in China and Japan—The Chinese Ishtar—Deluge Legend—Tree Spirits—Story of Little Peachling—"Soul Substance" in Dragon Bones, Trees, and Pearls.

The quest of the "elixir of life", the "water of life", or "the food of life" is as prominent a feature of ancient religious literature as is the quest of the Holy Grail in the Arthurian romances. As has been shown in the last chapter, the belief that prompted the quest was widely prevalent, and of great antiquity. The Babylonian hero, Gilgamesh, whose story is told in the oldest epic in the world, undertook his long and perilous journey to the Otherworld, in quest of the Plant of Life, because the thought of death was sorrowful to him. When his friend, Ea-bani, had expired,

Gilgamesh wept bitterly, and he lay stretched out upon the ground. He cried, "Let me not die like Ea-bani. . . . I fear death."[1]

[1] L. W. King, *Babylonian Religion* (London, 1903), p. 171.

131

In the Babylonian myth of Adapa reference is made to the " water of life " and the " food of life ", which give wisdom and immortality to the gods and to the souls of those mortals who win their favour.   The sacred tree in Babylonian art is evidently the Tree of Life.[1]

We seem to meet with the history of the immemorial quest in the Pyramid Texts of Ancient Egypt.   The ancient priests appear to have concerned themselves greatly regarding the problem how the dead were to be nourished in the celestial Paradise.   " The chief dread felt by the Egyptian for the hereafter," says Breasted, " was fear of hunger."[2]   In Egypt, as in other lands offerings of food were made at the tombs, and these were supposed to be conveyed to the souls by certain of the gods.   But those who hoped to live for ever knew well that the time would come when grave-offerings would cease to be made, and their own names would be forgotten on earth.   Some Pharaohs endowed their chapel-tombs for all time, but revolutions ultimately caused endowments to be appropriated.

The Babylonians believed that if the dead were not fed, their ghosts would prowl through the streets and enter houses, searching for food and water.[3]   In Polynesia the homeless and desolate ghosts were those of poor people, " who during their residence in the body had no friends and no property ".[4]   The custom of including food-vessels and drinking-cups in the funerary furniture of prehistoric graves in different countries was no doubt connected with the fear of hunger in the hereafter.   The custom was widespread of giving the dead food offerings

[1] L. W. King, *Legends of Babylon and Egypt* (London, 1918), p. 136.

[2] *Religion and Thought in Ancient Egypt*, p. 130.

[3] *Myths of Babylonia and Assyria*, p. 71.

[4] Westervelt, *Legends of Gods and Ghosts (Hawaiian Mythology)*, p. 245.

at regular intervals.   Once a year the living held feasts
in the burial-grounds, and invited the dead to partake
of their share.   Among the Hallowe'en beliefs in the
British Isles is one that ghosts return home during the
year-end festival to attend "the feast of all souls".   The
Hebridean custom, which lingered even in the nineteenth
century, of placing food and water, or milk, beside a
corpse while it lay in a house, and outside the door or at
the grave after the burial took place, was no doubt a
relic of an ancient custom, based on the haunting belief
that the dead were in need of nourishment, if not for all
time, at any rate until the journey to the Otherworld was
completed.

As has been said, it was the provision of food in
the celestial Paradise, far removed from the earth and its
produce, that chiefly concerned the Egyptians.   In the
Underworld Kingdom, presided over by Osiris, the souls
grew corn and gathered fruit.   But the Paradise of the
solar cult was above or beyond the sky.   Some of the
sun-worshippers are found in the Pyramid Texts to have
placed their faith in the food-supplying Great Mother,
the goddess Hathor, who gave them corn and milk
during their earthly lives.   As son of Re, born of
the sky - goddess, he (the Pharaoh) is frequently
represented as suckled by one of the sky-goddesses, or
some other divinity connected with Re, especially the
ancient goddesses of the prehistoric kingdoms of South
and North.   These appear as "the two vultures with
long hair and hanging breasts; . . . they draw their breasts
over the mouth of King Pepi, but they do not wean
him forever. . . ."   Another text invokes the mother-
goddess: "Give thy breast to this King Pepi, . . . suckle
this King Pepi therewith".   As a result, perhaps, of the
prevalence of Osirian beliefs, the solar cult adopted

the idea that food, such as is found in Egypt, might be provided in the regions above or beyond the sky. The sun-god was appealed to: "Give thou bread to this King Pepi, from this thy eternal bread, thy everlasting beer".[1]

But the chief source of nourishment in the celestial Paradise was the Tree of Life (a form of the mother-goddess) on the great isle in the mythical lake or sea beyond the Eastern horizon.[2] Egyptian artists depicted this tree as a palm, or sycamore, with a goddess rising from inside it, pouring water from a vessel on the hands of the Pharaoh's soul, which might appear in human form, or in the man-bird form called the *ba*. In the funeral ritual the ceremony of pouring out a libation was performed with the object of restoring the body moisture (the water of life) to the mummy.[3] A Biblical reference to the ceremony is found in 2 Kings, iii, 11, in which it is said of Elisha that he "poured water on the hands of Elijah". No doubt the Egyptian soul received water as nourishment, as well as to ensure its immortality, from the tree-goddess.

In the Book of the Dead (Chapter LIX), the Tree of Life is referred to as "the sycamore of Nut" (the sky-goddess). Other texts call the tree "the Western Tree" of Nut or Hathor. It may be that the solar cult of the East took over the tree from the Osirian cult of the West.

This mythical tree figures in many ancient mythologies. The goddess Europa was worshipped at Gortyna, in Crete, during the Hellenic period, as a sacred tree.[4] The tree may be traced from the British Isles to India, and there are numerous legends of spirits entering or leaving

[1] Breasted, *Religion and Thought in Ancient Egypt*, pp. 120 *et seq.*
[2] *Ibid.*, p. 134.   [3] G. Elliot Smith, *The Evolution of the Dragon*, pp. 23 *et seq.*
[4] Farnell, *Cults of the Greek States*, Vol. III, pp. 14, 30; Cook, *Zeus*, Vol. I, p. 537.

it.   The Polynesians have stories of this kind.   Their
Tree of Life was the local bread-fruit tree which "became
a god", or, as some had it, a goddess.   "Out of this
magic bread-fruit tree," a legend says, "a great goddess
was made."[1]

It may be that the island Paradise with its Tree of
Life was specially favoured after maritime enterprise
made strong appeal to the imagination of the Egyptians.
No doubt the old sailors who searched for "soul-substance" in the shape of pearls, precious stones, and
metals had much to do with disseminating the idea of
the Isles of the Blest.   At any rate, it became, as we
have seen, a tradition among seafarers to search for
the distant land in which was situated the "water of
life".   The home-dwelling Osirians clung to their idea
of an Underworld Paradise, and belief in it became fused
with that of the floating island, or Islands of the Blest.
Those who dwelt in inland plains and valleys, and those
accustomed to cross the great mysterious deserts on
which the oasis-mirage frequently appeared and vanished
like the mythical floating island, conceived of a Paradise
on earth.   There are references in more than one land to
a Paradise among the mountains.   It figures in the fairy
stories of Central Europe, for instance, as "the wonderful
Rose Garden" with its linden Tree of Immortality, the
hiding-place of a fairy lady, its dancing nymphs and
its dwarfs; the king of dwarfs has a cloak of invisibility
which he wraps round those mortals he carries away.[2]

At first only the souls of kings entered Paradise.
But, in time, the belief became firmly established that
the souls of others could reach it too, and be fed there.
The quest of the "food of life" then became a popular

---

[1] Westervelt, *Legends of Old Honolulu*, pp. 22 et seq., and p. 29.
[2] *Teutonic Myth and Legend*, pp. 424-32.

theme of the story-tellers, and so familiar grew the idea of the existence of this fruit that people believed it could be obtained during life, and that those who partook of it might have their days prolonged indefinitely. For, as W. Schooling has written, "a few simple thoughts on a few simple subjects produce a few simple opinions common to a whole tribe" (and even a great part of mankind), "and are taught with but little modification to successive generations; hence arises a rigidity that imposes ready-made opinions, which are seldom questioned, while such questioning as does occur is usually met with excessive severity, as Galileo and others have found out".[1]

The apple, as we have seen, was to the Celts the fruit of immortality: the Chinese favoured the peach—that is, it was favoured by the Chinese cult of the West. As all animals were supposed to be represented in the Otherworld by gigantic prototypes—the fathers or mothers of their kind—so were trees represented by a gigantic tree.[2] This tree was the World Tree that supported the Universe. In Egypt the World Tree was the sycamore of the sky-goddess, who was the Great Mother of deities and mankind. The sun dropped into the sycamore at eventide; when darkness fell the swallows (star-gods) perched in its branches. In Norse mythology the tree is the ash, called Ygdrasil, and from the well at its roots souls receive the Hades-drink of immortality, drinking from a horn embellished with serpent symbols. The Tree figures prominently in Iranian mythology: the Aryo-Indian Indra constructs the World-house round

---

[1] *Westminster Review*, November, 1892, p. 523.

[2] When, some years ago, an ass was acquired by a tenant on a Hebridean island, a native, on seeing this animal for the first time, exclaimed, "It is the father of all the hares".

it.   This Tree is, no doubt, identical with the sacred tree in Assyrian art, which is sometimes the date, the vine, the pomegranate, the fir, the cedar, and perhaps the oak.   It may be that the Biblical parable about the talking trees is a memory of the rivalries of the various Assyrian tree cults:

The trees went forth on a time to anoint a king over them; and they said unto the olive tree, Reign thou over us.   But the olive tree said unto them, Should I leave my fatness, wherewith by me they honour god and man, and go to be promoted over the trees? And the trees said to the fig tree, Come thou, and reign over us. But the fig tree said unto them, Should I forsake my sweetness, and my good fruit, and go to be promoted over the trees?   Then said the trees unto the vine, Come thou, and reign over us.   And the vine said unto them, Should I leave my vine, which cheereth God and man, and go to be promoted over the trees?   Then said all the trees unto the bramble, Come thou, and reign over us.   And the bramble said unto the trees, If in truth ye anoint me King over you, then come and put your trust in my shadow: and if not, let fire come out of the bramble, and devour the cedars of Lebanon.

As in Assyria, there was in China quite a selection of life-giving trees.

The Chinese gigantic Peach Tree, whose fruit was partaken of by gods and men, grew in the Paradise among the Kwun-lun mountains in Tibet, and, like the Indian Mount Meru ("world spine"), supported the Universe. Its fruit took three thousand years to ripen.   The tree was surrounded by a beautiful garden, and was under the care of the fairy-like lady Si Wang Mu, the queen of immortals, the "Mother of the Western King", and the "Royal Mother of the West".   She appears to have originally been the mother-goddess—the Far-Eastern form of Hathor.   In Japan she is called Seiobo.   Her Paradise, which is called "the palace of exalted purity", and "the metropolis of the pearl mountain", or of "the jade mountain", and is entered through "the golden door",[1] was originally that of the cult of the West. Sometimes Si Wang Mu is depicted as quite as weird a deity as the Phigalian Demeter, with disordered hair, tiger's teeth, and a panther's tail. Her voice is harsh, and she sends and cures diseases. Three blue birds bring food to her.

Chinese emperors and magicians were as anxious to obtain a peach from the Royal Mother's tree in the Western Paradise, as they were to import the " fungus of immortality" from the Islands of the Blest in the Eastern Sea.

There once lived in China a magician named Tung Fang So, who figures in Japanese legend as Tobosaku, and is represented in Japanese art as a jolly old man, clasping a peach to his breast and performing a dance, or as a dreamy sage, carrying two or three peaches, and accompanied by a deer—an animal which symbolized longevity. Various legends have gathered round his name. One is that he had several successive rebirths in various reigns, and that originally he was an avatar of the planet Venus. He may therefore represent the Far-Eastern Tammuz, the son of the mother-goddess. Another legend tells that he filched three peaches from the Tree of Life, which had been plucked by the " Royal Mother of the West".

Tung Fang So was a councillor in the court of Wu Ti, the fourth emperor of the Han Dynasty, who reigned for over half a century, and died after fasting for seven days in 87 B.C. In Japanese stories Wu Ti is called Kan no Buti. He was greatly concerned about finding the " water of life" or the " fruit of life", so that his days might be prolonged. In his palace garden he caused to be erected a tower over 100 feet high, which appears to

---

[1] Dr. Joseph Edkins, *Religion in China*, p. 151.

have been an imitation of a Babylonian temple. On its summit was the bronze image of a god, holding a golden vase in its hands. In this vase was collected the pure dew that was supposed to drip from the stars. The emperor drank the dew, believing that it would renew his youth.

One day there appeared before Wu Ti in the palace garden a beautiful green sparrow. In China and Japan the sparrow is a symbol of gentleness, and a sparrow of uncommon colour is supposed to indicate that something unusual is to happen. The emperor was puzzled regarding the bird-omen, and consulted Tung Fang So, who informed him that the Queen of Immortals was about to visit the royal palace.

Before long Si Wang Mu made her appearance. She had come all the way from her garden among the Kwun-lun mountains, riding on the back of a white dragon, with seven of the peaches of immortality, which were carried on a tray by a dwarf servant. Her fairy majesty was gorgeously attired in white and gold, and spoke with a voice of bird-like sweetness.

When she reached Wu Ti there were only four peaches on the tray, and she lifted one up and began to eat it. The peach was her symbol, as the apple was that of Aphrodite. Tung Fang So peered at her through a window, and when she caught sight of his smiling face, she informed the emperor that he had stolen three of her peaches. Wu Ti received a peach from her, and, having eaten it, became an immortal. A similar story is told regarding the Chinese Emperor, Muh Wang.

In her " Jade Mountain " Paradise of the West (the highest peak of the Kwun-lun mountains) this goddess is accompanied by her sister, as the Egyptian Isis is by Nephthys, and the pair are supposed to flit about in

Cloud-land, followed by the white souls of good women of the Taoist cult. Her attendants include the Blue Stork, the White Tiger, the Stag, and the gigantic Tortoise, which are all gods and symbols of longevity in China.

Among the many stories told about Tung Fang So is one regarding a visit he once paid to the mythical Purple Sea. He returned after the absence of a year, and on being remonstrated with by his brother for deserting his home for so long a period, he contended that he had been away for only a single day. His garments had been discoloured by the waters of the Purple Sea, and he had gone to another sea to cleanse them. In like manner heroes who visit Fairyland find that time slips past very quickly.

The Purple Sea idea may have been derived from the ancient Well of Life story about El Khidr,[1] whose body and clothing turned green after he had bathed in it. Purple supplanted green and blue as the colour of immortality and royalty after murex dye became the great commercial asset of sea-traders. Tung Fang So may have had attached to his memory a late and imported version of the El Khidr story.

The reference to Wu Ti's dew-drinking habit recalls the story of the youthful Keu Tze Tung, a court favourite, who unwittingly offended the emperor, Muh Wang, and was banished. As the Egyptian Bata, who similarly fell into disgrace in consequence of a false charge being made against him, fled to the "Valley of the Acacia", Keu Tze Tung fled to the "Valley of the Chrysanthemum". There he drank the dew that dropped from the petals of chrysanthemums, and became an immortal. The Buddhists took over this story, and

[1] *Myths of Babylonia and Assyria*, pp. 185 *et seq.*

told that the youth had been given a sacred text, which he painted on the petals. This text imparted to the dew its special qualities. In the Far East the chrysanthemum is a symbol of purity. The chrysanthemum with sixteen petals is the emblem of the Mikado of Japan.

A Chinese sage, who, like the Indian Rishis, practised *yogi* until he became immortal, engaged his spare moments in painting fish. He lived on the bank of a stream for over two hundred years. In the end he was carried away to the Underworld Paradise of the Lord of Fish, who was, of course, the dragon-god. He paid one return visit to his disciples, riding like the Chinese "Boy Blue" in the dragon story, on the back of a red carp.

Another Chinese "tree-cult" favoured, instead of the peach tree, a cassia tree. This cassia-cult must have been late. The peach tree is indigenous. "Of fruits," says Laufer, "the West is chiefly indebted to China for the peach (*Amygdalus persica*) and the apricot (*Prunus armeniaca*). It is not impossible that these two gifts were transmitted by the silk-dealers, first to Iran (in the second or first century B.C.) and thence to Armenia, Greece, and Rome (in the first century A.D.)." In India the peach is called *cinani* ("Chinese fruit"). "There is no Sanskrit name for the tree (peach); nor does it play any rôle in the folk-lore of India, as it does in China." . . . Persia "has only descriptive names for these fruits, the peach being termed *saft alu* ('large plum'), the apricot, *zard alu* ('yellow plum')."[1]

It is difficult to identify the cassia tree of Chinese religious literature. "The Chinese word *Kwei* occurs at an early date, but it is a generic term for *Lauraceæ;* and there are about thirteen species of *Cassia,* and about sixteen species of *Cinnamomum* in China. The essential

[1] Laufer, *Sino-Iranica* (Chicago, 1919), pp. 539 *et seq.*

point is that the ancient texts maintain silence as to cinnamon; that is, the product from the bark of the tree. *Cinnamomum cassia* is a native of Kwan - si, Kwan-tun, and Indo-China; and the Chinese made its first acquaintance under the Han, when they began to colonize and to absorb southern China." The first description of this tree goes no farther back than the third century. " It was not the Chinese, but non-Chinese peoples of Indo-China who first brought the tree into civilization, which, like all other southern cultivations, was simply adopted by the conquering Chinese."[1] It has been suggested that the cinnamon bark was imported into Egypt from China as far back as the Empire period (*c.* 1500 B.C.) by Phœnician sea-traders.[2] Laufer rejects this theory.[3] Apparently the ancient Egyptians imported a fragrant bark from their Punt (Somaliland, or British East Africa). At a very much later period cinnamon bark was carried across the Indian Ocean from Ceylon.

The Egyptians imported incense-bearing trees from Punt to restore the " odours of the body" of the dead, and poured out libations to restore its lost moisture.[4] "When", writes Professor Elliot Smith, " the belief became well established that the burning of incense was potent as an animating force, and especially a giver of life to the dead, it naturally came to be regarded as a divine substance in the sense that it had the power of resurrection. As the grains of incense consisted of the exudation of trees, or, as the ancient texts express it, ' their sweat', the divine power of animation in course of time became transferred to trees. They were no

[1] Laufer, *Sino-Iranica*, p. 543.
[2] *Transactions Am. Phil. Association*, Vol. XXIII, 1892, p. 115.
[3] *Sino-Iranica*, pp. 542–3.
[4] G. Elliot Smith, *The Evolution of the Dragon*, pp. 36 *et seq.*

longer merely the source of the life-giving incense, but were themselves animated by the deity, whose drops of sweat were the means of conveying life to the mummy. . . . The sap of trees was brought into relationship with life-giving water. . . . The sap was also regarded as the blood of trees and the incense that exuded as sweat." As De Groot reminds us, "tales of trees that shed blood, and that cry out when hurt are common in Chinese literature (as also in Southern Arabia, notes Elliot Smith); also of trees that lodge, or can change into maidens of transcendant beauty."[1]

Apparently the ancient seafarers who searched for incense-bearing trees carried their beliefs to distant countries. The goddess-tree of the peach cult was evidently the earliest in China. It bore the fruit of life. The influence that led to the foundation of this cult probably came by an overland route. The cassia-tree cult was later, and beliefs connected with it came from Southern China; these, too, bear the imprint of ideas that were well developed before they reached China.

There are references in Chinese lore to a gigantic cassia tree which was 10,000 feet high. Those who ate of its fruit became immortal. The earlier belief connected with the peach tree was that the soul who ate one of its peaches lived for 3000 years.

This cassia world-tree appears first to have taken the place of the peach tree of the " Royal Mother of the West ". It was reached by sailing up the holiest river in China, the Hoang-Ho (Yellow River), the sources of which are in the Koko-Nor territory to the north of Tibet. It wriggles like a serpent between mountain barriers before it flows northward; then it

---

[1] *Religious System of China*, Vol. IV, pp. 272-6: and Elliot Smith, *The Evolution of the Dragon*, pp. 38-9.

flows southward for 200 miles on the eastern border
of Shensi province (the Chinese homeland), and then
eastward for 200 miles, afterwards diverging in a north-
easterly direction towards the Gulf of Chihli, in which
the Islands of the Blest were supposed to be situated.

It was believed that the Hoang-Ho had, like the
Ganges of India and the Nile of Egypt, a celestial
origin. Those sages who desired to obtain a glimpse
of Paradise sailed up the river to its fountain head.
Some reached the tree and the garden of Paradise.
Others found themselves sailing across the heavens.
The Western Paradise was evidently supposed by some
to be situated in the middle of the world, and by others
to have been situated beyond the horizon.

Chang Ki'en, one of the famous men attached to
the court of Wu Ti, the reviver of many ancient beliefs
and myths, was credited with having followed the course
of the sacred river until he reached the spot where the
cassia tree grew. Beside the tree were the immortal
animals that haunt the garden of the " Royal Mother of
the West". In addition, Chang Ki'en saw the moon-rabbit
or moon-hare, which is adored as a rice-giver. In the Far
East, as in the Near East and in the West, the moon is
supposed to ripen crops. The lunar rabbit or hare is
associated with water; in the moon grow plants and
a tree of immortality. There is also, according to Chinese
belief, a frog in the moon. It was originally a woman,
the wife of a renowned archer, who rescued the moon
from imprisonment in masses of black rain-clouds. The
" Royal Mother of the West" was so grateful to the archer
for the service he had rendered that she gave him a jade
cup filled with the dew of immortality. His wife stole
the cup and drank the dew. For this offence the " Royal
Mother of the West" transformed her into a frog, and

imprisoned her in the moon. In Egypt the frog was a symbol of resurrection or rebirth, and the old frog-goddess Hekt is usually regarded as a form of Hathor, the Great Mother.

The lunar tree is sometimes identified with the cassia tree of immortality. Its leaves are red as blood, and the bodies of those who eat of its fruit become as transparent as still water.

The moon-water which nourishes plants and trees (eight lunar trees of immortality are referred to in some legends), and the dew of immortality in the jade cup, appear to be identical with the Indian soma and the nectar of the classical gods. In Norse mythology the lunar water-pot (a symbol of the mother-goddess) was filled at a well by two children, the boy Hyuki and the girl Bil,[1] who were carried away by the moon-god Mani. Odin was also credited with having recovered the moon-mead from the hall of Suttung, "the mead wolf", after it had been stolen from the moon. The god flew heaven-ward, carrying the mead, in the form of an eagle.[2] Zeus's eagle is similarly a nectar-bringer.

In Indian mythology the soma was contained in a bowl fashioned by Twashtri, the divine artisan, and was drunk by the gods, and especially by Indra, the rain-bringer. A Vedic frog-hymn was chanted by Aryo-Indian priests as a rain-charm when Indra's services were requisitioned. In one of the Indian legends an eagle or falcon carries the soma to Indra. The souls who reach Paradise are made immortal after they drink of the soma. In India the soma was personified, and the lunar god, Soma, became a god of love, immortality, and fertility. The soma juice was obtained by the Vedic priests from

[1] The Jack and Jill of the nursery rhyme.
[2] *Teutonic Myth and Legend*, pp. 22 *et seq.*

some unknown plant. There are also references in Indian mythology to the "Amrita", which was partaken of by the gods. It was the sap of sacred trees that grew in Paradise. Trees and plants derived their life and sustenance from water. The Far-Eastern beliefs in "the dew of immortality", "the fungus of immortality", and "the fruit of immortality" have an intimate connection with the belief that the mother-goddess was connected with the moon, which exercised an influence over water. The mother-goddess was also the love-goddess, the Ishtar of Babylonia, the Hathor of Egypt, the Aphrodite of Greece. Her son, or husband, was, in one of his phases, the love-god.

The sage of the Chinese Emperor Wu Ti, who followed the course of the Yellow River so as to reach the celestial Paradise, saw, in addition to the moon-rabbit, or hare, the "Old Man of the Moon", the Chinese Wu Kang and Japanese Gekkawo, the god of love and marriage. He is supposed to unite lovers by binding their feet with invisible red silk cords. The "Old Man in the Moon" is, in Chinese legend, engaged in chopping branches from the cassia tree of immortality. New branches immediately sprout forth to replace those thus removed, but the "Old Man" has to go on cutting till the end of time, having committed a sin for which his increasing labour is the appropriate punishment.

A Buddhist legend makes Indra the old man. He asked for food from the hare, the ape, and the fox. The hare lit a fire and leapt into it so that the god might be fed. Indra was so much impressed by this supreme act of friendship and charity that he placed the exemplary hare in the moon. A version of this story is given in the *Mahábhárata*.

In European folk-lore the "Old Man" is either a

thief who stole a bundle of faggots, or a man who "broke the Sabbath" by cutting sticks on that holy day.

> See the rustic in the Moon,
> How his bundle weighs him down;
> Thus his sticks the truth reveal
> It never profits man to steal.

Various versions of the Man in the Moon myth are given by S. Baring-Gould,[1] who draws attention to a curious seal "appended to a deed preserved in the Record office, dated the 9th year of Edward the Third (1335)". It shows the "Man in the Moon" carrying his sticks and accompanied by his dog. Two stars are added. The inscription on the seal is, "Te Waltere docebo cur spinas phebo gero (I will teach thee, Walter, why I carry thorns in the moon)". The deed is one of conveyance of property from a man whose Christian name was Walter.

Wu Ti's sage travelled through the celestial regions until he reached the Milky Way, the source of the Yellow River. He saw the Spinning Maiden, whose radiant garment is adorned with silver stars. She had a lover, from whom she was separated, but once a year she was allowed to visit him, and passed across the heavens as a meteor. This Spinning Maiden, who weaves the net of the constellations, is reminiscent of the Egyptian sky-goddess, Hathor (or Nut), whose body is covered with stars, and whose legs and arms, as she bends over the earth, "represent the four pillars on which the sky was supposed to rest and mark the four cardinal points". Her lover, from whom she was separated, was Seb.[2] In China certain groups of stars are referred to as the

---

[1] *Curious Myths of the Middle Ages,* pp. 190 *et seq.*
[2] Budge, *Gods of the Egyptians,* Vol. II, p. 104.

"Celestial Door", the "Hall of Heaven", &c. Taoist saints dwell in stellar abodes, as well as on the "Islands of the Blest"; some were, during their life on earth, incarnations of star-gods. The lower ranks of the western - cult immortals remain in the garden of the "Royal Mother"; those of the highest rank ascend to the stars.

Wu Ti's sage, according to one form of the legend, never returned to earth. His boat, which sailed up the Yellow River and then along the "Milky Way", was believed to have reached the Celestial River that flows round the Universe, and along which sails the sun-barque of the Egyptian god Ra (or Re). One day the Chinese sage's oar—apparently his steering oar— was deposited in the Royal Palace grounds by a celestial spirit, who descended from the sky. Here we have, perhaps, a faint memory of the visits paid to earth from the celestial barque by the Egyptian god Thoth, in his captivity as envoy of the sun-god Ra.

There is evidence in Far-Eastern folk-tales that at a very remote period the beliefs of the cult of the sky-goddess, which placed the tree of immortality in the "moon island", and the beliefs of the peach cult of "the Westerners" were fused, as were those of the Osirian and solar cults in Egypt.

A curious story tells that once upon a time a man went to fish on the Yellow River. A storm arose, and his boat was driven into a tributary, the banks of which were fringed with innumerable peach trees in full blossom. He reached an island, on which he landed. There he was kindly treated by the inhabitants, who told that they had fled from China because of the oppression of the emperor. This surprised the fisherman greatly. He asked for particulars, and was given the name of an emperor who had died about 500 years before he himself was born.

"What is the name of this island?" he asked. The inhabitants were unable to tell him. "We came hither," they said, "just as you have come. We are strangers in a strange land."

Next day the wanderer launched his boat and set out to return by the way he had come. He sailed on all day and all night, and when morning came he found himself amidst familiar landmarks. He was able to return home.

When the fisherman told the story to a priest, he was informed that he had reached the land of the Celestials, and that the river fringed by peach trees in blossom was the Milky Way.

In this story the Chinese Island of the Blest is, like the Nilotic "green bed of Horus", a river island.

Another memory of the Celestial River and the Barque of the Sun is enshrined in the story of Lo Tze Fang, a holy woman of China who ascended to heaven by climbing a high tree — apparently the "world-tree". After reaching the celestial regions she was carried along the Celestial River in a boat. According to the story, she still sails each day across the heavens.

Other saintly people have been carried to the celestial regions by dragons. According to Chinese belief the "Yellow Dragon" is connected with the moon. The reflection of the moon on rippling water is usually referred to as the "Golden Dragon", or "Yellow Dragon", the chief of Chinese dragons, and usually associated with the sun.

One of the classes of Chinese holy men of the Spirit-world, the Sien Nung, who bear a close resemblance to Indian Rishis, is connected with the moon cult. They are believed to prolong their lives by eating the leaves of the lunar plants.

In an Egyptian legend it is told that Osiris was the son of the Mother Cow, who had conceived him when a fertilizing ray of light fell from the moon. In like manner a moon-girl came into being in Japan. She was discovered by a wood-cutter. One day, when collecting bamboo, he found inside a cane a little baby, whose body shone as does a gem in darkness. He took her home to his wife, and she grew up to be a very beautiful girl. She was called "Moon Ray", and after living for a time on the earth returned to the moon. She had maintained her youthful appearance by drinking, from a small vessel she possessed, the fluid of immortality.

As the dragon was connected with the moon, and the moon with the bamboo, it might be expected that the dragon and bamboo would be closely linked. One of the holy men is credited with having reached the lunar heaven by cutting down a bamboo, which he afterwards transformed into a dragon. He rode heavenwards on the dragon's back.

Saintly women, as a rule, rise to heaven in the form of birds, or in their own form, without wings, on account of the soul-like lightness of their bodies, which have become purified by performing religious rites and engaging in prayer and meditation. Their husbands have either to climb trees or great mountains. Some holy women, after reaching heaven, ride along the clouds on the back of the K'ilin, the bisexual monster that the soul of Confucius is supposed to ride. It is a form of the dragon, but more like the *makara* of the Indian god Varuna than the typical "wonder beast" of China and Japan. Some of these monsters resemble lions, dogs, deer, walruses, or unicorns. They are all, however, varieties of the *makara*.

Sometimes we find that the attributes of the Great Mother, who, like Aphrodite, was a "Postponer of Old Age" (*Ambologera*), being the provider of the fruit of immortality and a personification of the World Tree, have been attached to the memory of some famous lady, and especially an empress. As the Egyptian Pharaoh, according to the beliefs of the solar cult, became Ra (the sun-god) after death, so did the Chinese empress become the "Royal Lady of the West". Nu Kwa, a mythical empress of China, was reputed to have become a goddess after she had passed to the celestial regions. She figures in the Chinese Deluge Myth. Like the Babylonian Ishtar, she was opposed to the policy of destroying mankind. She did not, however, like Ishtar, content herself by expressing regret. When the demons of water and fire, aided by rebel generals of her empire, set out to destroy the world, Nu Kwa waged war against them. Her campaign was successful, but not until a gigantic warrior had partly destroyed the heavens by upsetting one of its pillars and the flood had covered a great portion of the earth. The empress stemmed the rising waters by means of charred reeds (a Babylonian touch), and afterwards rebuilt the broken pillar, under which was placed an Atlas-tortoise. Like Marduk (Merodach), she then set the Universe in order, and formed the channel for the Celestial River. Thereafter she created the guardians of the four quarters, placing the Black Tortoise in the north, and giving it control over winter; the Blue Dragon in the east, who was given control over spring; the White Tiger in the west, who was given control over autumn; and the Red Bird in the south, who was given control over summer, with the Golden Dragon, whose special duty was to guard the sun, the moon being protected by the White

Deity of the west.   The broken pillar of heaven was built up with stones coloured like the five gods.

Among the gifts conferred on mankind by this Empress-Goddess was jade, which she created so that they might be protected against evil influence and decay.

In this Deluge Myth, which is evidently of Babylonian origin, the gods figure as rebels and demons.   The Mother Goddess is the protector of the Universe, and the friend of man.   Evidently the cult of the Mother Goddess was at one time very powerful in China.   In Japan the Empress Nu Kwa is remembered as Jokwa.

The Tree of Immortality, as has been seen, is closely associated with the Far Eastern Mother Goddess, who may appear before favoured mortals either as a beautiful woman, as a dragon, or as a woman riding on a dragon, or as half woman and half fish, or half woman and half serpent.   It is from the goddess that the tree receives its "soul substance"; in a sense, she is the tree, as she is the moon and the pot of life-water, or the mead in the moon.   The fruits of the tree are symbols of her as the mother, and the sap of the tree is her blood.

Reference has been made to Far Eastern stories about dragons transforming themselves into trees and trees becoming dragons.   The tree was a "kupua" of the dragon.   The mother of Adonis was a tree—Myrrha—the daughter of King Cinyras of Cyprus, who was transformed into a myrrh tree.   A Japanese legend relates that a hero, named Manko, once saw a beautiful woman sitting on a tree-trunk that floated on the sea.   She vanished suddenly.   Manko had the tree taken into his boat, and found that the woman was hidden inside the trunk.   She was a daughter of the Dragon King of Ocean.

A better-known Japanese tree hero is Momotaro

(*momo*, peach, *taro*, eldest son), whose name is usually rendered in English as " Little Peachling ". He is known in folk-stories as a slayer of demons—a veritable Jack the Giant-Killer.

The legend runs that one day an old wood - cutter went out to gather firewood, while his wife washed dirty clothes in a river. After the woman had finished her work, she saw a gigantic peach drifting past. Seizing a pole, she brought it into shallow water, and thus secured it. The size of the peach astonished her greatly, and she carried it home, and, having washed it, placed it before her husband when he returned home for his evening meal. No sooner did the wood-cutter begin to cut open the peach than a baby boy emerged from the kernel. The couple, being childless, were greatly delighted, and looked upon the child as a gift from the Celestials, and they believed he had been sent so as to become their comfort and helper when they grew too old to work.

Momotara, " the elder son of the peach ", as they called him, grew up to be a strong and valiant young man, who performed feats of strength that caused everyone to wonder at him.

There came a day when, to the sorrow of his foster-parents, he announced that he had resolved to leave home and go to the Isle of Demons, with purpose to secure a portion of their treasure. This seemed to be a perilous undertaking, and the old couple attempted to make him change his mind. Momotara, however, laughed at their fears, and said: " Please make some millet dumplings for me. I shall need food for my journey."

His foster-mother prepared the dumplings and muttered good wishes over them. Then Momotara bade the old couple an affectionate farewell, and went on his way.

The young hero had not travelled far when he met a dog, which barked out: "Bow-wow! where are you going, Peach-son?"

"I am going to the Isle of Demons to obtain treasure," the lad answered.

"Bow-wow! what are you carrying?"

"I am carrying millet dumplings that my mother made for me. No one in Japan can make better dumplings than these."

"Bow-wow! give me one and I shall go with you to the Isle of Demons."

The lad gave the dog a dumpling, and it followed at his heels.

Momotara had not gone much farther when a monkey, perched on a tree, called out to him, saying: "Kia! Kia! where are you going, Son of a Peach?"

Momotara answered the monkey as he had answered the dog. The monkey asked for a dumpling, promising to join the party, and when he received one he set off with the lad and the dog.

The next animal that hailed the lad was a pheasant, who called out: "Ken! Ken! where are you going, Son of a Peach?"

Momotara told him, and the bird, having received the dumpling he asked for, accompanied the lad, the dog, and the monkey on the quest of treasure.

When the Island of Demons was reached they all went together towards the fortress in which the demon king resided. The pheasant flew inside to act as a spy. Then the monkey climbed over the wall and opened the gate, so that Momotara and the dog were able to enter the fortress without difficulty. The demons, however, soon caught sight of the intruders, and attempted to kill them. Momotara fought fiercely, assisted by the friendly animals, and slew or scattered in flight the demon warriors. Then they found their way into the royal palace and made Akandoji, the king of demons, their prisoner. This great demon was prepared to wield his terrible club of iron, but Momotaro, who was an expert in the jiu-jitsu system of wrestling, seized the demon king and threw him down, and, with the help of the monkey, bound him with a rope.

Momotaro threatened to put Akandoji to death if he would not reveal where his treasure was hidden.

The king bade his servants do homage to the Son of the Peach and to bring forth the treasure, which included the cap and coat of invisibility, magic jewels that controlled the ebb and flow of ocean, gems that shone in darkness and gave protection against all evil to those who wore them, tortoise-shell and jade charms, and a great quantity of gold and silver.

Momotara took possession of as much of the treasure as he could carry, and returned home a very rich man. He built a great house, and lived in it with his foster-parents, who were given everything they desired as long as they lived.

In this story may be detected a mosaic of myths. The Egyptian Horus, whose island floated down the Nile, had white sandals which enabled him to go swiftly up and down the land of Egypt. There are references in the Pyramid Texts to his youthful exploits, but the full story of them has not yet been discovered. The Babylonian Tammuz, when a child, drifted in a "sunken boat" down the River Euphrates. No doubt this myth is the one attached to the memory of Sargon of Akkad,[1] the son of a vestal virgin, who was placed in an ark and set adrift on the river. He was found by a gardener,

[1] *Babylonian Myth and Legend*, p. 126-7.

and was afterwards raised to the kingship by the goddess Ishtar.   Karna, the Aryo-Indian Hector, the son of Surya, the sun-god, and the virgin-princess Pritha, was similarly set adrift in an ark, and was rescued from the Ganges by a childless woman whose husband was a charioteer.   The poor couple reared the future hero as their own son.[1]

Adonis, the son of the myrrh tree, was a Syrian form of Tammuz.   Horus was the son of Osiris, whose body was enclosed by a tree after Set caused his death by setting him adrift in a chest.   When Isis found the tree, which had been cut down for a pillar, the posthumous conception of the son of Osiris took place.[2] The Momotara legend has thus a long history.

The friendly animals figure in the folk-tales of many lands.   Momotara's fight for the treasure, including the cloak of invisibility, bears a close resemblance to Siegfried's fight for the treasure of the Nibelungs.[3]   In western European, as in Far Eastern lore, the treasure is guarded by dragons as well as by dwarfs and giants and other demons.   When the dragon-slayer is not accompanied by friendly animals, he receives help and advice from birds whose language he acquires by eating a part of the dragon, or, as in the Egyptian tale, after getting possession of the book of spells, guarded by the "Deathless Snake".   When the Egyptian hero reads the spells he understands the language of birds, beasts, and fishes.   The treasure-guarding dragon appears, as has been suggested, to have had origin in the belief that sharks were the guardians of pearl-beds and preyed upon the divers who stole their treasure.

[1] *Indian Myth and Legend*, pp. 173 *et seq.*, and 192–94.
[2] *Egyptian Myth and Legend*, p. 19 *et seq.*
[3] *Teutonic Myth and Legend*, pp. 352 (*n.*), 376, 383, 389, 391, 446.

The beliefs connected with the life-giving virtues of the tree of the Mother Goddess were attached to shells, pearls, gold, and jade. The goddess was the source of all life, and one of her forms was the dragon. As the dragon - mother she created or gave birth to the dragon - gods. Dragon - bones were ground down for medicinal purposes; dragon-herbs cured diseases; the sap of dragon-trees, like the fruit, promoted longevity, as did the jade which the goddess had created for mankind.

The beliefs connected with jade were similar to those connected with pearls, which were at a remote period emblems of the moon in Egypt. In China the moon was "the pearl of heaven". One curious and widespread belief was that pearls were formed by raindrops, or by drops of dew from the moon, the source of moisture, and especially of nectar or soma. Pearls and pearl-shells were used for medicinal purposes. They were, like the sap of trees, the very essence of life—the soul-substance of the Great Mother.[1]

That the complex ideas regarding shells, pearls, dew, trees, the moon, the sun, the stars, and the Great Mother were of "spontaneous generation" in many separated countries is difficult to believe. It is more probable that the culture-complexes enshrined in folk-tales and religious texts had a definite area of origin in which their history can be traced. The searchers for precious stones and metals and incense - bearing trees must have scattered their beliefs far and wide when they exploited locally-unappreciated forms of wealth.

[1] For beliefs connected with pearls and shells, see *Shells as Evidence of the Migrations of Early Culture*, I. Wilfrid Jackson (London, 1917).

CHAPTER XI
Tree-, Herb-, and Stone-lore

"Soul Substance" in Medicinal Plants—Life-fire in Water and Plants—
"The Blood which is Life"—Colour Symbolism in East and West—Charm
Symbolism—Gems as Fruit—Jade and Vegetation—Far Eastern Elixirs of Life
—Links between Pine, Cypress, Mandrake, and Mugwort—Story of Treasure-
finding Dog—The Far Eastern Artemis—Her Mugwort, Lotus, and Fruit
Basket—Herbs and Pearl-shell—Goats and Women's Herb—Chinese and
Tartar's Fight for Mandrake—Tea as an Elixir—Far Eastern Rip Van
Winkles—Problem of the Date Tree—"Tree Tears" and "Stone Tears"—
Weeping Deities—Goats and Thunder-gods—Goats and Sheep become Stones
—Gems and Herbs connected with Moon—Graded Herbs, Deities, and Stones
—Foreign Ideas in China.

In the ancient medical lore of China, as in the medical
lores of other lands, there are laudatory references to
"All-heal" plants and plants reputed to be specific
remedies for various diseases. Not a few of these medicinal
plants have been found to be either quite useless or
positively harmful, but some are included in modern
pharmacopœias, after having been submitted to the closest
investigations of physiological science.

The old herbalists, witch - doctors, and hereditary
"curers", who made some genuine discoveries that have
since been elaborated, were certainly not scientists in
the modern sense of the term. Their "cures" were
a quaint mixture of magic and religion. They searched
for those plants and substances that appeared, either
by their shape or colour, to contain in more concentrated
form than others the "essence of life", the "soul
substance" that restored health and promoted longevity.

This "soul substance" was concentrated in body-odours and body-moistures. It was a something mixed in water which had colour, odour, and heat—a something derived from the Great Mother, who had herself sprung from water, as did the Egyptian Hathor and the Greek Aphrodite, or, if not directly from the Great Mother, from one or other of her offspring. The "soul substance" of the goddess was in vegetation; the sap of trees was identified with her blood—the "blood which is life". Blood was one kind of body-moisture; other kinds were sweat, tears, saliva, &c. All these moistures had fertilizing properties. The Mother, as the sky-goddess, provided the world's supply of fertilizing water. In China the supply was controlled by the dragon-gods, who caused the thunder and lightning that released the rain and flooded the rivers.

Winter is the Chinese dry season. It was believed that during this period the dragons were concealed and asleep. No growth was possible during winter because of the scarcity of water—the life-giving water that caused Nature to "renew her youth" in the spring season. When the dragons awoke and rose fighting and thundering, parched wastes were soaked and fertilized by rain. Then the old, decaying world renewed her youth and fresh vegetation appeared, because "soul substance" in the form of rain had entered the soil and furnished plants with "blood-sap", and at the same time with vital energy, vital odours, and vital colours. Thus life, which had its origin in water, was sustained by the products of water and by the properties in water.

The plants that were supposed to store up most "soul substance" were those that grew in water, like the lotus, those that constantly absorbed moisture, like the "fungus of immortality", or those that sprang up suddenly during a thunder-storm, like the "Red Cloud herb". The latter required a heavy deluge to bring it into existence. It was a special gift of the dragon-god—or an "avatar" of that deity—and had concentrated in it the essence of much rain, and, in addition, the essence of lightning —the "fire of heaven", ejected by the rain - dragon. The lightning was the "dragon's tongue", and had therefore substance, moisture, and heat, as well as brilliance. To the early thinkers the life fluid was not only blood, but warm blood—blood pulsating with the "vital spark", the "fire of life". These men would have accepted in the literal sense the imagery of the modern Irish poet, who wrote:

> O, there was lightning in my blood,
> Red lightning lighten'd through my blood,
>   My Dark Rosaleen.

The "fire of life" might be locked up in vegetation, in stone, or in red earth, and be made manifest by its colour alone.

The genesis of this idea can be traced at a very early period in the history of modern man (*Homo sapiens*). In Aurignacian times in western Europe (that is, from ten till twenty thousand years ago) blood was identified with life and consciousness. The red substance in "the blood which is life" was apparently regarded as the vitalizing agency, and was supposed to be the same as red earth (red ochre). It is found, from the evidence afforded by burial customs, that the Aurignacian race originated or perpetuated the habit of smearing the bodies of their dead with red ochre. After the flesh had decayed, the red ochre fell on and coloured the bones and the pebbles around the bones. Whether or not the red ochre was supposed to be impregnated with the essence of fire, or of the sun, the source of fire, it is impossible to say. Behind the corpse - painting custom there was, no doubt, a body of definite beliefs. As much is suggested by the fact that shell - amulets and spine-amulets were laid on or about the dead. The belief that the first man had been formed of red clay mixed with water may well have been in existence in Aurignacian times. The amulets associated with Aurignacian ceremonial burials suggest, too, that ideas had been formulated regarding the after-life. Was it believed that the painted, and therefore reanimated, body would rise again, or that the soul could be assisted to travel to the Otherworld? These questions cannot yet be answered. We can do no more than note here that Colour Symbolism, and especially Red Symbolism and all it entails, had origin in remote antiquity.

In China red flowers and red berries were supposed, because of their colour, to be strongly impregnated with "soul substance" or "vital essence", or, to use the Chinese term, with *shen*. These flowers and berries had curative qualities. In western Europe the red holly berry was in like manner regarded as an "All-heal". The tree on which the red berry appears is so full of divine life that it is an evergreen. In Gaelic folk-lore holly is associated with the Mother Goddess and with the water-beast (dragon) and its "avatar", the red-spotted salmon, which is supposed to swallow the holly berries that drop into its pool.

The red substance which is in the blood was not necessarily confined, however, to vegetation. As it was of the earth, earthy, or a product of some mysterious agency at work in the earth, it might be found in coagulated form as a ruby, or any other red stone, or as a stone streaked or spotted with red; it might be found in water

as a shell, wholly or partly red, or as a red or yellow
pearl inside a shell. It might likewise be found concentrated in the red feathers of a bird. A bird with
red feathers was usually recognized as a "thunder bird"
—Robin Red-breast is a European "thunder bird"[1]—and
the red berry as a "thunder berry"—a berry containing
the "soul substance" of the god of lightning and fire.
Fire was obtained by friction from trees associated with
the divine Thunderer; his spirit dwelt in the tree. One
of the "fire sticks" was invariably taken from a red-
berried tree.

The red vital substance might likewise be displayed
by a sacred fish—the "thunder fish". In the Chinese
"Boy Blue" story the thunder-dragon in human form
rides on the back of a red carp.

Yellow is, like red, reputed to be a vital colour.
Lightning is yellow; the flames of wood fires are yellow,
while the embers are red. Early man appears to have
recognized the close association of yellow and red in
fire. Gold is yellow, and it was connected, as a substitute
for red and yellow shells, with the sun, which at morning
and evening sends forth red and yellow rays. The fire
which is in the sun "warms the blood" and promotes
the growth of plants, as does the moisture in the moon—
the moon which controls the flow of sap and blood.
The combination of sun-fire, lunar-fire, and moisture,
or of fire-red earth and rain, constituted, according to
early man's way of thinking, the mystery called life.
Yellow berries and yellow flowers were as sacred to him,
and had as great life-prolonging and curative qualities,
as red berries, red flowers, red feathers, and the skins
and scales of red fish. Yellow gems and yellow metals
were consequently valued as highly as were red gems

---

[1] Some thunder birds are dark as thunder-clouds.

and red metals. In China yellow is the earth colour.
In Ceylon, Burmah, Tibet, and China it is the sacred
colour of the Buddhists.

Blue, the sky colour, and therefore the colour of
the sky-deity, was likewise holy. Torquoise and lapis-
lazuli were connected with the Great Mother. The
sacredness of green has a more complex history. It
was not reverenced simply because of the greenness of
vegetation. The mysterious substance that makes plants
green was derived from the supreme source of life —
the green form of the water-goddess or god—and was
to be found in concentrated form in green gems and
stones, including green jade. White was the colour of
day, the stars, and the moon, and black the colour of
night and of death, and therefore the colour of deities
associated with darkness and the Otherworld. In China
black is the colour of the north, of winter, and of drought.
The combination of the five colours (black, white, red,
yellow, and blue or green) was displayed by all deities.
This conception is enshrined in the religious text which
De Visser gives without comment:

> "A dragon in the water covers himself with five colours;
> *Therefore he is a god.*"[1]

In China, as in several other countries, the colour
of an animal, plant, or stone was believed to reveal its
character and attributes. A red berry was regarded with
favour, because it displayed the life colour. A red stone
was favoured for the same reason. When it is nowadays
found that some particular berry or herb, favoured of
old as an "All-heal", is really an efficacious medicine,
an enthusiast may incline to regard it as a wonderful
thing that modern medical science has not achieved, in

[1] De Visser, *The Dragon in China and Japan*, p. 63.

some lines, greater triumphs than were achieved by the "simple observers" of ancient times. But it may be that the real cures were of accidental discovery, and that the effective berry or herb would, on account of its colour alone, have continued in use whether it had cured or not.

In China not only the berry with a "good colour" was used by "curers", but even the stone with a "good colour". The physicians, for instance, sometimes prescribed ground jade, and we read of men who died, because, as it was thought, the quantities of jade-medicine taken were much too large. Some ancient writers assert, in this connection, that although a dose of ground jade may bring this life to a speedy end, it will ensure prolonged life in the next world.

The berries and stones which were reputed to be "All-heals" were not always devoured. They could be used simply as charms. The vital essence or "soul substance" in berry or stone was supposed to be so powerful that it warded off the attacks of the demons of disease, or expelled the demons after they had taken possession of a patient. Medicines might be prepared by simply dipping the charms into pure well water. These charms were often worn as body-ornaments. All the ancient personal ornaments were magic charms that gave protection or regulated the functions of body organs. When symbols were carved on jade, the ornaments were believed to acquire increased effectiveness. Gold ornaments were invariably given symbolic shape. Like the horse-shoe, which in western Europe is nailed on a door for "luck"—that is, to ward off evil—these symbolic ornaments were credited with luck - bringing virtues. The most ancient gold ornaments in the world are found in Egypt, and these are models of shells, which had been worn as "luck-bringers" long before

gold was worked.[1] These shells had an intimate association with the Mother Goddess, who, in one of her
aspects, personified the birth-aiding and fertilizing
shell.

The idea that the coloured fruits and the coloured
stones were life-giving "avatars" of the Mother Goddess
is well illustrated in the glowing accounts of the Chinese
Paradise. The Tree of Life might bear fruit or gems.
The souls swallowed gems as readily as fruit. In the
Japanese Paradise the immortals devour powdered mother-
of-pearl shells as well as peaches, dried cassia pods, cinnabar, pine needles, or pine cones.

Jade was connected with vegetation on this earth
as well as in Paradise. As we have seen, the Great
Mother goddess created this famous mineral for the
benefit of mankind. It contained her "soul substance",
as did the trees, their blossoms, and their fruit, and
even their leaves and bark. This quaint belief is enshrined in the following quotation from the *Illustrated
Mirror of Jades*, translated by Laufer and given without
comment:

"In the second month, the plants in the mountains receive a
bright lustre. When their leaves fall, they change into jade.
The spirit of jade is like a beautiful woman."[2]

It is obvious that the "beautiful woman" is the
Goddess of the West. Reference to coral trees in
Paradise are numerous. It was believed not only in
China but in western Europe, until comparatively recent
times, that coral was a marine tree—the tree of the water-
goddess. The Great Mother was connected with the

---

[1] G. A. Reisner, *Early Dynastic Cemeteries of Naga-ad-Dêr*, Vol. I, 1908, Plates 5 and
7, and *Shells as Evidence of the Migrations of Early Culture*, 1917, p. xxi.
[2] *Jade*, p. 1.

water above and beyond the firmament, as well as the rivers and the sea.

"Good health" in the Otherworld was immortality or great longevity. A soul which ate of a peach from the World Tree was assured of 3000 years of good health. He renewed his youth, and never grew old, so long as the supply of peaches was assured.[1]

In China men lengthened their days by partaking of "soul substance" in various forms. The pine-tree cult made decoctions of pine needles and cones, or of the fungus found at the roots of pines. "The juice of the pine", says one Chinese sage, "when consumed for a long time, renders the body light, prevents man from growing old, and lengthens his life. Its leaves preserve the interior of the body; they cause a man never to feel hunger, and increase the years of his life." The cypress was also favoured. "Cypress seeds," the same writer asserts, "if consumed for a long period, render a man hale and healthy. They endow him with a good colour, sharpen his ears and eyes, cause him never to experience the feeling of hunger, nor to grow old." The camphor tree comes next to the pine and cypress as "a dispenser and depository of vital power".[2]

Apparently the fact that pines and cypresses are evergreens recommended them to the Chinese, although it was not for that reason only the belief arose about their richness of "soul substance". An ancient Chinese sage has declared: "Pines and cypresses alone on this earth are endowed with life, in the midst of winter as

[1] The Norse gods grew old when the apples of immortality, kept by the goddess Idun, were carried away. After the apples were restored, they ate of them and grew young again.—*Teutonic Myth and Legend*, p. 57.

[2] De Groot, *The Religious System of China*, Vol. I, p. 300.

well as in summer they are evergreen. Pines 1000 years old resemble a blue ox, a blue dog, or a blue human being. Cypresses 1000 years old have deep roots *shaped like men in a sitting posture.* . . . When they are cut they lose blood. . . . Branches of pines which are 3000 years old have underneath the bark accumulations of resin in the shape of dragons, which, if pounded and consumed in a quantity of full ten pounds, will enable a man to live 500 years."[1]

Here we have the tree connected with the blue dragon. As has been stated, ancient pines were transformed into dragons. The assertion that the pines and cypresses were the only trees possessed of "vital power" does not accord with the evidence regarding the peach-tree cult. The peach, although not an evergreen, was credited with being possessed of much "soul substance".

No doubt the ideas connected with evergreens had a close association with the doctrines of colour symbolism. The Chinese "Tree of Heaven" (*Ailanthus glandulosa*) appears to have attracted special attention, because in spring its leaves are coloured reddish-violet or reddish-brown before they turn green. The walnut, cherry, and peony similarly show reddish young leaves, and these trees have much lore connected with them.

One seems to detect traces of the beliefs connected with the mandrake in the reference to the human-shaped roots of the 1000-year-old cypress tree. The mandrake was the plant of Aphrodite, and its root, which resembles the human form, was used medicinally; it has narcotic properties, and was believed also to be a medicine which promoted fertility, assisted birth, and caused youths and girls to fall in love with one another. According to

[1] De Groot, *The Religious System of China*, Vol. I, p. 295.

mandrake-lore, the plant shrieks when taken from the earth, and causes the death of the one who plucks it.[1] Dogs were consequently employed to drag it out of the ground, and they expired immediately. The "mandrake apple" is believed by Dr. Rendel Harris to have been the original "love apple".[2]

In like manner the mugwort, the plant of Artemis, was connected in China and Japan with the pine which had virtues similar to those of the herb. Although the mandrake-dog is not associated with the cypress, it is found connected in a Japanese folk-story with the pine. The hero of the tale, an old man called Hana Saka Jijii, acquired the secret how to make withered trees blossom. He possessed a wonderful dog, named Shiro, which one day attracted his attention by sniffing, barking, and wagging his tail at a certain spot in the cottage garden. The old man was puzzled to know what curious thing in the ground attracted the dog, and began to dig. After turning up a few spadefuls of earth he found a hoard of gold and silver pieces.

A jealous neighbour, having observed what had happened, borrowed Shiro and set the animal to search for treasure in his own garden. The dog began to sniff and bark at a certain spot, but when the man turned over the soil, he found only dirt and offal that emitted an offensive smell. Angry at being deceived by the dog, he killed it and buried the body below the roots of a pine tree. Hana Saka Jijii was much distressed on account of the loss of Shiro. He burned incense below the pine tree, laid flowers on the dog's grave, and shed

---

[1] Shrieks like mandrakes torn out of the earth.—*Romeo and Juliet*, iv, 3.
  Give me to drink mandragora . . .
  That I may sleep out the great gap of time
  My Anthony is away.—*Anthony and Cleopatra*.
[2] *The Ascent of Olympus*, pp. 107 *et seq.*

tears. That night he dreamed a wonderful dream. The ghost of Shiro appeared before him, and, addressing him, said: "Cut down the pine tree above my grave and make a rice mortar of it. When you use the mortar think of me."

The old man did as the dog advised, and discovered to his great joy that when he used the pine-tree mortar each grain of rice was transformed into pure gold. He soon became rich.

The envious neighbour discovered what was going on and borrowed the mortar. In his hands, however, it turned rice into dirt. This enraged him so greatly that he broke the mortar and burned it.

That night the ghost of Shiro appeared once again in a dream, and advised Hana Saka Jijii to collect the ashes of the burnt mortar and scatter them on withered trees. Next morning he did as the dog advised him. To his astonishment he found that the ashes caused withered trees to come to life and send forth fresh and beautiful blossoms. He then went about the country and employed himself reviving dead plum and cherry trees, and soon became so renowned that a prince sent for him, asking that he should bring back to life the withered trees in his garden. The old man received a rich reward when he accomplished the feat.

The jealous neighbour came to know how Hani Saka Jijii revived dead trees, so he collected what remained of the ashes of the pine-tree mortar. Then he set forth to proclaim to the inhabitants of a royal town that he could work the same miracle as Hani Saka Jijii. The prince sent for him, and the man climbed into the branches of a withered tree. But when he scattered the ashes no bud or blossom appeared, and the wind blew the dust into the eyes of the prince and nearly blinded him. The impostor was seized and soundly beaten; and the dog Shiro was, in this manner, well avenged.

In this story the dog is a searcher for and giver of treasure. It is of special interest, therefore, to find that Artemis, the mugwort-goddess of the West, "was not only the opener of treasure-houses, but she also possessed the secret of the Philosopher's Stone; she could transmute base substances into gold". She could therefore grant riches to those whom she favoured. Dr. Rendel Harris, quoting from an old English writer, records the belief "that upon St. John's eve there are coals (which turn to gold) to be found at midday under the roots of mugwort, which after or before that time are very small, or none at all". The gold cures sickness.[1]

A similar belief was attached to the mandrake. A French story tells of a peasant who regularly "fed" a mandrake that grew below a mistletoe-bearing oak. The mandrake, when fed, would, it was believed, "make you rich by returning twice as much as you spent upon it. . . . The plant had become an animal."[2]

If Shiro's prototype was the mandrake-dog which sacrificed itself for the sake of lovers, and was itself an "avatar" of the deity, we should expect to find the pine tree connected with the love-goddess.[3] Joly, in his *Legend in Japanese Art* (p. 147), tells that "at Takasago there is a very old pine tree, the trunk of which is bifurcated; in it dwells the spirit of the Maiden of Takasago, who was seen once by the son of Izanagi, who fell in love and wedded her. Both lived to a very great age, dying at the same hour on the same day, and since

[1] Elliot Smith, *The Evolution of the Dragon*, p. 184; Rendel Harris, *The Ascent of Olympus*, p. 73. [2] *The Ascent of Olympus*, p. 126.

[3] Artemis, as goddess of birth, was a specialized form of the Great Mother, who was herself the goddess of love and birth, of treasure, &c.—the All-mother.

then their spirits abide in the tree, but on moonlight nights they return to human shape and revisit the scene of their earthly life and pursue their work of gathering pine needles." The needles were promoters of longevity, as we have seen.

Another Japanese pair associated with the pine trees are Jo and Uba, a couple of old and wrinkled spirits. They gathered pine needles, Jo using a rake and Uba a besom and fan.

The goddess of the pine was evidently a Far Eastern Aphrodite, as well as a Far Eastern Artemis—an Artemis who provided medicine for women in the form of the mugwort, was a goddess of birth, a guardian of treasure, and a goddess of travellers and hunters. The Romans associated with Diana (Artemis) her loved one, Dianus or Janus,[1] as the tree-goddess in Japan was associated with a deified human lover.

The pine may have been "a kind of mugwort" (and apparently, like the cypress, a "kind of mandrake"), but it did not displace the mugwort as a medicinal plant. Dr. Rendel Harris quotes a letter from Professor Giles, the distinguished Chinese scholar, who says: "There is quite a literature about *Artemisia vulgaris*, L. (the mugwort), which has been used in China from time immemorial for cauterizing as a counter-irritant, especially in cases of gout. Other species of Artemisia are also found in China."[2]

The Far Eastern Artemis appears to be represented by the immortal lady known in China as Ho Sien Ku, and in Japan as Kasenko. She is shown "as a young woman clothed in mugwort, holding a lotus stem and flower" (like a western Asiatic or Egyptian goddess), "and talking to a phœnix", or "depicted carrying a

---

[1] *The Ascent of Olympus*, p. 87.   [2] *Ibid.*, p. 86.

basket of loquat fruits which she gathered for her sick
mother. She was a woman who, having been promised
immortality in a dream, fed on mother-of-pearl, and
thereafter moved as swiftly as a bird."[1] The Mexican
god Tlaloc's wife was similarly a mugwort goddess.

In the pine-tree story the Japanese representative
of the tree- and lunar-goddess of love appears with her
spouse on moonlight nights. The moon was the
"Pearl of Heaven". It will be noted that the mugwort
is connected with pearl-shell—the lady Ho Sien Ku
having acquired the right to wear mugwort, in her
character as an immortal, by eating mother-of-pearl.
This connection of pearl-shell with a medicinal plant is
a more arbitrary one than that of the mugwort with
the pine, or the mandrake with the cypress.

The lotus was a form of the ancient love-goddess,
as was also the cowry. In Egypt the solar-god Horus
emerges at birth from the lotus-form of Hathor as it
floats on the breast of the Nile. Ho Sien Ku's basket of
fruit is also symbolic. "A basket of sycamore figs"
was in Ancient Egypt "originally the hieroglyphic sign
for a woman, a goddess, or a mother". It had thus the
same significance as the Pot, the lotus, the mandrake-apple,
and the pomegranate. The latter symbol supplanted the
Egyptian lotus in the Ægean area.[2]

Mugwort, as already stated, was a medicine, and
chiefly a woman's medicine. "The plant (mugwort)",
says Dr. Rendel Harris, "is Artemis, and Artemis is the
plant. Artemis is a woman's goddess and a maid's goddess,
because she was a woman's medicine and a maid's
medicine.[3] The mugwort promoted child-birth, and con-

---

[1] Joly, *Legend in Japanese Art*, p. 165.
[2] Elliot Smith, *The Evolution of the Dragon*, pp. 183, 199 *et seq.*
[3] *The Ascent of Olympus*, 79–80.

trolled women like the moon, and was used for women's ailments in general. It was a healing plant, and was "good for gout" among other troubles.

The women's herb in China is called the "san tsi". An eighteenth-century writer[1] says it is "efficacious in women's disorders and hæmorrhages of all sorts". It is found "only on the tops of high, steep mountains", as is the scented Edelraut (*Artemisia mutellina*), an alpine plant like the famous and beautiful Edelweiss.

Continuing his account of the "san tsi" herb, the eighteenth-century writer and compiler says: "A kind of goat of a greyish colour is very fond of feeding upon this plant, insomuch that they (the Chinese) imagine the blood of this animal is endowed with the same medicinal properties. It is certain that the blood of these goats has surprising success against the injuries received by falls from horses, and other accidents of the same kind. This the missionaries have had experience of several times. One of their servants that was thrown by a vicious horse, and who lay some time without speech or motion, was so soon recovered by this remedy that the next day he was able to pursue his journey." It is also "a specific against the smallpox". The author of *The Chinese Traveller*, touching again on the blood substitute for this plant, which is "not easy to be had", says: "In the experiments above mentioned, the blood of a goat was made use of that had been taken by hunters".

The goat appears to be the link between Artemis "the curer" and Artemis as "Diana the huntress". As the virtues of rare curative herbs passed into the blood of animals who ate them, the goddess, like her worshippers, hunted the animals in question, or became their protector.

[1] *The Chinese Traveller* (London, 1772), Vol. I, p. 247.

Pliny, in his twenty-eighth book, having, as Dr. Rendel Harris notes, " exhausted the herbals", shows that "a larger medicine is to be found in animals and in man ".[1]

In China the stag or deer, the stork, and the tortoise are associated with the Tree of Life as "emblems of longevity". One is reminded in this connection of the Western, Eastern, and Far Eastern legends about birds that pluck and carry to human beings leaves of "the plant of life" or "fungus of immortality", and of Mykenæan and Ancient Egyptian representations of bulls, goats, deer, &c., browsing on vines and other trees or bushes that were supposed to contain the elixir of life, being sacred to the goddess and shown as symbols of her or of the god with whom she was associated as mother or spouse.

Another famous Far Eastern curative "wort" is the *ginseng*. Like the fungus of immortality, it grew on one of the Islands of the Blest. Taken with mermaid's flesh, it was supposed to lengthen the life of man for several centuries.

"As described by Father Jartoux", says the eighteenth-century English writer, already quoted,[2] "it has a white root, somewhat knotty, about half as thick as one's little finger; and as it frequently parts into two branches, not unlike the forked parts of a man, it is said from thence to have obtained the name of *ginseng*, which implies a resemblance of the human form, though indeed it has no more of such a likeness than is usual among other roots. From the root arises a perfectly smooth and roundish stem, of a pretty deep-red colour, except towards the surface of the ground, where it is somewhat whiter. At the top of the stem is a sort of joint or knot, formed by

---

[1] *The Ascent of Olympus*, p. 82.   [2] *The Chinese Traveller*, Vol. I, p. 239.

the shooting out of four branches, sometimes more, sometimes less, which spread as from a centre.   The colour of
the branches underneath is green, with a whitish mixture,
and the upper part is of a deep red like the stem. . . .
Each branch has five leaves," and the leaves "make
a circular figure nearly parallel to the surface of the
earth".   The berries are of "a beautiful red colour".

Here we have hints of the mandrake without a doubt.
As a matter of fact, the *ginseng* has been identified with
the mandrake.   The plant evidently attracted attention
because of its colours and form.   As it has a red stem
and red berries, it is not surprising to learn that "it
strengthens the vital spirits, is good against dizziness
in the head and dimness of sight, and prolongs life to
extreme old age", and that "those who are in health
often use it to render themselves more strong and
vigorous".   The four-leaved *ginseng*, like the four-leaved
clover, was apparently a symbol of the four cardinal
points.   Its "five leaves" and the "circular figure formed
by them" must have attracted those who selected five
colours for their gods and adored the sun.

The *ginseng* is found "on the declivities of mountains
covered with thick forests, upon the banks of torrents or
about the roots of trees, and amidst a thousand other
different forms of vegetables".

Conflicts took place between Tartars and Chinese for
possession of the *ginseng*, and one Tartar king had "the
whole province where the *ginseng* grows encompassed by
wooden palisades".   Guards patrolled about "to hinder
the Chinese from searching for it (*ginseng*)".

Tea first came into use in China as a life-prolonger.
The shrub is an evergreen, and appears to have attracted
the attention of the Chinese herbalists on that account.
Our eighteenth-century writer says: "As to the properties

of tea, they are very much controverted by our physicians; but the Chinese reckon it an excellent diluter and purifier of the blood, a great strengthener of the brain and stomach, a promoter of digestion, perspiration, and cleanser of the veins and urethra". Large quantities of tea were in China given "in fevers and some sorts of colics". Our author adds: "That the gout and stone are unknown in China is ascribed to the use of this plant".[1]

Apparently we owe not only some valuable medicines, but even the familiar cup of tea, to the ancient searchers for the elixir of life and curative herbs. Intoxicating liquors (*aqua vitæ*, i.e. "water of life") have a similar history. They were supposed to impart vigour to the body and prolong life. Withal, like the intoxicating "soma", drunk by Aryo-Indian priests, they had a religious value as they produced "prophetic states". Even the opium habit had a religious origin. *Aqua vitæ* was impregnated with "soul substance", as was the juice of grapes, or, as the Hebrews put it, "the blood of grapes".[2]

As Far Eastern beliefs associated with curative plants and curative stones (like jade) have filtered westward, so did Western beliefs filter eastward. Dr. Rendel Harris has shown that myths and beliefs connected with the ivy and mugwort, which were so prevalent in Ancient Greece, can be traced across Siberia to Kamschatka. The Ainus of Japan regard the mistletoe as an "All-heal", as did the ancient Europeans. "The discovery of the primitive sanctity of ivy, mugwort, and mistletoe", says Dr. Harris, "makes a strong link between the early Greeks and other early peoples both East and West, and it is probable that we shall find many more contacts between peoples

---

[1] *The Chinese Traveller*, Vol. I, pp. 237 *et seq.*   [2] *Genesis*, xlix, 11.

that, as far as geography and culture go, are altogether remote."[1]

There are many Far Eastern stories about men and women who have escaped threatened death by eating herbs, or pine resin, or some magic fruit.

One herb, called *huchu*, was first discovered to have special virtues by a man who, when crossing a mountain, fell into a deep declivity and was unable to get out of it, not only on account of the injuries he had sustained, but because the rocks were as smooth as glass. He looked about for something to eat, and saw only the *huchu* herb. Plucking it out of the thin soil in which it grew, he chewed the root and found that it kept his body at a temperature which prevented him feeling cold, while it also satisfied his desire for food and water. Time passed quickly and pleasantly. He felt happy, slept well, and did not weary.

One day the earth was shaken by a great earthquake that opened a way of escape for him. The man at once left his mountain prison and set off for home.

On reaching his house he found, to his surprise, that it was inhabited by strangers. He spoke to them, asking why they were there, and inquiring regarding his wife and children. The strangers only scoffed at him. Then he wandered through the village, searching for old friends, but could not find one. He, however, interested a wise old man in his case. An examination was made of the family annals, and it was discovered that the name given by the man had been recorded three centuries earlier as that of a member of the family who had mysteriously disappeared.

The Chinese Rip Van Winkle then told the story of his life in the mountain cavity, and how he had been

---

[1] *The Ascent of Olympus* (note on *Ivy and Mugwort in Siberia*), pp. 96 *et seq.*

sustained by the *huchu* herb. In this manner, according to Chinese tradition, the discovery was made that the herb "prolongs life, cures baldness, turns grey hair black again, and tends to renew one's youth". Great quantities of *huchu* tea must be drunk for a considerable time, and no other food taken, if the desired results are to be fully achieved.

Other Rip Van Winkle stories tell of men who have lived for centuries while conversing with immortals met by chance, or while taking part in their amusements like the men in Western European stories, who enter fairy knolls and dance with fairy women, and think they have danced for a single hour, but find, when they come out, that a whole year has gone past.

One day a Taoist priest, named Wang Chih, entered a mountain forest to gather firewood. He came to a cave in which sat two aged men playing chess, while others looked on. The game fascinated Wang Chih, so he entered the cave, laid aside his chopper, and looked on. When he began to feel hungry and thirsty he moved as if to rise up and go away, although the game had not come to an end. One of the spectators, however, divining his intention, handed him a kernel, which looked like a date stone, saying, "Suck that".

Wang Chih put the kernel in his mouth and found that it refreshed him so that he experienced no further desire for food or drink.

The chess-playing continued in silence, and several hours, as it seemed, flew past. Then one of the old men spoke to Wang Chih, saying: "It is now a long time since you came to join our company. I think you should return home."

Wang Chih rose to his feet. When he grasped his chopper he was astonished to find that the handle crumbled to dust. On reaching home, he discovered, like the man who fed on the *huchu* herb, that he had been missing for one or two centuries. The old men with whom he had mingled in the cave were the immortals, known to the Chinese as *Sten Nung*, to the Japanese as *Sennin*, and to the Indians as *Rishis*—a class of demi-gods who once lived on earth and achieved great merit, in the spiritual sense, by practising austerities in solitude and for long periods.

The reference to the date stone is of special interest. In Babylonia and Assyria the date palm was one of the holy trees. It was cultivated in southern Persia, and may have been introduced into China from that quarter. Another possibility is that the seeds were got from dates carried by Arab traders to China, or obtained from Arabs by Chinese traders. One of the Chinese names for the date resembles the Ancient Egyptian designation, *bunnu*. Laufer, who discusses this problem,[1] refers to early Chinese texts that make mention of Mo-lin, a distant country in which dark-complexioned natives subsist on dates. Mo-lin, earlier Mwa-lin, is, Laufer thinks, "intended for the Malindi of Edrīsī or Mulanda of Yāqūt, now Malindi, south of the Equator, in Seyidieh Province of British East Africa". The lore connected with other Trees of Life in China appears to have been transferred to the imported date palm. One of its names is "jujube of a thousand years", or "jujube of ten thousand years". Laufer quotes a Chinese description of the date palm which emphasizes the fact that it "remains ever green", and tells that "when the kernel ripens, the seeds are black. In their appearance they resemble dried jujubes. They are good to eat, and as sweet as candy."[2]

Another Chinese Rip Van Winkle story relates that

[1] *Sino-Iranica* (Chicago, 1919), pp. 385 *et seq.*   [2] *Ibid.*, p. 386.

two men who wandered among the mountains met two pretty girls. They were entertained by them, and fed on a concoction prepared from hemp. Seven generations went past while they enjoyed the company of the girls.

The hemp (old Persian and Sanskrit *bangha*) was cultivated at a remote period in China and Iran. A drug prepared from the seed is supposed to prolong life and to inspire those who partake of it to prophesy, after seeing visions and dreaming dreams. The "bang" habit is as bad as the opium habit.

In the tree-lore of China there are interesting links between trees and stones. It has been shown that jade was an "avatar" of the mother-goddess, who created it for the benefit of mankind; that tree foliage was identified with jade; that dragons were born from stones; certain coloured stones were "dragon eggs", the eggs of the "Dragon Mother", the mother-goddess herself, who had "many forms and many colours". Sacred stones were supposed to have dropped from the sky, or to have grown in the earth. Pliny refers to a stone that fell from the sun.

In Ancient Egypt it was believed that the creative or fertilizing tears of the beneficent deities, like those of Osiris and Isis, caused good shrubs to spring up, and that the tears of a deity like Set, who became the personification of evil, produced poisonous plants. The weeping Prajapati of the Ayro-Indians resembles the weeping sun-god Ra of Egypt. At the beginning, Prajapati's tears fell into the water and "became the air", and the tears he "wiped away, upwards, became the sky".[1]

It is evident that the idea of the weeping deity reached China, for there are references to "tree tears"

[1] *Indian Myth and Legend*, p. 100.

and to "stone tears". Both the tree and stone "avatars" of the Great Mother or Great Father shed creative tears.

The Chinese appear to have discovered their wonderful "weeping tree" in Turkestan in the second century B.C., but the beliefs connected with it were evidently of greater antiquity. They already knew about the weeping deities who created good and baneful vegetation, and the discovery of the tree, it would appear, simply afforded proof to them of the truth of their beliefs.

The tree in question (the *hu t'un* tree) has been identified by Laufer as the balsam poplar. "This tree", he quotes from a Chinese commentator, "is punctured by insects, whereupon flows down a juice, that is commonly termed *hu t'un lei* ('*hu t'un* tears'), because it is said to resemble human tears. When this substance penetrates earth or stone it coagulates into a solid mass, somewhat on the order of rock salt." Laufer notes that Pliny "speaks of a thorny shrub in Ariana, on the borders of India, valuable for its tears, resembling the myrrh, but difficult of access on account of the adhering thorns. It is not known what plant is to be understood by the Plinian text; but the analogy of the tears," comments Laufer, "with the above Chinese term is noteworthy."

An ancient Chinese scholar, dealing with the references to the weeping trees, says that "its sap sinks into the earth, and is similar to earth and stone. It is used as a dye, like the ginger stone" (a variety of stalactite). Ta Min, who lived in the tenth century of our era, wrote regarding the tree, "There are two kinds—a tree sap, which is not employed in the Pharmacopœia, and a stone sap collected on the surface of stones; this one only is utilized as medicine. It resembles in appearance small pieces of stone, and those coloured like loess take the first place. The latter was employed as a remedy for toothache."[1]

In Babylonia toothache was supposed to be caused by the marsh-worm demon which devours "the blood of the teeth" and "destroys the strength of the gums". The god Ea smites the worm, which is a form of the dragon Tiamat.[2]

The antique conception enshrined in the " weeping tree" is that the mother-goddess of the sky sheds tears, which cause the tree to grow, and that, as the tree, she sheds tears that become stones, while the stones shed tears that provide soul substance to cure disease by removing pain and promoting health. In Egypt the stone specially sacred to the sky-goddess Hathor was the turquoise, in which was, apparently, concentrated the vital essence or "soul substance" of the sky. The goddess sprang from water, and her tears were drops of the primeval water from which all things that are issued forth. Those stones that contained water were in China "dragon stones" or "dragon eggs". In various countries there are legends about deities, and men and women have sprung from moisture - shedding stones. The mother-goddess of Scotland, who presides over the winter season, transforms herself at the beginning of summer into a stone that is often seen to be covered with moisture. In Norse mythology the earliest gods spring from stones that have been licked by the primeval mother-cow. Mithra of Persia sprang from a rock. Indonesian beliefs regarding moist stones, from which issue water and human beings, are fairly common.[3]

The Kayan of Sumatra are familiar with the beliefs that connect stones and vegetables with the sky and water.

---

[1] Sino-Iranica, pp. 339–42.   [2] Myths of Babylonia and Assyria, pp. 234–5.
[3] Perry, Megalithic Culture of Indonesia, p. 68.

They say that "in the beginning there was a rock.   On
this rain fell and gave rise to moss, and the worms, aided
by the dung beetles, made soil by their castings.   Then
a sword handle came down from the sun and became
a large tree.   From the moon came a creeper which,
hanging from the tree, mated through the action of the
wind."   From this union of tree and creeper, i.e. sun
and moon, "the first men were produced".[1]

The connection between sky, plant, and animals is
found in the lore regarding the Chinese *sant si* mountain
herb which is eaten by goats.   This herb, like other
herbs, is produced from the body-moisture of the goddess;
it is the goddess herself—the goddess who sprang from
water.   The plant is guarded by the mountain goat as
the pearls are guarded by the shark, and the goat, which
browses on the plant, is, like the shark, an avatar of the
goddess.   Goat's blood is therefore as efficacious as the
sap of the herb.

The goat or ram is the vehicle of the Indian fire
and lightning god Agni; the Norse god Thor has a car
drawn by goats.   Dionysos, as Bromios (the Thunderer),
has a goat "avatar", too, and he is the god of wine
(Bacchus)—the wine, the "blood of grapes", being the
elixir of life.   Osiris, who had a ram form, was to the
Ancient Egyptians "Lord of the Overflowing Wine".
European witches ride naked on goats or on brooms;
the devil had a goat form.

In China, as has been shown, the dragon-herb, peach,
vine, pine, fungus of immortality, *ginseng*, &c., received
their sap, or blood, or "soul substance" from rain
released by dragon gods, who thundered like Bromios-
Dionysos.   The inexhaustible pot from which life-giving
water came was in the moon.   This Pot was the mother-

---

[1] *Megalithic Culture of Indonesia*, p. 92.

goddess, who had a star form. A fertilizing tear from the goddess-star, which falls on the "Night of the Drop", is still supposed in Egypt to cause the Nile to rise in flood.

We should expect to find the Chinese mythological cycle completed by an arbitrary connection between the goat or ram and sacred stones.

There are, to begin with, celestial goats. Some of the Far Eastern demi-gods, already referred to, ride through "Cloud-land" on the backs of goats or sheep. One of the eight demi-gods, who personify the eight points of the compass, is called by the Chinese Hwang Ch'u-P'ing, and by the Japanese Koshohei. He is said to be an incarnation of the "rain-priest", Ch'ih Sung Tze, who has for his wife a daughter of the Royal Mother of the West, the mother-goddess of the Peach Tree of Life.

The Japanese version of the legend of the famous Koshohei is given by Joly as follows: "Koshohei, when fifteen years old, led his herd of goats to the Kin Hwa mountains, and, having found a grotto, stayed there for forty years in meditation. His brother, Shoki, was a priest, and he vowed to find the missing shepherd. Once he walked near the mountain and he was told of the recluse by a sage named Zenju, and set out to find him. He recognized his brother, but expressed his astonishment at the absence of sheep or goats. Koshohei thereupon touched with his staff the white stones with which the ground was strewn, and as he touched them they became alive in the shape of goats."[1]

Goats might become stones. The Great Mother was a stone, rock, or mountain, having the power to assume many forms, because she was the life of all things and the

[1] *Legend in Japanese Art*, p. 195.

substance of all things. The goddess was the Mountain of Dawn in labour that brought forth the mouse-form of the sun (Smintheus Apollo), or the antelope form of the sun, or the hawk or eagle form, or the human form, or the egg containing the sun-god. She was also the sun-boat—the dragon-ship of the sun. The five holy mountains of China appear to have been originally connected with the goddess and her sons—the gods of the four quarters.

In China deities might on occasion take the form of stones or reptiles. During the Chou Dynasty (756 B.C.) "one of the feudal dukes", says Giles, "saw a vision of a yellow serpent which descended from heaven, and laid its head on the slope of a mountain. The duke spoke of this to his astrologer, who said, ' It is a manifestation of God; sacrifice to it '. In 747 B.C. another duke found on a mountain a being in the semblance of a stone. Sacrifices were at once offered, and the stone was deified and received regular worship from that time forward."[1]

Giles states further in connection with Chinese god-stones: "Under 532 B.C. we have the record of a stone speaking. The Marquis Lu inquired of his chief musician if this was a fact, and received the following answer: " Stones cannot speak. Perhaps this one was possessed by a spirit. If not, the people must have heard wrong. And yet it is said that when things are done out of season and discontents and complaints are stirring among the people, then speechless things do speak."[2]

Precious stones were, like boulders or mountains, linked with the Great Mother. In Egypt the red jaspar amulet, called "the girdle of Isis", was supposed to be a precious drop of the life-blood of that goddess. Herbs were connected with precious stones, and were credited

[1] *Religions of Ancient China*, pp. 24–5.   [2] *Ibid*, pp. 38–9.

with the attributes and characteristics of these stones. There are many references in Chinese, Indian, and other texts and folk-lores to gems that gleam in darkness. No gems do. The mandrake was similarly believed to shine at night. Both gem and herb were associated with the moon, a form of the mother-goddess, and were supposed to give forth light like the moon,[1] just as stones associated with the rain-mother were supposed to become moist, or to send forth a stream of water, or to shed tears like the "weeping trees", and like the sky from which drop rain and dew. The attributes of the goddess were shared by her "avatars".

The amount or strength of the "soul-substance" in trees, herbs, well-water, stones, and animals varied greatly. Some elixirs derived from one or other of these "avatars" might prolong life by a few years; other elixirs might ensure many years of health.

The difference between a medicinal herb and the herb of immortality was one of degree in potency. The former was imbued with sufficient "soul-substance" to cure a patient suffering from a disease, or to give good health for months, or even years; the latter gave extremely good health, and those who partook of it lived for long periods in the Otherworld.

Even the "spiritual beings" (*ling*) of China were graded. The four *ling*, as De Visser states, are "the unicorn, the phœnix, the tortoise, and the dragon". The dragon is credited with being possessed of "most *ling* of all creatures".[2]

Stones were likewise graded. Precious stones had more *ling* than ordinary stones. Precious stones are sometimes referred to as *pi-si*. One Chinese writer says

---

[1] See Chapter XIII *re* shining gems, jade, coral, &c.
[2] *The Dragon in China and Japan*, pp. 39 and 64.

that "the best *pi-si* are deep-red in colour; that those
in which purple, yellow, and green are combined, and
the white ones take the second place; while those half
white and half black are of the third grade".[1]

Stones that displayed five colours combined apparently
all the virtues of the five deities—the gods of the four
quarters, and the sun, their chief. These were all children
of the sixth deity, the Great Mother, who was the water
on earth and the water above the firmament and the
moon. The moon contained, as has been said, the "Pot"
of fertilizing water which created all the water that flows
into the Earth "Pot".   In China, as in Egypt and
Western Europe, the Great Mother was the reproductive
principle in Nature, the source of the moisture of life, the
blood which is life, the sap of trees, the soul-substance in
herbs, in fruit, in pearls, and in precious stones and
precious metals—precious because of their close association with her.

It was the human dread of death and pain, the human
desire for health and long life, and for the renewal of
youth that instigated early man to search for the well of
life, the plant of life, the curative herb, the pearl, and
precious stones and precious metals. But before the search
began, the complex ideas about the origin of life and the
means by which it might be prolonged, which are reviewed
in this chapter, passed through a long process of development in the most ancient centres of civilization.   In
China we meet not only with primitive ideas regarding
life-giving food and water, but with ideas that had gradually
developed for centuries outside China after the earliest
attempts had been made to reanimate the corpse, not
merely by painting it, but by preventing the body from
decaying.   In the history of mummification in Egypt

----

[1] Laufer, *Sino-Iranica*, p. 568.

may be found the history of complex beliefs that travelled far and wide.[1] Even those peoples who did not adopt, or, at any rate, perpetuate the custom of mummification, adopted the belief that it was necessary to preserve the corpse. This belief is still prevalent in China, as will be shown, but magic takes the place of surgery.

In the next chapter evidence will be provided to indicate how the overland "drift" of culture towards China was impelled by the forces at work in Babylonia and Egypt.

[1] Elliot Smith, *The Migration of Early Culture* (London, 1915), and *The Evolution of the Dragon* (London, 1919).

CHAPTER XII

How Copper-culture reached China

Metals connected with Deities—Introduction of Copper—Struggles for the First "Mine-Land"—Early Metal-working in Caucasus, Armenia, and Persia—Civilizations of Trans-Caspian Oases—Babylonian Influence in Mid Asia—Bronze and Jade carried into Europe—Ancient "Gold Rushes" to Siberia—Discoveries in Chinese Turkestan—Jade carried to Babylonia—Links between China, Iran, and Siberia—Bronze-links between China and Europe— Evidence of Ornaments and Myths—Early Metal-working—Far Eastern and European Furnaces Identical—Chinese Civilization dates from 1700 B.C.— Culture-mixing in Ancient Times.

The persistent and enterprising search for wealth in ancient times, which, as will be shown in this chapter, had so much to do with the spread of civilization, may seem quite a natural thing to modern man. But it is really as remarkable, when we consider the circumstances, to find the early peoples possessed of the greed of gold as it would be to find hungry men who have been shipwrecked on a lonely island more concerned about its mineral resources than the food and water they were absolutely in need of. What was the good of gold in an ancient civilization that had no coinage? What attraction could it possibly hold for desert nomads?

The value attached to gold, which is a comparatively useless metal, has always been a fictitious value. As we have seen, it became precious in ancient times, not because of its purchasing power, but for the reason that it had religious associations. The early peoples regarded the precious metal as an "avatar" of the life-giving and life-sustaining Great Mother goddess — the "Golden Hathor", the "Golden Aphrodite".

In Egypt, Babylonia, Greece, India, and China the cow- and sky-goddess, the source of fertilizing water, was, in the literal sense, a goddess of gold. In India one of the five Sanskrit names for gold is Chandra[1] ("the moon"), and the Indus was called "Golden Stream", not merely because gold was found in its sand, but because of its connection with the celestials. "Gold is the object of the wishes of the Vedic singer, and golden treasures are mentioned as given by patrons, along with cows and horses. Gold was used for ornaments for neck and breast, for ear-rings, and even for cups. Gold is always associated with the gods. All that is connected with them is of gold; the horses of the sun are 'gold skinned', and so on." This summary by two distinguished Sanskrit scholars emphasizes the close connection that existed in India between gold and gold ornaments and religious beliefs.[2]

"Gold", a reader may contend, "is, of course, a beautiful metal, and the ancients may well have been attracted by its beauty when they began to utilize it for ornaments." But is there any proof that ornaments were adopted, because, in the first place, they made appeal to the æsthetic sense, which, after all, is a cultivated sense, and not to be entirely divorced from certain mental leanings produced by the experiences and customs of many generations? Do ornaments really beautify those who wear them? Was it the æsthetic sense that prompted the early peoples to pierce their noses and ears; and to extend the lobes of their ears so as to

---

[1] The other names are Jāta-rūpa, Su-varna, Harita, and Hiranya.
[2] Macdonell and Keith, *Vedic Index of Names and Subjects* (London, 1912), Vol. II, p. 504. See also for moon and gold, Vol. I, 254.

"adorn" themselves with shells, stones, and pieces of metal? Can we divorce the practice of mutilation from its association with crude religious beliefs? Inherited ideas of beauty may be wrong ideas, and it can be said of the modern lady who wears collections of brilliant and costly jewels that she is not necessarily made more beautiful by perpetuating a custom rooted in the grossest superstitions of antiquity, for these jewels were originally charms to preserve health, to regulate the flow of blood, to promote fertility and birth, and, generally speaking, to secure "luck" by bringing the wearer into close touch with the "deities", whose "soul-substance" was contained in them.

When the æsthetic sense of mankind reached that high stage of development represented by Greek sculpture, the so-called ornaments were discarded and the human form depicted in all its natural beauty and charm.

Whatever was holy seemed beautiful to the early people, and that is why in a country like India, with its wealth of exquisitely coloured flowers, the Sanskrit names for gold include *Jāta-rūpa* (native beauty), and *Su-varna* (good, or beautiful colour). The gold colour was really a luck-bringing colour, and therefore beautiful to Aryan eyes.

Having attached in their homelands a fictitious religious value to gold, the early prospectors and miners carried their beliefs and customs with them wherever they went, and these were in time adopted by the peoples with whom they came into contact.

When Columbus crossed the Atlantic he and his followers greatly astonished the unsophisticated natives of the New World by their anxiety to obtain precious metals. They found, to their joy, that "the sands of the mountain streams glittered with particles of gold;

these", as Washington Irving says,[1] "the natives would skilfully separate and give to the Spaniards, without expecting a recompense".

No doubt the early searchers for gold in Africa and Asia met with many peoples who were as much amused and interested, and as helpful, as were the natives of the New World, who welcomed the Spaniards as visitors from the sky.

Gold was the earliest metal worked by man. It was first used in Egypt to fashion imitation sea-shells, and the magical and religious value attached to the shells was transferred to the gold which, in consequence, became "precious" or "holy".

Copper was the next metal to be worked. It was similarly used for the manufacture of personal ornaments and other sacred objects, being regarded apparently, to begin with, as a variety of gold. But in time—some centuries, it would appear, after copper was first extracted from malachite—some pioneer of a new era began to utilize it as a substitute for flint, and copper knives and other implements were introduced. This discovery of the usefulness of copper had far-reaching effects, and greatly increased the demand for the magical metal. Increasing numbers of miners were employed, and search was made for new copper-mines by enterprising prospectors who, in Egypt, were employed, or, at any rate, protected, by the State. This search had much to do with promoting race movements, and introducing not only new modes of life but new modes of thought into lands situated at great distances from the areas in which these modes of life and thought had origin. The metal-workers were the missionaries of a New Age. In this chapter it will be shown how they reached China.

[1] *Life and Voyages of Christopher Columbus* (London, 1703 Edition), p. 243.

Archæologists are not agreed as to where copper was first used for the manufacture of weapons and implements. Some favour Egypt, and others Mesopotamia. In the former country the useful metal was worked in pre-Dynastic times, that is, before 3500 B.C. or 4500 B.C. " Copper ornaments and objects, found in graves earlier than the middle pre-Dynastic period", wrote the late Mr. Leonard W. King, " are small and of little practical utility as compared with the beautifully flaked flint knives, daggers, and lances. . . . At a rather later stage in the pre-Dynastic period, copper dagger-blades and adzes were produced in imitation of flint and stone forms, and these mark the transition to the heavy weapons and tools of copper which, in the early Dynastic period, largely ousted flint and stone implements for practical use. The gradual attainment of skill in the working of copper ore on the part of the early Egyptians had a marked effect on the whole status of their culture. Their improved weapons enabled them by conquest to draw their raw materials from a far more extended area."[1]

Copper was found in the wadis of Upper Egypt and on the Red Sea coast—in those very areas in which gold was worked for generations before copper was extracted from malachite. At a later period the Pharaohs sent gangs of miners to work the copper-mines in the Sinaitic peninsula. King Semerket, of the early Dynastic age, had men extracting copper in the Wadi Maghara. " His expedition was exposed to the depredations of the wild tribes of Beduin . . . and he recorded his punishment of them in a relief on the rocks of the Wadi." There is evidence that at this remote period the Pharaohs " maintained foreign relations with far remote peoples".[2] A record of a later age (c. 2000 B.C.) affords us a vivid

[1] *History of Sumer and Akkad,* pp. 326–7.   [2] Breasted, *A History of Egypt,* p. 48.

glimpse of life in the "Mine-Land". An official re-corded in an inscription that he had been sent there in what he calls the "Evil summer season". He complained, "It is not the season for going to this Mine-Land. . . . The highlands are hot in summer, and the mountains brand the skin." Yet he could boast that "he extracted more copper than he had been ordered to obtain".[1]

The transition from stone to copper cannot be traced in ancient Babylonia. Sumerian history begins at the seaport Eridu, when that centre of civilization was situated at the head of the Persian Gulf—a fact that suggests the settlement there of seafaring colonists. At the dawn of Sumerian culture, copper tools and weapons had come into use. No metals could be found in the alluvial "plain of Shinar".

The early Babylonians (Sumerians) had to obtain their supplies of copper from Sinai, Armenia, the Caucasus area, and Persia. It may be that their earliest supplies came from Sinai, and that the battles in that "Mine-Land", recorded in early Egyptian inscriptions, were fought between rival claimants of the ore from the Nile valley and the valley of the Tigris and Euphrates. One ancient Pharaoh refers in an inscription to his "first occurrence of smiting the Easterners" in Sinai. "This designation", comments Breasted, "of the event as the 'first occurrence' would indicate that it was a customary thing for the kings of the time (First Dynasty, c. 3500 B.C.) to chastise the barbarians."[2] But were they really "barbarians"? Is it likely that barbarians would be found in such a region, especially in summer? It is more probable that the "Easterners" came from an area in which the demand for copper was as great as it was in Egypt.

[1] Breasted, *A History of Egypt*, p. 190.   [2] *Ibid*, p. 48.

The regular battles between the ancient "peggers-out" of "claims" in Mine-Land no doubt forced the "Easterners" to search for copper elsewhere. By following the course of the Tigris the Sumerian prospectors were led to the rich mineral area of the Armenian Highlands, and it is of special significance in this connection to find that the earliest Assyrian colonies were founded by Sumerians. Apparently Nineveh (Mosul) had origin as a trading centre at which metal ores were collected and sent southward some time before the Semitic Akkadians obtained control of the northern part of the Babylonian plain.

The copper obtained from Armenia and other western Asiatic areas was less suitable than Sinaitic copper, being much softer. Sinaitic and Egyptian copper is naturally hard on account of the proportion of sulphur it contains. But after tin was found, and it was discovered that, when mixed with copper, it produced the hard amalgam known as bronze, the Sumerians appear to have entirely deserted the Sinaitic Mine-Land, and left it to the Egyptians.

The Egyptians continued in their Copper Age until their civilization ceased to be controlled by native kings.

Babylonia had likewise a Copper Age to begin with, but copper was at an early period entirely supplanted by bronze, except for religious purposes—a fact which is of great importance, especially when it is found that the religious beliefs associated with copper and gold were disseminated far and wide by the early miners—the troglodytes of Sinai in the early Egyptian texts—who formed colonies that became industrial and trading centres. Votive images found in Babylonia are of copper. A good example of early Sumerian religious objects is the interesting bull's head in copper from Tello, which is dated c. 3000 B.C. The eyes of this image of the bull-god—

the "Bull of Heaven", the sky-god, whose mother or spouse was the "Cow of Heaven"—"are inlaid with mother-of-pearl and lapis-lazuli". A "very similar method is met with in the copper head of a goat which was found at Fara".[1] Here we find fused in early Sumerian religious objects complex religious beliefs connected with domesticated animals, sea-shells, and metals.

The opinion, suggested here by the writer, that the battles between rival miners in Sinai compelled the Sumerians to search for copper elsewhere and to discover means whereby the softer copper could be hardened, appears to accord with the view that bronze was first manufactured in Babylonia, or in some area colonized by Babylonia. In his able summary of the archæological evidence regarding the introduction of bronze, Sir Hercules Read shows that "the attribution of the discovery to Babylonia is preferred as offering fewest difficulties".[2]

Recent archæological finds make out a good case for Russian Turkestan as the "cradle of the bronze industry".

In Troy and Crete bronze supplanted flint and obsidian. There was no Copper Age in either of these culture centres. The copper artifacts found in Crete are simply small and useless votive axes and other religious objects.

Whence did the Babylonians receive, after the discovery was made how to manufacture bronze, the necessary supplies of tin? Armenia and the Caucasus "appear", as Read says, "to be devoid of stanniferous ores". Apparently the early metal-searchers had gone as far as Khorassan in Persia before their fellows had ceased to wage battles with Egyptians in the Sinaitic "Mine-Land". Tin

---

[1] L. W. King, *A History of Sumer and Akkad*, pp. 74, 75.
[2] *British Museum Guide to the Antiquities of the Bronze Age*, p. 10.

has been located at Khorassan and "in other parts of Persia, near Asterabad and Tabriz.[1] . . . From such areas as these", Reid says, "the tin used in casting the earliest bronze may have been derived." We are now fairly on our way along the highway leading to China. "In Eastern Asia, beyond the radius of the ancient civilizations of Mesopotamia", Read continues, "there would seem to be no region likely to have witnessed the discovery (of how to work bronze) nearer than Southern China; for India, which has copper implements of a very primitive type, is poor in tin . . . while the Malay peninsula, an extremely rich stanniferous region, does not appear to have been mined in very ancient times".[2] It is unlikely that bronze was first manufactured in China, considering the period of its introduction into Babylonia, which antedates by several centuries the earliest traces of civilization in the Far East.

The history of the development of the industries and commerce of early Babylonia is the history of the growth and dissemination of civilization, not only in western Asia, but in the "Mid East" and the "Far East".

Babylonia, the Asiatic granary of the ancient world, lay across the trade routes. Both its situation and its agricultural resources gave it great commercial importance. It had abundant supplies of surplus food to stimulate trade, and its industrial activity created a demand for materials that could not be obtained in the rich alluvial plain. "Over the Persian Gulf", says Professor Goodspeed,[3] "teak-wood, found in Eridu (the seaside "cradle" of Sumerian culture), was brought from India. Cotton also made its way from the same source to the southern cities. Over Arabia, by way of Ur, which stood at the

---

[1] *British Museum Guide to the Antiquities of the Bronze Age*, p. 9.
[2] *Ibid.*, p. 9. [3] *A History of the Babylonians and Assyrians*, p. 74.

foot of a natural opening from the desert . . . were led the caravans laden with stone, spices, copper, and gold[1] from Sinai, Yemen, and Egypt.   Door-sockets of Sinaitic stone found at Nippur attest this traffic."   Cedar wood was imported from the Syrian mountains "for the adornment of palaces and temples.   From the east, down the pass of Holwan, came the marble and precious metal of the mountains.   Much of this raw material was worked over by Babylonian artisans and shipped back to less-favoured lands, along with the grain, dates, and fish, the rugs and cloths of native production.   All this traffic was in the hands of Babylonian traders, who fearlessly ventured into the borders of distant countries, and *must have carried with them thither the knowledge of the civilization and wealth of their own home, for only thus can the widespread influence of Babylonian culture in the earliest periods be explained.*"

It was evidently due to the influence of the searchers for metals and the traders that the culture of early Sumeria spread across the Iranian plateau.   As Laufer has shown,[2] "the Iranians were the great mediators between the West and the East".   The Chinese "were positive utilitarians, and always interested in matters of reality; they have bequeathed to us a great amount of useful information on Iranian plants, products, animals, minerals, customs, and institutions".   Not only plants but also Western ideas were conveyed to China by the Iranians.[3]

The discoveries of archæological relics made by the De Morgan Expedition in Elam (western Persia), and by the Pumpelly Expedition in Russian Turkestan, have provided further evidence that Sumero-Babylonian civiliza-

[1] In the Tell-el-Amarna letters, Western-Asian monarchs are eloquent in their requests for gold from Egypt.   In one a Babylonian king "asks for much gold" and complains that the last supply was base, and that there was "much loss in melting".

[2] *Sino-Iranica: Chinese Contributions to the History of Civilization in Ancient Iran.* Chicago, 1919.   [3] *Ibid.,* p. 185.

tion exercised great influence over wide areas in ancient times. Unfortunately no such records as those made by the Egyptians who visited Mine-Land have been discovered either in Babylonia or beside the mineral workings exploited by the Sumerians or Akkadians. The Egyptian Pharaohs, as we have seen, had to send military forces to protect their miners, and on one occasion found it necessary to conduct mining operations in the hot season instead of in the cool season, a fact which suggests that the opposition shown by rivals was at times very formidable. It does not follow that the Babylonians had to contend with similar opposition in Armenia and Persia. They appear to have won the co-operation of the native peoples in the mid-Asian mining districts, and to have made it worth their while to keep up the supply of gold, and copper, and tin. Babylonia had corn and manufactured articles to sell, and they made it possible for native chiefs to organize their countries and to acquire wealth and a degree of luxury. Nomadic pastoral peoples became traders, and commmunities of them adopted Babylonian modes of life. Mr. W. J. Perry has shown that in districts where minerals were anciently worked, the system of irrigation, which brought wealth and comfort in Babylonia and the Nile valley, was adopted, and that megalithic monuments were erected.[1]

The early searchers for metals and pearls and precious stones were apparently the initiators of cultural intermingling in many a district outside their native lands.

The mineral area to the south-east of the Caspian Sea appears to have been exploited as early as the third millenium B.C., as was also the mineral area stretching from the Caspian to the eastern coast of the Black Sea.

---

[1] *The Relationship between the Geographical Distribution of Megalithic Monuments and Ancient Times.* Manchester, 1915.

New trade routes were opened up and connections established, not only with Elam and Babylonia in the south,
but with Egypt, through Palestine, and with Crete and
with the whole Ægean area. Troy became the "clearing-
house" of this early trade flowing from western Asia
into Europe. The enterprising sea-kings of Crete appear
to have penetrated the Dardanelles and reached the
eastern shores of the Black Sea, where they tapped the
overland trade routes.[1] Dr. Hubert Schmidt, who accompanied the Pumpelly expedition to Russian Turkestan in 1903–4, found Cretan Vasiliki pottery in one
of the excavated mounds, and, in another, "three-sided
seal-stones of Middle Minoan type (c. 2000 B.C.), engraved with Minoan designs".[2] There is evidence which
suggests that this trade in metals between western Asia
and the Ægean area was in existence long before 2500
B.C., and not long after 3000 B.C.

One of the great centres of Mesopotamian culture in
the south-eastern Caspian area was Anau, near Askabad, on
the Merve-Caspian railway route. Another was Meshed,
which lies to the south-east of Anau in a rich metalliferous
mountain region. One of the "Kurgans" (mounds)
excavated at Anau yielded archæological relics that indicated an early connection between Turkestan and Elam in
south-western Persia. In another "Kurgan" were found
traces of a copper-culture. The early searchers for metals
were evidently the originators or introducers of this culture, and as the stratum contained baked clay figurines
of the Sumerian mother-goddess, the prototype of Ishtar,
little doubt can remain whence came the earliest miners.
This region of desolate sand-dunes was in ancient times
irrigated by the Mesopotamian colonists who sowed not
only the seeds of barley, wheat, and millet, but also the

[1] Mrs. Hawes, *Gournia*, p. 33.   [2] *The Dawn of Mediterranean Civilization*, pp. 62–3.

seeds of civilization, and stimulated progress among the native tribes. The settlers built houses of bricks which had been sun-dried in accordance with the prevailing Babylonian fashion. The Egyptian potter's wheel was introduced—another indication that regular trading relations between Babylonia and Egypt were maintained at a very early period.

Mr. Pumpelly, in the first flush of enthusiasm aroused by the mid-Asia revelations, urged the claim that the agricultural mode of life originated in the Transcaspian Oases, and that it passed thence to Babylonia and Egypt. But the discovery of husks of barley in the stomachs of naturally mummified bodies found in the hot dry sands of Upper Egypt affords proof that cannot be overlooked in this connection.[1] Agriculture was practised in the Nile valley long centuries before the Transcaspian Copper Age was inaugurated. Besides, barley and millet grow wild in the Delta area.

The early Mesopotamian searchers for metals, and their pupils from the Transcaspian region, continued the explorations towards the east. They appear to have wandered to the north-west of the Oxus and the south-east of the Lake Balkash and apparently to the very borders of China. This eastward drift must have been in progress long before the introduction of bronze into central Europe, which had a Stone Age culture for three or four centuries after bronze implements had become common in Troy and Crete. The traders who carried bronze into Hungary carried jade too, and the beliefs which had been connected with jade in Asia. The earliest supplies of European jade objects must have come, as will be shown, from Chinese Turkestan.

There was good reason for the early gold rush to-

[1] Elliot Smith, *The Ancient Egyptians*, pp. 41 *et seq.*

wards the east. Gold can still be easily found "every-where and in every form" in Siberia. The Altai means "gold mountains", and these yield silver and copper as well as gold. Indeed, eastern Siberia is a much richer metalliferous area than western Siberia, and this fact appears to have been ascertained at a very remote period. The searchers for metals not only collected gold, copper, and silver on the Altai Mountains and the area of the upper reaches of the Yenesei River, but also penetrated into Chinese Turkestan, where, as in Russian Turkestan, trading colonies were founded, the metals were worked, and the agricultural mode of life, including the system of irrigation, adopted with undoubted success.[1] Important archæological excavations, conducted by Dr. Stein in Chinese Turkestan, "on behalf of the Indian Govern-ment", have revealed traces of the far-reaching influences exercised by Mesopotamian culture in a region now covered by the vast and confusing sand-dunes of the Taklamakan Desert. At Khotan the discoveries made were of similar character to those at Anau.

Khotan is the ancient trading centre which connected central Asia and India, and India and China. One of the most important products of Khotan is jade—that is, important from the historical point of view. It is un-certain at what period the importation of jade into China from the Khotan area was inaugurated. But there can be no doubt about the antiquity of the jade trade between Chinese Turkestan and Babylonia. Some of the Baby-lonian cylinder-seals were of jade, others being of "marble, jasper, rock-crystal, emerald, amethyst, topaz, chalcedony, onyx, agate, lapis-lazuli, hæmatite, and steatite"[2]—all

---

[1] It seems ridiculous to suggest that irrigation had origin in mid-Asia and not in areas like the deltas of Egypt and Sumeria.
[2] *British Museum Guide to the Babylonian and Assyrian Antiquities*, p. 157.

relics of ancient trade and mining activity. Turquoise was imported into Babylonia from Khotan and Kashgar. The archæological finds made on the site of the ancient Sumerian city at Nippur include cobalt, " presumably from China ".[1] At Nippur was found, too, Persian marble, lapis-lazuli from Bactria, and cedar and cypress from Zagros.

When it is borne in mind that the chief incentive behind the search for precious metals and precious stones was a religious one, we should not express surprise to find that not only the products of centres of ancient civilization were carried across Asia to outlying parts, but also myths, legends, and religious beliefs of complex character. These were given a local colouring in different areas. In northern Siberia, for instance, the local fauna displaced the fauna of the southern religious cults, the reindeer or the goat taking the place of the gazelle or the antelope. Mythological monsters received new parts, just as the dolphin-god of Cretan and other seafaring peoples received an elephant's head in northern India and became the *makara*; and the seafarers' shark-god received in China the head of a lion, although the lion is not found in China. No doubt the lion was introduced into China as a religious art *motif* by some intruding cult. Touching on this phase of the problem of early cultural contact, Ellis H. Minns[2] suggests a number of possibilities to account for the similarities between Siberian and Chinese art. One is that " the resemblance may be due to both (Siberians and Chinese) having borrowed from Iranian or some other Central Asian art. . . . In each case," he adds, " we seem to have an intrusion of monsters ultimately derived from Mesopotamia, the great breeding-ground of monsters." The data sum-

<hr>

[1] Peter, *Nippur II*, p. 134.   [2] *Scythians and Greeks* (1913), p. 280.

marized in a previous chapter[1] dealing with the Chinese dragon affords confirmation of this view.

Dr. Joseph Edkins, writing in the seventies of last century as a Christian missionary who made an intensive study of Chinese religious beliefs at first hand, had much to say about the "grafting process" or culture-mixing. "Every impartial investigator", he wrote, "will probably admit that the ceremonies and ideas of the Chinese sacrifices link them with Western antiquity. The inference to be drawn is this, that the Chinese primeval religion was of common origin with the religions of the West. But if the religion was one, then the political ideas, the mental habits, the sociology, the early arts and knowledge of nature, should have been of common origin also with those of the West."[2]

No doubt the stories brought from Siberia by the early explorers tended to stimulate the imaginations of the myth-makers of Mesopotamia, India, and China. The mineral and hot springs in the cold regions may have been regarded as proof that " the wells of life " had real existence. Some of these wells are so greatly saturated with carbonic acid gas that they burst skin and stone bottles. " Here is living water indeed!" the early explorer may have exclaimed when he attempted to carry away a sample. "The feathers in the air", as Herodotus puts it when referring to the snow, and the aurora borealis must have greatly impressed the early miners in the mysterious Altai region — a region possessing so much mineral wealth that it must have been regarded as a veritable wonderland of the gods by the early prospectors. Who knows but that the story of Gilgamesh's pilgrimage through the dark mountain to the land in which trees bore gems instead of fruit owes something

[1] Chapter V.   [2] *Religion in China* (London 1878, 2nd Ed.), p. 38.

to the narratives of the early explorers who reached mysterious regions rich in metals and gems, where the strange murmurings that fill the air on still winter nights are still referred to as " the whisperings of the stars ", and the aurora borealis, which scatters the darkness and illumines snow-clad mountain ranges and valleys, displays wonderful and vivid colours in great variety.

That the early culture which was disseminated eastward across Siberia to China and westward into Europe was of common origin, is clearly indicated by the archæological remäins.

Dealing with the bronzes of Russia and Siberia, Sir Hercules Read writes: " At both extremities of the vast area stretching from Lake Baikal through the Southern Siberian Steppes across the Ural Mountains to the basin of the Volga, and even beyond to the valleys of the Don and Dnieper, there have been found, generally in tombs, but occasionally on the surface of the ground, implements and weapons marked by the same peculiarities of form, and by a single style of decoration. These objects exhibit an undoubted affinity with those discovered in China; but some of the distinctive features have been traced in the bronze industry of Hungary and the Caucasus; for example, pierced axes and sickles have a close resemblance to Hungarian and Caucasian forms. The Siberian bronzes have this relationship both in the East and West, but their kinship with Chinese antiquities being the more obvious, it is natural to assume that the culture which they represent is of East Asiatic origin." Read notes, however, that " most of the Chinese bronze implements are of developed, and therefore not of primitive forms. . . . Such forms can only have been reached after a long period of evolution, but their prototypes are found neither in the Ural-Altaic region itself, where some objects may indeed be simpler in design than others, but cannot be described as quite primitive; nor as yet within the limits of China."[1]

The evidence afforded by ancient religious beliefs and customs tends to show that the cultural centre in Asia, which stimulated the growth of civilization, was Babylonia, while Egyptian influence flowed northward through Palestine and into Syria. In time the influence of Cretan civilization made itself felt on the eastern shores of the Black Sea. The ebb and flow of cultural influences along the trade routes at various periods renders the problem of highly complex character. But one leading fact appears to emerge. The demand for metals and precious stones in the earliest seats of civilization—that is, in Babylonia and Egypt—stimulated exploration and the spread of a culture based on the agricultural mode of life. Not only was the system of irrigation, first introduced in the Nilotic and Tigro-Euphratean valleys, adopted by colonies of miners and traders who settled in mid-Asia and founded sub-cultural centres that radiated westward and eastward; the religious ideas and customs that had grown up with the agricultural mode of life in the cradles of ancient civilization were adopted too. New experiences and new inventions imparted "local colour" to colonial culture, but the leading religious principles that veined that culture underwent little change. The immemorial quest for the elixir of life was never forgotten. It was not to purchase their daily bread alone that men lived laborious days washing gold dust from river sands, crushing quartz among the Altai Mountains, or quarrying and fishing jade in Chinese Turkestan; they were chiefly concerned about "purchasing" the "food of life" so as to secure immortality. The fear of death, which sent

[1] *British Museum Guide to the Antiquities of the Bronze Age*, p. 107.

Gilgamesh on his long journey, caused many a man in ancient times to wander far and wide in search of life-giving metals, precious stones, pearls, and plants. And so we find in China as in Egypt, in Babylonia as in western Europe, that the quest of immortality was the chief incentive that stimulated research, discovery, and the spread of civilization. The demand for the wood of sacred trees, incense-bearing trees and plants, precious metals and precious stones in the temples of Egypt and Babylonia, had much to do with the development of early trade. The Pharaohs of Egypt and the Patesies of Sumeria fitted out expeditions to obtain treasure for their holy places, and to keep open the trade routes along which the treasure was carried.

That the system of metal-working had anciently an area of origin is emphasized by the investigations conducted by Professor Gowland.[1] He deals first with the Japanese evidence. "The method which was practised, and the furnace employed by the early workers, still", he writes, "survive in use at several mines in Japan at the present time." A hole in the ground forms the furnace, and a bellows is used to introduce the blast from the top. After the copper is smelted it is allowed to cool off, and when it is nearly solidified it is taken out and broken up. "The copper thus produced in Japan is never cast direct from the smelting furnaces into useful forms, but is always resmelted in crucibles, a mode of procedure which undoubtedly prevailed in Europe during the early Metal and the Bronze Ages." The Japanese clay crucibles "are analogous to those found in the pile-dwellings of the Swiss and Upper Austrian lakes".

Dealing with iron-furnaces, the Professor shows that

---

[1] *Archæologia*, p. 276.

the Ancient Egyptian furnace resembled " the Japanese furnace for copper, tin, and lead". The Etruscan furnace also resembled the Egyptian one. " From metallurgical considerations only", Gowland adds, " we would certainly be led to the inference that the Etruscans had obtained their knowledge of the method of extracting metal from that (the Egyptian) source." British evidence suggests that the methods obtaining in ancient times were introduced from " the Mediterranean region of Europe. . . . The actual process for the extraction of iron from its ores in Europe, *in fact in all countries in early times*, was practically the same."

Elsewhere, Professor Gowland has written : " It is important to note . . . that the type of furnace which survives in India among the hill tribes of the Ghats is closely analogous to the prehistoric furnace of the Danube, and of the Jura district in Europe".[1]

" Culture-drifts" can thus be followed in their results. Backward communities that adopted inventions in early times continue to use them in precisely the same manner as did those ancient peoples by whom they were first introduced. In like manner are early beliefs and customs still perpetuated in isolated areas. But it does not follow that all these beliefs had origin among the peoples who still cling to them. Some so-called " primitive" beliefs are really of highly complex character, with as long a history of development as has the primitive type of furnace utilized by the hill tribes of India.

In the next chapter it will be shown that in the jade beliefs of China traces survive of ideas not necessarily of Chinese origin—ideas that, in fact, grew up and passed through processes of development in countries in which jade was never found. For, as the Chinese bronze

---

[1] *Journal of the Royal Anthropological Institute*, Vol. XLII, p. 279.

implements are "not of primitive forms", and therefore not indigenous, neither are all Chinese beliefs and customs "primitive" in the same sense, or, in the real sense, indigenous either. As the stimulus to work metals in China came from an outside source, so, apparently, did the stimulus to search for such a "life-giving" and "luck-conferring" material as jade come from other countries, and from races unrelated to those that occupied China in early times.

The beliefs associated with jade were developed in China, although they did not originate there; and these beliefs were similar to those attached to the pearls, the precious stones, and the precious metals searched for by the ancient prospectors who discovered and first worked jade in Chinese Turkestan and on the borders of China.

To sum up, it would appear that the elements of a religious culture, closely associated with the agricultural mode of life, and common to Sumeria and Egypt, passed across Asia towards China, reaching the Shensi province about 1700 B.C. At a much later period the complex culture of the Egyptian Empire period gradually drifted along the sea route and left its impress on the Chinese coast. Iranian culture, which was impregnated with Babylonian and Egyptian ideas, likewise exercised a persisting influence, and was renewed again and again.

One of the ultimate results of the rise of Persia as a world-power, and of the invasion of Asia by Alexander, was to bring China into direct touch with the Hellenistic world.

Indian influence is represented chiefly by Buddhism. In northern India Buddhism had been blended with Naga (serpent) worship, and when it reached China, the local beliefs regarding dragons were given a Buddhistic colouring. The Chinese Buddhists mixed the newly-imported religious culture with their own.   The "Islands of the Blest" were retained by the cult of the East, and the Western Paradise by the cult of the West.   The latter paradise is unknown to the Buddhists in Burmah and Ceylon, but has never been forgotten by the Buddhists of northern China.   A Buddha called "Boundless Age" was placed in the garden of the Royal Lady of the West, but that goddess still lingered beside the Peach Tree of Immortality, while the sky-goddess continued to weave the web of the constellations, and the pious men and women of the Taoist faith were supposed to reach her stellar Paradise by sailing along the Celestial River in dragon-boats or riding on the back of dragons.   The Chinese Buddhists found ideas regarding Nirvana less satisfying than those associated with the Paradise of the "Peaceful Land of the West" and the higher Paradise of the "Palaces of the Stars", in which dwelt the gods and the demi-gods of the older faiths.

Writing in this connection, Dr. Joseph Edkins says: "A mighty branch of foreign origin has been grafted in the old stock.   The metaphysical religion of Shakyamuni was added to the moral doctrines of Confucius.   Another process may then be witnessed.   A native twig was grafted in the Indian branch.   Modern Taoism has grown up on the model supplied by Buddhism.   That it is possible to observe the *modus operandi* of this repeated grafting, and to estimate the amount of gain and loss to the people of China, resulting from the varied religious teaching which they have thus received, is a circumstance of the greatest interest to the investigator of the world's religions."[1]

[1] *Religion in China,* p. 6.

CHAPTER XIII

The Symbolism of Jade

Jade in Early Times—Used to Reanimate and Preserve the Dead—Jade as a Night-shining Jewel—Connection with the Pearl, Coral, Mandrake, Moon, Dragon, Fish, &c.—Jade Beliefs in Japan—Jade Amulets—The Chinese Cicada Amulet and Egyptian Search—Butterfly, Frog, and Bird Amulets—Jade and the Mother-goddess—The Chinese Universe—Great Bear and "World Mill"—Babylonian Astronomy in China—Star Deities—The Fung-shui Doctrine—Jade Symbols of Deities—Tigress as a Mother-goddess—Links with the West—The Two Souls in China and Egypt—Jade as an Elixir—Jade and Herbs—Jade and Babylonian Nig-gil-ma—Jade and Rhinoceros Horn—Jade Beliefs in Prehistoric Europe—Jade and Colour Symbolism—Jade contains Heat and Moisture—Jade as "The Jewel that Grants all Desires".

One's thoughts at once turn to China when mention is made of jade, for in no other country in the world has it been utilized for such a variety of purposes or connected more closely with the social organization and with religious beliefs and ceremonies.

This tough mineral, which is also called nephrite and "axe-stone", and is of different chemical composition to jadeite, was known to the Chinese at the very dawn of their history. It was used by them at first like flint or obsidian for the manufacture of axes, arrow-heads, knives, and chisels, as well as for votive objects and personal ornaments of magical or religious character, and then, as time went on, for mortuary amulets, for images or symbols of deities, for mirrors,[1] for seals and symbols

---

[1] Jade and other stone mirrors are referred to in ancient texts. No doubt these were religious symbols. None survives. Jade shoes are mentioned too, but there are

of rank, and even for musical instruments, possessing, as it does, wonderful resonant qualities. The latter include jade flutes and jade "luck gongs", which have religious associations.

Native artisans acquired great skill in working this tenacious mineral, and the finest art products in China are those exquisite jade ornaments, symbols, and vessels that survive from various periods of its history. Not only did the accomplished and patient workers, especially of the Han period (200 B.C.–200 A.D.), achieve a high degree of excellence in carving and engraving jade, and in producing beautiful forms; they also dealt with their hard mineral so as to utilize its various colours and shades, and thus increase the æsthetic qualities of their art products. The artistic genius, as well as the religious beliefs, of the Chinese has been enshrined in nephrite.

When the prehistoric Chinese settled in Shensi, they found jade in that area. "All the Chinese questioned by me, experts in antiquarian matters, agree", Laufer writes, "in stating that the jades of the Chou and Han Dynasties are made of indigenous material once dug on the very soil of Shensi Province, that these quarries have been long ago exhausted, no jade whatever being found there nowadays. My informant pointed to Lan-t'ien and Fêng-siang-fu as the chief ancient mines."[1]

But although the early Chinese made use of indigenous jade, it does not follow, as has been noted, that the early beliefs connected with this famous mineral were of indigenous origin. It cannot be overlooked that the symbolism

---

no surviving specimens. In Ireland bronze shoes were worn in ancient times—perhaps in connection with religious ceremonies. Obsidian mirrors were used in Mexico for purposes of divination, and there were stone mirrors in Peru.

[1] *Jade: A Study in Chinese Archæology and Religion*, Berthold Laufer (Field Museum of Natural History, Publication 154, Anthropological Series, Vol. X, Chicago, 1912, p. 23).

of jade is similar in character to the older symbolism of pearls, precious stones, and precious metals, and that the associated beliefs can be traced not in China alone, but in such widely-separated countries as India, Babylonia, and Egypt. There was evidently a psychological motive for the importance attached by the early Chinese to jade, which they called *yu*.[1] It had been regarded elsewhere as a precious mineral before they began to search for it and make use of it, especially for religious purposes.

It is not necessary to go back to the "Age of Stone" to theorize regarding Chinese jade beliefs. It has yet to be established that China had a Neolithic Age. "As far as the present state of our archæological knowledge and the literary records point out", says Laufer, "the Chinese have never passed through an epoch which, for other culture regions, has been designated as a Stone Age."[2]

Stone implements have been found, but, as in ancient Egypt, these were still being manufactured long after metals came into general use.

The fact that the same beliefs were connected with jade as with pearls, shells, gold, &c., is brought out very clearly in Chinese records regarding ancient burial customs. It was considered to be as necessary in ancient China as in ancient Egypt that the bodies of the dead should be preserved from decay. The Egyptians mummified their dead, and laid on and beside them a variety of charms that were supposed to afford protection and assist in the process of reanimation; withal, food offerings were provided. The Chinese, who have long been noted for their tendency to find substitutes for religious offerings, including paper money, believed that the bodies of the dead could be preserved by magic. At any rate, they did not

---

[1] Laufer notes that *yu* included nephrite, jadeite, bowenite, and sometimes "beautiful kinds of serpentine, agalmatolite, and marble".—*Jade*, p. 22.   [2] *Ibid.*, p. 29.

consider it necessary to practise the science of mummification. In the *Li Ki* (chapter 56) the orthodox treatment of the bodies of the Emperor and others is set forth as follows :

"The mouth of the Son of Heaven is stuffed with nine cowries, that of a feudal lord with seven, that of a great officer with five, and that of an ordinary official with three".[1]

Gold and jade were used in like manner. Laufer quotes from Ko Hung the significant statement: "If there is gold and jade in the nine apertures of the corpse, it will preserve the body from putrefaction". A fifth-century Chinese writer says: "When on opening an ancient grave the corpse looks like alive, then there is inside and outside of the body a large quantity of gold and jade. According to the regulations of the Han Dynasty, princes and lords were buried in clothes adorned with pearls and with boxes of jade for the purpose of preserving the body from decay."[2]

According to De Groot, pearls were introduced into the mouth of the dead during the Han Dynasty. "At least", he says, "it is stated that their mouths were filled with rice, and pearls and jade stone were put therein, in accordance with the established ceremonial usages." And *Poh hu thung i*, a well-known work, professedly written in the first century, says: "On stuffing the mouth of the Son of Heaven with rice, they put jade therein; in the case of a feudal lord they introduce pearls; in that of a great officer and so downwards, as also in that of ordinary officials, cowries are used to this end".

De Groot, commenting on the evidence, writes: "The same reasons why gold and jade were used for stuffing the mouth of the dead hold good for the use of pearls in this

[1] De Groot, *The Religious System of China*, Book I, pp. 275 *et seq.*   [2] *Jade*, p. 299.

connection ". He notes that in Chinese literature pearls were regarded as "depositories of Yang matter", that medical works declare "they can further and facilitate the procreation of children", and "can be useful for recalling to life those who have expired, or are at the point of dying".[1]

In India, as a Bengali friend, Mr. Jimut Bahan Sen, M.A., informs me, a native medicine administered to those who are believed to be at the point of death is a mixture of pounded gold and mercury. It is named *Makara-dhwaja*. The *makara*[2] is in India depicted in a variety of forms. As a composite lion-legged and fish-tailed "wonder beast" resembling the Chinese dragon, it is the vehicle of the god Varuna, as the Babylonian "sea goat" or "antelope fish" is the vehicle of the god Ea or of the god Marduk (Merodach). The *makara* of the northern Buddhists is likewise a combination of land and sea animals or reptiles, including the dolphin with the head of an elephant, goat, ram, lion, dog, or alligator.[3]

In China the lion-headed shark, a form of the sea-god, is likewise a *makara* or sea-dragon. Gold and night-shining pearls are connected with the *makara* as with the dragon. The Chinese dragon, as we have seen, is born from gold, while curative herbs like the "Red Cloud herb" and the "dragon's whiskers herb" are emanations of the dragon. Gold, like the herb, contains "soul substance" in concentrated form. Pounded gold, the chief ingredient in the *makara-dhwaja* medicine, is believed in India to renew youth and promote longevity like pounded jade and gold in China.

"In Yung-cheu, which is situated in the Eastern Ocean, rocks exist," wrote a Chinese sage in the early

---

[1] *The Religious System of China*, Book I, pp. 274 *et seq.* [2] Pronounced *muk'ära*.
[3] See illustrations in Professor Elliot Smith's *The Evolution of the Dragon*, pp. 88, 89.

part of the Christian era. "From these rocks there issues a brook like sweet wine; it is called the Brook of Jade Must. If, after drinking some pints out of it, one suddenly feels intoxicated, it will prolong life. . . . Grease of jade," we are further told, "is formed inside the mountains which contain jade. It is always to be found in steep and dangerous spots.[1] The jade juice, after issuing from those mountains, coagulates into such grease after more than ten thousand years. This grease is fresh and limpid, like crystal. If you find it, pulverize it and mix it with the juice of herbs that have no pith; it immediately liquefies; drink one pint of it then and you will live a thousand years. . . . He who swallows gold will exist as long as gold; he who swallows jade will exist as long as jade. Those who swallow the real essence of the dark sphere (heavens) will enjoy an everlasting existence; the real essence of the dark sphere is another name for jade. Bits of jade, when swallowed or taken with water, can in both these cases render man immortal."[2]

As we have seen, the belief prevailed in China that pearls shone by night. The mandrake root was believed elsewhere to shine in like manner. The view is consequently urged by the writer that the myths regarding precious stones, jade, pearls, and herbs of nocturnal luminosity owe their origin to the arbitrary connection of these objects with the moon, and the lunar-goddess or sky-goddess. In China *Ye Kuang* ("light of the night") "is", Laufer notes, "an ancient term to designate the moon".[3]

The intimate connection between the Mother deity and precious metals and stones is brought out by Lucian in his *De Dea Syria*. He refers to the goddess Hera

[1] Like the *ginseng* (mandrake) in the Kang-ge mountains in northern Korea. (See Chapter XVII.)
[2] De Groot, *The Religious System of China*, Book I, Vol. I, pp. 272-3.
[3] *The Diamond*, pp. 55, 56, *n*.

of Hierapolis, who has "something of the attributes of Athene, and of Aphrodite, and of Selene, and of Rhea, and of Artemis, and of Nemesis, and of the Fates", and describes her as follows:

"In one of her hands she holds a sceptre, and in the other a distaff;[1] on her head she bears rays and a tower, and she has a girdle wherewith they adorn none but Aphrodite of the sky. And without she is gilt with gold, and gems of great price adorn her, some white, some sea-green, others wine-dark, others flashing like fire. Besides these there are many onyxes from Sardinia, and the jacinth and emeralds, the offerings of the Egyptians and of the Indians, Ethiopians, Medes, Armenians, and Babylonians. But the greatest wonder of all I will proceed to tell: she bears a gem on her head, called a Lychnis; it takes its name from its attribute. From this stone flashes a great light in the night-time, so that the whole temple gleams brightly as by the light of myriads of candles, but in the day-time the brightness grows faint; the gem has the likeness of a bright fire."[2]

Laufer notes in his *The Diamond*[3] that "the name *lychnis* is connected with the Greek *lychnos* ("a portable lamp"), and that, "according to Pliny, the stone is so called from its lustre being heightened by the light of a lamp". He thinks the stone in question is the tourmaline. Laufer reviews a mass of evidence regarding precious stones that were reported to shine by night, and comes to the conclusion that there is no evidence on record "to show that the Chinese ever understood how to render precious stones phosphorescent". He adds: "Since this experiment is difficult, there is hardly reason to believe that they should ever have attempted it. Altogether," he concludes, "we have to regard the traditions about gems luminous at night, not as a result

---

[1] She is thus the divine spinner as the god Ptah of Egypt is the divine potter.
[2] *The Syrian Goddess*, Strong and Garstang (London, 1913), pp. 71, 72.
[3] Chicago, 1915, p. 58.

of scientific effort, but as folk-lore connecting the Orient with the Occident, Chinese society with the Hellenistic world." As Laufer shows, the Chinese imported legends regarding magical gems from Fu-lin ("the forest of Fu"), an island in the Mediterranean Sea, which was known to them as "the Western Sea" (*Si hai*).[1] At a very much earlier period they imported other legends and beliefs regarding metals and minerals.

Pearls and gold having been connected with the *makara* or dragon, it is not surprising to find that their lunar attributes were imparted to jade. Laufer quotes Chinese references to the "moonlight pearl" and the "moon-reflecting gem",[2] while De Groot deals with Chinese legends about "effulgent pearls", about "pearls shining during the night", "flaming or fiery pearls", and "pearls lighting like the moon". De Groot adds, "Similar legends have always been current in the empire (of China) about jade stone", and he notes in this regard that "at the time of the Emperor Shen-nung (twenty-fifth century B.C.) there existed", according to Chinese records, "jade which was obtained from agate rocks, under the name of 'Light shining at night'. If cast into the waters in the dark it floated on the surface, without its light being extinguished."[3]

The wishing jewel (" Jewel that grants all desires") of India, Japan, and China is said to be "the pupil of a fish eye". In India it was known in Sanskrit as the *cintimani*, and was believed to have originated from the *makara*.[4] The Chinese records have references to "moon-light pearls" from the eyes of female whales, and from the eyes of dolphins.[5] It does not follow that this belief

[1] *The Diamond*, p. 7. *Lesser Fu-lin* was Syria, and *Greater Fu-lin* the Byzantine Empire.   [2] *Ibid.*, pp. 55, n. 2, 56.

[3] *The Religious System of China*, Book I, Vol. I, pp. 277–8.

[4] Laufer, *The Diamond*, p. 22 and n. 3, and p. 69 and n. 7.   [5] *Ibid.*, pp. 68–9.

about the origin of shining pearls had a connection with observatious made of the phosphorescing of parts of marine animals, because the Chinese writers refer too, for instance, to the nocturnal luminosity of rhinoceros horn.[1] Even coral, which, like jade, was connected with the lunar- or sky-goddess, was supposed to shine by night. Laufer quotes from the work, *Si King tsa* (*Miscellaneous Records of the Western Capital*, i.e. Si-ngan-fu), in this connection:

"In the pond Tsi-ts'ui there are coral trees twelve feet high. Each trunk produces three stems, which send forth 426 branches. These have been presented by Chao T'o, King of Nan Yūe (Annam), and were styled 'beacon-fire trees'. *At night they emitted a brilliant light as though they would go up in flames.*"[2]

The "coral tree" here links with the pine, peach, and cassia trees, and the shining mandrake, as well as with jade, gold, precious stones, and pearls. In Persia the pearl and coral are called *margan*, which signifies "life-giver" or "life-owner". Lapis-lazuli was called *Kin tsin* ("essence of gold") during the Tiang period in China.[3]

As the metal associated with the moon was usually silver, gold being chiefly, although not always, the sun metal, we should expect to find silver connected with jade and pearls.

De Groot, who is frankly puzzled over Chinese beliefs regarding pearls, and has to "plead incompetency" to solve the problem why they were "considered as depositories and distributors of vital force",[4] provides the translation of a passage in the *Ta Ts'ing thung li* that connects

---

[1] Laufer, *Chinese Clay Figures*, pp. 138, 151.   [2] *The Diamond*, p. 71.
[3] Elliot Smith, *The Evolution of the Dragon*, p. 157, *n.* 1. Laufer, *Sino-Iranica*, pp. 520 and 525.
[4] *The Religious System of China*, Book II, Vol. IV, p. 331.

silver with pearls.   It states in reference to burial customs that "in the case of an official of the first, second, or third degree, five small pearls and pieces of jade shall be used for stuffing the mouth; in that of one of the fourth, fifth, sixth, or seventh rank, five small pieces of gold and of jade.   The gentry shall use three bits of broken gold or silver; among ordinary people the mouth shall be stuffed with three pieces of silver."

De Groot insists that the principal object of the practice of stuffing the mouths of the dead was "to save the body from a speedy decay".[1]

It is significant therefore to find references in Chinese literature to "Pearls of Jade", to "Fire Jade" that sheds light or even "boils a pot", and to find silver being regarded as a substitute for jade.   Shells, pearls, gold, silver, and jade contained "soul substance" derived from the Great Mother.   As we have seen, Nu Kwa, the mythical Chinese Empress (the sister of Fu Hi, the "Chinese Adam"), who stopped the Deluge, took the place of the ancient goddess in popular legend.   She was credited, as has been indicated, with planning the course of the Celestial River, with creating dragons, with re-erecting one of the four pillars that supported the firmament, and with creating jade for the benefit of mankind.   In Japan Nu Kwa is remembered as Jokwa.

The Japanese beliefs connected with jade are clearly traceable to China.   A Tama may be a piece of jade, a crystal, a tapering pearl, or the pearl carried on the head of a Japanese dragon.   "The Tama", says Joly, "is associated not only with the Bosatsu and other Buddhist deities or saints, but also with the gods of luck."[2]   There are a number of heroic legends in which

---

[1] *The Religious System of China*, Book I, pp. 278–9.
[2] *Legend in Japanese Art*, pp. 354, 355.

the Tama figures.   In a story, relegated to the eighth
century B.C., a famous jade stone is called "the Tama".
It tells that Pien Ho (the Japanese Benwa) saw an eagle
standing on a large block of jade which he took possession
of and carried to his king.   The royal magicians thought
it valueless, and Benwa's right foot was cut off.   He
made his way to the mountains and replaced the jade,
and soon afterwards observed that the same eagle returned and perched upon it again.   When a new king
came to the throne Benwa carried the jade to the court,
but only to have his left foot cut off.   A third king
came to the throne, and on seeing Benwa weeping by the
gate of the palace he inquired into the cause of his grief,
and had the stone tested, when it was found to be a perfect
gem.   This Tama was afterwards regarded so valuable
that it was demanded as "a ransom for fifteen cities".[1]

Here the eagle is associated with the gems containing
"soul substance".   Joly notes that "foxes are also shown
holding the Tama", and he wonders if the globe "held
under their talons by the heraldic lions has a similar
meaning".[2]   Foxes and wolves were, like dragons, capable
of assuming human form and figure among the were-
animals of the Far East.   As these were-animals include
the tiger, which is a god in China, it is possible that they
were ancient deities.   The lion is associated with the Babylonian goddess Ishtar, with the Cretan mother-goddess,
while the Egyptian Tefnut has a lioness form.   Tammuz
of Babylon is, as Nin-girsu of Lagash, a lion-headed
eagle.   The Indian Vishnu has a lion-headed avatar.

The connection of the precious jewel and of gold
with the supreme deity is traceable to the ancient beliefs
regarding the shark-guardian of pearls.   As the beliefs
associated with pearls were transferred to jade, it need

[1] *Legend in Japanese Art*, pp. 355-6.   [2] *Ibid.*, p. 355.

not surprise us to find the sacred fish—a form of the Great Mother—connected with jade. A significant text is quoted by Laufer, without comment, which brings out this connection. He says that "Lü Pu-wei, who died in B.C. 235, reports in his book *Lu-shih Ch'un Ts'iu* : 'Pearls are placed in the mouth of the dead, and fish-scales are added ; these are now utilized for interment with the dead.' The Commentary to this passage explains : 'To place pearls in the mouth of the dead (*han chu*) means to fill the mouth with them ; the addition of fish-scales means, to enclose these in a jade casket which is placed on the body of the deceased, as if it should be covered with fish-scales.'"[1] Jade fish-symbols figure among the Chinese mortuary amulets.

Light is thrown on Chinese beliefs regarding resurrection by the cicada mortuary amulet which was made of jade. It was placed on the tongue of the dead and seems therefore to have been like the Egyptian scarab amulet, a guarantee of immortality.

One of the important ceremonies in connection with the process of reanimating an Egyptian corpse was "the opening of the mouth". It was necessary that the re-animated corpse should speak with "the true voice" and justify itself in the court of Osiris, judge of the dead, when the heart was weighed in the balance.

Tongue and heart were closely connected. According to the beliefs associated with the cult of Ptah, which was fused with the cult of Osiris, the heart was "the mind", and the source of all power and all life. The tongue expressed the thoughts of the mind.

> Ptah, the great, is the mind and tongue of the gods.
> Ptah, from whom proceeded the power
> Of the mind,

[1] *Jade*, p. 21, n. 4.

And of the tongue. . . .
It (the mind) is the one that bringeth forth every successful
   issue.
It is the tongue that repeats the thoughts of the mind.[1]

The mind was the essence of life : the tongue, which formed the word, was the active agent of the mind (heart).

As " the stuffing of the corpse with jade took the place of embalming " [2] in China, the custom of placing a jade amulet on the tongue is of marked significance. It is quite evidently an imported custom. The cicada takes the place of the Egyptian scarabæus, the beetle-god of Egypt, named Khepera and called in the texts " father of the gods ". In ancient Egypt scarabs were placed on the bodies and in the tombs of the dead to protect heart (mind) and tongue and ensure resurrection. A text sets forth in this connection : " And behold, thou shalt make a scarab of green stone, with a rim of gold, and this shall be placed in the heart of a man, and it shall perform for him the ' Opening of the Mouth ' ". The scarab is to be anointed with " ānti unguent" and then "words of power" are to be recited over it. In " words of power " the deceased addresses the scarab as " my heart, my mother : my heart whereby I came into being".

The beetle-god, in whose form the scarab was made, " becomes ", as Budge says, " in a manner a type of the dead body, that is to say, he represents matter containing a living germ which is about to pass from a state of inertness into one of active life. As he was a living germ in the abyss of Nu (the primeval deep) and made himself emerge therefrom in the form of the rising sun, so the germ of the living soul, which existed in the dead body of man, and was to burst into new life in a new world by

[1] Breasted, *A History of Egypt*, p. 357.   [2] Laufer, *Jade*, p. 299, *n.* 1.

means of the prayers recited during the performance of appropriate ceremonies, emerged from its old body in a new form either in the realm of Osiris or in the boat of Ra (the sun-god)."[1]

This Egyptian doctrine was symbolized by the beetle which rolls a bit of dung in the dust into the form of a ball, and then, having dug a hole in the ground, pushes it in and buries it. Thereafter the beetle enters the sub-terranean chamber to devour the ball. This beetle also collects dung to feed the larvæ which ultimately emerge from the ground in beetle form.

As the Chinese substituted jade for pearls, so did they substitute the cicada for the dung-beetle.

The cicada belongs to that class of insect which feeds on the juices of plants. It is large and broad with brightly-coloured wings. The male has on each side of the body a sort of drum which enables it to make that chirping noise called "the song of the cicada", referred to by the ancient classical poets. When the female lays her eggs she bores a hole in a tree and deposits them in it. Wingless larvæ are hatched, and they bore their way into the ground to feed on the juices of roots. After a time— in some cases after the lapse of several years—the cicada emerges from the ground, the skin breaks open, and the winged insect rises in the air. The most remarkable species of the cicada is found in the United States, where it passes through a life-history of seventeen years, the greater part of that time being spent underground—the larval stage. In China the newly-hatched larva sometimes bores down into the earth to a depth of about twenty feet.

"The observation of this wonderful process of nature," says Laufer, "seems to be the basic idea of this (cicada) amulet. The dead will awaken to a new life from his

[1] Budge, *The Gods of the Egyptians*, Vol. I, pp. 357-8.

grave as the chirping cicada rises from the pupa buried in the ground. This amulet, accordingly, was an emblem of resurrection." Laufer quotes in this connection from the Chinese philosopher Wang Ch'ung, who wrote : "Prior to casting off the exuviæ, a cicada is a chrysalis. When it casts them off, it leaves the pupa state, and is transformed into a cicada. The vital spirit of a dead man leaving the body may be compared to the cicada emerging from the chrysalis." [1]

The fact that the cicada feeds on the juices of plants apparently connected it with the idea of the Tree of Life, the source of " soul substance ".

Another insect symbol of resurrection was the butterfly, which was connected with the Plum Tree of Life. Laufer notes that some butterflies carved from jade, which were used as mortuary amulets, have a plum-blossom pattern between the antennæ and plum-blossoms " carved à jour in the wings ".[2]

He notes that " in modern times the combination of butterfly and plum-blossom is used to express a rebus with the meaning " Always great age ". This amulet is of great antiquity.

The butterfly symbol of resurrection is found in Mexico. The Codex Remensis shows an anthropomorphic butterfly from whose mouth a human face emerges. Freyja, the Scandinavian goddess, is connected with the butterfly, and in Greece and Italy the same insect was associated with the idea of resurrection. Psyche (a name signifying "soul") has butterfly wings. Apparently the butterfly, like the cicada, was supposed to derive its vitality from the mother-goddess's Tree of Life.

Another important Chinese mortuary jade object was the frog or toad amulet. As we have seen, the frog was

[1] *Jade*, p. 301 and n. 1.   [2] *Ibid.*, p. 310.

connected with the moon and the lunar goddess, and in
China, as in ancient Egypt, was a symbol of resurrection.

Among the interesting jade amulets shown by Laufer
are two that roughly resemble in shape the Egyptian
scarabs. "The two pieces", he writes, "show traces of
gilding, and resemble helmets in their shape, and are
moulded into the figures of a curious monster which it is
difficult to name. It seems to me that it is possibly some
fabulous giant bird, for on the sides, two wings, each
marked by five pinions, are brought out, a long, curved
neck rises from below, though the two triangular ears do
not fit the conception of a bird."[1] The figure apparently
represents a "composite wonder beast". Fishes and composite quadrapeds were also depicted in jade and placed in
graves. Human figures are rare.

Stone coffins were used in ancient times. The books
of the later Han Dynasty (at the beginning of our era) tell
about a pious governor, Wang Khiao, who receives a jade
coffin from heaven. It was placed by unseen hands in his
hall. His servants endeavoured to take it away, but found
it could not be moved.

De Groot,[2] who translates the story, continues: "Khiao
said, 'Can this mean that the Emperor of Heaven calls
me towards him?' He bathed himself, put on his official
attire with its ornaments, and lay down in the coffin, the
lid being immediately closed over him. When the night
had passed, they buried him on the east side of the city,
and the earth heaped itself over him in the shape a
tumulus. All the cows in the district on that evening
were wet with perspiration and got out of breath, and
nobody knew whence this came. The people thereupon
erected a temple for him."

De Groot quotes from another work written in the

[1] *Jade*, pp. 306-7.   [2] *The Religious System of China*, Book I, p. 284.

fifth century, which relates that " at Lin-siang there is in the water a couch of stone, upon which stand two coffins of solid stone, green like copper mirrors. There is nobody who can give information regarding them."[1]

Here we have jade used for the preservation of the dead, associated with the sky, with cows, water, and stone, and, in addition, a reference to green copper. Jade has taken the place of pearls, and pearls were, as has been shown, connected with the mother-goddess, the sky and cow deity who was the source of fertilizing and creative moisture and " soul substance ". The standing stones of the mother-goddess were supposed to perspire, and to split and give birth to dragons or gods. This idea appears to lie behind the story regarding the perspiring cows. An influence was at work on the night when the sage was buried in the jade coffin, and that influence came from the sky, and was concentrated in jade. It is necessary, therefore, at this point, to get at Chinese ideas regarding the connection between jade and the mysterious influence or influences in what we call " Nature ".

Behind all mythologies lie basic ideas regarding the universe. To understand a local or localized mythology, it is necessary that we should know something regarding the world in which lived those who invented or perpetuated the myths.

The Chinese world was flat, and over it was the dome of the firmament supported by four pillars. These pillars were situated at the four cardinal points, and were each guarded by a sentinel deity. The deities exercised an influence on the world and on all living beings in it, and their influence was particularly strong during their seasons.

Like the ancient Egyptians and Babylonians the Chinese believed that their world was surrounded by

---

[1] *The Religious System of China*, Book I, p. 284.

water.   There are references in the texts to the "Four Seas", and to what the Egyptians called the "Great Circle" (Okeanos).

The Babylonians believed the world was a mountain, and their temples were models of their world.   Thus the temple of Enlil, as the world-god, was called E-Kur, which signifies "mountain house".   His consort Ninlil was also called Nin-Kharsag, "the lady of the mountain".[1] The Babylonian and Egyptian temples were not only places of worship, but seats of learning, and they had workshops in which the dyers, metal-workers, &c., plied their sacred trades.

Chinese palaces and universities were in ancient times models of the world.   One of the odes says of King Wu:

"In the capital of Hao he built his hall with its circlet of water.   From the west to the east, from the south to the north, there was not a thought but did him homage."[2]

This hall was a royal college, "built", says Legge, "in the middle of a circle of water".   Colleges might also have semicircular pools in front of them, "as may now be seen in front of the temples of Confucius in the metropolitan cities of the provinces".[3]   Ceremonies were studied in these institutions.   There were also grave-pools.   In Singapore these grave-pools have had to be abolished because they were utilized for hatching purposes by mosquitoes.

Much attention was paid by the Chinese to the shape and situation of a temple, college, palace, or grave.   Each was subjected to good and bad influences, and as seafarers set their sails to take full advantage of a favourable breeze, so did the Chinese construct edifices and graves to take full advantage of favourable influences emanating

---

[1] *Myths of Babylonia and Assyria*, p. 332.   [2] Legge, *The Shih King*, p. 395.
[3] *Ibid.*, p. 338.

from what may be called the "magic tanks" of the universe—the cardinal points and the sky.

The beliefs involved in this custom are not peculiar to China. In Scottish Gaelic, for instance, there is the old saying :

> Shut the north window,
>   And quickly close the window to the south ;
> And shut the window facing west ;
>   Evil never came from the east.

Another saying is : "Shut the windows to the north, open the windows to the south, and do not let the fire go out". Both in Scottish and Irish Gaelic the north is the "airt" (cardinal point) of evil influence, and is coloured black, as is the north in China, and the south in India. The black Indian south is "Yama's gate", that is the "gate" of the god of death. One cannot say anything worse to a Hindu than "Go to Yama's gate". The north is the good and white "airt" of Indian mythology ; the good go northward to Paradise, as in Scotland they go southward. A Japanese poet has written: "The Paradise is in the south; only fools pray towards the west".[1]

In the Pyramid Texts of ancient Egypt the east is held by the solar cult "to be the most sacred of all regions", while the west is the sacred "airt" of the Osirian cult.[2] In the east the sun-god, to whom the soul of the dead Pharaoh went, was supposed to be reborn every morning. The Chinese regarded the east "as the quarter", says De Groot, "in which is rooted the life of everything, the great genitor of life (the sun) being born there every day".[3] As we have seen, there was in China, as in Egypt, a rival cult of the west.

[1] Joly, *Legend in Japanese Art*, p. 297.
[2] Breasted, *Religion and Thought in Ancient Egypt*, p. 100.
[3] *The Religious System of China*, Book I, Vol. III, p. 962.

The gods of the four quarters of China, from whom influences flowed, were: The Blue (or Green) Dragon (east), the Red Bird (south), the White Tiger (west), and the Black Tortoise (north). The east is the left side, and the west is the right side; a worshipper therefore faces the south. In Irish and Scottish Gaelic lore the south is the right side, and the north is the left side; a worshipper therefore faces the east.

According to Kwang-tze, the Taoist, it was believed in China that "the breath (or influence) of the east is wind, and wind creates wood"; that "the breath of the south is Yang, which creates fire"; that "the centre is earth"; that "the breath of the west is Yin, which gives birth to metal"; and that the breath of the north "is cold, by which water is produced". Another native pre-Christian writer says that "the east appertains to wood, the south to fire, the west to metal, and the north to water".[1] Thus taking in the seasons we have the following combinations, showing the organs of the body influenced by the gods of the "airts":

East—the Blue Dragon, Spring, Wood; Planet, Jupiter; liver and gall.
South—the Red Bird, Summer, Fire, the Sun; Planet, Mars; heart and large intestines.
West—the White Tiger, Autumn, Wind, Metal; Planet, Venus; lungs and small intestine.
North—the Black Tortoise, Winter, Cold, Water; Planet, Mercury; kidneys and bladder.

The good influence (or breath) was summed up in the term Yang, and bad influence in the term Yin. Yang refers to what is bright, warm, active, and life-giving; and Yin to what is inactive, cold, and of the earth earthy. "When", says a Chinese writer, "we speak of the Yin

[1] De Groot, *op. cit.*, Book I, Vol. III, p. 983.

and the Yang, we mean the air (or ether) collected in the Great Void. When we speak of the Hard and Soft, we mean that ether collected and formed into substance."[1] Says De Groot in this connection: "In China vital power is specially assimilated with the Yang, the chief part of the Cosmos, identified with light, warmth, and life". Yin is "the principle of darkness, cold, and death, standing in the universe diametrically opposite to Yang".[2] The chief source of Yang is the sun, which gives forth "shen" or "soul substance"; the chief source of Yin is the moon. Yang strengthens the vital energy, and is the active principle in various elixirs of life, including, as De Groot notes, "the cock, jade, gold, pearls, and the products of pine and cypress trees".[3]

Yin and Yang are controlled by the constellation, the Great Bear, called in China "the Bushel". In the *Shi Ki* there is a reference to "the seven stars of the Bushel", styled "the Revolving Pearls or the Balance of Jasper", and arrayed "to form the body of seven rulers". This constellation is "the chariot of the Emperor (of Heaven). Revolving around the pole, it descends to rule the four quarters of the sphere and to separate the Yin and the Yang; by so doing it fixes the four seasons, upholds the equilibrium between the five elements, moves forward the subdivisions of the sphere, and establishes all order in the Universe."[4]

An ancient Chinese writer says in this connection that when the handle (tail) of the Bushel (Great Bear) points to the east (at nightfall), it is spring to all the world. When the handle points to the south it is summer, when it points to the west it is autumn, and when it points to the north it is winter. In the *Shu King*

---

[1] Legge, *The Yi King*, pp. 43–44.　　[2] *The Religious System of China*, Book I, p. 327.
[3] *Op. cit.*, p. 327.　　[4] De Groot, *op. cit.*, p. 317.

(Part II, Book I) the Great Bear is referred to as "the pearl-adorned turning sphere with its transverse tube of jade".[1] The Polar Star is the "Pivot of the Sky", which revolves in its place, "carrying round with it all the other heavenly bodies". In like manner the Taoists taught that "the body of man is carried round his spirit and by it". The spirit is thus the "Pivot of Jade". That is why the Pivot of Jade is used in the ritual services of Taoism.[2]

In Norse-Icelandic mythology the World Mill controls the seasons and the movements of the heavenly bodies. The heavens revolve round the Polar Star, *Veraldar Nagli* ("the world spike"). Nine giant maids turn the world mill.[3]

The Babylonians, who were the pioneer astronomers and astrologers of Asia, identified the stable and controlling spirit of the night sky with the Polar Star, which was called "Ilu Sar" ("the god Shar") or "Anshar" ("Star of the Height" or "Star of the Most High").[4]

Isaiah (xiv, 4–14) refers to the supreme star-god when he makes Lucifer declare: "I will ascend unto heaven, I will exalt my throne above the stars of God; I will sit also upon the mount of the congregation, in the sides of the north; I will ascend above the heights of the clouds; I will be the most High".

Chinese astronomy and the Chinese calendar are undoubtedly of Babylonian origin. The Babylonian god of the Pole Star has not been forgotten. Dr. Edkins once asked a Chinese schoolmaster: "Who is the Lord of heaven and earth?" He replied "that he knew none but the Pole Star, called in the Chinese language Teen-hwang-ta-te, *the great imperial ruler of heaven*.[5]

---

[1] Legge, *Texts of Taoism*, Vol. II, p. 265.   [2] Legge, *The Shu King*, pp. 38, 39.
[3] *Teutonic Myth and Legend*, p. 5.   [4] *Myths of Babylonia and Assyria*, pp. 330, 331.
[5] *Religion in China* (London, 1878), p. 109.

There is a god and a goddess in the Great Bear. "Among the liturgical works used by the priests of Tao", says Edkins, "one of the commonest consists of prayers to Towmoo, a female divinity supposed to reside in the Great Bear. A part of the same constellation is worshipped under the name Kwei-sing. A small temple is erected to this deity on the east side of the entrance to Confucian temples, and he is regarded as being favourable to literature." But the chief god of literature is "Wen-chang, who is identified with a constellation near the Great Bear which bears his name. He is prayed to by scholars to assist them in their examinations. Temples were erected to him on elevated earthen terraces. "Wen-chang", says Edkins, "is said to have come down to our world during many generations at irregulai intervals. Virtuous and highly-gifted men were chosen from history as likely to have been incarnations of this divinity."[1]

The five elements controlled by the Great Bear as it swings round the Polar Star are in China (1) water, (2) fire, (3) wood, (4) metal, and (5) earth. These elements compose what we call Nature. As we have seen, they were placed under the guardianship of animal gods. The White Tiger of the West, for instance, is associated with metal. When, therefore, metal is placed in a grave, a ceremonial connection with the tiger-god is effected. "According to the Annals of Wu and Yueh, three days after the burial of the king, the essence of the element metal assumed the shape of a white tiger and crouched down on the top of the grave."[2] Here the tiger is a protector—a preserver.

Jade being strongly imbued with Yang or "soul

[1] *Religion in China,* p. 107.
[2] Quoted by De Groot, *The Religious System of China,* Book I, Vol. III, p. 983.

substance" was intimately associated with all the gods,
and the various colours of jade were connected with the
colours of the "airts" and of the heavens and earth.
Laufer quotes from the eighteenth chapter of *Chou li*,
which deals with the functions of the Master of Religious
Ceremonies:

"He makes of jade the six objects to do homage to Heaven,
to Earth, and to the Four Points of the compass.   With the
round tablet *pi* of bluish (or greenish) colour, he does homage
to Heaven.   With the yellow jade tube *ts'ung*, he does homage to
Earth.   With the green[1] tablet *Kuei*, he renders homage to the
region of the East.   With the red tablet *chang*, he renders homage
to the region of the South.   With the white tablet in the shape of
a tiger (*hu*), he renders homage to the region of the West.   With
the black jade piece of semicircular shape (*huang*), he renders
homage to the region of the North.   The colour of the victims
and of the pieces of silk for these various spirits correspond to that
of the jade tablet."[2]

The shape, as well as the colours, of the jade symbols
was of ritualistic importance.

What would appear to be the most ancient Chinese
doctrine regarding the influences or "breaths" that
emanated from Nature, and affected the living and the
dead, is summed up in the term Fung-shui.   "Fung"
means wind, and "shui" means "the water from the
clouds which the wind distributes over the world".
Certain winds are good, and certain winds are bad.

The importance attached to wind and water appears
to be connected with the ancient belief, found in Babylonia and Egypt, that wind is the "breath of life", the
soul, and that water is the source of all life—"the water
of life".

"Fung-shui", says De Groot, "denotes the atmos-

---

[1] Green and blue are interchangeable in China.
[2] Biot, Vol. I, pp. 434, 435, quoted by Laufer in *Jade*, p. 120.

pherical influences which bear absolute sway over the fate of man, as none of the principal elements of life can be produced without favourable weather and rains." It also means, he adds, "a quasi-scientific system, supposed to teach men where and how to build graves, temples, and dwellings, in order that the dead, the gods, and the living may be located therein exclusively, or as far as possible, under the auspicious influences of Nature".[1]

The controllers of wind and water are the White Tiger god of the West, and the Blue (or green) Dragon god of the East. "These animals", says De Groot, "represent all that is expressed by the word Fung-shui, viz., both æolian and aquatic influences, Confucius being reputed to have said that 'the winds follow the tiger', and the dragon having, since time immemorial, in Chinese cosmological mythology played the part of chief spirit of water and rain."[2]

When the dead were buried it was considered necessary, according to Fung-shui principles, to have graves facing the south, and the Dragon symbol on the left (east) side of the coffin, and the Tiger symbol on the right (west) side, while the Red Bird of the south was on the front, and the Black Tortoise of the north on the back.

These symbols were, so to speak, set amidst natural surroundings that allowed the "free flow" of auspicious influences or "breaths". A site for a burial-ground was carefully selected, due account being taken of the con-figurations of the surrounding country and the courses followed by streams.[3]

Not only graves, but houses and towns, were so placed

---

[1] *The Religious System of China*, Book I, Part III, p. 935.
[2] *Ibid.*, Book I, Vol. III, p. 949.
[3] In Scotland south-flowing water is specially good and influential.

as to secure the requisite balance between the forces of Nature. De Groot notes that Amoy is reputed by Chinese believers of the Fung-shui system to owe its prosperity to two knolls flanking the inner harbour, called " Tiger-head Hill" and " Dragon-head Hill". Canton is influenced by the " White clouds", a chain of hills representing the Dragon on one side of its river, and by undulating ground opposite representing the Tiger. " Similarly", he says, " Peking is protected on the north-west by the Kin-shan or Golden Hills, which represent the Tiger and ensure its prosperity, together with that of the whole empire and the reigning dynasty. These hills contain the sources of a felicitous watercourse, called Yu-ho or 'Jade River', which enters Peking on the north-west, and flows through the grounds at the back of the Imperial Palace, then accumulates its beneficial in-fluences in three large reservoirs or lakes dug on the west side, and finally flows past the entire front of the inner palace, where it bears the name of the Golden Water."[1]

Here we find jade and gold closely associated in the Fung-shui system.

As we have seen, white jade was used when the Tiger god of the West was worshipped; it is known as " tiger jade"; a tiger was depicted on the jade symbol. To the Chinese the tiger was the king of all animals and " lord of the mountains", and the tiger-jade ornament was specially reserved for commanders of armies. The male tiger was, among other things, the god of war, and in this capacity it not only assisted the armies of the emperors, but fought the demons that threatened the dead in their graves.

There are traces in China of a tigress shape of the

[1] *The Religious System of China*, Book I, Vol. III, pp. 949, 950.

goddess of the West. Laufer refers to an ancient legend of the country of Chu, which tells of a prince who in the eighth century B.C. married a princess of Yün. A son was born to them and named Tou Po-pi. The father died and the widow returned to Yün, where Tou Po-pi, in his youth, had an intrigue with a princess who bore him a son. " The grandmother ordered the infant to be carried away and deserted on a marsh, but a tigress came to suckle the child. One day when the prince of Yün was out hunting, he discovered this circumstance, and when he returned home terror-stricken, his wife unveiled to him the affair. Touched by this marvellous incident, they sent messengers after the child, and had it cared for. The people of Ch'u, who spoke a language differing from Chinese, called suckling *nou*, and a tiger they called *yü-t'u*; hence the boy was named Nou Yü-t'u ('Suckled by a Tigress'). He subsequently became minister of Ch'u." [1]

This Far Eastern legend recalls that of Romulus and Remus, who were thrown into the Tiber but were preserved and rescued; they were afterwards suckled by a she-wolf. The Cretan Zeus was suckled, according to one legend, by a sow, and to another by a goat. A Knossian seal depicts a child suckled by a horned sheep. Sir Arthur Evans refers, in this connection, to the legends of the grandson of Minos who was suckled by a bitch; of Miletos, " the mythical founder of the city of that name", being nursed by wolves.[2] Vultures guarded the Indian heroine Shakuntala, the Assyrian Semiramis was protected by doves, while the Babylonian Gilgamesh and the Persian patriarch Akhamanish were protected and rescued at birth by eagles. Horus of Egypt was nourished and concealed by the serpent goddess Uazit, and in his boyhood made

1 *Jade*, pp. 182–3.   2 *Journal of Hellenic Studies*, Vol. XXI, pp. 128–9.

friends of wild animals, as did also Bharata, the son of the Indian vulture-guarded Shakuntala. Horus figures in the constellation of Argo as a child floating in a chest or boat like the abandoned Moses, the abandoned Indian Karna, the abandoned Sargon of Akkad, and, as it would appear, Tammuz who in childhood lay in a "sunken boat". Horus of the older Egyptian legends was concealed on a green floating island on the Nile—the "green bed of Horus".[1]

The oldest known form of the suckling legend is found in the Pyramid Texts of Ancient Egypt. When the soul of the Pharaoh went to the Otherworld he was suckled by a goddess or by the goddesses of the north and south. The latter are referred to in the Texts as " the two vultures with long hair and hanging breasts ".[2] Here the vultures take the place of the cow-goddess Hathor. In Troy the cow-mother, covered with stars, becomes the star-adorned sow-mother.[3] Demeter had a sow form and Athene a goat form, and other goddesses had dove, eagle, wolf, bitch, &c., forms. The Chinese tigress-goddess is evidently a Far Eastern animal form of the Great Mother who suckles the souls of the dead and the abandoned children who are destined to become notables. Thus behind the wind-god, in the Chinese Fung-shui system, we meet with complex ideas regarding the source of the " air of life ", and the source of the food-supply. The Blue Dragon of the East is the Naga form of the Aryo-Indian Indra,[4] the rain-controller, the fertilizer, who is closely associated with Vayu, the wind-god; the dragon

---

[1] See *Egyptian Myth and Legend*, *Myths of Babylonia and Assyria*, *Myths of Crete and Pre-Hellenic Europe*, and *Indian Myth and Legend*.

[2] Breasted, *Religion and Thought in Ancient Egypt*, p. 130.

[3] See terra-cotta image of pig marked with stars in Schliemann's *Troy and its Remains* (translation by Smith, London, 1875), p. 232.

[4] Elliot Smith, *The Evolution of the Dragon*, p. 96.

is the thunderer, too, like Indra.   The close association
of the tiger- and dragon-gods in the Fung-shui system
may account for the custom of decorating jade symbols
of the tiger with the thunder pattern.[1]

In jade-lore, as will be seen, we touch on complex
religious beliefs and conceptions not entirely of Chinese
origin.   Indeed, it is necessary to leave China and investigate the religious systems of more ancient countries
to understand rightly Chinese ideas regarding jade as a
substitute for gold, pearls, precious stones, &c., and its
connection with vegetation and the Great Mother, the
source of all life.

It remains with us to deal with Chinese ideas regarding the soul which was protected by jade, the concentrated form of "soul substance".

The Chinese believed that a human being had two
souls.   One was the *Kwei*, that is the soul which partook
of the nature of the element Yin and returned to the
earth from which it originally came;[2] the other soul was
the *shen* which partook of the element Yang.   When the
shen is in the living body, it is called *Khi* or "breath";
after death "it lives forth as a refulgent spirit, styled
ming".   The other soul, called *Kwei*, is known as the
p'oh during life; after death it lives on in the grave
beside the body, which is supposed to be protected against
decay by the jade, gold, pearls, shells, &c., and the good
influences "flowing" from east and west.

The *shen*, like the cicada, may also dwell for a time
in the grave or in the gravestone before it rises on wings
to the Sky Paradise, or passes to the Western Paradise
or the Eastern "Islands of the Blest".   Ancient local

---

[1] Laufer, *Jade* (for illustrations of tigers with thunder pattern), pp. 180–4.
[2] De Groot, *Religious System of China*, Vol. I, Book I, pp. 94 and 110; Book II,
pp. 5 *et seq.*

and tribal beliefs and beliefs imported at different periods from different culture centres were evidently fused in China, and we consequently meet with a variety of ideas regarding the destiny of the *shen*. "Departed souls", says De Groot, "are sometimes popularly represented as repairing to the regions of bliss on the back of a crane."[1] The soul may sail to the Western Paradise in a boat. "Thou hast departed to the West, from whence there is no returning in the barge of mercy", runs an address to the corpse.[1] Here we have the Ra-boat of Egypt conveying the soul to the Osirian Paradise. As has been shown, souls sometimes departed on the backs of dragons, or rose in the air towards cloudland, there to sail in boats or ride on the backs of birds or kirins, or reached the moon or star-land by climbing a gigantic tree. Belief in transmigration of souls can also be traced in China, the result apparently of the importation of pre-Buddhist as well as Buddhist beliefs from India.

The living performed ceremonies to assist the soul of the dead on its last journey. Priests chanted:

I salute Ye, Celestial Judges of the three spheres constituting the higher, middle, and lower divisions of the Universe, and Ye, host of Kings and nobles of the departments of land and water and of the world of men! Remember the soul of the dead, and help it forward in going to the Paradise of the West.[2]

Egyptian, Babylonian, and Indian ideas regarding the Western Paradise are here significantly mingled.

During life the soul might leave the body for a period, either during sleep or when one fainted suddenly.

This belief is widespread. The soul, in folk-stories, is sometimes seen, as in Scotland, as a bee, or bird, or serpent, as in Norway as an insect or mouse, as in Indonesia

---

[1] *The Religious System of China*, Book I, Vol. I, p. 226, *n.* 2.
[2] De Groot, op. cit., Book I, p. 72.

and elsewhere as a worm, snake, butterfly, or mouse, and even, as in different countries, as deer, cats, pigs, crocodiles, &c.   Chinese beliefs regarding souls as butter-flies, cicadas, &c., have already been referred to.

The wandering soul could be "called back" by repeating the individual's name.   In China, even the dead were called back, and the ceremony of recalling the soul is prominent in funeral rites, as De Groot shows.[1] Peoples as far separated as the Mongolian Buriats and the inhabitants of England, Scotland, and Ireland believed that ghosts could be enticed to return to the body.[2]   The "death-howl" in China and Egypt, and elsewhere, is evidently connected with this ancient belief.

Of special interest is the evidence regarding Korean customs and beliefs.   Mrs. Bishop writes: "Man is sup-posed to have three souls.   After death one occupies the tablet, one the grave, and one the unknown.   During the passing of the spirit there is complete silence.   The under-garments of the dead are taken out by a servant, who waves them in the air, and calls him by name, the relations and friends meantime wailing loudly.   After a time the clothes are thrown upon the roof."   When a man dies, one of his souls is supposed to be seized and carried to the unknown and placed on trial before the Ten Judges, who sentence it "either to 'a good place' or to one of the manifold hells".[3]

Professor Elliot Smith, reviewing the Chinese ideas regarding the two souls, comes to the conclusion that "the early Chinese conceptions of the soul and its functions are essentially identical with the Egyptian, and must have been derived from the same source".[4]   As the Chinese

[1] *The Religious System of China*, Book I, Vol. I, pp. 241 *et seq.*
[2] See references in *Myths of Babylonia and Assyria*, pp. 69, 70, and 70 *n.*
[3] Mrs. Bishop, *Korea and Her Neighbours*, Vol. II, pp. 84-5.
[4] *The Evolution of the Dragon*, p. 50.

have the *shen* and the *Kwei*, so had the Egyptians the *Ka* and the *ba*. The *Ka* was the spirit of the placenta, "which was accredited with the attributes of the life-giving and birth-promoting Great Mother and intimately related to the moon and the earliest totem ".[1]   In China the beliefs and customs connected with the placenta and the moon are quite Egyptian in character.[2]

Even in the worship of ancestors in China one can trace the influence of Ancient Egyptian ideas.   When the Pharaoh died, he was identified with the god.   King Unis, in the Pyramid Texts, becomes Osiris, who controls the Nile.   "It is Unis ", we read, "who inundates the land."   Pepi I, in like manner, supplanted the god, and he is addressed as Osiris, as is also King Mernere—" Ho this Osiris, King Mernere!" runs a Pyramid Text.[3]   The sun-god Ra was similarly supplanted by his son, the dead Pharaoh.

The souls of Chinese ancestors, who passed to the Otherworld, became identified with the deities who protected households.   Emperors became, after death, emperors in heaven and their souls were the deified preservers of their dynasties.   Clan and tribal ancestors were protectors of their clans and tribes, and families were ever under the care of the souls of their founders. The belief became deeply rooted in China that the ancestral soul exercised from generation to generation a beneficent influence over a home.   It is not surprising to find, therefore, that gods are exceedingly numerous in China, and that it is sometimes difficult to distinguish an ancestor from a god and a god from an ancestor. The State religion was something apart from domestic

---

[1] *The Evolution of the Dragon*, pp. 51–2.
[2] De Groot, op. cit., p. 396, and Elliot Smith, op. cit., p. 48, and *n.* 1.
[3] Breasted, *Religion and Thought in Ancient Egypt*, p. 19.

religion. Emperors worshipped the deities that controlled the nation's destinies, and families worshipped the
deities of the household.

Local and imported beliefs were fused and developed
on Chinese soil, and when, in time, Buddhism was introduced it was mixed with pre-existing religious systems.
Chinese Buddhism is consequently found to have local
features that distinguish it from the Buddhism of Tibet,
Burmah, and Japan, in which countries there was, in like
manner, culture-mixing.

Beliefs connected with jade, which date back to the
time when the jade fished from the rivers of Chinese
Turkestan was identified with pearls and gold, were
similarly developed in China. At first the jade was used
to assist birth and to cure diseases. It likewise brought
luck, being an object that radiated the influence of the
All-Mother. As the living had their days prolonged and
their youth revived by jade, so were the dead preserved
from decay by the influence of the famous mineral. The
custom ultimately obtained of eating jade, as has already
been noted in these pages. Ground jade or " pure extract
of jade " was not only supposed to promote longevity, but
to effect a ceremonial connection between the worshipper
and the spirits or deities. In the *Chou li* it is stated that
" when the Emperor purifies himself by abstinence, the
chief in charge of the jade works prepares for him the
jade which he is obliged to eat ".[1] It is explained by
commentators that " the emperor fasts and purifies himself
before communicating with the spirits; he must take the
pure extract of jade ; it is dissolved that he may eat it ".
Jade was also pounded with rice as food for the corpse.
" A marvellous kind of jade ", says Laufer, " was called
Yü ying, ' the perfection of jade ', " which ensured eternal

---

[1] Biot, Vol. I, p. 125.

life. " In 163 B.C. a jade cup of this kind was discovered on which the words were engraved ' May the sovereign of men have his longevity prolonged '." Immortality was secured by eating from jade bowls, or, as we have seen, by drinking dew from a jade bowl.[1]

As has been shown, the Great Mother created jade for the benefit of mankind, and " the spirit of jade is like a beautiful woman ".[2] Jade was also " the essence of the purity of the male principle ".[3]

Apparently the god who was husband and son of the Great Mother was connected with jade. The Mother was the life-giver, and the son, as Osiris, was "the imperishable principle of life wherever found ".[4] If men died, the seed of life in the body was preserved by jade amulets; the plants might shed their leaves, but the life of the plants was perpetuated by the spirit of jade. " In the second month", says *The Illustrated Mirror of Jade*, "the plants in the mountains receive a brighter lustre. When their leaves fall, they change into jade." [5] The mountain plants in question appear to be the curative herbs that contained, like jade, the elixir of life, and the chief of these plants was the *ginseng* (mandrake), an avatar of the Great Mother. The plant, or ground jade, or food or moisture from the jade vessel renewed youth and prolonged life. All the elixirs were concentrated in jade ; the vital principle in human beings and plants was derived from and preserved by jade.

It is of special interest to find that the Chinese Nu Kwa who caused the flood to retreat was the creator of the jade which protected mankind and ensured longevity by preserving the seed or *shen* of life, being impregnated with *Yang*, the male principle. In Babylonia, the seed of

---

[1] Laufer, *Jade*, pp. 296 *et seq.*   [2] *Ibid.*, p. 1.   [3] *Ibid.*, p. 296.
[4] Breasted, *Religion and Thought in Ancient Egypt*, p. 23.   [5] Laufer, *Jade*, p. 1.

mankind was preserved during the flood by the *nig-gil-ma*.

In the Sumerian version of the Creation legend, the three great gods Anu, Enlil, and Enki, assisted by the Great Mother goddess Ninkharasagga, first created mankind, then the *nig-gil-ma*, and lastly the four-legged animals of the field.   The mysterious *nig-gil-ma* is referred to in the story of the Deluge as " Preserver of the seed of mankind", while the ship or ark is " Preserver of Life", literally " She that preserves life".   A later magical text refers to the creation after that of mankind and animals of " two small creatures, one white and one black".   Man and animals were saved from the flood and the *nig-gil-ma* played its or their part " in ensuring their survival".

Leonard W. King, who has gathered together the surviving evidence regarding the mysterious *nig-gil-ma*[1] points out that the name is sometimes preceded by " the determinative for ' pot', ' jar', or ' bowl' ", and is identical with the Semitic word *mashkhalu*.   In the Tell-el-Amarna letters there are references to a *mashkhalu* of silver and a *mashkhalu* of stone (a silver vessel and a stone vessel).   The *nig-gil-ma* may be simply a " jar " or " bowl".   " But", says Mr. L. King, " the accompanying references to the ground, to its production from the ground, and to its springing up . . . suggest rather some kind of plant; and this, from its employment in magical rites, may also have given its name to a bowl or vessel which held it.   A very similar plant was that found and lost by Gilgamesh, after his sojourn with Ut-napishtim[2] ; it too had potent magical power, and bore a title descriptive of its peculiar virtue of transforming old age to youth."   The *nig-gil-ma* may

---

[1] *Legends of Babylonia and Egypt in relation to Hebrew Tradition* (The Schweich Lectures), London, 1918, pp. 56 *et seq* and pp. 88 *et seq*.

[2] The Babylonian Noah, who became an immortal and lived on an "Island of the Blest " and near the island on which were the Plant of Life and the Well of Life.

therefore be a plant, a ship, a stone bowl or jar, or a vessel
of silver (the moon metal). If we regard it as a symbol
or avatar of the mother-goddess it was any of these things
and all of these things—the Mother Pot, the inexhaustible
womb of Nature, the Plant of Life containing " soul
substance", the red clay, the moon-silver, or, as in China,
the jade of'which the sacred vessel was made. The Great
Mother's herb-avatar was the *ginseng* (mandrake), as in
the Egyptian Deluge story it was the red earth *didi* from
Elephantine placed in the beer prepared for the slaughtering goddess Hathor-Sekhet as a surrogate of blood and a
soporific drink; the mixture was " the giver of life", the
red *aqua vitae*, like the red wine and the juice of red
berries in different areas.[1] The mandrake was the *didi* of
southern Europe and of China. Dr. Rendel Harris shows
that the early Greek magicians and doctors referred to the
male mandrake, which was white, and the female mandrake,
which was black. The black mandrake was personified as
the Black Aphrodite.[2]

The Babylonian reference in a magical text to the
nig-gil-ma as " two small creatures, one white and one
black " is therefore highly significant. Apparently, like
jade, the *nig-gil-ma* symbolized " the male principle ", and
" the spirit " of " a beautiful woman". Thus mandrake
(*ginseng*), the Plant of Life, red earth, jade, the pearl and
the pot or jar or bowl, and the Deluge ship, and the ship
of the sun-god, were forms, avatars, or manifestations of
the Great Mother who preserved the seed of mankind
and the elixir of life—in the Pot it grew the Plant of
Life, and from it could be drunk the dew of life, the
water of life, plant and water being impregnated with the
" spirit " of jade. Jade-lore is of highly complex character

---

[1] Elliot Smith, *The Evolution of the Dragon*, p. 205.
[2] *The Ascent of Olympus*, pp. 120-1.

because, as has been indicated, the early instructors of the Chinese attached to the mineral the Egypto-Babylonian doctrines regarding the Great Mother and her shells, pearls, precious stones, gold, silver and copper, herbs, trees, cereals, red earth, &c. The Babylonian evidence regarding the *nig-gil-ma* as a herb, and as a silver or stone jar, pot, or cup, in which was preserved the seed of mankind ("soul substance") may explain why in the Chinese Deluge myth there is no ark or ship. The goddess provided jade instead of a boat and she created dragons to control the rain-supply, so that the world might not again suffer from the effects of a flood.

The virtues of jade were shared to a certain degree by rhinoceros horn, which, as we have seen, was reputed to shine by night.

Laufer has gathered together sufficient evidence to prove that the rhinoceros was one of the wild animals known in ancient China.[1] A hero of the Chou Dynasty, who subdued rebels and established peace throughout the Empire, "drove away also the tigers, leopards, rhinoceroses and elephants—and all the people were greatly delighted".[2] A native writer says: "To travel by water and not avoid sea-serpents and dragons—this is the courage of a fisherman. To travel by land and not avoid the rhinoceros and the tiger—this is the courage of hunters." In ancient times certain of the lords attending on the emperor had a tiger symbol on each chariot wheel, while other lords had on their wheels crouching rhinoceroses.[3] Laufer expresses the view that "the strong desire prevailing in the epoch of the Chou for the horn of the animal (rhinoceros) which was carved into ornamental cups, and for its valuable skin,

---

[1] *History of the Rhinoceros* in Chinese clay figures (Field Museum of Natural History, Publication 177), Chicago, 1914, pp. 73 *et seq.*

[2] Legge, *The Chinese Classics*, Vol. II, p. 281.   [3] Laufer, op. cit., pp. 160-1.

which was worked up into armour, had . . . contributed to its final destruction." [1]   The rhinoceros-horn cups were used, like jade cups, chiefly for religious purposes.   Rice-wine was drunk from them when vows were made, and from them were poured libations to ancestors.   The animal's skin was used not only for armour, because of its toughness and durability, but because the rhinoceros was a longevity animal, and a form of the god of longevity (shou-sing).   It was used, too, for the coffin of the " Son of Heaven " (the Emperor).   " The innermost coffin was formed by hide of water buffalo and rhinoceros."   This case was enclosed in white poplar timber and the two outer cases were of catalpa wood. [2]   The jade coffin was similarly a protecting life-giver.

As there were black and white *nig-gil-ma*, and black and white deities, so were there black and white rhinoceroses and black and white elephants.   Gautama Buddha entered his mother's right side "in the form of a superb white elephant ".[3]

The water-rhinoceros had " pearl-like armour " (a significant comparison when it is remembered that pearl-lore and jade-lore are so similar), but not the mountain rhinoceros.   It was the horn of the male animal that had special virtues.   The markings on it included a red line, which was a result of his habit of gazing at the moon; the spots were stars.   As the animal was connected with the " material sky ", the horn was impregnated with the Yang principle.   A horn that " communicated with the sky " was of the " first quality ".   Laufer quotes the statement : " If the horn of the rhinoceros ' communicating with the sky ' emits light, so that it can be seen by night,

[1] Op. cit., p. 161.
[2] Legge, *Sacred Books of the East*, Vol. XXVII, p. 158, and Laufer, *Chinese Clay Images*, p. 172.   [3] Rhys David, *Buddhism* (London, 1903), p. 183.

it is called 'horn shining at night' (*ye ming si*): hence it can communicate with the spirits and open a way through the water". A man who carried in his mouth a piece of rhinoceros horn found, it was alleged, on diving into the sea, that the water gave way so as to allow a space for breathing.[1] The pearl-fishers may therefore have used the magic horn, believing that it protected and assisted them.

It is recorded of a horn presented to an emperor of the T'ang Dynasty that " at night it emitted light so that a space of a hundred paces was illuminated. Manifold silk wrappers laid around it could not hide its luminous power. The emperor ordered it to be cut into slices and worked up into a girdle; and whenever he went out on a hunting expedition, he saved candle light at night." With the aid of the horn it was possible " to see super-natural monsters in water ".[2]

There was warm rhinoceros horn and cold rhinoceros horn, as there was warm jade and cold jade. A Chinese work of the eighth century mentions "cold-dispelling rhinoceros horn (*pi han si*), whose colour is golden.[3] . . . During the winter months it spreads warmth which imparts a genial feeling to man." Another work speaks of "heat-dispelling rhinoceros horn (*pi shu si*). . . . During the summer months it can cool off the hot temperature." Girdles of " wrath-dispelling " horn caused men " to abandon their anger "; hair-pins, combs, &c., were made from " dust dispelling " horn. Rhinoceros horn had, like jade, healing properties. A fourth-century Chinese writer tells that " the horn can neutralize poison because the animal devours all sorts of vegetable poisons with its food ". Chinese drug stores still stock shavings of the horn to

---

[1] Laufer, op. cit., p. 138.   [2] *Chinese Clay Images*, pp. 150 *et seq.*
[3] Like the "golden sun".

cure fever, smallpox, ophthalmia, &c.[1]   According to
S. W. Williams[2] " a decoction of the horn shavings is
given to women just before parturition and also to frighten
children ".   A medicine is prepared from rhinoceros skin,
too.   Laufer states that " the skin, as well as the horn,
the blood, and the teeth, were medicinally employed in
Cambodja, notably against heart diseases. . . . In Japan
rhinoceros horn is powdered and used as a specific in fever
cases of all kind."   Dragon bones were used in like
manner in China.   It is of importance to note that the
rhinoceros horn derived its healing qualities because the
animal fed on plants and trees provided with thorns.[3]
Like the dragon, the rhinoceros had an intimate connection
with certain plants; like the ginseng-devouring goat, it
carried in its blood the virtue of the plants and herbs it
devoured.   In Tibet and China the rhinoceros became
confused with the stag, antelope, and goat with one horn.
It was the prototype of the unicorn.   In India and Iran
it was confused with the horse.   There is in Chinese lore
a " spiritual rhinoceros (ling si)" with the body of an ox,
the hump of a zebu, cloven feet, the snout of a pig, and a
horn in front.[4]   It may be that in ancient times the lore
connected with the hippopotamus was transferred by the
searchers for pearls, precious stones, and metals to the
Chinese " water-rhinoceros ".   Like the composite wonder-
beast in the Osirian hall of judgment, which tore the
unworthy soul to pieces, the rhinoceros had its place in
judicial proceedings in China.   In its goat form it solved
a difficult case when Kas Yas administered justice by butt-
ing the guilty party and sparing the innocent.[5]

---

[1] *Chinese Clay Images*, pp. 152-3 and p. 153 *n.* 2.
[2] *The Chinese Commercial Guide*, p. 95 (Hong-Kong, 1863).
[3] *Chinese Clay Images*, p. 139.   [4] *Ibid.*, p. 108.
[5] Referred to by the philosopher Wang Ch'ung in his work *Lun hêng* (A.D. 82 or 83),
quoted by Laufer, op. cit., p. 171 *n.* 3.

The importance attached to jade in prehistoric Europe raises an interesting problem. Jade artifacts have been found associated with the Swiss lake-dwellings, and at "Neolithic sites" in Brittany and Ireland, as well as in Malta and Sicily, and other parts of Europe. Schliemann found votive axes of green and white jade (nephrite) in the stratum of the first city of Troy. It was believed at the time that the European jade artifacts had been imported from the borders of China, and Professor Fischer expressed the wish "that before the end of his life the fortune might be allotted to him of finding out what people brought them to Europe".[1] Professor Max Muller believed that the Aryans were the carriers of jade. "If", he wrote, "the Aryan settlers could carry with them into Europe so ponderous a tool as their language, without chipping a single facet, there is nothing so very surprising in their having carried along and carefully preserved from generation to generation so handy and so valuable an instrument as a scraper or a knife, made of a substance which is *Aere perennuis*".[2]

After a prolonged search, European scientists have located nephrite (jade proper) or jadeite in situ in Silesia, Austria, North Germany, Italy, and among the Alps. "A sort of nephrite workshop was discovered in the vicinity of Maurach (Switzerland), where hatchets chiselled from the mineral and one hundred and fifty-four pieces of cuttings were found."[3]

Laufer writes in this connection : "If we consider how many years, and what strenuous efforts it required for European scientists to discover the actual sites of jade in Central Europe, which is geographically so well explored, we may realize that it could not have been quite such an

---

[1] Schliemann's *Ilios*, p. 242.   [2] Letter to the *Times*, 18th December, 1879.
[3] Laufer's *Jade*, p. 2.

easy task for primitive man to hunt up these hidden places". Laufer thinks that in undertaking to overcome the difficulties experienced in discovering jade in Europe, early man "must have been prompted by a motive pre-existing and acting in his mind; the impetus of searching for jade he must have received somehow from somewhere. . . . Nothing", he says, "could induce me to believe that primitive man of Central Europe incidentally and spontaneously embarked on the laborious task of quarrying and working jade. The psychological motive for this act must be supplied. . . . From the standpoint of the general development of culture in the Old World there is absolutely no vestige of originality in the prehistoric cultures of Europe which appear as an appendix to Asia."[1]

Apparently the "psychological motive" for searching for jade in China and Europe came from the Khotan area in Chinese Turkestan, whence jade was carried to Babylonia during the Sumerian period. It is probable that bronze was first manufactured in the jade-bearing area of Asia, and that the people who carried "the knowledge of bronze-making into Europe", as Professor Elliot Smith suggests, "also introduced the appreciation of jade". Laufer comments in this connection: "Originality is certainly the rarest thing in the world, and in the history of mankind the original thoughts are appallingly sparse. There is, in the light of historical facts and experience, no reason to credit the prehistoric and early populations of Europe with any spontaneous ideas relative to jade." After receiving jade and adopting the beliefs attached to it, they set out to search for it, and found it in Europe.

The polished axe pendants of jade found in Malta were evidently charms. Among the Greeks jade was "the kidney stone"; it cured diseases of the kidneys. The Spaniards brought jade or jadeite from Mexico, and called it "the loin stone" (*piedra de hijada*). Sir Walter Raleigh introduced it into England, and used the Spanish name from which "jade" is derived.

Red, green, blue, white, grey, and black jade were used, by reason of their colours, for various deities in China, and to indicate the rank of officials. "White jade, considered the most precious, was the privileged ornament of the emperor; jade green like the mountains was reserved for the princes of the first and second ranks; water-blue jade was for the great prefects; the heir apparent had a special kind of jade."[1] Mottled jades—some resembling granite—were likewise favoured for a variety of purposes.

Jade played an important part in Chinese rain-getting ceremonies. Dragon jade symbols, decorated with fish-scales, were placed on the altar as offerings and for the purpose of invoking the rain-controlling "composite wonder beast" and god. Sometimes bronze and silver dragon symbols were used. According to Laufer, "the jade image of the dragon remained restricted to the Han period, and was substituted at later ages by prayers inscribed on jade or metal tablets. A survival of the ancient custom", he adds, "may be seen in the large paper or papier mâché figures of dragons carried around in the streets by festival processions in times of drought to ensure the benefit of rain."[2] In front of these dragons are carried the red ball, which symbolizes the moon, the source of fertilizing moisture—of dew, of rain, and therefore of the streams and rivers that flow to the sea.

Jade links with pearls in the ocean surrounding the world, in which lies a gigantic oyster that gapes after rain

[1] Laufer's *Jade*, p. 196.   [2] *Ibid.*, pp. 186–9.

falls, and sends forth the gleaming rainbow. The Greek historian, Isidorus of Charace (*c.* 300 B.C.), referring to the pearl-fishing in the Persian Gulf, relates a story about the breeding of pearls being influenced by thunder-storms.[1] The jade ceremonial object, which roused the dragon, had thus indirectly a share in pearl production. Pearls were, as we have seen, likewise produced by dragons, who spat them out during storms. As certain pearls were supposed to be formed by dew that dropped from the moon, it may be that the Chinese gigantic oyster was, when it gaped to send forth the rainbow, receiving the substance of a gigantic pearl from the celestial regions. The life-prolonging and youth-renewing "Red Cloud herb" came into existence during a thunder- and rain-storm.

As we have seen, jade contains, according to Far Eastern belief, the essence of heat as well as of moisture. It contains, too, the essence of cold—not the cold of winter but the coolness desired in hot weather.[2] In the *Tu yang tsa pien*, a Chinese work of the ninth century, it is recorded that the Emperor of China received from Japan "an engraved gobang board of warm jade, on which the game could be played in winter without getting cold, and that it was most highly prized". It is told in this connection that "thirty thousand *li* (leagues) east of Japan is the island of *Tsi-mo*, and upon this island the Ninghia Terrace, on which terrace is the Gobang Player's Lake. This lake produces the chess-men which need no carving, and are naturally divided into black and white. They are warm in winter, cool in summer, and known as cool and warm jade. It also produces the catalpa-jade, in structure like the wood of the catalpa tree, which

[1] *Athenæus Deipnos*, Book III, chap. xlvi; and Jackson, *Shells as Evidence of the Migrations of Early Culture*, p. 77.
[2] Like rhinoceros horn.

is carved into chess-boards, shining and brilliant as mirrors."[1]

Jade is, in short, a "luck stone": the giver of children, health, immortality, wisdom, power, victory, growth, food, clothing, &c. It is "the jewel that grants all desires" in this world and the next, and is therefore connected with all religious beliefs, while it also plays its part as a symbol in the social organization, being the medium through which the mysterious forces of nature exercise their influence in every sphere of human thought and activity.

[1] Heber R. Bishop, *Investigations and Studies in Jade* (New York, 1906), Vol. I, p. 47; and A. Wylie, *Notes on Chinese Literature* (Shanghai, 1901), p. 194.

CHAPTER XIV

Creation Myths and the God and Goddess Cults

Although some exponents of the stratification theory
incline to regard Chinese religion as a stunted outcrop of
animistic ideas, and chiefly because of the remarkable
persistence through the ages of the worship of ancestors
—the worship of ghost-gods and ghosts identified with
gods—there is really little trace of what is usually referred
to as "the primitive state of mind". Under the term
"animism" have been included ideas that are less primitive than was supposed to be the case about a generation
ago. The belief, for instance, that there are spirits in
stones, or that the soul of the dead enters a megalithic
monument, or a statue placed in the tomb, may not, after
all, belong to a primitive stage of thought; nor does it
follow that because it is found to be prevalent among
various tribes isolated on lonely islands it is a product

merely of the early "workings of the human mind" when man, as if by instinct, framed his "first crude philosophy of human thought". The fact that settlers reached isolated islands, such as, for instance, Easter Island, where stone idols were erected, indicates clearly that they had acquired a knowledge of shipbuilding and navigation directly or indirectly from a centre of ancient civilization. It may be, therefore, that they likewise acquired from the same source ideas regarding the soul and the origin of things, and that these, instead of being "simple" and "primitive", are really of complex character, and have remained in a state of arrested development, simply because they have been detached from the parent stem, to be preserved like flower petals pressed in a book, that still retain a degree of their original brightness and characteristic odour.

In outlying areas, like Australia and Oceania, are found not only "primitive beliefs", but definite burial customs that have a long history elsewhere, including cremation and even mummification. "You get the whole bag of tricks in Australia", the late Andrew Lang once declared to the writer when contending that certain beliefs and customs found in Egypt, Babylonia, India, and Europe were "natural products of the primitive mind". But is it likely that such a custom as mummification should have "arisen independently" in Australasia? Let us take, for instance, the case of the mummy from the Torres Straits, which is preserved in the Mackay Museum in the University of Sydney. It was examined by Professor G. Elliot Smith, who, during his ten years' occupancy of the Chair of Anatomy in the Government School of Medicine in Cairo, had unique opportunities of studying Ancient Egyptian surgery as revealed by the mummies preserved in Gizeh museum. When he examined the

Papuan mummy at Sydney he found that undeniable Egyptian methods of a definite period in Egyptian history had been employed.   He communicated his discovery to the Anthropological Section of the British Association in Melbourne in 1914, and, as an anatomist, was astonished to hear Professor Myres contending that it seemed to him natural that people should want to preserve their dead! "If", Professor Elliot Smith has written, "Professor Myers had known anything of the history of anatomy he would have realized that the problem of preserving the body was one of extreme difficulty which for long ages had exercised the most civilized peoples, not only of antiquity, but also of modern times.   In Egypt, where the natural conditions favouring the successful issue of attempts to preserve the body were largely responsible for the possibility of such embalming, it took more than seventeen centuries of constant practice and experimentation to reach the stage and to acquire the methods exemplified in the Torres Straits mummies."[1]   Arm-chair theories vanish like mist when the light of scientific evidence is released.

In like manner may be found in the folk-lore and religious literature of China "mummies" of imported myths, as well as early myths of local invention that, ancient as they may be, cannot be regarded as "primitive" in the real sense of the term.   The following myth, found in the literature of Taoism, may be more archaic than the writings of Kwang-tze, who gives it.

At the beginning of time there were two oceans—one in the south and one in the north, and there was land in the centre.   The Ruler of the southern ocean was Shu (Heedless), and the Ruler of the northern ocean was Hu

---

[1] *The Migration of Early Culture : A Study of the Significance of the Geographical Distribution of the Practice of Mummification*, &c., pp. 20 et seq.

(Hasty), while the Ruler of the Centre was Hwun-tun (Chaos).

"Heedless" and "Hasty" were in the habit of paying regular visits to the land, and there they met and became acquainted. "Chaos" treated them kindly, and it was their desire to confer upon him some favour so as to give practical expression to their feelings of gratitude. They discussed the matter together, and decided what they should do.

Now Chaos was blind, his eyes being closed, and he was deaf, his ears being closed, and he could not breathe, having no nostrils, nor eat, because he was mouthless.

"Hasty" and "Heedless" met daily in the Central land, and each day they opened an orifice. On the seventh day their work was finished. But when he had eyes and ears opened, and could see and hear, and could breathe through his nostrils, and had a mouth with which to eat, old Chaos died.

The meaning of this Chinese parable seems to be that the Universe had, in the space of seven days, been "set in order", Chaos having been transformed into Kosmos.

Although Taoism has been referred to by some writers of the "Evolution School" as "an elaboration of animistic lore", this myth is really a product of the years that bring the philosophic mind. The three "Rulers" may have originally been giants, and the story may owe something to the Babylonian myth of Ea-Oannes, the sea-god, who came daily from the Persian Gulf to instruct the early Sumerians how to live civilized lives; but it was evidently some Far Eastern Socrates who first named the sea-gods "Heedless" and "Hasty", and tinged the fable with Taoistic cynicism.

Creation myths are not as "primitive" as some writers

would have us suppose. Considerable progress was achieved before mankind began to theorize regarding the origin of things. Even the widespread and so-called "primitive myth" about the egg from which the Universe, or the first god, was hatched by the "Primeval Goose" may belong to a much later stage of human development than is supposed by some of those writers who speculate with so much confidence regarding "the workings of the human mind". Even the metaphysicians of Brahmanic India were prone to speak in parables and fables.

"At the beginning there was nothing", the Chinese philosophers taught their pupils. "Long ages passed by. Then nothing became something." The something had unity. Long ages passed by, and the something divided itself into two parts—a male part and a female part. These two somethings produced two lesser somethings, and the two pairs, working together, produced the first being, who was named P'an Ku. Another version of the myth is that P'an Ku emerged from the cosmic egg.

It is not difficult to recognize in P'an Ku a giant god or world-god. He was furnished with an adze, or, as is found in some Chinese prints, with a hammer and a chisel. With his implement or implements P'an Ku moves through the universe as the Divine Artisan, who shapes the mountains and hammers or chisels out the sky, accompanied by the primeval Tortoise, and the Phœnix, and a dragon-like being who may represent the primeval "somethings"—the symbols of water, earth, and air. The sun, moon, and stars have already appeared.

Another version of the P'an Ku myth represents him as the Primeval World-giant, who is destroyed so that the material universe may be formed. From his flesh comes the soil, from his bones the rocks; his blood is the waters of rivers and the ocean; his hair is vegetation;

while the wind is his breath, the thunder his voice, the rain his sweat, the dew his tears, the firmament his skull, his right eye the moon, and his left eye the sun. P'an Ku's body was covered with vermin, and the vermin became the races of mankind.

A somewhat similar myth is found in Tibet. When M. Huc sojourned in that country, he had a conversation with an aged nomad, who said:

"There are on the earth three great families, and we are all of the great Tibetan family. This is what I have heard the Lamas say, who have studied the things of antiquity. At the beginning there was on the earth only a single man; he had neither house nor tent, for at that time the winter was not cold, and the summer was not hot; the wind did not blow so violently, and there fell neither snow nor rain; the tea grew of itself on the mountains, and the flocks had nothing to fear from beasts of prey. This man had three children, who lived a long time with him, nourishing themselves on milk and fruits. After having attained to a great age, this man died. The three children deliberated what they should do with the body of their father, and they could not agree about it; one wished to put him in a coffin, the other wanted to burn him, the third thought it would be best to expose the body on the summit of a mountain. They resolved then to divide it into three parts. The eldest had the body and arms; he was the ancestor of the great Chinese family, and that is why his descendants have become celebrated in arts and industry, and are remarkable for their tricks and stratagems. The second son had the breast; he was the father of the Tibetan family, and they are full of heart and courage, and do not fear death. From the third, who had inferior parts of the body, are descended the Tartars, who are simple and timid, without head or heart, and who know nothing but how to keep themselves firm in their saddles."[1]

P'an Ku, with his implements, links with the Egyptian artificer god Ptah of Memphis, who used his hammer to beat out the metal firmament. Ptah's name means "to open" in the sense of "to engrave, to carve, to chisel"; the sun and moon were his eyes; he was "the great artificer in metals, and he was at once smelter, and caster, and sculptor, as well as the master architect and designer of everything that exists in the world". In the *Book of the Dead* he (or Shu) is said to have performed "the ceremony of opening the mouth of the gods with an iron knife",[2] as "Hasty" and "Heedless" opened the mouth, eyes, ears, and nostrils of Chaos in the Chinese myth. The high priest of Memphis was called *Ur Kherp hem*, "the great chief of the hammer". As we have seen, he was closely associated with the Egyptian potter's wheel, which reached China at an early period. Like Ptah, P'an Ku is sometimes depicted as a dwarf, and sometimes as a giant.

Other hammer-gods include the Aryo-Indian Indra, who builds the world house; the Anatolian Tarku, the Mesopotamian Rammon or Adad, the northern European Thor. The hammer is apparently identical with adze and axe, and in Egypt the axe is an exceedingly ancient symbol of a deity; in Crete the double axe has a similar significance. In Scotland the hammer is carried by the Cailleach (Old Wife) in her character as Queen of Winter; she shapes the mountains with it, and causes the ground to freeze hard when she beats it. The hammer-god is in many countries a thunderer; to the modern Greeks light-

---

[1] *Recollections of a Journey through Tartary, Tibet, and China*, by M. Huc (English translation, London, 1852), pp. 219-20.

[2] Budge, *Gods of the Egyptians*, Vol. I, p. 500 *et seq.*

ning flashes are caused by blows of the " sky-axe " (*astro-peléki*); in Scottish Gaelic mention is made of the "thunder-ball" (*peleir-tarnainach*). A thunder-ball is carried by the Japanese thunder-god, but it is often replaced by the thunder-drum.

P'an Ku plays no conspicuous part in Chinese mythology; he is evidently an importation. In his character as a world-god he resembles the primeval giant Ymir of Norse-Icelandic myth, who was similarly cut up or ground in the "World Mill", so that the universe might be set in order.

> From the flesh of Ymir the world was formed,
> From his blood the billows of the sea,
> The hills from his bones, the trees from his hair,
> The sphere of heaven from his skull.
>
> Out of his brows the blithe powers made
> Midgarth for sons of men,
> And out of his brains were the angry clouds
> All shaped above in the sky.[1]

Ymir was, like P'an Ku, born from inanimate matter. He was nourished by Audhumbla (Darkness and Vacuity), the cow mother, the Scandinavian Hathor.

> From stormy billow sprang poison drops,
> Which waxed into Jotum (giant) form,
> And from him are come the whole of our *Kin*;
> All fierce and dread is that race.[2]

Another version of the Ymir myth makes the giant come into existence like the self-created Ptah:

> 'T was the earliest of times when Ymir lived;
> Then was sand, nor sea, nor cooling wave,
> Nor was Earth found even, nor Heavens on high;
> There was Yawning of Deeps, and nowhere grass.[3]

---

[1] *The Elder Edda*, translation by O. Bray, p. 19.
[2] *Ibid.*, p. 51.   [3] *Ibid.*, p. 277.

The black dwarfs were parasites on Ymir's body, as human beings were parasites on the body of P'an Ku.

It may be that the idea of a primeval giant like P'an Ku, or Ymir, was derived from the conception of Osiris as a world-god, which obtained in Egypt as far back as the Empire period.   Erman translates a hymn in which it is said of the god: "The soil is on thy arm, its corners are upon thee as far as the four pillars of the sky.   When thou movest, the earth trembles. . . .[1] The Nile comes from the sweat of thy hands.   Thou spewest out the wind that is in thy throat into the nostrils of men, and that whereon men live is divine.   It is[2] [alike in] in thy nostrils, the tree and its verdure, reeds, plants, barley, wheat, and the tree of life."   Everything constructed on earth lies on the "back" of Osiris.   "Thou art the father and mother of men, they live on thy breath, they eat of the flesh of thy body.   The 'Primæval' is thy name."[3]

The body of Osiris was cut into pieces by Set.   As the bones of P'an Ku and Ymir are the rocks, so are the bones of Set the iron found in the earth, but no myth survives of the cutting up of Set's body.   The black soil on the Nile banks is the body of Osiris, and vegetation springs from it.

It may be, however, that it was in consequence of the fusion in some cultural centre of the Babylonian myth regarding the cutting up of the dragon Tiamat and the cutting up of the body of Osiris that the northern Europeans came to hear of an Ymir and the Chinese of a P'an Ku from the early traders in amber, jade, and metals.

[1] In Norse mythology the earth trembles when Loki moves.
[2] The "breath" which is "soul substance".
[3] Quoted by Breasted, *Religion and Thought in Ancient Egypt*, pp. 21–2.

When Tiamat was slain, Marduk "smashed her skull".

He cut the channels of her blood,
He made the North Wind bear it away into secret places. . . .

. . . .

He split her up like a flat fish into two halves,
One half of her he set in place as a covering for the heavens.

With the other part of Tiamat's body Marduk made the earth. Then he fashioned the abode of the god Ea in the deep, the abode of the god Anu in high heaven, and the abode of Enlil in the air.[1]

In India is found another myth that appears to have contributed to the Chinese mosaic. At the beginning the Universal Soul assumed "the shape of a man". This was Purusha.

"He did not feel delight. Therefore nobody, when alone, feels delight. He was desirous of a second. He was in the same state as husband (Pati) and wife (Patni). . . . He divided this self two fold. Hence were husband and wife produced. Therefore was this only a half of himself, as a split pea is of the whole. . . . The void was completed by woman."[2]

It may be that India and China derived the god-splitting idea from a common source in Central Asia, where such "culture-mixing" appears to have taken place.

In China itself there are many traces of blended ideas. In the *Texts of Confucianism*, for instance, the symbol of the *Khien* stands for heaven, and that of the *Khwan* for earth.

In one of the native treatises it is stated:

"*Khien* suggests the idea of heaven; of a circle; of a ruler; of a father; of jade; of metal; of cold; of ice; of deep red; of a good horse; of an old horse; of a thin horse; of a piebald horse; and of the fruit of trees.

"*Khwan* suggests the idea of the earth; of a mother; of cloth;

[1] *Babylonian Myth and Legend*, pp. 146–7.   [2] *Indian Myth and Legend*, p. 95.

of a caldron; of parsimony; of a turning lathe; of a young heifer; of a large waggon; of what is variegated; of a multitude; and of a handle and support.   Among soils it denotes what is black."[1]

Here we have the Great Father, the god of heaven, who is red and is a circle (the sun); and the Great Mother, the goddess of Earth, who is black.

The sky-god is connected with jade and metal. As we have seen, the cult of the west attributed the creation of jade to the Chinese Ishtar. Precious metals were in several countries associated with sun, moon, and stars. The horse is one of the animals associated with sky-gods; it was, of course, later than the bull, stag, antelope, goat, ram, &c. Cold as well as warmth was sent by the sky-god, who controls the seasons.

The mother-goddess is the Caldron—the "Pot", which, as has already been noted, was in Ancient Egypt the symbol of the inexhaustible womb of nature personified by deities like Hathor, Rhea, Aphrodite, Hera, Ishtar, &c. The "young heifer" has a similar connection, while the "waggon" seems to be another form of the "Pot". Cloth was woven by men and women, but the production of thread was always the work of women in Ancient Egypt and elsewhere. Apparently the turning lathe was female, because the chisel was male; it may be that it was because the potter's wheel was female that it had to be operated by a man. "A multitude" may refer to the reproductivity of the Great Mother of all mankind. The goddess was, perhaps, parsimonious because during a period of the year the earth gives forth naught, and stores all it receives.

The egg from which P'an Ku emerged appears to have been a symbol of the Mother Goddess of the sacred

---

[1] James Legge, *The Texts of Confucianism*, Part II, p. 430 (*Sacred Books of the East*).

West, remembered in Chinese legends as Si Wang Mu, "the mother of the Western King", and in Japanese as Seiobo, who was guardian of the World Tree, the giant peach, or the lunar, cassia tree (Chapter X). Other references to her, under various names, are scattered through ancient Chinese writings. In the "Annals of the Bamboo Books" mention is made of "the Heavenly lady Pa". She favoured the Chinese monarch, Hwang Ti, who is supposed to have reigned during 2688 B.C. by stopping "the extraordinary rains caused by the enemy".[1]

Here we seem to meet with a vague reference to the Deluge legend. The Babylonian Ishtar was angered at the gods for causing the flood and destroying mankind, as is gathered from the Gilgamesh epic:

> Then the Lady of the gods drew nigh,
> And *she lifted up the great jewels*[2] which Anu had made accord-
>   ing to her wish (and said):
> "What gods these are! By the jewels of *lapis lazuli* which are
>   upon my neck, I will not forget!
> These days I have set in my memory, never will I forget them!
> Let the gods come to the offering,
> But Bel shall not come to the offering,
> Since he refused to ask counsel and sent the deluge,
> And handed over my people unto destruction."[3]

A goddess who protests against the destruction of her human descendants by means of a flood, caused by the gods, was likely to protect them against "extraordinary rains", caused by their human or demoniac enemies.

As we have seen in previous chapters, the Chinese Deluge legend, in one of its forms, was attached to the memory of the mythical Empress Nu Kwa, the sister

---

[1] Legge, *The Chinese Classics*, Vol. III, Part I, p. 108.
[2] This reference to the use of personal ornaments is highly significant.
[3] King, *Babylonian Religion*, p. 136.

of the mythical Emperor Fuh-hi, sometimes referred to as
"the Chinese Adam". Three rebels had conspired with
the demons or gods of water and fire to destroy the world,
and a great flood came on. Nu Kwa caused the waters to
retreat by making use of charred reeds (quite a Babylonian
touch!). Then she re-erected one of the four pillars
of the sky against which one of the rebels, a huge giant,
had bumped his head, causing it to topple over.

According to Chinese chronology, this world-flood
occurred early in the "Patriarchal Period" between
2943 B.C. and 2868 B.C.

Another reference to the mother-goddess crops up
in a poem by "the statesman poet, Chu Yuan, 332–
295 B.C., who drowned himself", Professor Giles writes,[1]
"in despair at his country's outlook, and whose body
is still searched for annually at the Dragon-boat Festival".
The poem in question is entitled "God Questions", and
one question is:

"As Nu-Chi had no husband, how could she bear nine sons?"

Professor Giles adds: "The Commentary tells us that
Nu Chi was a 'divine maiden', but nothing more seems
to be known about her". It is evident that she was
a virgin goddess, who, like the Egyptian Nut, was the
spirit of the cosmic waters.[2] It is of interest to find
the memory of the poet associated with the Dragon-boat
Festival, which, according to Chinese belief, had origin
because he drowned himself in the Ni-ro River. There
is evidence, however, that the festival had quite another
origin. Dragon-boats were used in China on the fifth
day of the fifth month at water festivals. They were

[1] *Religions of Ancient China*, pp. 43–44.
[2] For a discussion on "Early Biological Theories" in this connection see Professor
G. Elliot Smith's *The Evolution of the Dragon*, pp. 26 *et seq.*, and pp. 178 *et seq.*

"big ships adorned with carved dragon ornaments", the yih bird being painted on the prow.[1] De Visser says that these boats were used by emperors for pleasure trips, and music was played on board them. "The bird was painted, not to denote their swift sailing, but to suppress the water-gods."[2] According to De Groot, dragon-boat races were "intended to represent fighting dragons in order to cause a real dragon fight, which is always accompanied by heavy rains. The dragon-boats carried through the streets may also serve to cause rain, although they are at the same time considered to be substitutes."[3]

Having drowned himself, the poet became associated with the river dragon. "Offerings of rice in bamboo", says Giles, "were cast into the river as a sacrifice to the spirit of their great hero."[4] In like manner, offerings were made to dragons in connection with rain-getting ceremonies long before the poet was born. It is evident that he took the place of the dragon-god as the mythical Empress Nu Kwa of the Patriarchial Period took the place of the Chinese Ishtar, and as Ishtar took the place of the earlier Sumerian goddess Ninkharasagga, who, with "Anu, Enlil, and Enki", "created the black-headed (i.e. mankind)".[5]

The same Chinese poet sings of the mother-goddess in his poem, "The Genius of the Mountain", which Professor Giles has translated:

"Methinks there is a Genius of the Hills clad in wistaria, girdled with ivy, with smiling lips, of witching mien, riding on the red pard, wild cats galloping in the rear, reclining in a chariot,

---

[1] Wells Williams, *Chinese-English Dictionary*, p. 1092.
[2] *The Dragon in China and Japan*, pp. 83-4.
[3] De Groot, *The Religious System of China*; and De Visser, *The Dragon in China and Japan*, p. 85.　　　　[4] *Chinese Literature*, p. 52.
[5] King, *Legends of Babylonia and Egypt* (1916), p. 56.

with banners of cassia, cloaked with the orchid, girt with azalea, culling the perfume of sweet flowers to leave behind a memory in the heart."

Like Ishtar, who laments for her lost Tammuz, this goddess laments for her " Prince ".

"Dark is the grove wherein I dwell. No light of day reached it ever. The path thither is dangerous and difficult to climb. Alone I stand on hill-top,[1] while the clouds float beneath my feet, and all around is wrapped in gloom."

This goddess is not only associated with ivy, the cassia tree, &c., but with the pine. "I shade myself", she sings, "beneath the spreading pine." The poem concludes:

"Now booms the thunder through the drizzling rain. The gibbons howl around me all the long night. The gale rushes fitfully through the whispering trees. And I am thinking of my Prince, but in vain; for I cannot lay my grief."[2]

The goddess laments for her prince, as does Ishtar for Tammuz.

The mother-goddess is found also in the "Book of Odes" (*The Shih King*). She figures as the mother of the Hau-Ki and "the people of Kau" in the ode which begins as follows:

"The first birth of (our) people was from Kian Yuan. How did she give birth to our people? She had presented a pure offering and sacrificed, that her childlessness might be taken away. She then trod on a toe-print made by God, and was moved in the large place where she rested. She became pregnant; she dwelt retired; she gave birth to and nourished (a son), who was Hau-Ki."[3]

Professor Giles refers to this birth-story "as an

---

[1] Like the mountain-goddess of Crete.   [2] *Chinese Literature*, pp. 52, 53.
[3] Legge, *Shu King, Shih King, Hsiao King (Sacred Books of the East)*, Vol. III, pp. 396, 397.

instance in Chinese literature, which, in the absence of any known husband, comes near suggesting the much-vexed question of parthenogenesis".[1]

Other Chinese references to miraculous conceptions, given below, emphasize how persistent in Chinese legend are the lingering memories of the ancient mother-goddess.

As was the case in Babylonia and Egypt, the rival biological theories of the god cult and the goddess cult were fused or existed side by side in ancient China.

The goddess cult influenced Buddhism even when it was adopted in China, and fused with local religious systems.   To the lower classes the "Poosa", who brings luck—that is, success and protection—may be either a Buddha or a goddess.   The name is "a shortened form of the Sanskrit term Bodhisattwa", and was originally "a designation of a class of Buddha's disciples. . . . The 'Poosa" feels more sympathy with the lower wants of men than the Buddha (Fuh) does."

One of the holy beings referred to in China as a "Poosa" is Kwan-yin, the so-called "goddess of mercy". Dr. Joseph Edkins[2] says that "this divinity is represented sometimes as male, at others as female. . . . She is often represented with a child in her arms, and is then designated the giver of children.   Elsewhere she is styled the 'Kwan-yin who saves from the eight forms of suffering' or 'of the southern sea', or 'of the thousand arms', &c.   She passes through various metamorphoses, which give rise to a variety in names."

The "Poosa" of Buddhism or the ancient Chinese faith is a powerful protector.   Dr. Edkins tells that "Chinese worshippers will sometimes say, for example, that they must spend a little money occasionally to obtain

---

[1] *Religions of Ancient China*, pp. 21–3.
[2] *Religion in China* (London, 1878, second edition), pp. 99 *et seq.*

a favour of Poosa, in order to prevent calamities from assailing them. I saw ", he relates, "an instance of this at a town on the sea-coast near Hangchow. The tide here is extremely destructive in the autumn.[1] It often overflows the embankment made to restrain it, and produces devastation in the adjoining cottages and fields. A temple was erected to the Poosa Kwan-yin, and offerings are regularly made to her, and prayers presented for protection against the tide."

A vision of this Chinese Aphrodite was beheld about two years before the British forces captured Canton. "The governor of the province to which that city belongs", says Dr. Edkins, "was engaged in exterminating large bands of roving plunderers that disturbed the region under his jurisdiction. He wrote to the Emperor on one occasion a dispatch in which he said that, at a critical juncture in a recent contest, a large figure in white had been seen beckoning to the army from the sky. It was Kwan-yin. The soldiers were inspired with courage, and won an easy victory over the enemy."

Edkins notes that "the principal seat of the worship of Kwan-yin is at the island of Poots". Here the deity " takes the place of Buddha, and occupies the chief position in the temples ". There are many small caves on the island dedicated to the use of hermits. " In several of them, high up on a hill-side ", Dr. Edkins "noticed a small figure of Buddha". Here we have an excellent instance of "culture-mixing" in China in our own day.

Shang-ti, the personal god who rules in the sky, is to the Chinese Buddhists identical with Indra, the Hindu god of thunder and rain. In India Indra was in Vedic times the king of the gods, but in the Brahmanic Age became a lesser being than Brahma, Shiva, and Vishnu.

[1] The season controlled by the White Tiger-god of the west.

When Buddha was elevated to the godhead these great deities shrank into minor positions.   In China they stand among the auditors of the supreme Buddha, as he sits on the lotus flower, and "occupy", as Edkins found, "a lower position than the personages called Poosa, Lohan, &c."[1]

In the next chapter it will be found that floating myths were attached to the memories of mythical and legendary monarchs in China, and that not a few of these myths resemble others found elsewhere.

[1] *Religion in China*, p. 104.

CHAPTER XV

Mythical and Legendary Kings

P'an Ku as the Divine Ancestor—The Mythical Age—Gods as Kings—
The Prometheus of China—Fu Hi as Adam—Doctrine of World's Ages in
China—Links with Babylonia and India—Legendary Kings—The Chinese
Osiris—Reign of the "Yellow God"—Empress and Silk-worm Culture—
Royal Sons of Star-gods—Yaou, Son of the Red Dragon—Shun, Son of the
Rainbow—The Hea Dynasty—The Emperor Yu—Star Myths—Yu and the
River God—Yu as P'an Ku—The Flood Myth in Legends of Yu—The
Dynasty of Shang—Moon and Egg Myths—The Wicked Wu—A Hated
Queen—The Dynasty of Chou—A Chinese Gilgamesh—The Pious King
Wen—Divination by Tortoise and Grass—The Chous as Invaders—Historical
Dynasties—Ancient Iranian Traders—Trade and Civilization promoted by the
Dread of Death.

P'an Ku, the first "man" or "god", was the ancestor
of three families—the rulers of Heaven, Earth, and Mankind. In Tibet, as we have seen, the first man had three
sons, who divided his body between them, and they were
the ancestors of the three human races. Like the Babylonians, the Chinese had dynastic lists of antediluvian
kings. P'an Ku's descendants ruled the nine divisions of
the prehistoric empire or world. There were ten dynastic
periods, the first being that of the "Nine Heads" (kings),
the second that of the "Five Dragons", and so on. The
five dragon kings were connected with the five planets:
Venus, Jupiter, Mercury, Mars, and Saturn, and therefore with the five elements, for Venus was the Star of
Metal, Jupiter that of Wood, Mercury that of Water,
Mars the Star of Fire, and Saturn the Star of Earth.

Thus every part of the terrestrial surface, when identified with one or more elements on account of its shape, is under the influence of the corresponding metals, and also under that of the constellations through which these planets move.[1] As we have seen, the spirits of dragon swords appeared in the sky as stars. The star-gods, like the dragons, were fathers of some of the famous kings of China.

Towards the end came the period "Having Nests", which indicates that houses were built. Then came the period of Sui-zan, "the Fire-producer", who has been referred to as the "Prometheus of China".

A new age was ushered in by Fu Hsia or Fu Hi, the so-called "Adam of China". He is the first monarch of China's legendary history, and was supposed to reign from 2953 till 2838 B.C. Some regard him as the leader of a colony which settled in Shensi. But he is more like a mythical culture hero. He was the offspring of a miraculous conception, and had dealings with dragons. Like the Babylonian Ea he instructed the people how to live civilized lives. Before Fu-hi came, they lived like animals; they knew their mothers but not their fathers, and they ate raw flesh. They kept records by means of knotted cords, and he instructed them in the mysteries of lineal figures, which had a mystic significance. These were eight in number— the eight kwâ or trigrams, which represented: (1) the sky; (2) water of lakes and marshes; (3) fire, lightning, and the sun; (4) thunder; (5) wind and wood; (6) water as in rain, springs, streams, clouds, and the moon; (7) a hill; (8) the earth.

Fu-hi also instructed the people to worship spirits, and he instituted sacrifices. He kept in a park six kinds of animals, and sacrificed twice a year at the two solstices,

[1] *The Religious System of China*, Book I, p. 959.

causing the days to be regarded as sacred, so that the people might show gratitude to heaven.

According to the Taoists, Fu-hi disturbed the primal unity, and caused the people to begin to deteriorate.

Here we touch on the doctrine of the World's Ages. Like the Indians of the Brahmanic period, the Chinese Taoists believed that the first age was a perfect one, and that mankind gradually deteriorated. In the Indian Krita Age "all men were saintly, and therefore they were not required to perform religious ceremonies. . . . There were no gods in the Krita Age, and there were no demons."[1]

Lao Tze, who will be dealt with more fully in the next chapter, exclaims : " I would make people return to the use of knotted cords". His disciple, Kwang Tze, lamented that the paradisaical state of the early ages had been disturbed by law - makers. Decadence set in with the " Prometheus " and the " Adam ", and continued until the people became " perplexed and disordered, and had no way by which they might return to their true nature, and bring back their original condition ".[2]

"It is remarkable", says Legge, "that at the commencement of Chinese history, Chinese tradition placed a period of innocence, a season when order and virtue ruled in men's affairs." This comment is made in connection with the following passage in the *Shu King* (Book XXVII, " The Marquis of Lu on Punishments ") : " The King said, ' According to the teachings of ancient times, Khih Yu was the first to produce disorder, which spread among the quiet, orderly people, till all became robbers and murderers, owl-like and yet self-complacent in their conduct, traitors and villains, snatching and filching, dissemblers and oppressors ".[3]

[1] *Indian Myth and Legend*, p. 107.   [2] Legge, *The Texts of Taoism*, Vol. I, pp. 370-1.
[3] Legge, *The Shu King (Sacred Books of the East)*, Vol. III, p. 255 and *n*. 1.

In some accounts of the early period, Fu Hi is succeeded by his sister, the Empress Nu Kwa, the heroine of the Deluge.

Fu Hi's usual successor, however, is Shen-nung (2838–2698 B.C.), the Chinese Osiris, who introduced the agricultural mode of life and instructed the people how to make use of curative herbs. He was worshipped as the god of agriculture. Thus an Ode sets forth :

> That my fields are in such good condition,
> Is matter of joy to my husbandmen.
> With lutes, and with drums beating,
> We will invoke the Father of Husbandry,
> And pray for sweet rain,
> To increase the produce of our millet fields,
> And to bless my men and their wives.[1]

Shen-nung was not content with two annual sacrifices, and fixed two others at the equinoxes, " that in spring to implore a blessing on the fruit of the earth, and that in autumn, after the harvest was over, to offer the first fruits to the ruler of heaven ".

After Shen-nung died the emperor Hwang-Ti (" The Yellow God ") ascended the throne. He was in the literal sense the " Son of Heaven ", for his real father was the thunder-god, and he had therefore " a dragon-like countenance ". As in the case of Osiris, who was reputed to have reigned over Egypt, it is difficult to conclude whether he was a deified monarch or a humanized deity. He belongs, of course, to the mythical period of the " five Tis " in Chinese legendary history.

The account of his origin sets forth that one night his mother witnessed a brilliant flash of lightning which darted from the vicinity of the star *ch'oo* in the Great Bushel (the " Great Bear ") and lit up the whole country.

---

[1] Giles, *Religions of Ancient China*, p. 22.

Her Majesty became pregnant, but did not give birth to her son until twenty-five months later. Hwang Ti was able to speak as soon as he was born. When he ascended the throne, he possessed the power of summoning spirits to attend at the royal palace, and his allies in battle included tigers, panthers, and bears, as those of Rama, the hero of the Indian epic, the *Ramáyana*, included bears and gigantic monkeys. Hwang Ti was a lover of peace, and because he caused peaceful conditions to prevail, phœnixes nested in his garden, or, like swallows, perched on the palace roof and terraces and sang in the courtyard. Other spirit-birds haunted the residence of the " Yellow God".

He built a large temple so that he might not be prevented by bad weather from offering up sacrifices and performing other religious ceremonies at any season of the year, and he instructed the people in their duties towards the spirits, their ancestors, and himself. He fixed the holy days and introduced music in temple worship. His wife undertook the duty of nourishing silk-worms and producing silk. An enclosure on the north side of the temple was planted with mulberry trees, and in this grove the Empress and the ladies of her court attended to the silk-worms specially kept for the silk required for religious ceremonies. Her Majesty was the goddess as her husband was the god, and had therefore to promote reproduction and growth. She therefore visited also the enclosure on the southern side of the temple in which grew the cereals and fruits offered to the deities.

Hwang Ti was specially favoured by the goddess known as " the heavenly lady Pao", who on one occasion stopped the heavy and destructive rains that had been caused by the enemy.

When the Emperor was in his seventy-seventh year, he retired from the world, like an Indian ascetic, to practise austerities beside the Jo water. He died in his one hundredth year. Some tell that when he was ascending to heaven an earthquake occurred; others hold that he never died but was transformed into a dragon. After he passed away, either as a soul or dragon, to associate with the immortals, a wooden image of him was made and worshipped by princes.

His successor is said to have been the Emperor Che, whose dynastic title was Shao-Hao. This monarch was the son of a star god. One night his mother beheld a star, which resembled a rainbow, floating on a stream in the direction of a small island. After retiring to rest she dreamed that she received the star, and, in due course, she gave birth to her son. Phœnixes visited the royal palace on the day that he ascended the throne. This monarch had some mysterious association with the west— probably with the goddess of the west—and is said to have commanded an army of birds.

He was followed by the Emperor Chuen-Heugh (Kao-Yang). He, too, was the son of a star-god. It chanced that his mother witnessed the *Yao-Kwang* star passing through the moon like a rainbow. She gave birth to her son in the vicinity of the Jo water. There was a shield and spear on his head at birth, a tradition which recalls that when the Indian princess Pritha gave birth to Karna, son of Surya, the sun-god, he was fully armed.

Chuen-Heugh was a great sage. "He invented calendaric calculations and delineations of the heavenly bodies," and composed a piece of music called "The Answer to the Clouds".

Next came the Emperor Kuh (Kao-sin) who, like Richard III, had teeth when he was born. He similarly rose from the rank of a State prince to the Imperial throne. The State of Yew-Kae was conquered by him. His son, named Che, proved to be unworthy, and his younger son, Yao, was selected as his successor.

The Emperor Yao was the son of a red dragon, as well as of the Emperor, and was not born until fourteen months after conception. He is said to have been ten cubits in height when full grown. There were two pupils in each of his eyes. He was a great sage and wonderful happenings occurred during his reign.

A mysterious grass grew on the palace stairs. It bore a pod on each day of the month. He selected as his colleague and successor the sage Shun, who had held an undistinguished position. It is told that this selection was approved by five star-gods whose spirits appeared as five old men and walked about among the islands of the River Ho. On another occasion a bright light came from the river; then beautifully-coloured vapours arose and a dragon-horse appeared, carrying in its mouth a scaly cuirass for Shun, whose appointment was thus definitely approved by Heaven. Thirty years later a tortoise rose from the water and rested on the altar. On its back was an inscribed order instructing Yao to resign in favour of Shun. This divine command was duly obeyed.

Shun's mother had conceived after seeing a rainbow. As has been stated, a rainbow was believed to emanate from the gigantic oyster that lay in mid ocean. When the child was born his mother and father detested him, because his body was black and his eyes had double pupils, and because he had a dragon face and a large mouth. When he became a youth he reached the height of six cubits, and was thus like the Egyptian Horus and the Norse hero Sigurd, a veritable giant. His parents endeavoured on more than one occasion to cause his death by giving him difficult tasks to perform, and acting treacherously towards him. On one occasion they ordered him to plaster a granary, and when he was engaged at the work they set fire to the building. But Shun was clad in "bird's work clothing", which seems to indicate that he had power to assume bird form, and he flew away. He was next ordered to deepen a well. He went to work obediently, and while engaged in his task the well was suddenly filled up with stones. But Shun had "dragon's work clothing", or was able to assume a dragon form, and contrived to escape through the side of the well. Like Hercules, he performed all his difficult tasks and escaped without injury.

Although Shun is usually said to have been selected by Yaou as his successor, a vague tradition states that he dethroned Yaou by force and kept him a prisoner. Before long, however, he degraded the young ruler and took his place.

On ascending the throne, Shun publicly worshipped the spirit of Shang Ti (Ruler of Heaven, the personal god). He enacted new laws, so that the government of the Empire might be regulated and strengthened, and he was the first monarch to create Mandarins. Shun is credited with selecting his successor Yu.

The Emperor Yu was the first monarch of the Dynasty of Hea. According to tradition he was the son of a star-god. It is told that one night his mother saw a falling star and became pregnant. She afterwards swallowed a pearl that had been dropped by a spirit. In due course she gave birth to Yu.

A similar myth is attached to the memory of the Irish Christian saint Ciaran of Saigir, which was probably taken over from some ancient Celtic hero, the son or grandson of Sirona (the aged one or star-goddess). A Gaelic poem, believed to have been composed in the ninth century, sets forth :

Liadaine (his mother) was asleep
On her bed (a saying not wrong).
When she turned her face to heaven
A star fell into her mouth.
Thence was born the marvellous child,
Ciaran of Saigir who is proclaimed to thee
And thence (a saying without pride)
Luaigne (Liadaine's husband) said he (Ciaran) was not his son.[1]

Osiris, as the son of the cow-goddess, was a son of the moon, from which fell a fertilizing ray of light. The Egyptian deities had star forms. As stars, they rose from malachite pools and perched in swallow-shape on the branches of the world-tree of the Great Mother. Hathor and Isis were personified as the star Sirius, from which fell the tear, or drop of dew, that caused the low Nile to have increase and rise in flood. As the morning star, the goddess was the mother of the rising sun. Much star-lore surviving from ancient times remains to be gleaned.

When the star-deity's son, the Chinese Emperor Yu, was born, he had the mouth of a tiger. "His ears had three orifices; his head bore the resemblance of the star *Kow* and *K'een*. On his breast seemed a figure in gem of the Great Bear." When he grew up he reached the height of 9 cubits, 6 inches.[2]

The Irish hero, Cuchullin, was likewise a marvellous youngster. He had "seven toes to each foot, and to either hand as many fingers; his eyes were bright, with seven pupils apiece", and so on.

Yu was probably a historical character, to whose memory many floating myths and legends were attached. He figures as the hero of a deluge. One night, during his youth, he dreamt that while bathing in the Ho (the

---

[1] *Three Irish Glossaries*, Whitley Stokes (London, 1862), p. lxxiii.
[2] Legge, *The Chinese Classics*, Vol. III, Part I, p. 117.

Yellow River) he drank up the water. He also beheld a white fox with nine tails—a particularly good omen. This was during the reign of Yau. Shun came to know about him and showed him special favour, causing him to be promoted until he became an influential man in the Empire.

The gods were well pleased because he was loved by them. One day, as Yu stood on the banks of the River Ho, gazing at the water, a god appeared as a tall, white-faced man, with the body of a fish, like the Babylonian Ea. He addressed Yu and said: "I am the spirit of the Ho. Wan-ming shall regulate the waters."

The god then gave Yu a plan of the Ho, which gave full details regarding the regulating of the waters, and sank into the river.

A good deal of controversy has been engaged in as to what Yu was supposed to have done. In the *Shu King* ("The Tribute of Yu" chapter) it is stated: "Yu divided the land, following the course of the hills, he cut down the trees. He determined the highest hills and largest rivers (in the several regions). . . . The (waters of the) Hang and Wei were brought to their proper channels." Other rivers were similarly controlled.[1]

In another section Yu says: "When the floods were lifted to the heavens, spreading far and wide, surrounding the hills and submerging the mounds, so that the common people were bewildered and dismayed, I availed myself of four vehicles,[2] and going up the hills I felled the trees. . . . After that I drained off the nine channels, directing them into the four seas; I dug out ditches and canals and brought them into rivers."[3]

[1] Legge, *The Shu King (Sacred Books of the East)*, pp. 64 *et seq.*
[2] Boats, carriages, sledges, and spiked boots.
[3] W. G. Old, *The Shu King* (London, 1904), pp. 36–7.

In the fourth book of the *Shu King*, "The Great Plan", it is said: "I have heard that in old time Khwan dammed up the inundating waters, and thereby threw into disorder the arrangement of the five elements.   God was consequently roused to anger, and did not give him the Great Plan with its nine divisions, and thus the unvarying principles (of Heaven's method) were allowed to go to ruin." [1]

In one of the Odes it is stated that " when the waters of the Deluge spread vast abroad, Yu arranged and divided the regions of the land". [2]

It has been suggested by some that Yu constructed a great embankment to prevent the Yellow River changing its course—a task even greater than constructing the Great Wall, and that he formed dams and opened irrigating channels.   It may be that he did much work in reclaiming land and regulating the government of the Empire.   But there can be little doubt that the traditions surviving from his age were mixed with the older traditions regarding the Babylonian flood.   Yu is no mere canal cutter.   He hews the rocks and forms chasms between the mountains, like P'an Ku, the Chinese Ptah or Indra, he constructs the embankments of lakes, and makes channels for the great rivers, and he drains the marshes. The grounds are made habitable and fit for cultivation. There are even faint echoes of the Osirian legend in the stories regarding his achievements.

After Yu had finished his work, Heaven presented him with a dark-coloured mace. [3]   He was destined to become Emperor of the nine provinces, we are told, but it is doubtful if the Empire was really so large during his reign.   After Shun resigned, Yu ascended the throne.

---

[1] Legge, *The Shu King*, p. 139.   [2] Legge, *Ibid.*, p. 309.
[3] The sky is the " dark sphere", and the mace is therefore a sky-mace.

The vegetation then became luxuriant, and green dragons lay on the borders of the Empire. Yellow dragons rose from the rivers when Yu crossed them. His reign lasted for forty-five years.

The sixth Emperor of the Hea Dynasty was another famous man. This was Shao-K'ang. His father had been murdered, and his mother took flight and concealed herself. She gave birth to her son during her reign in Shan-tung, when he became a herdsman. Like Horus, he was searched for by the monarch who had usurped the throne, and he had to take to flight and become a cook. In time he was able to collect an army and win a great victory, which enabled him to regain the throne of his father.

The last few emperors of the Dynasty of Hea were weak and licentious men. It is told of K'ung-Kea, the fourteenth of his line, that he was the cause of much misfortune, and caused the government to decay. Among the terrible things he did was to eat a female dragon which had been slain and pickled for him. Kwei, the seventeenth emperor, was the first to introduce men-drawn carriages, but the omens of his reign foretold the approaching doom of the dynasty; the five planets wandered from their courses, and stars fell like rain in his tenth year. He was overthrown by T'ang, the founder of the Dynasty of Shang.

T'ang had seven names, one of which was Li. He was descended from the Empress Keen-tieh, who, having prayed for a son, entered a river to bathe. A dark swallow came nigh and dropped a variegated egg from her mouth, which the Empress swallowed. She became pregnant, and gave birth to a son named See, who, when he grew up, was appointed by Yao, Minister of Instruction, and was given the principality of Shang.

Thirteen generations later the wife of one of See's descendants gave birth to T'ang, the future Emperor. She had become pregnant after seeing a white vapour passing through the moon. The child had whiskers at birth, and his arms had four joints. He grew to the height of nine cubits.

Wonderful things happened to prove that T'ang was the chosen by Heaven to reign over the Empire. When he visited the altar of Yao, he dropped a jewel into the water. "Lo! yellow fishes leapt up in pairs; a blackbird followed him, and stood on the altar, where it changed into a black gem." There also appeared a black tortoise, which had on its back characters intimating that T'ang was to become the Emperor. A spirit appeared on Mount Pei at the same time. "Another spirit, dragging a white wolf, with a hook in his mouth, entered the court of Shang. The virtue of metal waxed powerful; silver overflowed from the hills." T'ang himself dreamed that "he went to the sky and licked it. After this he became possessor of the Empire."[1]

When the Dynasty of Shang began to decline, the rulers became weak and profligate. It is told of Wu-Yih, who reigned for only four years (1198–1194 B.C.), he was "without any right principle. He made an image of a man, and called it 'the Spirit of Heaven'. Then he 'gamed with it' (played dice, or at chess), causing someone to play for the image. 'The Spirit of Heaven' was unsuccessful, on which he disgraced it, and made a leather bag, which he filled with blood, and then placed aloft and shot at (the image was probably in the bag as well), calling this 'shooting at Heaven'. . . . In the fourth year of his reign, while hunting between

---

[1] Legge, *The Annals of the Bamboo Book*, pp. 128, 129 (*The Chinese Classics*, Vol. III, Part 1).

the Ho and the Wei, Wu-Yih suddenly died. Ts'een says that he was struck dead by lightning; and people recognize in that event the just and appropriate vengeance of Heaven which he had insulted."[1]

The Kafirs of Africa "play at a game of chance before their idols, and, should chance be against them, kick and box their idols; but if, after this correction, on pursuing their experiments they should continue unsuccessful, they burn the hands and feet off them in the fire; should ill fortune still attend them, they cast the idols on the ground, tread them under foot, dash them about with such force as to break them to pieces. Some, indeed, who show greater veneration for the images, content themselves with fettering and binding them until they have obtained their end; but should this not take place as early as their impatience looks for, they fasten them to a cord and gradually let them down into the water, even to the bottom, thus trusting to force them to be propitious".[2] It may be that Wu-Yih (Wuh-I) was engaged in some such ceremony when he disgraced and tortured his god.

A successor is remembered as the first man who used ivory chop-sticks. The Viscount of Ke admonished him, saying: "Ivory chop-sticks will be followed by cups of gem; and then you will be wanting to eat bears' paws and leopards' wombs, and proceed to other extravagances. Your indulgence of your desires may cost you the Empire." This was Chou-sin, an intemperate and extravagant tyrant. He came under the influence of a beautiful but wicked woman, called Ta-ke, whom he

---

[1] Legge, *The Shu King*, n. 5, p. 269 (*The Chinese Classics*, Vol. III, p. 1). Herodotus tells (Book II, chapter 122) that Pharaoh Rhampsinitus (? Rameses) of Egypt descended to Hades and played dice with Ceres (Isis), "sometimes winning and sometimes suffering defeat". A curious festival celebrated the event.

[2] Pinkerton, *A General Collection of the Best and Most Interesting Voyages and Travels* (London, 1814), XVI, 696.

married. "The most licentious songs were composed for her amusement and the vilest dances exhibited." A park was laid out for her amusement. "There was a pond of wine; the trees were hung with flesh; men and women chased each other about quite naked." Drinking bouts were common in the palace, and when the princes began to rebel, new and terrible tortures were introduced. The queen had constructed a copper pillar, which was greased all over. It was laid above a charcoal fire, and culprits were ordered to walk on it. When they slipped and fell into the fire, Ta-ke was "greatly delighted".

The Dynasty of Shang was overthrown by King Wu, the founder of the Dynasty of Chou. Wu was descended from the famous lady Kian Yuan, already referred to (see Index). After treading in the toe-print (or foot-print) made by God, she gave birth to her son, Hau Ki, suffering no pain. Like Gilgamesh, Sargon, Romulus and Remus, Karna, and other famous heroes, the child was exposed after birth, the lady's husband, according to one Chinese commentator, having been displeased with what had taken place. In the *Shih King* the ode, which relates the legend of Hau Ki, says:

> He was placed in a narrow lane,
> But the sheep and oxen protected him with loving care.
> He was placed in a wide forest,
> Where he was met by the wood-cutters.
> He was placed on the cold ice,
> And a bird screened and supported him with its wings.
> When the bird went away,
> Hau Ki began to wail.
> His cry was long and loud,
> So that his voice filled the whole way.[1]

[1] Legge, *The Shih King*, p. 397.

The ode goes on to tell that when Hau Ki grew up he promoted husbandry and founded the sacrifices of his house. Some of the Osirian - Tammuz traditions were attached to his memory, but, as Legge says, " he has not displaced the older Shan-nung, with whom, on his father's side, he had a connexion as ' the Father of Husbandry ' ".[1]

Before Wu became Emperor, a red man came out of the river to secure the support of allies, and phœnixes brought messages to the effect that the reigning dynasty was doomed. The empire could not be enjoyed by the Shang King; " the powerful spirits of the earth have left it; all the spirits are whisked away; the conjunction of the five planets in Fang brightens all within the four seas ".[2] King Wen, the father of Wu, to whom this revelation had been made, was a ruler in the west, and knew that his son's mission in life was the regeneration of the empire.

The dynasties of Hsia (Hea) and Shang
Had not satisfied God with their government;
So throughout the various States
He sought and considered
For a State on which he might confer the rule.

God said to King Wen:
I am pleased with your conspicuous virtue,
Without noise and without display,
Without heat and without change,
Without consciousness of effort,
Following the pattern of God.

God said to King Wen:
Take measures against hostile States,
Along with your brethren,
Get ready your engines of assault,
To attack the walls of Ts'ung.[3]

[1] Legge, *The Shih King*, p. 398, *n.*   [2] Legge, *The Annals of the Bamboo Books*, p. 143.
[3] Giles, *Religions of Ancient China*, p. 20.

After Wu became the Emperor the worship of ancestors was promoted, and dragons, tortoises, and phœnixes made regular appearances, while vegetation flourished, and the mugwort grew so plentifully that a palace could be erected from it.

After Wu died spirit-birds appeared, and a mysterious bean, which was an elixir, grew up. The Crown Prince was still a minor, and for seven years the Duke of Chou acted as regent. Accompanied by the young king the duke visited the Ho and the Lo. The king dropped a gem into the water, and after day declined "rays of glory came out and shrouded all the Ho (Yellow River), and green clouds came floating in the sky. A green dragon came to the altar, and went away. They did the same at the Lo, and the same thing happened." A tortoise appeared, and on its shell were writings that told of the fortunes of the empire till the dynasties of Ts'in and Han.[1]

The tortoise-shell and stalks of a variety of grass were long used in China for purposes of divination. What the tortoise and the grass revealed was supposed to be the will of the spirits. Nowadays lots are drawn, spirit-writing is believed in, and revelations are supposed to be made when a bean symbol is tossed in the air, as is a coin in the West; when the flat side is uppermost the tosser is supposed to receive a refusal to his prayer.

The Chou Dynasty was founded, according to Chinese dating, in 1122 B.C., and lasted until 249 B.C. It has been suggested that although the Chous claimed to be descended from one of Shun's ministers, they were really foreigners partly or wholly of Tartar origin. King Wu introduced the sacrifice of human beings to the spirits of ancestors, and favoured the magicians, whom he appointed to high positions in his court. His empire consisted of a con-

[1] *The Annals of the Bamboo Books*, p. 147.

federacy of feudal states, and its strength endured so long as the central state remained sufficiently powerful to exact tribute.

After holding sway for about eight hundred years, the Chou Dynasty, and with it the Feudal Age, came to an end. The State of Chin or Ts'in, which had been absorbing rival states, became so powerful that, in 221 B.C., its king, Shih-huang-ti, became the first Emperor of China. He resolved that the future history of China should begin with himself, and issued a decree commanding that all existing literature should be burned, except medical and agricultural books, and those dealing with divination. Those who disobeyed his order and attempted to conceal the forbidden books were put to death. Fortunately, however, some devoted scholars succeeded in preserving for posterity a number of the classics which would otherwise have perished. This extraordinary decree has cast a shadow over the fame of the first emperor, who was undoubtedly a great man.

During the early years of the Chin or Ts'in Dynasty the Great Wall to the west and north of China was constructed, so as to protect the empire against the barbarians who were wont to raid and pillage the rich pastoral and agricultural lands, and impose their sway on the industrious Chinese. "The building of the Great Wall", says Kropotkin, "was an event fraught with the greatest consequences, and one may say without exaggeration that it contributed powerfully to the premature downfall of the Roman Empire." The Mongolian and Turki peoples who had been attempting to subdue China were forced westward, and tribal and racial movements were set in motion that ultimately led to the invasions of Europe by nomadic fighting pastoralists from Asia.[1]

[1] Geographical Journal, XXII, 1904, pp. 24, 176, 331, 772.

The Great Wall is said to have been built in ten years in a straight line of about 1200 miles, the average width at the base being 25 feet, and the average height 30 feet. Strong "block-house" towers were constructed in the wall for the accommodation of bodies of troops.

It was during this Dynasty that China and related forms of that name, based on "Ts'in" or "Chin", came into use in the west. The dynasties that followed the Chin or Ts'in (221–200 B.C.) are as follows:

The Han Dynasty	200 B.C.– 200 A.D.
The Minor Dynasties	200 A.D.– 600 „
The T'ang Dynasty	600 „ – 900 „
The Sung Dynasty	900 „ –1200 „
The Mongol Dynasty	1200 „ –1368 „
The Ming Dynasty	1368 „ –1644 „
The Manchu Dynasty	1644 „ –1900 „

The evidence afforded by Chinese archæology, and Chinese religious beliefs, symbols, and customs tends to emphasize that the early inhabitants of Shensi province were strongly influenced by culture-drifts from the mid-Asian colonies of the ancient civilizations. Hunting and pastoral peoples adopted the agricultural mode of life, and with it the elements of a complex civilization which had origin in those areas where grew wild the cereals first cultivated by man.

The Chinese are a mixed race. In the north the oblique-eyed, yellow-skinned element predominates. Like the Semites, who overran Sumeria and adopted Sumerian modes of thought and life, so did the Mongoloid tribes overrun northern China and became a sedentary people. Petty kingdoms grew up, and in time found it necessary to unite against the hordes who invaded and plundered their lands. The invaders included Siberian nomads, Manchus, Mongolo-Turki peoples, the sacae (western Scythians), and the blue-eyed Usuns or Wusuns who are believed to have been congeners of the kurgan-builders of southern Siberia and southern Russia. It was against Manchus and Mongols that the Great Wall was erected, after northern China had been united as a result of those conquests which made petty kings over-lords of ever-widening areas. During the Han Dynasty southern China was subdued. There the brownish-skinned Man-tze stock is most in prominence. Ancient Indonesian intrusions have left their impress on the racial blend.

Along the sea-coasts of China the sea-traders exercised their influence, and in time their mode of life was adopted by the conquerors from the inland parts of the growing empire. The types of vessels used by the ancient Egyptians, the Phœnicians, the peoples of the Persian Gulf, the Indians, Burmese, Indonesians, and Polynesians became common on the Chinese coast and rivers. Maritime enterprise was stimulated, as we have seen, by the Far Eastern Columbuses who searched for the elixir of life and the fabled "Islands of the Blest". "The Chinese," writes Mr. Kebel Chatterton, "in their own independent way went on developing from the early Egyptian models (of ships), and have been not inaptly called the Dutchmen of the east in their nautical tendencies." [1] It is believed that they were the inventors of the rudder, which took the place of the ancient steering-oar.

Along their coastal sea-routes the Chinese were brought into touch with southern peoples, with whom they traded. Chinese records throw light on the articles that were in demand at markets. "In Nan-čao", [2] an ancient text reveals, "there are people from P'o-lo-men (Burma), Pose (Malay), Še-po (Java), P'o-ni (Borneo), K'un-lun (a Malayan country), and of many other heretic tribes, meeting

[1] *Sailing Ships and their Story*, p. 310.   [2] In Yün-nan.

at one trading-mart, where pearls and precious stones in great number are exchanged for gold and musk."[1]   The early traders by sea and land attached great importance to medicines and elixirs, and precious stones and metals, and pearls.

The overland trade-routes through Iran brought the Chinese into direct touch with Lesser Fu-lin (Syria), and ultimately with Greater Fu-lin (the Byzantine Empire). The vine and other plants with ancient religious associations were imported into China, and the Chinese peach tree reached Europe.   With the peach went silk.   "It is not impossible," says Laufer, "that these two gifts were transmitted by the silk-dealers, first to Iran (in the second or first century B.C.), and thence to Armenia, Greece, and Rome (in the first century A.D.)."[2]

As the cuckoos hatched in the nests of hedge-sparrows, meadow-pipits, and wagtails overcome and eject the off-spring of their foster-parents, so did the vigorous nomadic peoples who absorbed the elements of ancient civilizations overcome and eject the offspring of their "foster-parents". The Babylonian Empire perished, and Irania, which had been stimulated by it to adopt civilized conditions of life, became, in turn, the nursery of vigorous states.   Recent discoveries have brought to light evidence which shows that the Iranian peoples "once covered an immense terri-tory, extending all over Chinese Turkestan, migrating into China, coming into contact with the Chinese, and exerting a profound influence on nations of other stock, notably Turks and Chinese.   The Iranians were the great media-tors between the West and the East, conveying the heritage of Hellenistic ideas to central and eastern Asia, and trans-mitting valuable plants and goods of China to the Medi-terranean area."[3]

---

[1] *Sino-Iranica*, p. 469.   [2] Pliny, XV, 11, 13, and *Sino-Iranica*, p. 539.
[3] *Sino-Iranica*, p. 185.

The laws of supply and demand operated then as now on the trade-routes, which brought communities of regular traders into touch after they had cultivated plants or manufactured articles to offer in exchange for what they received. Before these routes could, however, have hummed with commerce, a considerable advance in civilization had to be achieved. States had to be organized and laws enforced for the protection of property and property owners.

The Iranians, who obtained silk from China, were not the originators of the culture represented by this commodity; they simply stimulated the demand for silk. Chinese civilization dates back to the time when the early prospectors and explorers came into touch with backward peoples, and introduced new modes and conditions of life. These pioneers did not necessarily move along the routes that were ultimately favoured by merchants, nor even those followed by migrating tribes in quest of green pastures. They wandered hither and thither searching for gold and gems and herbs, sowing as they went the seeds of civilization, which did not, however, always fall on good ground. But in those places where the seed took root and the prospects of development were favourable, organized communities gradually grew up with an assured food-supply. This was the case in Shensi province, in which was settled the "little leaven" that ultimately "leavened the whole lump" of northern China. It was after the empire became united under the Ts'in Dynasty that organized trade with the west assumed great dimensions, and was regularly maintained under assured protection.

Myths as well as herbs and gems and garments were exchanged by traders. With the glittering jewel was carried the religious lore associated with it; with the curative herb went many a fable of antiquity. Laufer has shown in his *The Diamond* how Hellenistic lore connected with that gem crept into Chinese writings. It is consequently possible to trace in the mosaic of Chinese beliefs and mythology certain of the cultural elements that met and blended and were developed on the banks of the Yellow River.

Elixirs and charms were in great demand in all centres of ancient civilizations. It can be held, therefore, that behind the commerce of early times, as behind the early religious systems, lay the haunting dread of death. Gems warded off evil, and imparted vitality to those who possessed them, and curative herbs renewed youth by restoring health. Even the dead were benefited by them. Progress was thus, in a sense, increasing efficiency in the quest of longevity in this world and the next.

In China, as elsewhere, the dread of death, as expressed in the religious system, promoted the arts and crafts; artists, engravers, architects, builders, jewellers, and scribes, as well as priests and traders, were engaged in the unceasing conflict against the all-dreaded enemy of mankind, the God of Death. The incentive that caused men to undertake perilous journeys by land and sea in quest of elixirs, to live laborious lives in workshops and temples, and to grasp at the mythical straws of hope drifted along trade-routes from other lands, was the same as that which sent the Babylonian Gilgamesh to explore the dark tunnel of the Mountain of Mashu and cross the Sea of Death, and it is found on the ninth tablet of the most ancient epic in the world:

> Gilgamesh wept bitterly, and he lay stretched out upon the ground.
> He cried: "Let me not die like Ea-bani!
> Grief hath entered into my body, and
> *I fear death. . . ."* [1]

[1] King, *Babylonian Religion*, p. 165.

CHAPTER XVI

Myths and Doctrines of Taoism

Taoism and Buddhism—The Tao—Taoism and Confucianism—Lao Tze
and Osiris—The "Old Boy" Myth—Lao Tze goes West—Kwang Tze—
Prince who found the Water of Life—The "Great Mother" in Taoism—
Taoism and Egyptian Ptahism—Doctrine of the Logos—Indian Doctrines in
China—Taoism and Brahmanism—Metal Searchers as Carriers of Egyptian
and Babylonian Cultures—The Tao and Water—The Tao as "Mother of
All Things"—Fertilizing Dew and Creative Tears—The Tao and Artemis—
The Gate Symbol—Tao and Good Order—The World's Ages in Taoism—
Taoists rendered Invulnerable like Achilles, &c.—The Tao as the Elixir of
Life—Breathing Exercises—The Impersonal God—Lao Tze and Disciples
deified and worshipped.

There are three religions in China, or, as native
scholars put it, "three Teachings", namely Taoism, Confucianism, and Buddhism. Pure Taoism, as taught by
Lao Tze, is, like the Buddhism of its founder, Siddhartha
Gautama, metaphysical and mystical. It is similarly
based on a vague and somewhat bewildering conception
of the origin of life and the universe; it recognizes a
creative and directing force which, at the beginning,
caused Everything to come out of Nothing. This force,
when in action, is called the Tao. It is so called from the
time when it began to move, to create, to cause Unity to
be. The Tao existed before then, but it was nameless,
and utterly incomprehensible. It existed, some writers
say, even when there was nothing. Others go the length
of asserting that it existed before there was nothing. We
can understand what is meant by "nothing", but we can-

not understand what the Nameless was before it was manifested as the Tao.

The Tao is not God; it is impersonal. Taoists must make unquestioning submission to the Tao, which must be allowed to have absolute sway in the individual, in society, in the world at large. Taoism does not, like Buddhism, yearn for extinction, dissolution, or ultimate loss of identity and consciousness in the nebulous Nirvana. Nor does it, like Buddhism, teach that life is not worth living—that it is sorrowful to be doomed to be reborn. Rather, it conceives of a perfect state of existence in this world, and of prolonged longevity in the next. All human beings can live happily if they become like little children, obeying the law (Tao) as a matter of course, following in "the way" (Tao) without endeavouring to understand, or having any desire to understand, what the Tao is. The obedient, unquestioning state of mind is reached by means of Inaction— mental Inaction. The Tao drifts the meritorious individual towards perfection, out of darkness into light. Those who submit to the Tao know nothing of ethical ideals; they are in no need of definite beliefs. It is unnecessary to teach virtue when all are virtuous; it is unnecessary to have rites and ceremonies when all are perfect; it is unnecessary to be concerned about evil when evil ceases to exist. The same idea prevailed among the Brahmanic sages of India, whose Krita or Perfect Age was without gods or devils. Being perfect, the people required no religion.

Confucianism is not concerned with metaphysical abstractions, or with that sense of the Unity of all things and all beings in the One, which is summed up in the term "Mysticism". It maintains a somewhat agnostic, but not irreligious frame of mind, confessing inability to deal with the spirit world, or to understand, or theorize about, its mysteries. It recognizes the existence of God and of spirits. "Respect the spirits," said Confucius, "but keep them at a distance. . . ." He also said: "Wisdom has been imparted to me. If God were to destroy this wisdom (his system of ethics) the generations to come could not inherit it."

Whether or not Confucius ever heard of the system of Lao Tze is uncertain. If he did, it certainly made no appeal to him. His own system of instruction was intensely practical. It was concerned mainly with ethical and political ideals—with political morality. He was no believer in Inaction. The salvation of mankind, according to his system, could be achieved by strict adherence to the ideals of right living and right thinking, and a robust and vigorous application of them in the everyday life of individuals and the State.

The reputed founder or earliest teacher of Taoism was Lao Tze, about whom little or nothing is known. He is believed to have been born in 604 B.C., and to have died soon after 532 B.C. Confucius was born in 551 B.C., and died in 479 B.C. There are Chinese traditions that the two sages met on at least one occasion, but these are not credited by Western or modern native Chinese scholars. Confucius makes no direct reference to Lao Tze in his writings.

Lao Tze[1] means "Old Boy", as Osiris, in his Libyan form, is said to mean the "Old Man".[2] He was given this name by his followers, because "his mother carried him in her womb for seventy-two years, so that when he was at length cut out of it his hair was already white". Julius Cæsar was reputed to have been born in like

---

[1] One of his names during his lifetime was Li Po-Yang: after his death he was Li Tan.
[2] *Journal of Egyptian Archæology.*

manner; so was the Gaelic hero, Goll MacMorna, who, as we gather from Dunbar, was known in the Lowlands as well as the Highlands; the poet makes one of his characters exclaim,

> My fader, meikle Gow mas Mac Morn,
> Out of his moderis (mother's) wame was shorn.

The same legend clings to the memory of Thomas the Rhymer, who is referred to in Gaelic as "the son of the dead woman" (*mac na mna marbh*), because his mother died before the operation was performed. Shakespeare's Macduff "was from his mother's womb untimely ripped".[1]

It may be that this widespread birth-story had its origin in Egypt. Plutarch, in his treatise on the Mystery of Osiris and Isis, tells that Set (the ancient god who became a devil) was "born neither at the proper time, nor by the right place", but that he "forced his way through a wound which he had made in his mother's side".

Different forms of the legend are found in China. According to the traditions preserved in the "Bamboo Books", which are of uncertain antiquity, the Emperor Yao was born fourteen months after he was conceived, the Emperor Yu emerged from his mother's back, and the Emperor Yin from his mother's chest. The Aryo-Indian hero, Karna, a prominent figure in the *Máhabhárata*, emerged from one of his mother's ears; he was a son of Surya, the sun-god.

According to Taoist lore (after Buddhism and Taoism were partly fused in China), Lao Tze appeared from time to time in China during the early dynasties in different forms, and with different names. He had the

---

[1] *Macbeth*, Act v, scene 7.

personal knowledge of the decline of the influence of the Tao from the Perfect Age. After Fu-hi and other sovereigns disturbed the harmonies of heaven and earth, "the manners of the people, from being good and simple, became bad and mean". He came to cleanse the stream of spiritual life at its source, and was ultimately reborn as Lao Tze, under the Plum Tree of Longevity, having been conceived under the influence of a star in the constellation of the Great Bear. Li (plum tree) was his surname.

Lao Tze is said to have held a position in the Royal Library of Kau. When he perceived that the State showed signs of decadence, he resolved to leave the world, like the Indian heroes, Yudhíshthira and his brothers. He went westwards, apparently believing, as did Confucius, "that the Most Holy was to be found in the West". On entering the pass of Hsien-Ku (in modern Ling-pao, Ho-nan province) the Warden, Yin Hsi, a Taoist, welcomed the sage and set before him a dish of tea. Lao Tze sat down to drink tea with his friend. This was the beginning of the tea-drinking custom between host and guest in China.[1]

Said the Warden, "And so you are going into retirement. I pray you to write me a book before you leave."

Lao Tze consented, and composed the *Tao Teh King*,[2] which is divided into two parts, and contains over 5000 words.

When he had finished writing, he gave the manuscript to the Warden, bade him farewell, and went on his way. It is not known where he died.

The most prominent of Lao Tze's disciples was Kwang Tze, who lived in the fourth century B.C. Sze-

---

[1] As has been stated, tea was an elixir.   [2] "King" signifies "classic".

ma Khien, the earliest Chinese historian of note, who died about 85 B.C., says that Kwang Tze wrote "with purpose to calumniate the system of Confucius and exalt the mysteries of Lao Tze". But although he wrote much, "no one could give practical application to his teaching". Other famous Taoist writers were Han Fei Tze, who committed suicide in 233 B.C., and Liu An, prince of Hwai-nan, and grandson of the founder of the Han Dynasty, who took his own life in 122 B.C., having become involved in a treasonable plot.

Another form of the legend is that this prince discovered the Water of Life. As soon as he drank of it, his body became so light that he ascended to the Celestial Regions in broad daylight and was seen by many. As he rose he let fall the cup from which he had drunk. His dogs lapped up the water and followed him. Then his poultry drank from the cup and likewise rose in the air and vanished from sight. Apparently it was not only the poor Indians "with untutored minds" who thought their dogs (not to speak of their hens) would be admitted to the "equal sky", there to bear them company.

It is generally believed by Oriental scholars that both Taoism and Confucianism are of greater antiquity than their reputed founders. Confucius insisted that he was "a transmitter, not a maker", and Lao Tze is found to refer to "an ancient", "a sage", and "a writer on war", as if he had been acquainted with writings that have not come down to us.

There is internal evidence in the Taoistic texts of Lao Tze and Kwang Tze that the idea of the Tao had an intimate association in early times with the ancient Cult of the West—the cult of the mother-goddess who had her origin in water. The priestly theorists instructed the worshippers of the Great Mother that at the beginning she came into existence as an egg, or a lotus bloom from which rose the Creator, the sun-god, or that she was a Pot containing water from which all things have come—the pot being the inexhaustible womb of Nature, and the symbol of the Great Mother-goddess.

But they themselves were not satisfied with this myth. They recognized that there was at work at the beginning a force—a law which "opened the way", a phrase which may have had a physical significance but ultimately became a mystical one. In Chinese Taoism, this force is the Tao which is manifested in order, stability, and rightness; it is Truth.

The Ancient Egyptian philosophers believed, at as remote a time as the Pyramid Texts period (*c.* 2500 B.C.), that everything had origin in Mind. The Universe was the idea of Ptah, the "opener"; he conceived it in his "Heart" (Mind); when he expressed the idea, the Universe came into existence.

> Ptah, the great, is the mind and tongue of the gods. . . .
> It (the mind) is the one that bringeth forth every successful issue.
> It is the tongue which repeats the thought of the mind :
> It (the mind) was the fashioner of all gods . . .
> At a time when every divine word
> Came into existence by the thought of the mind,
> And the command of the tongue.[1]

Although Breasted first thought that this fragment was a survival from the Empire period (*c.* 1500 B.C.), he has since become convinced, like Erman, that it must, on the basis of orthography, be relegated to the Pyramid Age. "Is there not here," Breasted asks, "the primeval germ of the later Alexandrian doctrine of the 'Logos'?"[2]

In India Brahma (neuter) was the World Soul, "that

---

[1] Breasted, *A History of Egypt*, p. 357.
[2] *Religion and Thought in Ancient Egypt*, pp. 46-7.

subtle essence " which, according to the composers of the *Upanishads*, exists in everything that is, but cannot be seen. The personal Brahma, as Prajapati, arose, at the beginning, from this impersonal World Soul. " Mind (or Soul, *manas*)," an Indian sage has declared, "was created from the non-existent. Mind created Prajapati. Prajapati created offspring. All this, whatever exists, rests absolutely on mind."

Another Indian sage writes :

"At first the Universe was not anything. There was neither sky, nor earth, nor air. Being non-existent, it resolved, ' Let me be.' It became fervent. From that fervour smoke was produced. It again became fervent. From the fervour fire was produced. Afterwards the fire became ' rays '[1] and the ' rays ' condensed into a cloud, producing the sea. A magical formula (Dasahotri) was created. Prajapati is the Dasahotri."

When the Rev. Dr. Chalmers of Canton translated the Taoist Texts into English in 1868[2], he wrote: " I have thought it better to leave the word ' Tao ' untranslated, both because it has given the name to the sect—the Taoists—and because no English word is its exact equivalent. Three terms suggest themselves—' the Way', ' Reason', and ' the Word'; but they are all liable to objection. Were we guided by etymology, ' the Way' would come nearest to the original, and in one or two passages the idea of a Way seems to be in the term; but this is too materialistic to serve the purpose of a translation. ' Reason' again seems to be more like a quality or attribute of some conscious Being than Tao is. I would translate it by ' the Word' in the sense of the Logos, but this would be like settling the question which I wish to leave open, viz. what amount of resemblance there is between the

---

[1] In Egypt the " rays " were the creative tears of the sun-god.
[2] *The Speculations in Metaphysics, Polity, and Morality of " The Old Philosopher"*.

Logos of the New Testament and this Tao, which is its nearest representative in Chinese."

The New Testament doctrine of the Logos may here be reproduced by way of comparison, the quotation being from Dr. Weymouth's idiomatic translation, which may be compared with the authorized versions : [1]

In the beginning was the Word, and the Word was with God, and the Word was God. He was in the beginning with God. All things came into being through Him, and apart from Him nothing that exists came into being. In Him was Life, and that Life was the Light of men. The Light shines in the darkness, and the darkness has not overpowered it.

There was a man sent from God, whose name was John. He came as a witness, in order that he might give testimony concerning the Light—so that all might believe through him. He was not the Light, but he existed that he might give testimony concerning the Light. The true Light was that which illumines every man by its coming into the world. He was in the world, and the world came into existence through Him, and the world did not recognize Him.

The meaning of the word "Tao", says Max Von Brandt, " has never been explained or understood," and he adds, " Like the Hellenistic ' Logos ', it is at once the efficient and the material cause." [2] Professor G. Foot Moore says, "Tao is literally 'way'; like corresponding words in many languages, 'course', 'method ', 'order', 'norm'." [3] Archdeacon Hardwick [4] was " disposed to argue" that the system of Taoism was founded on the idea of " some power resembling the ' Nature' of modern speculators. The indefinite expression 'Tao' was adopted to denominate an abstract cause, or the initial principle of life and order,

---

[1] *The Modern Speech New Testament* (London, 1903): John, Chap. i, verse 1 *et seq.*
[2] *The Ancient Faiths of China*, p. 49.   [3] *History of Religions* (Edinburgh, 1914), p. 49.
[4] *Christ and Other Masters*, Vol. II, p. 67.

to which worshippers were able to assign the attributes of immateriality, eternity, immensity, invisibility."

Canon Farrar has written in this connection: "We have long personified under the name of Nature the sum total of God's law as observed in the physical world ; and now the notion of Nature as a distinct, living, independent entity seems to be ineradicable alike from our literature and our systems of philosophy." [1]

Dr. Legge comments on this passage: "But it seems to me that this metaphorical use of the word 'nature' for the Cause and Ruler of it implies the previous notion of Him, that is, of God, in the mind." [2]

Dr. Legge notes that in Lao Tze's treatise "Tao appears as the spontaneously operating cause of all movement in the phenomena of the universe. . . . Tao is a phenomenon, not a positive being, but a mode of being." [3]

Others have rendered Tao as "God". But "the old Taoists had no idea of a personal God," says Dr. Legge.

De Groot [4] refers to Tao as "the 'Path', the unalterable course of Nature," and adds that the "reverential awe of the mysterious influences of Nature is the fundamental principle of an ancient religious system usually styled by foreigners Tao-ism."

The idea of the Chinese Tao resembles somewhat that of the Indian Brahma (neuter). Lao Tze says: "It (Tao) was undetermined and perfected, existing before the heaven and the earth. Peaceful was it and incomprehensible, alone and unchangeable, filling everything, the inexhaustible mother of all things. I know not its name, and therefore I call it Tao. I seek after its name and I call

---

[1] *Language and Languages*, pp. 184-5.   Jowett, in a letter to Mrs. Asquith in 1893, wrote, "I think also that you might put religion in another way, as absolute resignation to the Will of God and the order of Nature" (*Autobiography of Mrs. Asquith*).

[2] *The Texts of Taoism* p. 13 (*Sacred Books of the East*).   [3] *Ibid.*, p. 15.

[4] *The Religious System of China*, Book I, p. 936.

it the Great.   In greatness it flows on for ever, it retires and returns.   Therefore is the Tao great."

In his chapter " The Manifestation of the Mystery", Lao Tze says :

"We look at it (Tao), and we do not see it, and we name it ' the Equable'.

We listen to it, and we do not hear it, and we name it ' the Inaudible'.

We try to grasp it, and do not get hold of it, and we name it ' the Subtle'.

With these three qualities, it cannot be made the subject of description; and hence we blend them together and obtain 'The One'."

Some scholars, like Joseph Edkins and Victor von Strauss, have contended that Lao Tze was attempting to express the ideas of Jehovah in Hebrew theology.   Others incline to the belief that the influence of Indian Brahmanic speculations had reached China at an early period and inaugurated the intuitional teaching found in Lao Tze's treatise.

The idea of the first cause had arisen in India before the close of the Vedic Age.   At the beginning :

> There was neither existence nor non-existence,
> The Kingdom of air, nor the sky beyond.
>
> What was there to contain, to cover, in—
> Was it but vast, unfathomed depths of water?
>
> There was no death there, nor Immortality:
> No sun was there, dividing day from night.
>
> Then was there only THAT, resting within itself.
> Apart from it, there was not anything.
>
> At first within the darkness veiled in darkness,
> Chaos unknowable, the All lay hid.
>
> Till straitway from the formless void made manifest
> By the great power of heat was born the germ.[1]

[1] *Rigveda*, X, 129.

The Great Unknown was by the later Vedic poets referred to by the interrogative pronoun "What?" (*Ka*).

In the Indian *Khandogya Upanishad*, the sage tells a pupil to break open a fruit. He then asks, "What do you see?" and receiving the reply, "Nothing", says, "that subtle essence which you do not perceive there, of that very essence this great Nyagrodha tree exists. Believe me, my son, that which is the subtle essence, in it all that exists has itself. It is the True. It is self; and thou, my son, art it."[1]

The idea of the oneness and unity of all things is the basic principle of mysticism.

> There is true knowledge. Learn thou it is this:
> To see one changeless Life in all the lives,
> And in the Separate, One Inseparable.[2]

Dr. Legge in his commentary on *The Texts of Taoism*, asks his readers to mark well the following predicates of the Tao:

"Before there were heaven and earth, from of old, there It was securely existing. From It came the mysterious existence of spirits; from It the mysterious existence of Ti (God). It produced heaven. It produced earth."[3]

Lao Tze had probably never been in India, but that passage from his writings might well have been composed by one of the Brahmanic sages who composed the Upanishads.

The explanation may be that in Brahmanism and Taoism we have traces of the influence of Babylonian and Egyptian schools of thought. No direct proof is available in this connection. It is possible, however, that the ancient sages who gave oral instruction to their pupils

---

[1] *Indian Myth and Legend*, pp. 97–9.   [2] *The Blagavad-Gita*, Book 18.
[3] *The Texts of Taoism*, p. 19.

were the earliest missionaries on the trade-routes. The search for wealth had, as has been shown, a religious incentive. It is unlikely, therefore, that only miners and traders visited distant lands in which precious metals and jewels were discovered. Expeditions, such as those of the Egyptian rulers that went to Punt for articles required in the temples, were essentially religious expeditions. It was in the temples that the demand for gold and jewels was stimulated, and each temple had its workshops with their trade secrets. The priests of Egypt were the dyers, and they were the earliest alchemists[1] of whom we have knowledge. Such recipes as are found recorded in the Leyden papyrus were no doubt kept from the common people.

Associated with the search for metals was the immemorial quest of the elixir of life, which was undoubtedly a priestly business—one that required the performance of religious ceremonies of an elaborate character. Metals and jewels, as we have seen, as well as plants, contained the "soul substance" that was required to promote health and to ensure longevity in this world and in the next. It was, no doubt, the priestly prospectors, and not the traders and working miners, who first imparted to jade its religious value as a substitute for gold and jewels.

When the searchers for wealth introduced into India and China the god Ptah's potter's wheel they may well have introduced too the doctrine of the Logos, found in the pyramid-age Ptah hymn quoted above, in which the World Soul is the "mind" of the god, and the active principle "the tongue" that utters "the Word".

If they did so—the hypothesis does not seem to be improbable—it may be that as Buddhism was in India

---

[1] The beginnings of Alchemy can be traced back to the early dynastic period in ancient Egypt.

mixed with Naga worship, and was imported into Tibet and China as a fusion of metaphysical speculations and crude idolatrous beliefs and practices, the priestly philosophies of Egypt and Babylonia were similarly associated with the debris of primitive ideas and ceremonies when they reached distant lands. As a matter of fact, it is found that in both these culture centres this fusion was maintained all through their histories. Ptah might be the "Word" to the priests, but to the common people he remained the artisan-god for thousands of years—the god who hammered out the heavens and set the world in order —a form of Shu who separated the heavens from the earth, as did P'an Ku in China.

In India and China, as in ancient Egypt, the doctrine of the Logos, in its earliest and vaguest form, was associated with the older doctrine that life and the universe emerged at the beginning from the womb of the mother-goddess, who was the active principle in water, or the personification of that principle.

In one of the several Indian creation myths, Prajapati emerges, like the Egyptian Sun-god Horus, from the lotus-bloom floating on the primordial waters. The lotus is the flower form of the Great Mother, who in Egypt is Hathor.

Another myth tells that after the heat caused the rays to arise, and the rays caused a cloud to form, and the cloud became water, the Self-Existent Being (here the Great Father) created a seed. He flung the seed into the waters, and it became a golden egg. From the egg came forth the personal Brahma (Prajapati).[1] Because Brahma came from the waters (Narah), and they were his first home or path (*ayana*), he is called Narayana.[2]

---

[1] The Egyptian gods Ra and Ptah similarly emerged from cosmic eggs.
[2] *Indian Myth and Legend*, pp. 100–2.

Here we have the "path" or "way", the Chinese Tao in one of its phases.

When the Tao (neuter) became "active", it did not manifest itself as a Great Father, however, but as a Great Mother. The passive Tao is nameless; the active Tao has a name. Lao Tze's great treatise, *The Tao Teh King*, opens:

> "The Tao that can be trodden is not the enduring and unchanging Tao.
> The name that can be named is not the enduring and unchanging name,
> (Conceived of as) having no name, it is the Originator of heaven and earth;
> (Conceived of as) having a name, it is the *Mother of all* things."[1]

The creation myths embedded in the writings of Lao Tze are exceedingly vague.

> "The Tao produced One; One produced Two; Two produced Three; Three produced All things. All things leave behind them the Obscurity (out of which they have come), and go forward to embrace the Brightness (into which they have emerged), while they are harmonized by the Breath of Vacancy."[2]

Another passage seems to indicate that the One, first produced, was the Mother, and that the two produced by her were Heaven and Earth—the god of the sky and the goddess of the earth:

> "Heaven and Earth (under the guidance of Tao) unite together and send down the sweet dew, which, without the direction of men, reaches equally everywhere as of its own accord."[3]

The fertilizing dew, like the creative tears of Egyptian and Indian deities, gave origin to earth and its plants, and to all living things. But no such details are given by Lao Tze. He is content to suggest that the Tao as "the

[1] Dr. Legge, *Taoist Texts*, p. 47.   [2] *Ibid.*, p. 85.   [3] *Ibid.*, pp. 74, 75.

Honoured Ancestor" appears to have been before God.

In his chapter, "The Completion of Material Forms", he refers to the female valley spirit. "The valley," says Legge, "is used metaphorically as a symbol of 'emptiness' or 'vacancy', and the 'spirit of the valley' is 'the female mystery'—the Tao which is 'the mother of all things'."

Chalmers renders Chapter VI as follows:

"The Spirit (like perennial spring) of the Valley never dies. This (Spirit) I call the abyss-mother. The passage of the abyss-mother I call the root of heaven and earth. Ceaselessly it seems to endure, and it is employed without effort."

Dr. Legge's rendering is in verse:

The valley spirit dies not, aye the same;
The female mystery thus do we name.
Its gate, from which at first they issued forth,
Is called the root from which grew heaven and earth.
Long and unbroken does its power remain,
Used gently, and without the touch of pain.[1]

The symbolism of this short chapter is of special interest, and seems to throw light on the origin of the myths that were transformed by Lao Tze into philosophical abstractions. We find the "female mystery" or "abyss mother" is at once a gate (or passage) and a "root". The Greek goddess Artemis was both. She was the guardian of the portals, and was herself the portals; she was the giver of the mugwort (the Chinese knew it), and was herself the mugwort (*Artemesia*), as Dr. Rendel Harris has shown.[2] She opened the gate of birth as the goddess of birth, her "key" being the mugwort, and she opened the portal of death as the goddess of death. As the goddess of riches she guarded the door of the treasure-house, and she possessed the "philosopher's stone", which trans-

[1] Dr. Legge, *Taoist Texts*, p. 51.   [2] *Ascent of Olympus*, p. 73.

muted base metals into gold. Artemis was a form of the Egyptian Hathor, Aphrodite being another specialized form. Hathor was associated with the lotus and other water plants, and was *Nub*, the lady of gold, who gave her name to Nubia; she was the goddess of miners, and therefore of the Sinaitic peninsula; she was the "gate" of birth and death. The monumental gateways of Egypt, India, China, and Japan appear to have been originally goddess portals.[1]

The goddess of the early prospectors and miners was, as has been said, a water-goddess. In the writings of Lao Tze, his female and active Tao, "the Mother of all Things", is closely associated with water. The chapter entitled "The Placid and Contented Nature" refers to water, and water as "an illustration of the way of the Tao, is", Dr. Legge comments, "repeatedly employed by Lao Tze".

"The highest excellence is like (that of) water. The excellence of water appears in its benefiting all things."[2]

Lao Tze, dealing with "The Attribute of Humility", connects "water" with "women":

"What makes a great state is its being (like a low-lying downflowing stream); it becomes the centre to which tend (all the small states) under heaven.

"(To illustrate from) the case of all females:—the female always overcomes the male by her stillness."[3]

Water is soft, but it wears down the rocks.

"The softest thing in the world dashes against and overcomes the hardest; that which has no (substantial) existence enters where there is no crevice."[4]

---

[1] For discussions on these gates see Elliot Smith in *Journal of the Manchester and Oriental Society* (1916), and *The Evolution of the Dragon*, pp. 184, 185.
[2] Dr. Legge, *Taoist Texts*, p. 52.　　[3] *Ibid.*, p. 104.　　[4] *Ibid.*, p. 87.

The Tao acts like water, and (The Tao) "which originated all under the sky is", Lao Tze says, "to be considered as the mother of all of them. When the mother is found, we know what her children should be."[1]

A passage which has puzzled commentators is,

"Great, it (the Tao) passes on (in constant flow). Passing on, it becomes remote. Having become remote, it returns. Therefore the Tao is great."[2]

The reference may be to the circle of water which surrounds the world. It is possible Lao Tze had it in mind, seeing that he so often compares the action of the Tao to that of water—the Tao that produces and nourishes "by its outflowing operation".

Like "soul substance", the Tao is found in all things that live, and in all things that exercise an influence on life. The Tao is the absolute, or, as the Brahmanic sages declared, the "It" which cannot be seen—the "It" in the fruit of the tree, the "It" in man. Lao Tze refers to the "It" as the "One".

In his chapter, "The Origin of the Law", he writes:

The things which from of old have got the One (the Tao) are:

> Heaven, which by it is bright and pure;
> Earth endowed thereby firm and sure;
> Spirits with powers by it supplied;
> Valleys kept full throughout their void;
> All creatures which through it do live;
> Princes and Kings who from it get
> The model which to all they give.[3]

The Tao may produce and nourish all things and bring them to maturity, but it "exercises no control over them".[4]

---

[1] Dr. Legge, *Taoist Texts*, pp. 94, 95.
[2] *Ibid.*, pp. 67–9.
[3] *Ibid.*, p. 82.
[4] *Ibid.*, p. 94.

Man must begin by taking control of himself: he must make use of the light that is within him. The wise man "does not dare to act" of his accord. When he has acted so that he reaches a state of inaction, the Tao will then drift him into a state of perfection. He must guard the mother (Tao) in himself by attending to the breath. "The management of the breath," says Dr. Legge, "is the mystery of the esoteric Buddhism and Taoism."[1] "When one knows," Tao Tze has written, "that he is his mother's child, and proceeds to guard (the qualities of) the mother that belongs to him, to the end of his life he will be free from peril. Let him keep his mouth closed, and shut up the portals (of his nostrils), and all his life he will be exempt from laborious exertion."[2]

By giving "undivided attention to the breath" (the vital breath), and bringing it "to the utmost degree of pliancy", he "can become as a (tender) babe. When he has cleansed away the most mysterious sights (of his imagination), he can become without a flaw."[3]

The doctrine of Inaction pervades the teaching of Lao Tze, which is quite fatalistic. Salvation depends on the individual and the state allowing the Tao to "flow" freely.

"If the Empire is governed according to Tao, evil spirits will not be worshipped as good ones.

"If evil spirits are not worshipped as good ones, good ones will do no injury. Neither will the Sages injure the people. Each one will not injure the other. And if neither injures the other, there will be mutual profit."

A native commentator writes in this connection:

"Spirits do not hurt the natural. If people are natural, spirits have no means of manifesting themselves, and if spirits do not manifest themselves, we are not conscious of their existence

---

[1] *The Texts of Taoism*, p. 96.   [2] *Ibid.*, p. 95.   [3] *Ibid.*, pp. 53, 54.

as such. Likewise, if we are not conscious of the existence of spirits as such, we must be equally unconscious of the existence of inspired teachers as such; and to be unconscious of the existence of spirits and of inspired teachers is the very essence of Tao." [1]

The scholarly sage thus reached the conclusion that it is a blessed thing to know nothing, to be ignorant. Good order is necessary for the workings of the Tao, and good order is secured by abstinence from action, and by keeping the people in a state of simplicity and ignorance, so that they may be restful and child-like in their unquestioning and complete submission to the Tao. " The state of vacancy," says Lao Tze, "should be brought to the utmost degree. . . . When things (in the vegetable world) have displayed their luxuriant growth, we see each of them return to its root. This returning to their root is what we call the state of stillness." [2]

There would be no virtues if there were no vices, no robberies if there were no wealth.

"If," the Taoists argued, "we would renounce our sageness and discard our wisdom, it would be better for the people a hundredfold. If we could renounce our benevolence and discard our rightness, the people would again become filial and kindly. If we could renounce our artful contrivances and discard our scheming for gain, there would be no thieves and robberies." [3]

Here we meet with the doctrine of the World's Ages, already referred to. Men were perfect to begin with, because, as Lao Tze says, "they did not know they were ruled". "In the age of perfect virtue," Kwang Tze writes, "they attached no value to wisdom. . . . They

---

[1] Herbert A. Giles, *Religions of Ancient China*, p. 47.   [2] *The Texts of Taoism*, p. 59.
[3] Giles, *Chuang Tzu, Mystic, Moralist, and Social Reformer.*

were upright and correct, without knowing that to be so was righteousness; they loved one another, without knowing that to do so was benevolence; they were honest and leal-hearted without knowing that it was loyalty; they fulfilled their engagements, without knowing that to do so was good faith; in their simple movements they employed the services of one another, without thinking that they were conferring or receiving any gift. Therefore their actions left no trace, and there was no record of their affairs."

To this state of perfection, Lao Tze wished his fellow-countrymen to return.

That the idea of the Tao originated among those who went far and wide, searching for the elixir of life, is suggested by Lao Tze's chapter, "The Value Set on Life". He refers to those "whose movements tend to the land (or place) of death", and asks, "For what reason?" The answer is, "Because of their excessive endeavours to perpetuate life".

He continues:

"But I have heard that he who is skilful in managing the life entrusted to him for a time travels on the land without having to shun rhinoceros or tiger, and enters a host without having to avoid buff coat or sharp weapon. The rhinoceros finds no place in him into which to thrust its horn, nor the tiger a place in which to fix its claws, nor the weapon a place to admit its point. And for what reason? Because there is in him no place of death."[1]

It would appear that Lao Tze was acquainted not only with more ancient writers regarding the Tao, but with traditions regarding heroes resembling Achilles, Siegfried, and Diarmid, whose bodies had been rendered invulnerable by dragon's blood, or the water of a river in the Otherworld; or, seeing that each of these heroes

[1] *The Texts of Taoism*, pp. 92, 93.

had a spot which was a "place of death", with traditions regarding heroes who, like El Kedir, plunged in the "Well of Life" and became immortals, whose bodies could not be injured by man or beast. The El Kedirs of western Asia and Europe figure in legends as "Wandering Jews" or invulnerable heroes, including those who, like Diarmid, found the "Well of Life", and those who had knowledge of charms that rendered them invisible or protected them against wounds. The Far Eastern stories regarding the inhabitants of the "Islands of the Blest", related in a previous chapter, may be recalled in this connection. Having drunk the waters of the "Well of Life" and eaten of the "fungus of immortality", they were rendered immune to poisons, and found it impossible to injure themselves. When, therefore, we find Lao Tze referring to men who had no reason to fear armed warriors or beasts of prey, it seems reasonable to conclude that these were men who had found and partaken of the elixir of life, or had accumulated "stores of vitality" by practising breathing exercises and drinking charmed water, or by acquiring "merit", like the Indian ascetics who concentrated their thoughts on Brahma (neuter).

In the chapter, "Returning to the Root", in his *Tao Teh King*, Lao Tze appears to regard the Tao as a preservative against death. He who in "the state of vacancy" returns to primeval simplicity and perfectness achieves longevity through the workings of the Tao.

"Possessed of the Tao, he endures long; and to the end of his bodily life is exempt from all danger of decay."[1]

Here the Tao acts like the magic water that restores

[1] *The Texts of Taoism*, p. 60.

youth. It is "soul substance", and is required by the Chinese gods as Idun's apples are required by the Norse gods. Says Lao Tze:

"Spirits of the dead receiving It (Tao) become divine; the very gods themselves owe their divinity to its influence; and by It both heaven and earth were produced ". [1]

There were floating traditions in China in Lao Tze's time regarding men who had lived for hundreds of years. One was "the patriarch Phăng", who is referred to by Confucius[2] as "our old Phăng". It was told that "at the end of the Shang Dynasty (1123 B.C.) he was more than 767 years old, and still in unabated vigour". We read that during his lifetime he lost forty-nine wives and fifty-four sons; and that, after living for about 1500 years, he died and left two sons, Wu and I, who "gave their names to the Wu-i or Bu-i Hills, from which we get our Bohea tea".[3]

Kwang Tze refers to Phăng. But instead of telling that he had discovered and partaken of the elixir of life, as he must have done in the original story, he says that he "got It (the Tao), and lived on from the time of the lord Yu to that of the five chiefs ".[4]

Others who got It (the Tao) in like manner were, according to Kwang Tze, the prehistoric Shih-wei who "adjusted heaven and earth", Fu-hsi who "by It penetrated to the mystery of the maternity of the primary matter", the sage Hwang-Ti who "by It ascended the cloudy sky", Fu Yueh, chief minister of Wu-ting (1324-1264 B.C.), who got It and after death mounted to the Eastern portion of the Milky Way, where, riding on Sagittarius and

---

[1] *Kwang Tze*, Book VI, par. 7 (Balfour's translation).
[2] *Analects* VII, 1.   [3] *The Texts of Taoism*, p. 167 n.
[4] *The Texts of Taoism* (The Writings of Kwang Tze), p. 245.

Scorpio, he took his place among the stars. Various spirits "imbibed" It likewise and owed their power and attributes to It (the Tao).[1]

Kwang Tze tells that a man once addressed a Taoist sage, saying, " You are old, sir, while your complexion is like that of a child ; how is it so ? "

The reply was, " I have become acquainted with the Tao ".[2]

Here the Tao is undoubtedly regarded as the elixir of life—as "soul substance" that renews youth and promotes longevity. It was not, however, a thing to eat and drink—the " plant of life " or " the water of life "—but an influence obtained like the spiritual power, the " merit ", accumulated by the Brahmanic hermits of India who practised " yogi ". As the mystery of creation was repeated at birth when a new soul came into existence, so did the Tao create new life when the devotee reached the desired state of complete and unquestioning submission to its workings.

There were some Taoists who, like the Brahmanic hermits, sought refuge in solitary places and endeavoured to promote longevity by management of the breath, adopting what Mr. Balfour has called a " system of mystic and recondite calisthenics ". As we have seen, Lao Tze makes reference to " breathing exercises ", but apparently certain of his followers regarded the performance of these exercises as the sum and substance of his teachings, whereas they were but an aid towards attaining the state of mind which prepared the Taoist for submission to the Tao. Kwang Tze found it necessary to condemn the practices of those " scholars " who, instead of pursuing " the path of self cultivation ", endeavoured to accumulate " the breath of life " so that they might live as long as the

---

[1] *The Texts of Taoism*, pp. 244 *et seq.*   [2] *Ibid.*, p. 245.

patriarch Phăng. In his chapter, "Ingrained Ideas", he writes :

"Blowing and breathing with open mouth ; inhaling and exhaling the breath ; expelling the old breath and taking in new ; passing their time like the (dormant) bear, and stretching and twisting (the neck) like a bird ; all this simply shows the desire for longevity ". [1]

The genuine devotees "enjoy their ease without resorting to the rivers and seas", they "attain to longevity without the management (of the breath)", they "forget all things and yet possess all things" by cultivating the qualities of placidity, indifference, silence, quietude, absolute vacancy and non-action". These qualities "are the substance of the Tao and its characteristics".[2]

It seems undoubted, however, that the system of Lao Tze, whereby "spiritual fluid" flowed into the placid, receptive mind, originated in the very practices here condemned—in the quest of "soul substance" contained in water, herbs, metals, and gems. As Indian and Chinese sages retired to solitudes and endured great privations, so that they might accumulate "merit", so did the searchers for herbs, metals, and gems penetrate desert wastes and cross trackless mountains, so as to accumulate the wealth which was "merit" to them. They were inspired in like manner by genuine religious enthusiasm.

The Taoists never forgot the "Elixir". Taoism began with the quest of that elusive and mystical "It" which renewed youth and ensured immortality, or prolonged longevity after death, and the later Taoists revived or, perhaps one should say, perpetuated the search for "the Water of Life", and the "Plant of Life", the "Peach of 3000 years", or "10,000 years", the gem trees, gold, pearls, jade, &c. The fear of death obsessed their minds.

---

[1] The Texts of Taoism, p. 364. [2] Ibid., pp. 364-5.

They wished to live as long as the Patriarch Phăng on this earth, or to be transferred bodily to the Paradise of the West, the Paradise of Cloudland or Star-land, or that of the "Islands of the Blest". Besides, it was necessary that the earthly life should be prolonged so that they might make complete submission to the Tao. Their lives had to be passed in tranquillity; they were not to reflect on the past or feel anxiety regarding the future. The fear of death in the future tended to disturb their peace of mind, and they were therefore in need of water which, like the water of Lethe, would make them forget their cares, or some other elixir that would inspire them with confidence and give them strength. Kwang Tze might censure the ascetics for confusing "the means" with "the end", but ordinary men have always been prone to attach undue importance to ceremonies and rites—to concentrate their thoughts on the performance of rites rather than in accumulating "merit", and to believe that "merit" can be accumulated by the performance of the rites alone.

The explanation of the state of affairs censured by Kwang Tze seems to be that the transcendental teachings of Lao Tze and himself, in which the vague idea of the Logos was fused with belief in a vague elixir of life, were incomprehensible not only to the masses but even to scholars, and that the practices and beliefs of the older faith on which Lao Tze founded his system were perpetuated by custom and tradition by other adherents to the cult of which he was a teacher. Ordinary men, who were not by temperament or mental constitution or training either mystics or metaphysicians, required something more concrete than the elusive Tao of Lao and Kwang; they clung to their beliefs in the efficacy of life-prolonging herbs, jewels, metals, coloured stones, water, fresh air, &c. Withal, they required something to worship, having always been accustomed to perform religious ceremonies and offer up sacrifices. They could not worship or sacrifice to an abstraction like the Tao. Nor could they grasp the idea of an impersonal God as expressed in the writings of Kwang Tze, who taught:

"God is a principle which exists by virtue of its own intrinsicality, and operates spontaneously without self-manifestation".

The people clung to their belief in a personal God, or personal gods including dragon-gods, and when the old deities believed in by their ancestors were discredited by their teachers, they deified Lao Tze and his disciples as the Indians deified Buddha and the Rishis. Lao Tze was sacrificed to in the second century B.C., and a superb temple was erected to him. One of the Emperors who embraced the Taoist faith caused the statue of Lao Tze to be carried into his palace, with pomp and ceremony. The ordinary priests in the temples of China were called Taoists.

When Buddhism began to exercise an influence in China between the third century B.C. and the first century A.D., the Taoists borrowed from the Buddhists, while the Buddhists, in turn, borrowed from the Taoists. The myth then arose that when Lao Tze "went west", he was reborn in India as the Buddha. But the Taoists clung also to the older myth that after Lao Tze died, he ascended to Cloudland and became the personal god of heaven, Shang Ti, the Supreme and Divine Emperor. It was as Shang Ti, a term which includes the spirits of deceased Emperors of China, he was worshipped not only in temples but at domestic shrines, along with the various groups of demi-gods, some of whom were identified with the disciples of Lao Tze. The Chinese Shang Ti, like the ancient Egyptian sun-god Ra and the Babylonian Marduk (Merodach), was the divine father of the living monarch.

CHAPTER XVII

Culture Mixing in Japan

There was not only "culture" mixing but also a mixing of races in ancient times throughout the Japanese Archipelago. Distinct racial types can be detected in the present-day population. "Of these," says the Japanese writer, Yei Ozaki,[1] "the two known as the patrician and the plebeian are the most conspicuous. The delicate oval face of the aristocrat or Mongoloid, with its aquiline nose, oblique eyes, high-arched eyebrows, bud-like mouth, cream-coloured skin, and slender frame, has been the favourite theme of artists for a thousand years, and is still the ideal of beauty to-day. The Japanese plebeian has the Malayan cast of countenance, high cheek-bones, large prognathic mouth, full, straight eyes, a skin almost as dark as bronze, and a robust, heavily-boned physique. The flat-faced, heavy-jawed, hirsute Ainu type, with

[1] *Customs of the World*, p. 380.

luxuriant hair and long beards, is also frequently met with among the Japanese.   Such are the diverse elements which go to comprise the race of the present time."

The oblique-eyed aristocrats—the Normans of Japan —appear to have come from Korea, and to have achieved political ascendancy as a result of conquest in the archæological "Iron Age", when megalithic tombs of the corridor type, covered with mounds, were introduced.[1]   They brought with them, in addition to distinctive burial customs, a heritage of Korean religious beliefs and myths regarding serpent- or dragon-gods of rivers and ocean, air and mountains.   After coming into contact with other peoples in Japan, their mythology grew more complex, and assumed a local aspect.   Chinese and Buddhist elements were subsequently added.

There was no distinct "Bronze Age" in Japan. "Ancient bronze objects are," says Laufer, "so scarce in Japan, that even granted they were indigenous, the establishment of a Bronze Age would not be justified, nor is there in the ancient records any positive evidence of the use of bronze."[2]   Although stone implements have been found, it is uncertain whether there ever was, in the strict Western European sense, a "Neolithic Age".   The earliest inhabitants of the islands could not have reached them until after ships came into use in the Far East, and therefore after the culture of those who used metals had made its influence felt over wide areas.

As we have seen (Chapter III), the most archaic ships in the Kamschatka area in the north, and in the Malayan area in the south, were of Egyptian type, having appar-

---

[1] The terraced mound tombs of the Emperors of Japan appear to be survivals of the ancient tombs.   Although true dolmens have been found in Korea, they do not, so far as is known, occur in Japan (*Journal Athrop. Inst.*, xxiv, p. 330, and 1907, pp. 10 et seq.).   [2] *Chinese Clay Figures*, p. 265, n. 3.

ently been introduced by the early prospectors who searched for pearls and precious stones and metals. In the oldest Japanese writings, the records of ancient oral traditions, gold and silver are referred to as "yellow" and "white" metals existing in Korea, while bronze, when first mentioned, is called the "Chinese metal" and the "Korean metal".[1]   "The bronze and iron objects found in the ancient graves have simply," says Laufer, "been imported from the mainland, and plainly are, in the majority of cases, of Chinese manufacture.   Many of these, like metal mirrors, certain helmets, and others, have been recognized as such ; but through comparison with corresponding Chinese material, the same can be proved for the rest."[2]   At the beginning of our era, the Japanese, as the annals of the Later Han Dynasty of China record, purchased iron in Korea.   The Chinese and Koreans derived the knowledge of how to work iron from the interior of Siberia, the Turkish Yakut there being the older and better iron-workers.[3]

The racial fusion in ancient Japan was not complete. Although the Koreans, Chinese, and Malayans inter-married and became "Japanese", communities of the Ainu never suffered loss of identity, and lived apart from the conquerors and those of their kinsmen who were absorbed by them.

An outstanding feature of Japanese archæology is that Culture A appears to have been a higher one than Culture B, which is represented by Ainu artifacts.   Culture A is that of a pre-Ainu people whom the Ainu found inhabiting parts of the archipelago, and called the Koro-pok-guru. The name signifies "the people having depressions", and

---

[1] *Transactions of the Asiatic Society of Japan*, Vol. X (supplement), p. xxxvi.
[2] *Chinese Clay Figures* (Chicago, 1914), p. 265, *n*. 3.
[3] *Ibid.*, p. 271 and *n*. 3, p. 272 and *n*. 1.

is usually rendered by Western writers as "Pit-dwellers". In the Japanese writings the Koro-pok-guru are referred to as " the small people" and "earth spiders ".

During the winter season the Koro-pok-guru lived in pit-houses, with conical or beehive roofs. The depth of these earth houses was greater on slopes and exposed heights than on low-lying ground. In summer they occupied beehive houses erected on the level. Their " kitchen-midden" deposits have yielded pottery, including well-shaped vases, and arrowheads of flint, obsidian, reddish jasper or dark siliceous rock. Like the " pit-dwellers" of Saghalin and Kamschatka, the Koro-pok-guru were seafarers and fishers. Their houses were erected on river banks and along the sea coast.

Culture B deposits are devoid of pottery. The Ainu have never been potters; their bowls and spoons were in ancient times made of wood. They claim to have exterminated the Koro-pok-guru, who appear to have had affinities with the present inhabitants of the northern Kuriles, a people of short stature, with roundish heads, the men having short, thick beards, and being quite different in general appearance from the " hairy Ainu" with long, flowing beards. Some communities of Ainu present physical characteristics that suggest the blending in ancient times of the "long beards" and "short beards". The pure Ainu are the hairiest people in the world. They are broad-headed and have brown eyes and black beards, and are of sturdy build. Their *tibia* and *humerus* bones are somewhat flat. In old age some resemble the inhabitants of Great Russia.

The Ainu[1] are hunters and fishers. Their women

---

[1] In their own language *Ainu-utara*: "utara" is the plural suffix. Their Japanese name is *Yemishi*; the Chinese came to know of them first in A.D. 659, and called them *Hia-i*. A later Chinese name is *Ku-hi*.

cultivate millet (their staple food) and vegetables, and gather herbs and roots among the mountains. According to their own traditions, they came from Sara, which means a "plain". Their "culture hero", Okikurumi, descended from heaven to a mountain in Piratoru,[1] having been delegated by the Creator to teach the Ainu religion and law. Before this hero returned to heaven, he married Turesh Machi,[2] and he left his son, Waruinekuru, to instruct the Ainu "how to make cloth, to hunt and fish, how to make poison and set the spring-bow in the trail of animals".

When Okikurumi first arrived among the Ainu, the crust of the earth was still thin and "all was burning beneath". It was impossible for people to go a-hunting without scorching their feet. The celestial hero arranged that his wife should distribute food, but made it a condition that no human being would dare to look in her face. She went daily from house to house thrusting in the food with her great hands.

An inquisitive Ainu, of the "Peeping Tom" order, resolved to satisfy his curiosity regarding the mysterious food-distributor. One morning he seized her and pulled her into his house, whereupon she was immediately transformed into a wriggling serpent-dragon. A terrible thunderstorm immediately broke out, and the house of "Peeping Tom" was destroyed by lightning.

This is an interesting Far Eastern version of the Godiva legend[3] of Coventry.

Greatly angered by the breaking of the taboo, Okikurumi returned to the celestial regions. His dragon-wife is not only a Godiva, but another Far Eastern Melusina.[4]

Okikurumi is said to have worn ear-rings. He had

---

[1] *Pira*, "cliff"; *toru*, "to stay".   [2] *Turesh*, "younger sister"; *machi*, "wife".
[3] For other versions, see Hartland, *The Science of Fairy Tales* (London, 1891), pp. 71 *et seq*.   [4] See Index under "Melusina".

therefore a solar connection. The Aryo-Indian hero, Karma, son of Surya, the sun-god, who emerged from an ear of his human mother, Princess Pritha, was similarly adorned at birth with ear-rings. The Ainu have from the earliest times considered it essential that they should all wear ear-rings, and the ears of males and females are bored in childhood. It was similarly a ceremonial practice in ancient Peru to bore the ears of Inca princes. Jacob objected to his wives wearing ear-rings, and buried those so-called "ornaments" with the gods of Laban under an oak at Shechem.[1] Bracelets and "ear-ornaments" were similarly favoured as religious charms and symbols by the Ainu.

It is of special interest to note that mummification was practised by some Ainu tribes or families. Whether or not they acquired this custom from the Koro-pok-guru is uncertain. Women tattooed their arms, their upper and lower lips, and sometimes their foreheads. Tattooing and mummification similarly obtained among the Aleutian Islanders. The same peculiar methods of preserving corpses obtained among the Ainu, the Aleutians, and certain Red Indian tribes of North America.[2] Another link between the Old and New Worlds is afforded by American-Asiatic bone plate armour.[3]

Like the Ostiaks and other Siberian tribes, the Ainu worship the bear. Their bear feasts are occasions for heavy drinking and much dancing and singing. Drunkenness is to them "supreme bliss".

The bear-goddess was the wife of the dragon-god. She had a human lover, and that is why bears, her descendants, "are half like a human being".

---

[1] Genesis, chapter xxxv, 4.
[2] Elliot Smith, *Distribution of Mummification*: Manchester Memories, Vol. LIX (1915), pp. 90 *et seq.*   [3] Laufer, *Chinese Clay Figures*, p. 269.

The salmon is divine, and its symbol is worshipped. Folk-tales are told regarding salmon taking human shape, as do the seals in Scottish Gaelic stories. As in China and Japan, the fox is the most subtle of all beasts. It supplanted the tiger as chief god, according to an Ainu folk-tale. There is a great tortoise-god in the sea and an owl-god on the land, and their children have intermarried. The cock is of celestial origin. It was, at the beginning, sent down from heaven by the Creator to ascertain what the world looked like, but tarried for so long a time, being well pleased with things, that it was forbidden to return. Hares are mountain deities.

The oldest trees are the oak and pine, and they are therefore sacred, and the oldest and most sacred herb is the mugwort. In Kamschatka the pine is associated with the mugwort. The mugwort is connected with goddesses of the Artemis order.[1] Sacred, too, was the willow, and specially sacred the mistletoe that grew on a willow tree. An elixir prepared from the mistletoe was supposed to renew youth, and therefore to prolong life and cure diseases. Siberians venerate the herb willow.[2] The drink prepared from it was a soporific for human beings, wild animals, and deities. Far Eastern deities had apparently to be soothed as well as invoked as, it may be recalled, was Hathor-Sekhet in the Egyptian "flood myth", when she was given beer poured out from jars, so that she might cease from slaughtering mankind.[3]

When the Ainu performed religious ceremonies, shavings and whittled sticks of willow were used, and libations of intoxicating liquors provided. Deities were made drunk, as in Babylonia,[4] and then provided with a

---

[1] Rendel Harris, *The Ascent of Olympus*, pp. 56 *et seq.*, with its *Note on Ivy and Mugwort in Siberia*, pp. 96 *et seq.*   [2] Rendel Harris, *op. cit.*, pp. 101-2.

[3] *Egyptian Myth and Legend*, pp. 6 *et seq.*

[4] *Myths of Babylonia and Assyria*, pp. 143-4.

soothing anti-intoxicant. The Ainu set up their willow sticks at wells and around their dwellings. They had no temples, and when they worshipped the sun, a shaven willow stick was placed at the east end of a house.

The moon-god came next in order to the sun-god. The fire-god was invoked to cure disease. There was a subtle connection between fire and mistletoe, perhaps because fire was obtained by friction of soft and hard wood, and an intoxicating elixir prepared from a tree or its parasite was believed to be "fire water"—that is, "water of life". Offerings were made to gods of ocean, rivers, and mountains.

The world was supposed to be floating on and surrounded by water, and to be resting on the spine of a gigantic fish which caused earthquakes when it moved. There were two heavens—one above the clouds and another in the Underworld. A hell, from which the volcanoes vomit fire, was reserved for the wicked.

Like the Chinese, the Ainu tell stories of visits paid to Paradise. A man, whose wife had been spirited away, appealed to the oak-god, who provided him with a golden horse on which he rode to the sky. He reached a beautiful city in which people went about singing constantly. They smelled a stranger, and, the smell being offensive to them, they appealed to the chief god to give him his wife. The god promised to do so if the visitor would agree to go away at once. He consented readily, and returned to the oak-god, who told him his wife was in hell, and that the place was now in confusion because the chief god had ordered a search to be made for her. Soon afterwards the lost woman was restored to her husband. This man was given the golden horse to keep, and all the horses in Ainu-land are descended from it.

Another man once chased a bear on a mountain side.

The animal entered a cave, and he followed it, passing through a long, dark tunnel. He reached the beautiful land of the Underworld. Feeling hungry, he ate grapes and mulberries, and, to his horror, was immediately transformed into a serpent. He crawled back to the entrance and fell asleep below a pine tree. In his dream the goddess of the tree appeared. She told him he had been transformed into a serpent because he had eaten of the food of Hades, and that, if he wished to be restored to human shape, he must climb to the top of the tree and fling himself down. When he awoke, the man-serpent did as the goddess advised. After leaping from the tree top, he found himself standing below it, while near him lay the body of a great serpent which had been split open. He then went through the tunnel and emerged from the cave. But later he had another dream, in which the goddess appeared and told him he must return to the Underworld because a goddess there had fallen in love with him. He did as he was commanded to do, and was never again seen on earth.

A story tells of another Ainu who reached this Paradise. He saw many people he had known in the world, but they were unable to see him. Only the dogs perceived him, and they growled and barked. Catching sight of his father and mother he went forward to embrace them, but they complained of being haunted by an evil spirit, and he had to leave them.

The Ainu have a Deluge Myth which tells that when the waters rose the vast majority of human beings were destroyed. Only a remnant escaped by ascending to the summit of a high mountain.[1]

[1] Batchelor, *The Ainu and their Folk-lore*. Batchelor, *Notes on the Ainu* (*Transactions of the Asiatic Society of Japan*), Vol. X, pp. 206 *et seq.* Milne, *Notes on the Koro-pok-guru* (*Transactions of the Asiatic Society of Japan*), Vol. X, pp. 187 *et seq.* Chamberlain, *Ainu Folk-tales* (Folk-lore Society's Publications, Vol. XXII, 1888).

Although the Ainu claimed to have exterminated the Koro-pok-guru, it is possible that they really intermixed with them and derived some of their religious ideas and myths from them, and that, in turn, the Japanese were influenced by both Ainu and Koro-pok-guru ideas and myths.   The aniconic pillars and the female goddess with fish termination (the Dragon Mother) figure in Japanese as well as Ainu religion.   Both are found in Kamschatka, too.   Dr. Rendel Harris, commenting on the pillar and fish-goddess idols of the Kamschatdals,[1] recalls "the various fish forms of Greek and Oriental religions, the Dagon and Derceto of the Philistines, the Oannes of the Assyrians,[2] Eurynome of the Greek legends, and the like".   The pillar, sometimes shown to be clad with ivy, links with the symbols of Hermes and Dionysos.   He adds : " The Kamschatdals and other Siberian tribes manufacture for themselves intoxicating and stupefying drinks which have a religious value, and are employed by their Shamans in order to produce prophetic states of inspiration".   The Japanese manufactured *sake* from rice with precisely the same motive, and, like the Ainu, offered their liquor to the gods.

What attracted the Koro-pok-guru and the Ainu to Japan ? As we have seen (Chapter III), the primary incentive for sea-trafficking and prospecting by sea and land was the desire to obtain wealth in the form of pearls, precious stones, and metals.   Now, pearls are found round the Japanese coasts.   Marco Polo has recorded that in his day the people of Japan practised the mortuary custom (obtaining also in China) of placing pearls in the mouths of the dead.   "In the Island of Zipangu[3] (Japan),"

---

[1] Note on *Ivy and Mugwort in Siberia* in *The Ascent of Olympus*, pp. 99–100.

[2] The god Ea of the Sumero-Babylonians.

[3] *Zipangu* and *Cipangu* are renderings of the Chinese Jih-pĕn ("the place the sun comes from"), with the word *Kuo*, "country", added. The Japanese *Nihon* or *Nippon*,

he says, "rose-coloured pearls were abundant, and quite as valuable as white ones." Kaempfer, writing in the eighteenth century, stated that the Japanese pearls were found in small varieties of oysters (*akoja*) resembling the Persian pearl oyster, and also in "the yellow snail-shell", the *taira gai* (*Placuna*), and the *awabi* or *abalone* (*Haliotis*). A pearl fishery formerly existed in the neighbourhood of Saghalin Island. As pearls have from the earliest times been fished from southern Manchurian rivers, in Kamschatka, and on the south coast of the Sea of Okhotsk, it may be that the earliest settlers in Japan were prehistoric pearl-fishers. It is of special interest to note here that, according to G. A. Cooke, pearls and *ginseng* (mandrake) were formerly Manchurian articles of commerce.[1] The herbs and pearls were, as we have seen, regarded as "avatars" of the mother-goddess.

In Korea *ginseng* is cultivated under Government supervision . "It is", Mrs. Bishop writes,[2] "one of the most valuable articles which Korea exports, and one great source of its revenue." A basket may contain *ginseng* worth £4000. "But," she adds, "valuable as the cultivated root is, it is nothing to the value of the wild, which grows in Northern Korea, a single specimen of which has been sold for £40! It is chiefly found in the Kang-ge Mountains, but it is rare, and the search so often ends in failure, that the common people credit it with magical properties, and believe that only men of pure lives can

---

and our *Japan*, are other renderings of the Chinese name which was first used officially in Japan in the seventh century A.D. Earlier Japanese names include *Yamato* and *Ō-mi-kuni*, "the great dragon (*mi*) land", &c.

[1] Yule, *The Book of Ser Marco Polo* (Book III, chapter iii), Vol. III, p. 200. Kunz, *Folk-lore of Precious Stones* (*Memoirs Internat. Congr. Anthrop.*, Chicago, 1894), pp. 147 *et seq.* G. A. Cooke, *System of Universal Geography*, Vol. I (1801), p. 574. J. W. Jackson, *Shells as Evidence of the Migrations of Early Culture* (London, 1917), pp. 106 *et seq.*

[2] *Korea and her Neighbours* (London, 1898), Vol. II, pp. 95 *et seq.*

find it." The dæmon who is "the tutelary spirit of *ginseng* . . . is greatly honoured" (p. 243). A ready market is found in China for Korean *ginseng*. "It is a tonic, a febrifuge, a stomachic, the very elixir of life, taken spasmodically or regularly in Chinese wine by most Chinese who can afford it" (p. 95).

In Japan, *ginseng*, mushroom, and fungus are, like pearls, promoters of longevity, and sometimes, says Joly, "masquerade as phalli": they are "Plants of Life" and "Plants of Birth", like the plants searched for by the Babylonian heroes Gilgamesh and Etana, and like the dragon-herbs of China.[1]

In Shinto, the ancient religion of the Japanese, prominence is given to pearls and other precious jewels, and even to ornaments like artificial beads, which were not, of course, used merely for personal decoration in the modern sense of the term; beads had a religious significance. A sacred jewel is a *tama*, a name which has deep significance in Japan, because *mi-tama* is a soul, or spirit, or double. *Mi* is usually referred to as an "honorific prefix" or "honorific epithet", but it appears to have been originally something more than that. A Japanese commentator, as De Visser notes, has pointed out in another connection[2] that *mi* is "an old word for snake", that is, for a snake-dragon. *Mi-tama*, therefore, may as "soul" or "double" be all that is meant by "snake-pearl" or "dragon-pearl".[3]

---

[1] The Chinese dragon, *K'üh-lung*, originated from a sea-plant called *hai-lü*. De Visser, *The Dragon in China and Japan*, p. 72.

[2] *The Dragon in China and Japan*, p. 137.

[3] The temple of the Mexican dragon- and rain-god, Tlaloc, was called "Ep-coatl", which signifies "pearl-serpent" or "serpent-pearl". Young children sacrificed to Tlaloc by being thrown into the whirlpool (*pan tit lan*) of the lake of Mexico, were also called "Ep-coatl". This sacrifice took place at the water festival in the first month of the Mexican year. The infants were sacrificed at several points, some being butchered on holy hills, including the "place of mugwort", sacred to the mugwort and gem-goddess Chalchihuitlicue, wife of Tlaloc. But only the children thrown into the lake were called "Ep-coatl".

The pearl, as we have seen, contained " soul substance ",
the "vital principle", the blood of the Great Mother, like
the "jasper of Isis" worn by women to promote birth,
and therefore to multiply and prolong life ; in China and
Japan the pearl was placed in the mouth of the dead to
preserve the corpse from decay and ensure longevity or
immortality.   The connection between jewels and medicine is found among the Maya of Central America.   *Cit
Bolon Tun* (the " nine precious stones ") was a god of
medicine.   The goddess *Ix Tub Tun* ("she who spits out
precious stones") was " the goddess of the workers in jade
and amethysts".   She links with Tlaloc's wife.

According to Dr. W. G. Aston[1] *tama* contains the
root of the verb *tabu*, "to give", more often met with in
its lengthened form *tamafu*.   "*Tama* retains its original
significance in *tama-mono*, a gift thing, and *toshi-dama*, a
new year's present.   *Tama* next means something valuable, as a jewel.   Then, as jewels are mostly globular in
shape,[2] it has come to mean anything round.   At the
same time, owing to its precious quality, it is used symboli-
cally for the sacred emanation from God which dwells in
his shrine, and also for that most precious thing, the
human life or soul. . . . The element *tama* enters into
the names of several deities.   The food-goddess is called
either *Ukemochi no Kami* or *Uka no mi-tama*."   Phallic
deities are also referred to as *mi-tama*.   The *mi-tama* is
sometimes used in much the same sense as the Egyptian
Ka: it is the spirit or double of a deity which dwells in a
shrine, where it is provided with a *shintai* ("god body")—
a jewel, weapon, stone, mirror, pillow, or some such
object.

The jewels (*tama*) worn by gods and human beings were

---

[1] *Shinto* (London, 1905), pp. 27 *et seq.*
[2] This does not seem to be the reason for the sanctity of a round object.

not, as already insisted upon, merely ornaments, but objects possessing "soul substance". These are referred to in the oldest Shinto books. In ancient Japanese graves archæologists have found round beads (*tama*), "oblong perforated cylinders" or "tube-shaped beads" (*kuda-tama*), and "curved" or "comma-shaped[1] beads" (*maga-tama*). According to W. Gowland, "the stones of which *maga-tama* are made are rock-crystal, steatite, jasper, agate, and chalcedony, and more rarely chrysoprase and nephrite (jade)". He notes that "the last two minerals are not found in Japan".[2]

Henri L. Joly, writing on the *tama*, says[3] it is also "represented in the form of a pearl tapering to a pointed apex, and scored with several rings. It receives amongst other names *Nio-i-Hojiu*, and more rarely of *Shinshi*, the latter word being used for the spherical jewel, one of the three relics left to *Ninigi no Mikoto*[4] by his grandmother, *Amaterasu*.[5] The necklace of *Shinshi*, mentioned in the traditions, was lost, and in its place a large crystal ball, some three or four inches in diameter, is kept and carried by an aide-de-camp of the Emperor on State occasions."

The pearl (*tama*) is "one of the treasures of the Takaramono, a collection of objects associated with the Japanese gods of luck, which includes the hat of invisibility (*Kakuregasa*), a lion playing with a jewel, a jar containing coral, coins, &c.; coral branches (*sangoju*), the cowrie shell (*kai*), an orange-like fruit, the five-coloured feather robe of the Tennins, the winged maidens of the Buddhist paradise, copper cash, &c."[6] But although the

---

[1] Or shaped like the teeth of tigers or bears.
[2] *Archæologia*, 1897 (*The Dolmens and Burial Mounds in Japan*), p. 478.
[3] *Legend in Japanese Art*, pp. 354–6.   [4] Ancestor of the Mikado.
[5] Goddess of the Sun.   [6] *Legend in Japanese Art*, pp. 350–1.

tama may correspond to the *mani* of the Indian Buddhists, it was not of Buddhist origin in Japan; the Buddhists simply added to the stock of Japanese "luck jewels".

The *tama* of jade has raised an interesting problem. Nephrite is not found in Japan. "It is difficult", says Laufer, "to decide from what source, how and when the nephrite or jadeite material was transmitted to Japan." Referring to jade objects found in the prehistoric Japanese graves, he says: "The jewels may go back, after all, to an early period when historical intercourse between Japan and China was not yet established; they[1] represent two clearly distinct and characteristic types, such as are not found in the jewelry of ancient China. If the Japanese *maga-tama* and *kuda-tama* would correspond to any known Chinese forms, it would be possible to give a plausible reason for the presence of jade in the ancient Japanese tombs; but such a coincidence of type cannot be brought forward. Nor is it likely that similar pieces will be discovered in China, as *necklaces were never used there anciently or in modern times*. We must therefore argue that the two Japanese forms of ornamental stones were either indigenous inventions or borrowed from some other non-Chinese culture sphere in south-eastern Asia, the antiquities of which are unknown to us."[2]

The *tama* is of great importance in Shinto religion. At Ise,[3] "the Japanese Mecca", which has long been visited by pious pilgrims, a virgin daughter of the Mikado used to keep watch over the three imperial insignia—the mirror, the sword, and the jewel (*tama*)—which had been handed down from Mikado to Mikado. There were no idols in the temples. The *Shintai* was carefully wrapped up and kept in a box in the "holy of holies", a screened-

---

[1] The *Maga-tama* and the *Kuda-tama*.   [2] *Jade*, pp. 353-4.

[3] Ise is the name of a province, and the nearest town to the "Mecca" is Yamada.

off part of the simple and unadorned wooden and thatched little temple. The temple was entered through a gateway—the *tori wi*, a word which means "bird-perch", in the sense of a hen-roost. "As an honorary gateway", says Dr. Aston, "the *tori-wi* is a continental institution identical in purpose and resembling in form the *turan* of India, the *pailoo* of China, and the *hong-sal-mun* of Korea.[1] When this symbol of Artemis[2] was introduced into Japan is uncertain. "Rock gates" were of great sanctity in old Japan. There is one at Ise—the "twin-rocks of Ise".

The mirror was the *shintai* (god-body) of the sun-goddess; the sword was the *shintai* of the dragon; and the jewel (*tama*) was the *shintai* of the Great Mother, who was the inexhaustible womb of nature. At sacred Ise, the chief deities worshipped were Ama-terâsu, the goddess of the sun, and Toyouke-hime, the goddess of food.[3] The high-priest was the Mikado, who was a *Kami* (a god), and called "the Heavenly Grandchild", his heir being "august child of the sun", and his residence "the august house of the sun".[4] After the Mikado had ascended the throne, the *Ohonihe* (great food offering) ceremony was performed. It was "the most solemn and important festival of the Shinto religion", says Aston, who quotes the following explanation of it by a modern Japanese writer:

"Anciently the Mikado received the auspicious grain from the Gods of Heaven and therewithal nourished the people. In the *Daijowe* (or *Ohonihe*) the Mikado, when the grain became ripe, joined unto him the people in sincere veneration, and, as in duty bound, made return to the Gods of Heaven. He thereafter partook of it along with the nation. Thus the people learnt that the

[1] *Shinto* (1905), pp. 231–2.   [2] See Index under *Artemis*.
[3] The temple of the sun-goddess is called *Naiku*, and that of the food-goddess *Geku*. These temples are of wood, with thatched roofs. Every twenty years the buildings are renewed.   [4] *Shinto*, p. 38.

grain which they eat is no other than the seed bestowed on them by the Gods of Heaven."

The Mikado was thus, in a sense, a Japanese Osiris.

Shinto religion was in pre-Buddhist days a system of ceremonies and laws on which the whole social structure rested. The name is a Chinese word meaning "the way of the gods", the Japanese equivalent being *Kami no michi*. But although the gods were numerous, only a small proportion of them played an important part in the ritual (*norito*), which was handed down orally by generations of priests until after the fifth century of our era, when a native script, based on Chinese characters, came into use.

Old Shinto was concerned chiefly with the food-supply, with child-getting, with the preservation of health, and protection against calamities caused by floods, droughts, fire, or earthquakes. It has little or nothing to say regarding the doctrine of immortality. There was no heaven and no hell. The spirits of some of these deities who died like ordinary mortals went to the land of Yomi, as did also the spirit of the Mikado, but little is told regarding the mysterious Otherworld in which dwelt the spirits of disease and death. "In one passage of the *Nihon-gi*," says Aston,[1] "Yomi is clearly no more than a metaphor for the grave." It thus resembled the dark Otherworld or Underworld of the Babylonians, from which Gilgamesh summoned the spirit of his dead friend, Ea-bani.[2] No spirit of a god could escape from Yomi after eating "the food of the dead". When the Babylonian god Adapa, son of Ea, was summoned to appear in the Otherworld, his father warned him not to accept of

---

[1] *Shinto* (1907), pp. 15–6.
[2] King, *Babylonian Religion and Mythology*, pp. 35, and 174 *et seq*.

the water and food which would be offered him.[1] The goddess Ishtar was struck with disease when she entered Hades in quest of her lover, the god Tammuz, and it was not until she had been sprinkled with the "water of life" that she was healed and liberated.[2]

The Mikado, being a god, had a spirit, and might be transferred to Yomi or might ascend to heaven to the celestial realm of his ancestress, the sun-goddess. Some distinguished men had spirits likewise. But there is no clear evidence in the *Ko-ji-ki* or the *Nihon-gi* that the spirits of the common people went anywhere after death, or indeed, that they were supposed to have spirits. Some might become birds, or badgers, or foxes, and live for a period in these forms, and then die, as did some of the gods. There are no ghosts in the early Shinto books.[3]

The ancient Pharaohs of Egypt, like the ancient Mikados of Japan, were assured of immortality. The mortuary Pyramid Texts "were all intended for the king's exclusive use, and as a whole contain beliefs which apply only to the king". There are vague references in these texts to the dead "whose places are hidden", and to those who remain in the grave.[4] The fate of the masses did not greatly concern the solar cult.

Before dealing with the myths of Japan, it is necessary to consider what the term *kami*, usually translated "gods", signified to the devotees of "Old Shinto". The *kami* were not spiritual beings, but many of them had spirits or doubles that resided in the *shintai* (god body). Dr. Aston reminds us that although *kami* "corresponds in a general way to 'god', it has some important limitations. The *kami* are high, swift, good, rich, living but not

---

[1] *Myths of Babylonia and Assyria*, pp. 72-3.   [2] *Ibid.*, p. 95.
[3] Aston, *Shinto* (1907), p. 14.
[4] Breasted, *Religion and Thought in Ancient Egypt*, pp. 99 *et seq.*

infinite, omnipotent, or omniscient.   Most of them had a
father and mother, and of some the death is recorded."[1]
It behoves us to exercise caution in applying the term
" animistic" to the numerous *kami* of Japan, or in assuming that they were worshipped, or reverenced rather,
simply because they were feared.   Some of the *kami* were
feared, but the fear of the gods is not a particular feature
of Shinto religion with its ceremonial hand-clappings and
happy laughter.

Dr. Aston quotes from Motöori, the great eighteenth
century Shinto theologian, the following illuminating
statement regarding the *kami* :

"The term *kami* is applied in the first place to the various
deities of heaven and earth who are mentioned in the ancient
records as well as to their spirits (*mi-tama*) which reside in the
shrines where they were worshipped.   Moreover, not only human
beings, but birds, beasts, plants, and trees, seas and mountains, and
all other things whatsoever which deserve to be dreaded and
revered for the extraordinary and pre-eminent powers which they
possess are called *kami*.   They need not be eminent for surpassing
nobleness, or serviceableness alone.   Malignant and uncanny
beings are also called *kami* if only they are objects of general dread.
Among *kami* who are human beings, I need hardly mention, first of
all, the successive Mikados—with reverence be it spoken. . . . Then
there have been numerous examples of divine human beings, both
in ancient and modern times, who, although not accepted by the
nation generally, are treated as gods, each of his several dignity,
in a single province, village, or family."

In ancient Egypt the reigning monarch was similarly
a god—a Horus while he lived and an Osiris after he died,
while a great scholar like Imhotep (the Imuthes of the
Greeks in Egypt who identified him with Asklepois)
might be deified and regarded as the son of Ptah, the god

---

[1] *Shinto* (1907), p. 6.

of Memphis.   Egypt, too, had its local gods like Japan;
so had Babylonia.

The Japanese theologian proceeds to say :

"Amongst *kami* who are not human beings, I need hardly
mention Thunder (in Japanese *Nuru kami* or the sounding-god).
There are also the Dragon and Echo (called in Japanese *Ko-dama*
or the Tree Spirit), and the Fox, who are *kami* by reason of their
uncanny and fearful natures.   The term *kami* is applied in the
Nihon-gi and *Manjoshiu* to the tiger and the wolf.   Isanagi (the
creator-god) gave to the fruit of the peach and to the jewels round
his neck names which implied that they were *kami*."[1]

Here we touch on beliefs similar to those that obtained
in China where the dragon and tiger figure so prominently
as the gods of the East and the West.   The idea that the
peach was a *kami* appears to be connected with the Chinese
conception of a peach world-tree, a form of the Mother
Goddess, the fruit of which contains her "life substance"
or *shen* as do the jewels like the pearl and jade objects;
the peach is a goddess symbol as the phallus is a symbol
of a god.

Motöori adds :

"There are many cases of seas and mountains being called
kami.   *It is not their spirits which are meant.*   The word was
applied directly to the seas or mountains themselves as being very
awful things."[2]

There were a beneficent class and an evil class of *kami*.
Beneficent deities provided what mankind required or
sought for; they were protectors and preservers.   Four
guardians of the world were called "Shi Tenno".   They
were posted at the cardinal points like the Chinese Black
Tortoise (north), the Red Bird (south), the White Tiger

---

[1] Here we have the sanctity of jewels and other so-called "ornaments" brought out
very clearly.   [2] Aston, *Shinto* (1907), pp. 6–7.

(west), and the Blue or Green Dragon (east). The Japanese colour scheme, however, is not the same as the Chinese. At the north is the blue god Bishamon or Tamoten; at the south the white-faced warrior Zocho; at the west the red-faced Komoku with book and brush or a spear ; and at the east the warrior with green face, named Jikoku, who is sometimes shown trampling a demon under foot.

In India the north is white and the south black, and in Ceylon the Buddhist colours of the cardinal points are yellow (north), blue (south), red (west), and white (east).

Although it is customary to regard the coloured guardians of the Japanese world as of Buddhist origin, it may well be that the original Japanese guardians were substituted by the Hindu and Chinese divinities imported by the Buddhists. The dragon-gods of China and Japan were pre-Buddhistic, as De Visser has shown,[1] but were given, in addition to their original attributes, those of the *naga* (serpent or dragon) gods introduced by Buddhist priests.

[1] *The Dragon in China and Japan.*

CHAPTER XVIII

Japanese Gods and Dragons

Japanese Version of Egyptian Flood Myth—A Far Eastern Merodach—
Dragon-slaying Story—The River of Blood—Osiris as a Slain Dragon—
Ancient Shinto Books—Shinto Cosmogony—Separation of Heaven and Earth
—The Cosmic "Reed Shoot" and the *Nig-gil-ma*—The Celestial Jewel Spear
—Izanagi and Izanami—Births of Deities and Islands—The Dragons of
Japan—The Wani—Bear, Horse, and other Dragons—Horse-sacrifice in
Japan—Buddhist Elements in Japanese Dragon Lore—Indian Nagas—Chinese
Dragons and Japanese Water-Snakes.

There is no Shinto myth regarding the creation of
man; the Mikados and the chiefs of tribes were descendants of deities. Nor is there a Deluge Myth like the
Ainu one, involving the destruction of all but a remnant
of mankind. The Chinese story about *Nu Kwa*, known to
the Japanese as Jokwa, was apparently imported with the
beliefs associated with the jade which that mythical queen
or goddess was supposed to have created after she had
caused the flood to retreat, but it does not find a place in
the ancient Shinto books. There is, however, an interesting version of the Egyptian flood story which has been
fused with the Babylonian Tiamat dragon-slaying myth.
Susa-no-wo,[1] a Far Eastern Marduk, slays an eight-headed
dragon and splits up its body, from which he takes a
spirit-sword—an avatar of the monster.

Hathor - Sekhet, of the Egyptian myth, was made
drunk, so that she might cease from slaying mankind,

[1] See Chapter XX.

and a flood of blood-red beer was poured from jars
for that purpose.   Susa-no-wo provides sake (rice beer)
to intoxicate the dragon which has been coming regularly
—apparently once a year—for a daughter of an earth god.
When he slays it, the River Hi is "changed into a river
of blood".

Another version of the Egyptian myth, as the Pyramid
Texts bear evidence, appears to refer to the "Red Nile"
of the inundation season as the blood of Osiris, who
had been felled by Set at Nedyt, near Abydos.[1]   Lucian
tells that the blood of Adonis was similarly believed to
redden each year the flooded River of Adonis, flowing
from Lebanon, and that "it dyed the sea to a large space
red".[2]   Here Adonis is the Osiris of the Byblians.
Osiris, as we have seen, had a dragon form; he was the
dragon of the Nile flood, and the world-surrounding
dragon of ocean.[3]   He was also the earth-giant; tree and
grain grew from his body.[4]   The body of the eight-
headed Japanese dragon was covered with moss and trees.

Susa-no-wo, as the rescuer of the doomed maiden,
links with Perseus, the rescuer of Andromeda from the
water-dragon.[5]   The custom of sacrificing a maiden to
the Nile each year obtained in Ancient Egypt.   In the
Tiamat form of the Babylonian myth, Marduk cut the
channels of the dragon's blood and "made the north
wind bear it away into secret places".[6]   The stories of
P'an Ku of China and the Scandinavian Ymer, each of

---

[1] Breasted, *Religion and Thought in Ancient Egypt*, p. 26.   The Texts referred to are:
"His brother Set felled him to the earth in Nedyt. . . . Osiris was drowned in his
new water (the inundation)."   [2] *De Dea Syria*, Chapter VIII.

[3] Breasted, *op. cit.*, p. 20.   Osiris was addressed: "Thou art great, thou art green, in
thy name of Great Green (Sea); lo, thou art round as the Great Circle (Okeanos); lo,
thou art turned about, thou art round as the circle that encircles the Haunebu
(Ægeans)".   [4] *Ibid.*, 22–3.

[5] For various versions of this legend see Hartland, *Legend of Perseus* and *River
deities* in Index.   [6] King, *Babylonian Religion*, p. 77.

whose blood is the sea, are interesting variants of the legend.[1]

The Japanese dragon-flood myth is merely an incident in the career of a hero in Shinto mythology, which is a mosaic of local or localized and imported stories, somewhat clumsily arranged in the form of a connected narrative.

Our chief sources of information regarding these ancient Japanese myths are the Shinto works, the *Ko-ji-ki* and the *Nihon-gi*.[2] Of these works, the *Ko-ji-ki* (" Records of Ancient Matters ") is the oldest; it was completed in Japanese in A.D. 712; the *Nihon-gi* (" Chronicles of Japan ") was completed in A.D. 720 in the Chinese language.

Although the myths, formerly handed down orally by generations of priests, were not collected and systematized until about 200 years after Buddhism was introduced into Japan, they were not greatly influenced by Indian ideas. Dragon-lore, however, became so complex that it is difficult to sift the local from the imported elements.

In the preface to the *Ko-ji-ki*, Yasumaro, the compiler, in his summary, writes:

" Now when chaos had begun to condense, but force and form were not yet manifest, and there was nought named, nought done, who could know its shape? Nevertheless Heaven and Earth first parted, and the Three Deities performed the commencement of Creation; the Passive and Active Essences then developed, and the Two Spirits became the Ancestors of all things."

---

[1] See Index under *Ymer* and *P'an Ku*.

[2] A translation into English of the *Ko-ji-ki*, by Professor B. H. Chamberlain, was printed as a supplement to Vol. X of the *Transactions of the Asiatic Society of Japan* (1893). The *Nihon-gi* was translated into English by Dr. Aston, and printed in the *Transactions of the Japan Society* for 1896.

The myth of the separation of Heaven and Earth dates back to remote antiquity in Egypt. Shu, the atmosphere-god, separated the sky-goddess Nut from the earth-god Seb. In Polynesian mythology Rangi (Heaven), and Papa (Earth), from whom "all things originated", were "rent apart" by Tane-mahuta, "the god and father of forests, of birds, of insects". But in this case the earth is the mother and the sky the father.[1]

About the "Three Deities" referred to by Yasumaro, we do not learn much. The idea of the trinity may have been of Indian origin. The Passive and Active Essences recall the male *Yang* and its female *Yin* principles of China. These are represented in the *Ko-ji-ki* by Izanagi ("Male who Invites") and Izanami ("Female who Invites").

Dr. Aston translates the opening passage of the *Nihon-gi* as follows:

"Of old, Heaven and Earth were not yet separated, and the In and the Yo not yet divided. They formed a chaotic mass like an egg, which was of obscurely defined limits, and contained germs. The purer and clearer part was thinly diffused and formed Heaven, while the heavier and grosser element settled down and became Earth. The finer element easily became a united body, but the consolidation of the heavy and gross element was accomplished with difficulty. Heaven was therefore formed first, and Earth established subsequently. Thereafter divine beings were produced between them."

Here we meet with the cosmic egg, from which emerged the Chinese P'an Ku, the Indian Brahma, the Egyptian Ra or Horus, and one of the Polynesian creators. It might be held that China is the source of the Japanese myth, because the *In* and the *Yo* are

[1] Grey, *Polynesian Mythology*, pp. 1 et seq.

here, quite evidently the *Yang* and the *Yin*, representing not Izanagi and Izanami as in the *Ko-ji-ki*, but the deities of heaven and earth.   But the *Ko-ji-ki* form of the myth may be the oldest, and we may have in the *Nihon-gi* evidence of Chinese ideas having been superimposed on those already obtaining in Japan, into which they were imported from other areas.

But to return to the Creation myth.   An ancient native work, the *Kiu-ji-ki*, which has not yet been translated into English, refers to seven generations of gods, beginning with one of doubtful sex, in whose untranslatable name the sun, moon, earth, and moisture are mentioned.   This First Parent of the deities was the offspring of Heaven and Earth.   The last couple is Izanagi and Izanami, brother and sister, like Osiris and Isis, who became man and wife.

According to the *Ko-ji-ki* the first three deities came into being in *Takama-no-hara*, the "Plain of High Heaven".   They were alone, and afterwards disappeared, i.e. died.   The narrative continues: "The names of the deities that were born next from a thing that sprouted up like unto a reed-shoot when the earth, young and like unto floating oil, drifted about medusa-like,[1] were the Pleasant - Reed - Shoot - Prince - Elder - Deity, next the Heavenly-Eternally-Standing-Deity.   These two Deities were likewise born alone, and hid their persons."[2]   Earth and mud deities followed, and also the other deities who were before Izanagi and Izanami.

It may be that the "reed-shoot" was the Japanese *nig-gil-ma*.   (See Chapter XIII.)   As in one of the early

---

[1] Like the Floating Island or Islands of the Blest.

[2] "Hid their persons" signifies, according to some commentators, that they died. But certain Egyptian deities were "hidden"; their influence remained: the Japanese hidden deity had a "mi-tama" (soul).

Sumerian texts, the mysterious plant, impregnated with preserving and perpetuating "life substance", was the second product of Creation.

Izanagi and Izanami were told by the elder deities that they must "make, consolidate, and give birth to this drifting land". They were then given the *Ame no tama-boko*, the "Celestial Jewel-spear". It is suggested that the spear is a phallic symbol. The jewel (tama) is "life substance". Izanagi and Izanami stood on "the floating bridge of heaven", which Aston identifies with the rainbow, or, as some Japanese scholars put it, the "Heavenly Rock Boat", or "Heavenly Stairs", and pushed down the *tama-boko* and groped with it until they found the ocean. According to the *Ko-ji-ki*, they "stirred the brine until it went curdle-curdle (*koworo-koworo*)", that is, as Chamberlain suggests, "thick and glutinous". Others think the passage should be translated so as to indicate that the brine gave forth "a curdling sound". When the primæval waters and the oily mud began to "curdle" or "cook", the deities drew up the spear. Some of the cosmic "porridge" dropped from the point and formed an island, which was named *Onogoro* ("self-curdling", or "self-condensed"). The deities descended from heaven and erected on the island an eight-fathom house[1] with a central pillar. Here we meet with the aniconic pillar, the "herm" of Kamschatkan religion, the pillar of the Vedic world-house erected by the Aryo-Indian god Indra, the "branstock" of Scandinavian religion, the pillar of the "Lion Gate" of Mycenæ; the "pillar" is the "world spine", like the Indian Mount Meru.[2] "The central pillar of a house (corresponding to our king-post) is," writes Dr. Aston, "at the present day, an object of

---

[1] Eight is a sacred number in Japan.
[2] See *Myths of Crete and pre-Hellenic Europe*, pp. 305–9.

honour in Japan as in many other countries.   In the case
of Shinto shrines, it is called *Nakago no mibashira* ('central
august pillar'), and in ordinary houses the *Daikoku-
bashira.*" [1]

Izanagi and Izanami become man and wife by performing the ceremony of going round the pillar and meeting
one another face to face.   Their first-born is Hiruko
(leech-child).   At the age of three he was still unable to
stand upright, and was in consequence placed in a reed
boat and set adrift on the ocean.

Here we have what appears to be a version of the
Moses story.   The Indian Karna, who is similarly set
adrift, was a son of Surya, god of the sun.   The Egyptian
Horus was concealed after birth on a floating island, and
he was originally a solar deity with a star form.[2]   Ra, the
Egyptian sun-god, drifted across the heavens on reed
floats before he was given a boat.   Osiris was, after death,
set adrift in a chest.   When the Egyptians paid more
attention to the constellations than they did in the early
period of their history, they placed in the constellation of
Argo the god Osiris in a chest or boat.   In the Greek
period Canopus, the chief star of the constellation of
Argo, is the child Horus in his boat.   Horus was a re-
incarnation of Osiris.   The Babylonian Ea originally
came to Eridu in a boat, which became transformed into
a fish-man.   As the sign for a god was a star, Ea was
apparently supposed to have come from one.   Lockyer
refers to Egyptian and Babylonian temples, which were
" oriented to Canopus".[3]   Sun-gods were the offspring
of the mother-star, or their own souls were stars by night.
" Hiruko," says Aston, " is in reality simply a masculine

[1] *Shinto* (1905), p. 90.
[2] He is the green falcon of the Morning Star in the Pyramid Texts.
[3] *The Dawn of Astronomy* (London, 1894), pp. 383 *et seq.*

form of Hirume, the sun female."[1]   The sun and moon
had not, however, come into existence when he was set
adrift, and it may be that as the "leech-child" he was
a star.   He became identified in time with Ebisu (or
Yebisu), god of fishermen, and one of the gods of
luck.

Izanagi and Izanami had subsequently as children the
eight islands of Japan, and although other islands came
into existence later, Japan was called "Land-of-the-Eight-
great-Islands" (Oho-ya-shima-kuni).   "When," continues
the Ko-ji-ki, "they (Izanagi and Izanami) had finished
giving birth to countries they began afresh, giving birth
to deities (kami)."   These included "Heavenly-Blowing
Male", "Youth of the Wind", the sea-kami, "Great-
Ocean-Possessor", "Foam Calm", "Foam Waves",
"Heavenly-Water-Divider", or "Water-Distributor"
(Ame-no-mi-kumari-no-kami), and the deities of mountains, passes, and valleys.

According to the Nihon-gi, the gods of the sea to
whom Izanagi and Izanami gave birth are called Wata-
tsumi, which means "sea children", or, as Florenz translates it, "Lords of the Sea".   Wata, so like our "water",
is "an old word for sea".   It is probable that, as De
Visser says, "the old Japanese sea-gods were snakes or
dragons".[2]

In the Ko-ji-ki two groups of eight deities are followed by "the Deity Bird's-Rock-Camphor-Tree-Boat",
another name for this kami being "Heavenly Bird-Boat".
Then came the food-goddess, "Deity Princess-of-Great
Food".   She was followed by the fire-god, kagu-tsuchi.
This deity caused the death of his mother Izanami,
having burned her at birth so severely that she sickened

---

[1] Shinto (1905), p. 132.   [2] The Dragon in China and Japan, p. 137.

and "lay down". Before she died, an interesting group
of deities, making a total of eight from "Heavenly Bird-
Boat" to the last named, "Luxuriant Food Princess",
came into being. From her vomit sprang "Metal-
Mountain Prince" and "Metal-Mountain Princess";
from her fæces came "Clay Prince" and "Clay Princess"
(earth deities); and from her urine crept forth *Mitsu-ha
no-Me*, which Japanese commentators explain as "Female-
Water-snake", or "The Woman who. produces the
Water". In the first rendering *ha* is regarded as meaning "snake" (dragon), and in the second as "to produce".
Neither Florenz nor De Visser can decide which explanation is correct.[1] The dragon was, of course, a
water-producer, or water-controller, or a "water-confiner", who was forced to release the waters, like the
"drought demon", slain by the Aryo-Indian god Indra,
and the water-confiner of the Nile, whose blood reddened
the river during inundation.

When Izanami died, the heart of Izanagi was filled
with wrath and grief. Drawing his big sabre, he, according to the *Ko-ji-ki*, cut off the head of the fire-god; or,
as the *Nihon-gi* tells, cut him into three pieces, each
of which became a god. Other gods sprang from the
pieces, from the blood drops that bespattered the rocks,
the blood that clung to the upper part of the sabre,
and the blood that leaked out between the fingers of
Izanagi.

According to the *Nihon-gi*, the blood dripping from
the upper part of the sword became the gods *Kura-okami*,
Kura-yama-tsumi, and *Kura-mitsu-ha*. The meaning of the
character *kura* is "dark", and Professor Florenz explains
it as "abyss, valley, cleft",[2] and notes that *okami* means

[1] De Visser, *The Dragon in China and Japan*, pp. 136–7; and Florenz, *Japanische Mythologie*, Chap. III, p. 33.   [2] *Japanische Mythologie*, p. 46.

"rain" and "dragon". According to De Visser, *Kura-okami* is a dragon- or snake-god who controls rain and snow, and had Shinto temples "in all provinces". Another reading in the *Nihon-gi* states that one of the three gods who came into being from the pieces of the fire-god's body was *Taka-okami*, a name which, according to a Japanese commentator, means "the dragon-god residing on the mountains", while *Kura-okami* means "the dragon-god of the valleys".[1] The second god born from the blood drops from the upper part of the sword, *Kura-yama-tsumi*, is translated "Lord of the Dark Mountains", and "Mountain-snake"; and the third, *Kura-mitsu-ha*, is "Dark-water-snake" or "Valley-water-snake". According to the *Ko-ji-ki*, the deities *Kura-okami* and *Kura-mitsu-ha* came from the blood that leaked out between Izanagi's fingers.

It is of interest to note here that other dragon deities to which Izanagi and Izanami gave origin, included the *mizuchi* or "water fathers", which are referred to as "horned deities", "four-legged dragons", or "large water-snakes". As Aston notes,[2] these "water fathers" had no individual names; they were prayed to for rain in times of drought. Another sea-dragon child of the great couple was the *wani*, which appears to have been a combination of crocodile and shark. Aston thinks that *wani* is a Korean word. De Visser, on the other hand, is of opinion that the *wani* is the old Japanese dragon-god or sea-god, and that the legend about the Abundant Pearl Princess (*Toyo-tama-bime*)[3] who had a human lover and, like Melusina, transformed herself from human shape into that of a *wani* (*Ko-ji-ki*) or a dragon (*Nihon-gi*), was originally a Japanese serpent-dragon, which was "dressed

---

[1] De Visser, *op. cit.*, pp. 135-6.   [2] *Shinto* (1905), p. 73.
[3] See Index under *wani*.

in Indian garb by later generations".[1]   Florenz, the German Orientalist, thinks the legend is of Chinese origin, but a similar one is found in Indonesia. "*Wani*," De Visser says, "may be an Indonesian word," and it is possible, as he suggests, that "foreign invaders, who in prehistoric times conquered Japan, came from Indonesia and brought the myth with them."[2]

There is a reference in the *Nihon-gi* (Chapter 1) to a "bear-wani, eight fathoms long", and it has been suggested that "bear" means here nothing more than "strong".[3]   The Ainu, however, as we have seen (Chapter XVII), associated bear and dragon deities; the bear-goddess was the wife of the dragon-god, and that goddess had, like the Abundant Pearl Princess, a human lover. "Bear-wani" may therefore have been a bear-dragon. There was a dragon-horse "with a long neck and wings at its sides", which flew through the air, and did not sink when it trod upon the water,[4] and there were withal Japanese crow-dragons, toad-dragons, fish-dragons, and lizard-dragons.

The horse played as prominent a part in Japanese rain-getting and rain-stopping ceremonies as did the bear among the Ainu.   White, black, or red horses were offered to bring rain, but red horses alone were sacrificed to stop rain.   Like the Buriats of Siberia and the Aryo-Indians of the Vedic period, the Japanese made use of the domesticated horse at the dawn of their history.   No doubt it was imported from Korea.   There is evidence that at an early period human beings were sacrificed to the Japanese dragon-gods of rivers, lakes, and pools.   Human sacrifices at tombs are also referred to.   In the *Nihon-gi*, under the legendary date 2 B.C., it is related that when a

---

[1] *The Dragon in China and Japan*, p. 140.   [2] *Ibid.*, pp. 141–2.
[3] De Visser, *op. cit.*, pp. 139–40.   [4] De Visser, *op. cit.*, pp. 147 *et seq.*

Mikado died his personal attendants were buried alive in an upright position beside his tomb.[1]

In his notable work on the dragon, M. W. de Visser[2] shows that the Chinese ideas regarding their four-legged dragon and Indian Buddhist ideas regarding *nagas* were introduced into Japan and fused with local ideas regarding serpent-shaped water-gods. The foreign elements added to ancient Japanese legends have, as has been indicated, made their original form obscure. In the dragon place-names of Japan, however, it is still possible to trace the locations of the ancient Shinto gods who were mostly serpent-shaped. An ancient name for a Japanese dragon is *Tatsu*. De Visser notes that *Tatsu no Kuchi* ("Dragon's mouth") is a common place-name. It is given to a hot spring in the Nomi district, to a waterfall in Kojimachi district, to a hill in Kamakura district, where criminals were put to death, and to mountains, &c., elsewhere. *Tatsu ga hana* ("Dragon's nose") is in Taga district; *Tatsu-kushi* ("Dragon's skewer") is a rock in Tosa province; and so on. Chinese and Indian dragons are in Japanese place-names "ryu" or "ryo". These include *Ryo-ga-mine* ("Dragon's peak") in Higo; *Ryu-ga-take* ("Dragon's peak") in Ise; *Ryu-kan-gawa* ("Dragon's rest river") in Tokyo, &c.

The worship of the Water Fathers or Dragons in Japan was necessary so as to ensure the food-supply.

---

[1] Aston, *Shinto* (1905), p. 56 and pp. 219–20.
[2] *The Dragon in China and Japan*, pp. 231 *et seq.*

CHAPTER XIX

Rival Deities of Life and Death, Sunshine and Storm

Izanagi visits Hades—Origin of Thunder Deities—The Flight from Hades—Japanese Version of the "Far-travelled Tale"—The Sacred Peach Tree—Izanami as Goddess of Death—Births of Sun and Moon from Eyes of Izanagi—The Sun-goddess's Necklace—Susa-no-wo as "Impetuous Male Deity"—Connection with Typhoon and Rain—A Japanese Indra—Vitalizing and Blighting Tears of Deities—Deities Born from Jewels and Sword—The Harrying of Heaven—Flight of Sun-goddess—How Light was Restored—The Sacred Mirror—Banishment of Susa-no-wo.

After Izanagi had slain his son, the fire-god, and brought into being new gods, including dragons, he was seized with longing to see Izanami once more. Accordingly he set out to find her in Yomi ("Yellow stream"), the dark Hades of the Underworld. "The orthodox Japanese derivation of Yomi," says Chamberlain, "is from *yoru*, 'night', which would give us for *Yomo-tsu-kuni* some such rendering as 'Land of Gloom'." Another view is that "Yomi" is a mispronunciation of "Yama", the name of the Aryo-Indian god of death.[1]

When Izanagi reached the gloomy dwelling of his sister, she raised the door, and he spoke to her, saying: "Thine Augustness, my lovely young sister! the lands that I and you made are not yet finished; so come back". She replied out of the darkness: "It is sorrowful that you did not come hither sooner, for I have eaten of the

[1] *Transactions of the Asiatic Society of Japan*, Vol. X (supplement), p. 34.

food of Yomi.   Nevertheless, it is my desire to return.
I will therefore speak with the *kami* of Yomi."[1]   She
added in warning, " Look not at me ! "

Izanami then went back to the place she had come
from.   She tarried there for so long a time that Izanagi
grew impatient.   At length he felt he could not wait any
longer, so he broke off the end tooth of his hair-comb,
which is called the " male pillar ", and thus made a light,
and entered.[2]   He found his sister.   Her body was
rotting, and maggots swarmed over it.   The *Ko-ji-ki*
proceeds :

" In her head dwelt the Great Thunder, in her breast dwelt
the Fire Thunder, in her belly dwelt the Black Thunder, in her
private parts dwelt the Cleaving Thunder, in her left hand dwelt
the Young Thunder, in her right hand dwelt the Earth Thunder,
in her left foot dwelt the Rumbling Thunder, in her right foot
dwelt the Couchant Thunder; altogether eight thunder deities
had been born and dwelt there."

Horrified at the spectacle, Izanagi drew back suddenly ;
whereupon his sister exclaimed, " You have put me to
shame ! " and became angry.

Here Izanagi has broken a taboo, as did the Japanese
youth who married the dragon-maid, Abundant Pearl
Princess, and as did the husband of Melusina in the
French legend.   It was an ancient custom in Japan to
erect " parturition houses ".   These were one-roomed
huts to which women retired so as to give birth to
children unseen.   Ernest Satow tells that on the island
of Hachijo, until comparatively recent times, " women,
when about to become mothers, were . . . driven out to
the huts on the mountain-side, and according to the

---

[1] The spirits of disease, decay, destruction, and darkness.
[2] This phallic symbol had, apparently, like jade, rhinoceros-horn, &c., nocturnal
luminosity.

accounts of native writers, left to shift for themselves, the result not infrequently being the death of the new-born infant".[1] It was taboo for a man to enter a "parturition house". Apparently Izanami had retired to a "parturition house" in Yomi.

Enraged against Izanagi, because he had put her to shame, Izanami commanded the Ugly Females of Yomi to pursue and slay him.

At this point in the mythical narrative begins a version of the widespread folk-story about the young man who makes escape from his enemy or enemies, and in the course of his flight throws down articles that are transformed into obstacles, or into things which tempt the pursuers to tarry and eat.[2]

The first article that Izanagi cast down behind him was his wreath or head-dress, which was instantly turned into grapes. This is according to the *Ko-ji-ki*; the *Nihon-gi* makes the head-dress the second obstacle. His pursuer (*Ko-ji-ki*) or pursuers (*Nihon-gi*), having devoured the grapes, resumed the chase. Then Izanagi, as he fled, broke his hair-comb and threw it down; it instantly turned into bamboo sprouts. While these were being pulled up and eaten, he continued his flight.

The *Ko-ji-ki* (but not the *Nihon-gi*) here introduces another set of pursuers. Izanami, finding that her brother had outwitted the Ugly Female (or Females), " sent the eight Thunder-Deities with a thousand and five hundred warriors of Hades to pursue him. Izanagi, drawing the ten-grasp sabre that was augustly girded on him, fled forward, brandishing it in his back hand (brandishing it behind him); and as the demons still

---

[1] *Transactions of Asiatic Society of Japan*, Vol. VI, Part III, pp. 455-6.

[2] For representative versions in various lands, see Andrew Lang's *Custom and Myth* (A Far-travelled Tale), pp. 87 *et seq*.

continued to pursue him, he took, on reaching the base of the Even Pass of Hades,[1] three peaches that were growing at its base, and waited and smote (his pursuers therewith) so that they all fled back."[2]

Having thus rid himself of his pursuers, Izanagi addressed the peaches, saying: "As you have helped me, so must ye help all living people in the Central Land of Reed-Plains, when they are troubled and harassed".

Here we have not only a native name of China ("Land of Reed-Plains") applied to Japan, but also the sacred Chinese peach, a symbol of the Great Mother, the Western Queen of Immortals (Si Wang Fu). The story of a hero's flight from the Underworld has not survived in China, if ever it existed there. It is, however, found in the myths of Scandinavia.

In the *Nihon-gi* (Aston) the comment is added to the peach incident: "This was the origin of the custom of exorcising evil spirits by means of peaches".

The peach, like the bean, was in Japan a symbol of the mother-goddess, as was the shell in Egypt and the pig-shell in Greece.

Izanami herself was the last to pursue Izanagi. When he saw her coming, Izanagi blocked up the Pass of Yomi with a huge boulder of rock, which it would take a thousand men to lift, and he stood on one side of it, while she stood on the other to "exchange leave-takings" (*Ko-ji-ki*), or to pronounce the formula of divorce (*Nihon-gi*).

In the *Ko-ji-ki* Izanami threatens to slay a thousand inhabitants in the land of the living, but Izanagi retorts

---

[1] Or "Flat Hill of Hades", the frontier line between the land of the living and the land of the dead.

[2] In the Ainu story about the man who visited the Underworld and was transformed into a snake, a pine tree, inhabited by a goddess, occupies the spot on which grows the peach tree in this Japanese myth.

that he will arrange for the birth of one thousand and five hundred, so that the number born may exceed the number who must die.

Izanami became thereafter *Yomo-tsu-oho-kami* (Yomi's Great Deity).[1] The rock which blocks the Pass of Yomi became the "Great-Deity-of-the-Road-Turning-back".

In the *Nihon-gi* (Aston's translation) it is related that Izanagi flung down various articles on leaving Hades, as the goddess Ishtar in Babylonian mythology flung down her clothing and ornaments on entering the dread abode of Erish-ki-gal (Persephone). Having pronounced the divorce formula:

"He also said, 'Come no farther', and threw down his staff, which was called *Funando-no-kami* (pass-not-place-deity), or *Kunado-no-kami* (come-not-place-deity). Moreover, he threw down his girdle, which was called *Nagachiha-no-kami*. Moreover, he threw down his upper garment, which was called *Wadzurahi-no-kami* (god of disease). Moreover, he threw down his trousers, which were called *Aki-guhi-no-kami*. Moreover, he threw down his shoes, which were called *Chi-shiki-no-kami*."

On returning to the land of the living, Izanagi exclaimed: "I have come from a hideous and polluted place. I will therefore perform the purification of my august body."

He went to bathe at a river mouth on a plain covered with bush-clover, beside a grove of orange trees confronting the sun. It is here, according to the *Ko-ji-ki*, that he flings down his staff and the various articles of clothing that are transformed into deities. Two evil deities were born from the filth of Hades that fell from his person when he entered the water. He dived, and three sea-gods came into being. He washed his left eye, and thus gave origin to the goddess of the sun, *Ama-terâsu-oho-mi-*

---

[1] The Japanese Persephone.

kami (The Heaven-Shining-Great-August-Deity). He washed his right eye, and there came into being the god of the moon, *Tsuki-yomi-no-kami* (Moon-Night-Possessor). He washed his nose, and from it was born *Take-haya-susa-no-wu-no-mikoto*[1] (His-Brave-Swift-Impetuous-Male-Augustness).

Izanagi took off his necklace of jewels or beads (tama), and, shaking it so that the beads jingled, bestowed it on Ama-terâsu, the sun kami or goddess, and set her to rule the "Plain of High Heaven". He commanded the moon-god to rule the night, and Susa-no-wo to rule the "Sea Plain".

"At this point," as Chamberlain says, "the story loses its unity. The moon-goddess is no more heard of, and the traditions concerning the sun-goddess diverge from those concerning the 'Impetuous-Male-Deity' in a manner which is productive of inconsistencies in the rest of the mythology."[2]

Chamberlain translates Susa-no-wo as "Impetuous-Male-Deity", connecting his name with *susama*, "to be impetuous". But, as Aston points out, the implied noun *susa*, "impetuosity", does not exist. There is, however, a town named Susa in Idzumo,[3] with which area the legends regarding the god are specially associated. Susa-no-wo may therefore have been simply "the god of Susa". Aston, following Dr. Buckley, Chicago, regards him as a personification of the rain-storm. Japanese writers, on the other hand, have connected him with Godzu Tenno, an Indian Hades deity, and with the moon-god, or regarded him as a war-god, while some European scholars have referred to him as a "rotating-heavens god". Having been born from the nose of

---

[1] "Susa-no-wo" for short.   [2] *Things Japanese*, p. 145.
[3] *Shinto* (1905), p. 141.

Izanagi, we should expect Susa-no-wo to have a connection with wind and "the air of life", as well as with rain and the sea. It is of special interest to note in this connection that, as Aston says,[1] "Japan is annually visited by destructive typhoons, accompanied by great darkness and a terrific downpour of rain". Susa-no-wo is "continually weeping, wailing, and fuming with rage", and is "a lover of destruction", and he is associated with *Yomi*, the habitation of the deities that work evil against mankind. Susa-no-wo may be the Japanese Indra, who brings rain. Japanese wind-gods were givers of rain, as well as wind.[2] Like Indra, Susa-no-wo is a dragon-slayer. A festival "celebrated in his honour at Onomochi in Bingo" is described by a Japanese writer in these words:[3]

"The procession is a tumultuous trial of speed and strength. Bands of strong men seize the sacred cars, race with them to the sea, and having plunged in breast-deep, their burden held aloft, dash back at full speed to the shrine. There refreshments are served out, and then the race is resumed, the goal being the central flag among a number set up in a large plain. Their feet beat time to a wildly shouted chorus, and they sweep along wholly regardless of obstacles or collisions."

Indra, with Agni, the fire-god, was the winner in a race of the gods; he links with Vayu or Vata, the wind-god, and he wages war against the Danavas, the demons of ocean.[4]

In China dragon-boat races were held so as to cause rain. Imitation boats were likewise carried through the streets to the seashore, and there burned so as to take away evil influences. The boats represented fighting dragons, and these were rain-bringers. The Japanese

---

[1] *Shinto* (1905), p. 137. [2] De Visser, *The Dragon in China and Japan*, pp. 153-4.
[3] *Shinto* (1905), p. 140. [4] *Indian Myth and Legend*, pp. 14, 15, 24, 64, 65.

imitated these Chinese customs, but not, however, until about the eleventh century.[1]

As a trickster among the gods, Susa-no-wo bears some resemblance to the Scandinavian Loki; he is, like that deity, an ally of the powers of darkness and destruction, and he similarly suffers banishment from the celestial land. Susa-no-wo also recalls Nergal, the Babylonian warrior-god, who conquered Hades, and was "the death spreader" (*Mushtabarrŭ-mûtanu*).

The deities of the sun and moon proceeded to rule the day and the night as commanded by their parent Izanagi, but Susa-no-wo did not depart to the ocean, which had been committed to his charge; instead, he cried and wept until his eight-grasp beard reached the pit of his stomach. Says the *Ko-ji-ki*:

"The fashion of his weeping was such as by his weeping to dry up all the rivers and seas. For this reason the sound of bad deities was like unto the flies of the fifth moon as they all swarmed, and in all things every portent of woe arose."

The reference to the god's tears causing the green mountains to wither and the waters to dry up has greatly perplexed Japanese commentators. But there are statements in Asian and American mythologies regarding "evil" or "poisonous rain" distributed, to the injury of vegetation, by dragons that may be sick or badly disposed towards mankind. De Visser refers to a Buddhist legend about a poisonous Naga that guarded a big tree and killed all those who took a branch from it; when angry it sent thunder and rain.[2] Central Asian legends tell that evil rains were sent out of season by disturbed and enraged dragons. A Chinese story tells of a sick dragon that,

[1] De Visser, *The Dragon in China and Japan*, pp. 83 et seq.
[2] *Ibid.*, p. 15.

having been roused by prayers, gave "a badly-smelling rain which would have spoiled the crops if a diviner had not discovered it in time and cured the dragon at the latter's request". Thereupon a fertilizing rain fell and a very clear spring dashed forth from a rock.[1]

In Ancient Egypt the deities wept vitalizing tears (see Index). Ra's tears gave life to gods and men, the tears of the god Shu and the goddess Tefnut became incense-bearing trees. The tears of Osiris and Isis caused life-giving herbs, &c., to grow, but the tears shed on the world by the evil Set and his partisans produced poisonous plants. When deities were enraged, their saliva, sweat, and blood on touching the earth germinated and produced poisonous plants, scorpions, serpents, &c.[2]

The Chinese Buddhists believed in a Naga that, by means of a single drop of water, could give rain to one or two kingdoms, and even prevent the sea from drying up.[3] Similarly a single tear from Isis-Hathor, as the star Sirius, that fell on the "Night of the Drop", caused the Nile to rise in flood.

The blighting and ocean-drying tears of Susa-no-wo were evidently those of an evil or angry deity, or of one who was sick with sorrow.

Izanagi, beholding the ocean-ruler in tears, asked him why he wailed and wept.

Susa-no-wo made answer: "I wail because I wish to depart to the land of my dead mother (Izanami) in the Nether-Distant Land (Yomi, i.e. Hades)".

Izanagi was very angry, and said: "If that be so, you

---

[1] *The Dragon in China and Japan*, p. 121.
[2] Maspero, *Dawn of Civilization*, pp. 156 *et seq.*
[3] De Visser, *The Dragon in China and Japan*, p. 13.

shall not dwell in the ocean domain". He then banished
Susa-no-wo to Afumi.[1]

Susa-no-wo made answer that he would first take leave
of his sister, Ama-terâsu, goddess of the sun. He rose
in the air, as does a thunder-bringing dragon. Says the
Ko-ji-ki :

"(With these words) he forthwith went up to Heaven, whereupon all the mountains shook, and every land and country quaked.
So Ama-terâsu, alarmed at the noise, said: 'The reason of the ascent
hither of His Augustness my elder brother[2] is surely no good intent.
It is only that he wishes to wrest my land from me.'"[3]

The goddess unbound her hair, twisted it into bunches,
put on her string of five hundred curved jewels (*maga-
tama*, i.e. claw-shaped),[4] and armed herself with bow and
arrows. She stood "valiantly like unto a mighty man",
and asked her brother why he had ascended. Susa-no-wo
declared he had no evil intention, and she asked him to
give proof of his sincerity and goodwill. He proposed
that they should pledge their faith and produce children. To this she consented, and they "swore to each
other from the opposite banks of the Tranquil River
of Heaven".[5]

Ama-terâsu asked Susa-no-wo for his sword. He gave
it to her and she broke it into three pieces. She then
made a jingling sound with her jewels, brandished and
washed them in the True-Pool-Well of Heaven[6] and
"crunchingly crunched them". Then from the mist (of

---

[1] The modern Omi, Afumi (Aha-humi), "Fresh-water Lake": Chamberlain,
Transactions of Asiatic Society of Japan, Vol. X (supplement), p. 45, *n.* 12.

[2] That is, the elder brother of her family. He was really younger than herself.

[3] As the Babylonian Nergal wrested Hades from Eresh-ki-gal (Persephone).

[4] The so-called "comma-shaped" beads, which represented the claws of tigers or
bears, or a cut sea-shell.

[5] The "Milky Way" by night, also called the "Heavenly River of Eight currents
(or 'reaches')".

[6] The ancient Egyptian Celestial Pool of the Gods.

her breath) were born the deities Torrent-Mist-Princess, Lovely-Island-Princess, and Princess-of-the-Torrent.

Susa-no-wo then asked for and obtained from Ama-terâsu the string of five hundred curved jewels[1] which was twisted in the left bunch of her hair. He made a jingling sound with the jewels, washed them in the Pool, and, having crunched them, "blew them away". From his breath were born the god "Truly-Conqueror-I-Conquer-Conquering-Swift-Heavenly-Great-Great-Ears", the god Ame-no-hohi,[2] the god "Prince-Lord of Heaven", the god "Prince-Lord of Life", and the god of Kumano. In all eight deities—three goddesses and five gods—were born.

From these deities the Japanese noble families have claimed descent. The Mikados were supposed to be descended from the Conquering God with Great Ears (*Masa-ya-a-katsu-kachi-haya-hi-ama-no-oshi-ho-mi-mi*). Another myth makes the Mikado a descendant of the sun-goddess and *Taka-mi-musubi* (the High, August God of Birth and Growth), who, in a sense, is a Japanese Osiris. He has been compared to the Hindu god Shiva. Aston says that "musubi" is "the abstract process of growth personified—that is, a power immanent in nature and not external to it".[3] Breasted similarly regards Osiris as "the imperishable principle of life wherever found".[4] Shiva, as "the fructifying principle", is represented by the phallus. It is believed that this symbol was the "shintai" (god body) of Musubi.[5]

After the three goddesses and five gods had come into being, Susa-no-wo declared, "I have undoubtedly gained

---

[1] Each jewel was eight feet long.
[2] The "hohi of Heaven". What "hohi" signifies is a puzzle.
[3] *Shinto* (1905), p. 172. [4] *Religion and Thought in Ancient Egypt*, p. 23.
[5] *Shinto* (1905), p. 174. Professor Benoy K. Sarkar compares Shiva to Osiris. See *The Folk-Element in Hindu Culture* (London, 1917), p. 7.

the victory". He then proceeded to harry the celestial regions. He broke down the divisions of the rice-fields, filled up the ditches, and fouled with excrement and urine the palace in which the goddess took food. He became even more violent. Having broken open a hole in the sacred house in which sat Ama-terâsu superintending the weaving of the garments of deities, he let fall into it a heavenly piebald horse that had been flayed backwards (a criminal offence). The celestial female weavers were terrified.

Alarmed by Susa-no-wo's doings, the sun-goddess entered her cave, the Heavenly Rock Dwelling,[1] shut the door and made it fast. All the land became dark.

Then the eight hundred myriad deities took counsel, sitting in the bed of the River of Heaven, so as to plan how they could entice the sun-goddess from her hiding-place. They made the cocks ("the long-singing birds of eternal night") to crow loud, they caused the Heavenly Smith to shape a mirror of iron (the "true metal") from the Heavenly Metal-Mountains (the mines), and charged the Jewel-Ancestor (*Tama-noya-no-mikoto*) to make a complete string of five hundred curved jewels. A tree was then taken from the celestial Mount Kagu[2] and on it were hung the mirror, the jewel, cherry bark, and other offerings. The ritual was recited, and thereafter *Ama-no-Uzume* (the Dread Celestial Female), wearing metal head-gear (flowers of gold and silver) and a sash of club-moss from the celestial mountain, and holding in her hands a posy of bamboo grass, danced on a tub[3] until the eight hundred myriad deities laughed. Wondering to hear sounds of merriment, instead of sounds of woe, the sun-

---

[1] In Ancient Egypt the mountain that splits when the sun emerges at dawn.

[2] The tree *Sakaki* (*Cleyera japonica*) planted beside Shinto shrines.

[3] The dance was a gross and indelicate one.

goddess opened the door of her cave a little and asked why they all laughed. She was told that the deities rejoiced because they had among them a more august goddess than herself.

One of the gods then held up the mirror, and the sun-goddess was astonished to behold a bright deity, not knowing it was her reflected image, and gradually came forth, fascinated by her own beauty and brightness. A strong deity took her hand and drew her out while another deity, Grand Jewel, drew a straw rope behind her so as to prevent her retreating.[1] In this manner the sun-goddess was enticed to return and light up the world.

The second expulsion of Susa-no-wo followed. He was fined an immense fine of table-offerings, his beard was shorn, and his finger and toe nails were drawn out.

According to the *Ko-ji-ki*, he begged for food from the food-goddess. She took "dainty things" from various parts of her body which he regarded as filth, so he slew her. Then from her head "were born silk-worms, in her two eyes were born rice-seeds, in her two ears were born millet, in her nose were born small beans, in her private parts were born barley, in her fundament were born large beans". These were used as seeds. According to the *Nihon-gi*, they were sown "in the narrow fields and in the long fields of Heaven".

The reason for keeping the mirror and jewels (*tama*) in the shrine of Ise, and for worshipping the sun-goddess and the food-goddess there, are thus explained in Shinto mythology. Virgin priestesses danced at religious ceremonies as did the tub-thumping goddess, and offerings

---

[1] This rope (*shime-naha*) is tied round trees at Shinto shrines. At Ise it stretches across a ravine, through which the sun is seen and adored at dawn. The straw is pulled up by the roots.

were suspended from trees as in the celestial regions, while the straw rope was utilized to keep back demons and to ensure the rising of the sun by preventing the retreat of the sun-goddess.

The finding of the dragon-sword is dealt with in the next mythical story.

CHAPTER XX

The Dragon-Slayer and His Rival

The Eight-headed Dragon—Sacrifices of Maidens—How the Dragon was intoxicated and slain—Finding of the Dragon-sword—The Nuptial House—Adventures of Ohonamochi—The Jealous Brothers—Flight of Ohonamochi to Hades—Susa-no-wo as Giant-god of Hades—Princess Forward—Far Eastern Version of Jack-and-the-Beanstalk Story—The Life-sword, Life-bow and arrows, &c.—Ohonamochi's Conquest of Japan—A Japanese Odin—Another Creation Myth—The Elfin Deity in Bird Skins—A Shining Sea-god.

After Susa-no-wo had been banished from heaven, he descended on *Tori-kami*, beside the river Hi, in the province of Idzumo. A chopstick came floating down the river, so he knew that people were dwelling near, and he set out to search for them. He soon met an old man and an old woman who were weeping bitterly; between them walked a lovely maiden.

"Who are you?" asked Susa-no-wo.

The old man made answer: "I am a god of earth, son of a mountain god, and my name is *Ashi-na-dzu-chi* ('foot-stroker'); this woman is my wife, and her name is *Te-na-dzu-chi* ('hand stroker'); the maiden is my daughter *Kush-inada-hime* ('Miraculous-rice-field-sun-maiden')."

"Why do you weep?" asked Susa-no-wo.

Said the old man: "I have had eight daughters, but each year the eight-forked serpent (dragon) of Koshi has come and devoured one after the other. I weep now because the time is at hand to give Kush-inada-hime to the serpent."

"What is the serpent like?"

371

"Its eyes are red as the winter cherry[1]; it has a body with eight heads and eight tails, and on its body grow moss and trees. It is so long that it stretches over eight valleys and eight hills. Its belly is constantly bloody and inflamed."[2]

"If this maiden is your daughter," said Susa-no-wo, "will you give her to me?"

"You honour me," the old man made answer, "but I do not know your name."

"I am the dear brother of the sun-goddess, and. have just descended from heaven."

"Most obediently do I offer my daughter to you," the old man said with reverence.

Susa-no-wo then transformed the girl into a comb, which he placed in his hair. Having done this, he bade the old couple to brew rice-beer (sake). They obeyed him, and he asked them to construct a fence with eight gates and eight benches, and to place on each bench a vat filled with the beer.

In time the eight-forked serpent came nigh. It dipped each of its heads into each of the vats, drank the sake, became drunk, and then lay down and slept. Susa-no-wo drew his two-handed sword,[3] and cut the serpent in pieces. The Hi River turned red with blood.

When Susa-no-wo cut the middle tail his sword broke. He marvelled at this. Taking the point of the sword in his hand, he thrust and split, and looked inside, and found a keen-cutting blade within this tail. He took it out and sent it to his sister, Ama-terâsu, the sun-

---

[1] The modern *hohodzuki* (*Physalis Alkekengi*).

[2] De Groot refers to a "venerable" Chinese dragon living in a pond; it had nine heads and eighteen tails, and "ate nothing but fever demons". *The Religious System of China*, Vol. VI, p. 1053. Another dragon is 1000 miles long; his breath causes wind; when he opens his eyes it is day, and when he closes them it is night. De Visser, *The Dragon in China and Japan*, p. 62.

[3] In the *Nihon-gi* this sword is called *Ama no-hawe-giri* (the heavenly fly-cutter).

goddess. This sword is the *Kusa-nagi-no-tachi* (the "herb-quelling" dragon-sword).

Susa-no-wo afterwards built a house in the land of Idzumo, at a place called Suga. Clouds rose up from that place. He made an ode regarding the eight clouds that formed an eight-fold fence for husband and wife to retire within the house. Then he appointed the maiden's father to be keeper, or head-man of the house.

In this nuptial house children were born to Susa-no-wo and the young woman he had rescued from the dragon. These children included *Oho-toshi-no-kami* (Great Harvest deity), *Uka-no-mitama* (the August Spirit of Food), and *Ohonamochi* ("Great Name Possessor"), the god of Idzumo,[1] who could assume snake form or human form at will.

Ohonamochi and his eighty brothers desired to marry the Princess of Yakami in Inaba. On their way thither the eighty brothers tricked a hare, which came by a distressing injury, but Ohonamochi caused it to be cured. The grateful hare of Inaba, now called "the Hare Deity", promised Ohonamochi, who carried the bag as a servant to his brothers, that he would get the princess for wife.

The princess afterwards refused to marry any of the eighty brothers, saying she favoured Ohonamochi. Being enraged, the brothers took counsel together and said to Ohonamochi: "There is a red boar on this mountain, named Tema, in the land of Hataki. When we drive it down, you must catch it. If you fail to catch it, we shall certainly slay you."[2]

Having thus spoken, the eighty deities kindled a fire, in which they heated a great boulder, shaped like to a boar. They rolled the stone down the mountain-side,

---

[1] Idzumo is the next holiest place to Ise. The god had other names including *Oho-kuni-nushi* ("Great Land Master").

[2] An incident that recalls the Diarmid story in Scottish and Irish Gaelic folk-tales.

and when Ohonamochi seized it he was so grievously burned that he died.

Then his mother wept and lamented, and ascending to heaven, appealed to *Kami-musu-bi-no-kami* (Divine-Producing Wondrous-Deity), one of the elder gods,[1] who sent *Kisa-gahi-hime* (Princess Cockle-Shell)[2] and *Umugi-hime* (Princess Clam)[3] to restore the dead deity to life. Kisa-gahi-hime "triturated and scorched her shell", and Umugi-hime "carried water and smeared him as with mother's milk".[4] Thereupon Ohonamochi came to life as a beautiful young man and walked again.

The eighty deities again deceived Ohonamochi. They led him to the mountains. There they cut down a tree, which they split, inserting a wedge in it, and having made him stand in the middle, they took away the wedge, and thus killed him.

Ohonamochi's mother again wailed and wept. She cut the tree, and, taking him out, restored him to life once more. Then he fled to the Land of Trees, escaping from his pursuers, who had fixed arrows in their bows, by dipping under the fork of a tree and disappearing.[5]

Ohonamochi was advised to seek refuge in the Nether-Distant-Land (Hades), where dwelt Susa-no-wo. Princess Forward met him, and they exchanged glances, and were married. She then informed her father, Susa-no-wo, that a very beautiful god had arrived. But Susa-no-wo was angry, and called the youthful deity "Ugly-

---

[1] One of the first three deities, the children of Heaven and Earth.

[2] The *Arca inflata*. [3] The *Cytherea meretrix*.

[4] Chamberlain, in his translation of the *Ko-ji-ki* (p. 70), says "the meaning is that a paste like milk was made of the triturated and calcined shell mixed with water". Mother (*omo*) may be read as "nurse" too. Mrs. Carmichael, widow of Dr. Alexander Carmichael, the Scottish folk-lorist, informs me that in the Outer Hebrides women burn and grind cockle-shells to make a "lime water" for delicate children. The clam is likewise used. The ancient Japanese and ancient Hebrideans may have received this folk-medicine from the ancient seafarers who searched for shells and metals.

[5] This was a magical act. He rendered himself invisible.

Male-God-of-Reed-Plain", and commanded him to sleep in the snake-house. The Princess Forward gave Ohonamochi a snake-scarf, instructing him to wave it thrice when the snakes threatened to bite him. This he did, and was protected. On the next night Susa-no-wo placed the young god in the house of centipedes and wasps, but the princess gave him another scarf that protected him against attack.

Next day Susa-no-wo shot a "humming arrow"[1] into the middle of a moor, and made Ohonamochi fetch it back. But when the young god went out on the moor Susa-no-wo set fire to it all round. Ohonamochi could perceive no way of escape. As he stood there, a mouse[2] came and told him of a hollow place in which he could shelter himself. Ohonamochi hastened to the hole and hid in it till the fire had gone past. Then the mouse discovered and brought the humming arrow to Ohonamochi. "The feathers of the arrows were brought in their mouths by all the mouse's children" (Ko-ji-ki, p. 73).[3]

Princess Forward lamented for her husband, and Susa-no-wo believed he was dead. But the princess found Ohonamochi, and took him to the house. He returned the arrow to Susa-no-wo. This god had many centipedes in his hair, and bade the youth take them out. Ohonamochi made pretence of doing this, and Susa-no-wo fell asleep.

Then Ohonamochi tied the hair of Susa-no-wo to the rafters, placed a great boulder against the door, and fled

---

[1] The "sounding arrow" with a whistling contrivance made of bone. It was known in China during the T'ang Dynasty, and was used by hunters to make birds rise, and by soldiers to scare enemies. Laufer thinks the Japanese sounding arrows were of Chinese origin.—*Chinese Clay Figures*, p. 224, n. 4.   [2] Or a rat.

[3] Here one is tempted to see mouse-Apollo, or the mouse of the Homeric Apollo who shoots the arrows of disease. The mice that strip the arrows of their feathers may be the arresters of disease. Mouse medicine is of great antiquity in Egypt.

away with Princess Forward on his back.   He carried away, too, Susa - no - wo's life-sword and life - bow and arrows, and the heavenly-speaking lute.[1]

As Ohonamochi fled, the lute touched a tree, and the earth resounded with its call.   Susa-no-wo was awakened by the spirit-call.   He pulled down the great house so as to get out, but was so long delayed in disentangling his hair from the rafters, that when he went in pursuit he did not get within call of Ohonamochi until he reached the Even Pass of Yomi (Hades).[2]

Susa-no-wo shouted to Ohonamochi, advising him to pursue the eighty half-brothers with the life-sword and life-bow and arrows until they were swept into the river rapids.   "Then, wretch," said he, "become *Oho-kuni-nushi* (Great Master god of the land), and make Princess Forward thy consort.   Set up the temple-pillars at the foot of Mount Uka on foundations of rock and raise the cross-beams to the Plain of High Heaven.   Dwell there, you villain."

Ohonamochi pursued and destroyed the eighty deities. "Then," the narrative continues, "he began to make the land."

Here we meet with another Creation myth.

Two children were born to Ohonamochi and Princess Forward; these were *Ki-no-mata-no-kami* (Tree-fork-deity) and *Mi-wi-no-kami* (Deity of August Wells).

Like Odin, Ohonamochi woos in the course of his career more than one goddess.   One of these, the Princess of *Nuna-kaha* (Lagoon-river), sings to him:

"Being a man probably (thou) hast on the various island headlands that thou seest, and on every beach headland that thou lookest

---

[1] "Divine messages," says Chamberlain, "were conveyed through a person playing on the lute."   The language of the "lute" was thus like the "language of birds".

[2] This is a Far Eastern version of the Jack-and-the-Beanstalk story.

on, a wife like the young herbs. But as for me, alas! being a woman, I have no man except thee."[1]

An elfin deity comes across the ocean to assist Qho-namochi to "make and consolidate the land". He is named *Sukuna-bikona* (the Little Prince god). Attired in bird[2] skins, the little god sailed in a boat of the heavenly *Kagami*.[3]

After Little Prince had for a time assisted to consolidate the land, he crossed over to *Toko-yo-no-kuni* (the Eternal Land).

Then came a deity illuminating the sea to assist in consolidating the land. He asked for a temple on Mount Mimoro and was afterwards worshipped there. He himself passed to the Eternal Land (*Toko-yo-no-kuni*), where grows the orange tree of life.[4] The deity there who revealed Little Prince is called Crumbling Prince; his legs do not walk, but he knows everything beneath the Heavens.[5]

---

[1] *Transactions of the Asiatic Society of Japan*, Vol. X (supplement), p. 81.

[2] Native commentators say "goose" or "wren"; some consider that owing to a copyist's error "insect" has been changed to bird, and that the reading should be "moth" or "silk-worm moth" or "fire insect".

[3] Some think this plant is one that bears a berry three or four inches long, and that the boat was a scooped-out berry.

[4] This is not Yomi, but either the Chinese Paradise of the West or the Paradise of the Buddhists.

[5] A Chinese phrase signifying anciently the Chinese world or empire. The "Crumbling Deity" may be the "leech-child", or the caterpillar worshipped by a Japanese cult.

CHAPTER XXI

Ancient Mikados and Heroes

End of Dynasty of Susa-no-wo—Dynasty of Sun-goddess—The First Emperor of Japan—Mikado as Descendant of the Sea-god, the "Abundant Pearl Prince"—A Japanese Gilgamesh—Quest of the Orange Tree of Life—The "Eternal Land"—The Polynesian Paradise and Tree of Life—Yamato-Take, National Hero of Japan—Conflicts with Gods and Rebels—Enchantment and Death of Hero—The Bird-soul—Empress Jingo—Mikado deified as God of War—Shinto Religion and Nature-worship—The Goddess Cult in Japan—Adoration of the Principle of Life in Jewels, Trees, Herbs, &c.—Buddhism—Revival of Pure Shinto—Culture-mixing in China and Japan—China "not a nation".

Many children were born to Ohonamochi, but the Celestials would not give recognition to the Dynasty of Susa-no-wo, and resolved that Ninigi, the august grand-child of the sun-goddess, should rule Japan. Ohona-mochi was deposed, and several deities were sent down from heaven to pacify the land for the chosen one.

Ninigi's wife was *Konohana-sakuyahime*, and two of their children were *Hohodemi*, the hunter, and *Ho-no-Susori*, the fisherman.

It was Hohodemi who wooed and wed the "Abundant Pearl Princess" and lived with her for a time in the land under the ocean.[1] After she gave birth to her child, she departed to her own land, deeply offended because her husband beheld her in dragon (*wani*) shape in the par-turition house he had built for her on the seashore.

This child was the father of the first Emperor of

[1] See Index.

Japan, Jimmu Tenno.[1] The Mikados were therefore descended from the sun-goddess Ama-terâsu and the Dragon-king of Ocean, the "Abundant Pearl Prince".

When engaged pacifying the land, Jimmu followed a gigantic crow[2] that had been sent down from heaven to guide him. He possessed a magic celestial cross-sword and a fire-striker. His two brothers, who accompanied him on an expedition across the sea, leapt overboard when a storm was raging so that the waves might be stilled. They were subsequently worshipped as gods.

Yamato now becomes the centre of the narrative, Idzumo having lost its former importance.

Jimmu Tenno reigned until he was 127 years of age, dying, according to Japanese dating, in 585 B.C. His successor was Suisei Tenno. There follows a blank of 500 years which is bridged by the names of rulers most of whom had long lives, some reaching over 120 years.

At the beginning of the Christian era, the Mikado was Sui-nin, who died at the age of 141 years. This monarch sent the hero Tajima-mori to the Eternal Land with purpose to bring back the fruit of the "Timeless (or Everlasting) Fragrant Tree". The Japanese Gilgamesh succeeded in his enterprise. According to the *Ko-ji-ki*:

"Tajima-mori at last reached that country, plucked the fruit of the tree, and brought of club-moss eight and of spears eight; but meanwhile the Heavenly Sovereign had died. Then Tajima-mori set apart of club-moss four and of spears four, which he presented to the Great Empress, and set up of club-moss four and of spears four as an offering at the door of the Heavenly Sovereign's august mausoleum, and, raising on high the fruit of the tree, wailed and wept, saying: 'Bringing the fruit of the Everlasting Fragrant Tree from the Eternal Land, I have come to serve thee.' At last he

---

[1] This is his posthumous name. During his life he was *Kamu-Yamato-Iware-Biko.*
[2] The golden crow of the sun had three legs. In the moon was the jewelled hare.

wailed and wept himself to death. This fruit of the Everlasting Fragrant Tree is what is now called the orange."

Chamberlain explains[1] that "club-moss oranges" signifies oranges as they grow on the branch surrounded by leaves, while spear-oranges are the same divested of leaves and hanging to the bare twig.

The location of the Eternal Land has greatly puzzled native scholars. Some suppose it was a part of Korea and others that it was Southern China or the Loocho Islands. According to the *Nihon-gi*, Tajima-mori found the Eternal Land to be inhabited by gods and dwarfs. As it lay somewhere to the west of Japan, it would appear to be identical with the Western Paradise which, according to Chinese belief, is ruled over by Si Wang Mu (the Japanese Seiobo), the "Royal Mother" and "Queen of Immortals". Instead of the Chinese Peach Tree of Life, the Japanese had in their own Western Paradise the Orange Tree of Life. The orange was not, however, introduced into Japan until the eighth century of our era.[2] Whether or not it supplanted in the Japanese paradise an earlier tree, as the cassia tree supplanted the peach tree in the Chinese paradise, is at present uncertain. It may be that the idea of the Western Paradise was introduced by the Buddhists. At the same time, it will be recalled that the Peach Tree of Life grew on the borderland of Yomi, which was visited by Izanagi.

A similar garden paradise was known to the Polynesians, and especially the Tahitians. It was called Rohutu noanoa ("Perfumed or Fragrant Rohutu"). Thither the souls of the dead were conducted by the god

[1] *Transactions of the Asiatic Society of Japan*, Vol. X (supplement), p. 199, *n.* 5.
[2] Chamberlain, *Things Japanese*, p. 57.

Urutaetae. This paradise "was supposed", writes Ellis,[1] "to be near a lofty and stupendous mountain in Raiatea, situated in the vicinity of Hamaniino harbour and called *Temehani unauna*, 'splendid or glorious Temehani'. It was, however, said to be invisible to mortal eyes, being in the *reva*, or aerial regions. The country was described as most lovely and enchanting in appearance, adorned with flowers of every form and hue, and perfumed with odours of every fragrance. The air was free from every noxious vapour, pure, and most salubrious. . . . Rich viands and delicious fruits were supposed to be furnished in abundance for the frequent and sumptuous festivals celebrated there. Handsome youths and women, *purotu anae*, all perfection, thronged the place."

Another Polynesian paradise, called Pulotu, was reserved for chiefs, who obtained "plenty of the best food and other indulgences". Its ruler, Saveasiuleo, had a human head. The upper part of his body reclined in a great house "in company with the spirits of departed chiefs", while "the extremity of his body was said to stretch away into the sea in the shape of an eel or serpent".[2]

The Japanese had thus, like the Polynesians, a garden paradise and a sea-dragon-king's paradise, as well as the gloomy Yomi. It may be that the beliefs and stories regarding these Otherworlds were introduced by the earliest seafarers, who formed pearl-fishing communities round their shores. The Ainu believe that Heaven and Hell are beneath the earth, "in *Pokna moshiri*, the lower world", but they have no idea what the rewards of the righteous are.[3] Nothing is definitely known regarding

---

[1] *Polynesian Researches* (First Edition, 1829), p. 327.
[2] Turner, *Nineteen Years in Polynesia* (1861), p. 237.
[3] Batchelor, *Notes on the Ainu* (*Transactions of the Asiatic Society of Japan*, Vol. X), p. 218.

the beliefs of the earlier people remembered as the Koro-pok-guru and their highly complex culture.

The Mikado Sui-nin was succeeded by the Mikado Kei-ko, who died in A.D. 130, aged 143 years. One of his sons, Yamato-Take, is a famous legendary hero of Japan. He performed many heroic deeds in battle against brigands and rebels. At Ise he obtained from his aunt, Yamato-hime, the priestess, the famous Kusanagi sword, and a bag which he was not to open except when in peril of his life. He then set out to subdue and pacify all savage deities and unsubmissive peoples. The ruler of Sagami set fire to a moor which Yamato entered in quest of a "Violent Deity". Finding himself in peril, he opened the bag and discovered in it a fire-striker (or fire-drill). He mowed the herbage with the dragon-sword, and, using the fire-striker, kindled a counter-fire, which drove back the other fire. The Kusanagi (herb-quelling) sword takes its name from this incident. Yamato-Take afterwards slew the wicked rulers of that land. He also slew a god in the shape of a white deer which met him in Ashigara Pass. He lay in ambush, and with a scrap of chive[1] hit the deer in the eye and thus struck it dead. Then he shouted three times "Adzuma ha ya" (Oh, my wife!). The land was thereupon called Adzuma.

Then follows the mysterious story of the death of the hero. He went to the land of Shinanu, in which Ohona-mochi had taken refuge when Japan was being subdued for the ruler chosen by the sun-goddess, and where, being pursued and threatened with death, Ohonamochi consented to abdicate and take up his abode in a temple. The country takes its name from *shina*, a tree resembling the lime,[2] and *nu* or *no*, "moor". Yamato-Take entered

---

[1] *Nira*, the *Allium odorum*.
[2] *Tilia cordata*. See Chamberlain's *Ko-ji-ki*, pp. 102 *n*. 26, and 215.

this land through Shinanu Pass (*Shinanu no saka*), between
the provinces of Shinano and Mino. He overcame the
deity of the pass, and went to dwell in the house of
Princess Miyazu, of fragrant and slender arms. She
welcomed him with love. In the house of the princess
he left the Kusanagi sword, and went forth against the
deity of evil breath (or influence) on Mount Ibuki. As
he climbed the mountain he met a white boar, big as
a bull. Believing it was a messenger of the deity, he
vowed he would slay it when he returned, and continued
to climb the mountain. But the boar was not a messenger;
it was the very deity in person, and it sent a heavy ice-
rain.[1] The rain-smitten and perplexed hero was thus
misled by the deity.

On descending the mountain, Yamato-Take reached
the fresh spring of *Tama-kura-be* (the "Jewel-store-tribe").
He drank from it, and revived somewhat. The spring
was afterwards called *Wi-same* (the "well of awakening"
or "resting").

Then Yamato-Take departed, and reached the moor
of *Tagi*,[2] lamenting the loss of bodily strength. He
passed on to Cape Wotsu in Ise, and there found a sword
he had left at a pine tree, and sang:

> "O pine tree, my brother,
> If thou wert a person,
> My sword and my garments
> To thee would I give".

Having sung this song, he proceeded on his way,
yearning for his native land, delightful Yamato, situated

---

[1] An evil rain which did harm like the evil rain sent by a sick or an angry and destroying dragon.
[2] The moor of the waterfall of the River Yoro in Mino.

behind Mount Awogaki.   His next song was one of love and regret.

> " How sweet o'er the skies
> From Yamato, my home,
> Do its white clouds arise,
> Do its white clouds all come. "

His sickness and weariness made him feel more and more faint, and he sang in his distress:

> " Oh! the sharp sabre-sword
> I left by the bedside
> Of Princess Miyazu—
> The sharp sabre-sword".[1]

Yamato-Take sank and died as soon as he had finished his song.

In time his wives came and built for him a mausoleum, weeping and moaning the while, because he could not hear them or make answer.   Then Yamato-Take was transformed into a white bird,[2] which rose high in the air and flew towards the shore.   The wives pursued the bird with lamentations and entered the sea.   They saw the bird flying towards the beach, and followed it.   For a time it perched on a rock.   Then it flew from Ise to Shiki, in the land of Kafuchi, where a mausoleum was built for it, so that it might rest.[3]   But the white bird rose again to heaven and flew away.   It was never again seen.

After Mikado Kei-ko, father of Yamato-Take, had passed away, Sei-mu reigned until he was 108 years old. Then followed the Mikado Chiu-ai.   His capital was in the south-west on the island of Kyushu.   A message

---

[1] Apparently the sword would have protected him against the fatal enchantment wrought by the white boar-god of Mount Ibuki.

[2] *Chidori*, a dotteril, plover, or sandpiper.

[3] As a god's *mi-tama* rests in a temple to be worshipped.

came from the goddess through the Empress Jingo, who was divinely possessed, promising him Korea, "a land to the westward" with "abundance of various treasures, dazzling to the eye, from gold and silver downwards".

The Mikado refused to believe there was a land to the west, and declared that the gods spoke falsely. Soon afterwards the heavenly sovereign was struck dead.

Now the Empress Jingo was with child. Having received the instructions of the deities to conquer Korea for her son, she delayed his birth by taking a stone and attaching it to her waist with cords. Korea was subdued, the Empress having made use of the "Jewels of flood and ebb", as related in a previous chapter. Her child was born after she returned to Japan.

Empress Jingo is further credited with subduing and uniting the Empire of Japan, and again establishing the central power at Yamato. She lived until she was 100 years old.

Her son Ojin Tenno,[1] who had a dragon's tail, lived until he was 110 years old, and died in A.D. 310. He was worshipped after death as a war-god, and the patron of the Minamoto clan. His successor, Nin-toku, who died at the age of 110, was the last of the mythical monarchs, or of the monarchs regarding whom miraculous deeds are related. Japanese history begins and myth ends about the beginning of the fifth century of the Christian era.

The cult of Hachiman (Ojin Tenno) came into prominence in the ninth century with the rise of the Minamoto family; its original seat was Usa, in Buzen province. Hachiman's *shintai* ("god body") is a white stone, or a fly-brush, or a pillow, or an arm-rest.

---

[1] His posthumous title. During life he was called Hachiman.

Jimmu Tenno, the Empress Jingo, and Yamato-Take were similarly deified and worshipped. A ninth century scholar, Sugahara Michizane, was deified as Temmangû, god of scholars. Living as well as dead Mikados were *kami* (deities). "The spirits of all the soldiers who died in battle," writes Yei Ozaki,[1] "are worshipped as deified heroes at the Kudan shrine in Tokyo."

The worship of human ancestors in Japan is due to Chinese influence, and had no place in old Shinto prior to the sixth century. In the *Ko-ji-ki* and *Nihon-gi*, the ancestors of the Mikados and the ruling classes are the deities and their avatars. As we have seen, the Mikados were reputed to be descended from the sun-goddess, and from the daughter of the Dragon King of Ocean, called the "Abundant-Pearl Princess", a Japanese Melusina.

It is far from correct, therefore, to refer, as has been done, to Shinto religion as "the worship of nature-gods and ancestors". Even the term "nature-worship" is misleading. The adoration in sacred shrines of the *mi-tama* (the "August jewel", or "Dragon-pearl", or "spirit", or "double") of a deity is not "the worship of Nature", but the worship of "the imperishable principle of life wherever found". At Ise, the "Mecca" of Japan, the goddess cult is prominent. Both the sun-goddess and the food-goddess are forms of the Far Eastern Hathor, the personification of the pearl, the shell, the precious jewel containing "life substance", the sun mirror, the sword, the pillow, the standing-stone, the holy tree, the medicinal herb, the fertilizing rain, &c. The Mikado, as her descendant, was the living Horus, an avatar of Osiris; after death the Mikado ascended, like Ra, to the celestial regions, or departed, like Osiris, to the Underworld of

---

[1] *Customs of the World* (Japan), pp. 380 *et seq.*

the Dead.   The Mikado of Japan, like the Pharaoh of Egypt, was a Son of Heaven.

After Buddhism had been introduced into Japan in the sixth century, it was fused with Shinto.   The Shinto deities figured as avatars of Buddha in the cult of Ryobu-Shinto.   Even the Mikados came under the spell of Buddhism.

In the eighteenth century began the movement known as the "Revival of Pure Shinto".   It was promoted chiefly by Motŏori and his disciple Hirata.   In time it did much to bring about the revolution which restored to supreme political power, as the hereditary high priest and living representative of the sun-goddess, the Mikado of Japan.   Shinto is the official religion of modern Japan; but Buddhism, impregnated with Shinto elements, is the religion of the masses.   "Pure Shinto", however, was not "pure" in the sense that Motŏori and Hirata professed to believe.   It was undoubtedly a product of culture mixing in early times.   "The *Ko-ji-ki* and *Nihon-gi*," as Laufer says, "do not present a pure source of genuine Japanese thought, but are retrospective records largely written under Chinese and Korean influence, and echoing in a bewildering medley continental-Asiatic and Malayo-Polynesian traditions."[1]   In China, Korea, Polynesia, &c., a similar process of culture mixing can be traced.   Buddha and Mohammed were not the earliest founders of cults which have left their impress on the religious systems of the Far East.   Vast areas were influenced by the cultures of Ancient Egypt and Babylonia.

The history of civilization does not support the hypothesis that the same myths and religious practices

[1] *Chinese Clay Figures*, Part I, p. 272 (*Field Museum of Natural History*, Publication 177; Anthropological Series, Vol. XIII, No. 2).   Chicago, 1914.

were of spontaneous generation in widely-separated countries. Culture complexes cannot be accounted for or
explained away by the application of the principles of
biological evolution. As has been shown in these pages,
there are many culture complexes in China and Japan,
and many links with more ancient civilizations.

Touching on the problem of culture mixing in China,
Laufer writes:

" In opposition to the prevalent opinion of the day, it
cannot be emphasized strongly enough on every occasion
that Chinese civilization, as it appears now, is not a unit
and not the exclusive production of the Chinese, but the
final result of the cultural efforts of a vast conglomeration
of the most varied tribes, an amalgamation of ideas
accumulated from manifold quarters and widely differentiated in space and time; briefly stated, this means China
is not a nation, but an empire, a political, but not an
ethnical unit. No graver error can hence be committed
than to attribute any culture idea at the outset to the
Chinese, for no other reason than because it appears
within the precincts of their empire."[1]

1 *Jade*, p. 57.

INDEX

rush of, 85; Chinese and Polynesian, 67; and Dragon Boat Festival, 269; Egyptian serpent-island story, 98; Five, as rulers of seasons, &c., 61; Fungus of Immortality and, 107; Garudas and Nagas and, 70; gods ride on, 65; herbs, &c., and, 183; human shapes of, 47; Indian Nagas and, 69; in pools, rivers, and sea, 54; as tide controllers, 54; iron dreaded by, 38, 64; as rain-bringers, 39; fond of gems, 38; Japanese dragon place-names, 356; Japanese sea-gods as, 352; Japanese "water snakes" as, 353; "Kingdom Under the Sea" legends of, 95; as Light-gods, 63; Melusina legend in lore of, 86, 87; mother of, 59; Pearl Princess legend, 97; pearls produced by, 39; Japanese mountains and, 39; Red Island of 95; skins of, shine by night, 64; the Chinese nine-headed dragon, 372, and also note 2; transformed dragons harmless, 105; vital spirit in eyes of, 64; Water of Life controlled by, 159; were-animals and, 221; whales and, 49; women as, in China, 86; boys become, in Japan, 86.

Dugong, dragon and, 50.

Dynasties, Chin or Ts'in, 291; Early and Mythical, 277; Han, Minor, T'ang, Sung, Mongol, Ming, and Manchu, 292; the Chinese, Chou Dynasty, 288; the Hea, 281; the Shang, 285.

Ea, Babylonian god, as sea-farer, 30; Dagan and Dagon and, 52; dragon and, 51; antelope, goat, gazelle and, 51; Oannes and, 31.

Eagle, jade and, 221.

Eagle-stone, 128, 129.

East, Cult of, 134, 210; Cult of, in China and Egypt, 60; sacredness of, in Egypt and China, 229.

East Indies, Egyptian millet in, 9.

Eel, as Polynesian dragon, 78; God of Samoa as, 68.

Eels as dragon-vampires, 64.

Egg, the Cosmic, 260, 266, 303; in Shinto, 348.

Egg, the Swallow's, Ancestress of

Emperor T'ang and, 285 (see *Dragon Eggs*).

Egypt, agriculture in, 6; beliefs of, regarding souls, in China, 239, 240; Bird and serpent myth in, 71; Chinese adopt inventions of, 13; potter's wheel of, 13; Chinese goddess and, 137; Chinese Horus, 285; Chinese Isis and Nephthys, 139; Chinese Shun and Horus, 280; cinnamon imported into, 142; corn, fruit, and milk in Paradise, 133; Cosmic Egg in, 348; cult of East and of West in, 60; Date Tree of Life, 179; Deathless Snake of, and Chinese and Japanese dragons, 78, and also note 3, 156; deities as fish, 59; deities create plants of life, 180; Dragon Isle story of, 98; Dragon-slayer of, 77, 78; Dragon-stones and mountain of dawn, 59; Frog goddess of, 145; god Ptah and Dragon, 63; goddess of turquoise, 58; gold plentiful in, 198, and also note 1; Hathor and Chinese Spinning Maiden, 147; Hathor and Taoism, 313; Hathor beer and Far Eastern intoxicants, 330; Heart and tongue connection in, 222; Heart as "mind" in, 77; Horus myth in Japan, 351; Horus story in Japan, 155; Indian links with, 74; influence of, in Asia, 206; iron as Set's metal, 64; Island of the Blest in Pyramid Texts of, 108; Japanese Deluge myth and Egyptian, 345; Pharaoh and Mikado, 341, 387; jasper of Isis and Japanese Tama, 336; kings of, as gods, 342; Mikado as Osiris and Horus, 386; Mikado and Osiris, 339, 340; myths of, in China, 148; myth of separation of Heaven and Earth, in Japan and Polynesia, 348; Nile flows from Milky Way in, 111; Nut and Chinese virgin goddess, 268; origin of agriculture in, 201; origin of mummification in, 257; connection of mummification with Animism, 256; Osiris and Chinese Shen-nung, 277; Osiris and Lao Tze, 299; Set and Lao Tze, 300;